Marpeck

Studies in
Anabaptist and Mennonite History
No. 44

Marpeck

Walter Klaassen
and
William Klassen

Studies in
Anabaptist and Mennonite
History

Series Editor Steven M. Nolt; with Editors Geoffrey L. Dipple, Marlene G. Epp, Rachel Waltner Goossen, Leonard Gross, Gerald J. Mast, Thomas J. Meyers, John D. Roth, Theron F. Schlabach, and Astrid von Schlachta.

The series Studies in Anabaptist and Mennonite History is sponsored by the Mennonite Historical Society. Beginning with volume 8, titles were published by Herald Press, Scottdale, Pennsylvania and Waterloo, Ontario unless otherwise noted.

1. Harold S. Bender. *Two Centuries of American Mennonite Literature, 1727-1928*. 1929.
2. John Horsch. *The Hutterian Brethren, 1528-1931: A Story of Martyrdom and Loyalty*. 1931; reprint, Macmillan Hutterite Colony, Cayley, Alberta. 1985.
3. Harry F. Weber. *Centennial History of the Mennonites in Illinois, 1829-1929*. 1931.
4. Sanford Calvin Yoder. *For Conscience' Sake: A Study of Mennonite Migrations Resulting from the World War*. 1940.
5. John S. Umble. *Ohio Mennonite Sunday Schools*. 1941.
6. Harold S. Bender. *Conrad Grebel, c. 1498-1526, Founder of the Swiss Brethren*. 1950.
7. Robert Friedmann. *Mennonite Piety Through the Centuries: Its Genius and Its Literature*. 1949.
8. Delbert L. Gratz. *Bernese Anabaptists and Their American Descendants*. 1953.
9. A. L. E. Verheyden. *Anabaptism in Flanders, 1530-1650: A Century of Struggle*. 1961.
10. J. C. Wenger. *The Mennonites in Indiana and Michigan*. 1961.
11. Rollin Stely Armour. *Anabaptist Baptism: A Representative Study*. 1966.
12. John B. Toews. *Lost Fatherland: The Story of Mennonite Emigration from Soviet Russia, 1921-1927*. 1967.
13. Grant M. Stoltzfus. *Mennonites of the Ohio and Eastern Conference, from the Colonial Period in Pennsylvania to 1968*. 1969.
14. John A. Lapp. *The Mennonite Church in India, 1897-1962*. 1972.
15. Robert Friedmann. *The Theology of Anabaptism: An Interpretation*. 1973.

16. Kenneth R. Davis. *Anabaptism and Asceticism: A Study in Intellectual Origins.* 1974.
17. Paul Erb. *South Central Frontiers: A History of the South Central Mennonite Conference.* 1974.
18. Fred R. Belk. *The Great Trek of the Russian Mennonites to Central Asia, 1880-1884.* 1976.
19. Werner O. Packull. *Mysticism and the Early South German-Austrian Anabaptist Movement, 1525-1531.* 1976.
20. Richard K. MacMaster, with Samuel L. Horst and Rubert F. Ulle. *Conscience in Crisis: Mennonites and Other Peace Churches in America, 1739-1789.* 1979.
21. Theron F. Schlabach. *Gospel Versus Gospel: Mission and the Mennonite Church, 1863-1944.* 1980.
22. Calvin Wall Redekop. *Strangers Become Neighbors: Mennonite and Indigenous Relations in the Paraguayan Chaco.* 1980.
23. Leonard Gross. *The Golden Years of the Hutterites: The Witness and Thought of the Communal Moravian Anabaptists during the Walpot Era, 1565-1578.* 1980; rev. ed., Pandora Press Canada. 1998.
24. Willard H. Smith. *Mennonites in Illinois.* 1983.
25. Murray L. Wagner. *Petr Chelcický: A Radical Separatist in Hussite Bohemia.* 1983.
26. John L. Ruth. *Maintaining the Right Fellowship: A Narrative Account of Life in the Oldest Mennonite Community in North America.* 1984.
27. C. Arnold Snyder. *The Life and Thought of Michael Sattler.* 1984.
28. Beulah Stauffer Hostetler. *American Mennonites and Protestant Movements: A Community Paradigm.* 1987.
29. Daniel Liechty. *Andreas Fischer and the Sabbatarian Anabaptists: An Early Reformation Episode in East Central Europe.* 1988.
30. Hope Kauffman Lind. *Apart and Together: Mennonites in Oregon and Neighboring States, 1876-1976.* 1990.
31. Paton Yoder. *Tradition and Transition: Amish Mennonites and Old Order Amish, 1800-1900.* 1991.
32. James R. Coggins. *John Smyth's Congregation: English Separatism, Mennonite Influence, and the Elect Nation.* 1991.
33. John D. Rempel. *The Lord's Supper in Anabaptism: A Study in the Theology of Balthasar Hubmaier, Pilgram Marpeck, and Dirk Philips.* 1993.
34. Gerlof D. Homan. *American Mennonites and the Great War, 1914-1918.* 1994.
35. J. Denny Weaver. *Keeping Salvation Ethical: Mennonite and Amish Atonement Theology in the Late Nineteenth Century.* 1997.

36. Wes Harrison. *Andreas Ehrenpreis and Hutterite Faith and Practice.* 1997. Copublished with Pandora Press Canada.
37. John D. Thiesen. *Mennonite and Nazi? Attitudes among Mennonite Colonists in Latin America, 1933-1945.* 1999. Copublished with Pandora Press Canada.
38. Perry Bush. *Dancing with the Kobzar: Bluffton College and Mennonite Higher Education, 1899-1999.* 2000. Copublished with Pandora Press U.S. and Faith & Life Press.
39. John L. Ruth. *The Earth Is the Lord's: A Narrative History of the Lancaster Mennonite Conference.* 2001.
40. Melanie Springer Mock. *Writing Peace: The Unheard Voices of Great War Mennonite Objectors.* 2003. Copublished with Cascadia Publishing House.
41. Mary Jane Lederach Hershey. *This Teaching I Present: Fraktur from the Skippack and Salford Mennonite Meetinghouse Schools, 1747-1836.* 2003. Published by Good Books.
42. Edsel Burdge Jr. and Samuel L. Horst. *Building on the Gospel Foundation: The Mennonites of Franklin County, Pennsylvania, and Washington County, Maryland, 1730-1970.* 2004.
43. Ervin Beck. *MennoFolk: Mennonite and Amish Folk Traditions.* 2004.
44. Walter Klaassen and William Klassen. *Marpeck: A Life of Dissent and Conformity.* 2008.

Marpeck

A LIFE OF DISSENT AND CONFORMITY

Walter Klaassen
and
William Klaassen

Herald Press
Waterloo, Ontario
Scottdale, Pennsylvania

Library and Archives Canada Cataloguing in Publication

Klaassen, Walter, 1926-
   Marpeck : a life of dissent and conformity / Walter Klaassen and William Klassen.
   (Studies in Anabaptist and Mennonite history ; no. 44)
   Includes bibliographical references and index.
   ISBN 978-0-8361-9423-4
   1. Marpeck, Pilgram, ca. 1495-1556. 2. Anabaptists—Europe—Biography.
3. Anabaptists—History—16th century. I. Klassen, William, 1930– II. Title. III. Series.
BX4946.M3K54 2008   284'.3092   C2008-903532-1

Art and photos on title page, pages 38, 56, 121, 123, 150, 152, 252: From Jan Gleysteen's Anabaptist Heritage Collection, Goshen, Indiana. Page 145: Courtesy of the Schwenkfelder Library & Heritage Center, Pennsburg, Pennsylvania. Page 264: Illustration by Jan Luiken, from *Martyrs Mirror* (Scottdale, Pa.: Herald Press, 1938). Used by permission. All rights reserved. Page 65: From page 383 of *De Re Metallica*, by Georgius Agricola, translated by Herbert C. Hoover and Lou H. Hoover, (Mineola, N.Y.: Dover Publications, 1950). Used courtesy of Dover Publications. Photos on pages 59, 61, 80, 99, 100, 108, 120, 238, 241, 249 by Dona Harvey. Map on page 35: "Holy Roman Empire, France and Spain," by Cliff Snyder, from page 179 of *Anabaptist History and Theology, an Introduction*, by C. Arnold Snyder (Kitchener, Ont.: Pandora Press, 1995). Map courtesy of Cliff Snyder. Map on pages 36-37 by Kerry Jean Handel.

MARPECK: A LIFE OF DISSENT AND CONFORMITY
Copyright © 2008 by Herald Press, Scottdale, Pa. 15683
   Published simultaneously in Canada by Herald Press,
   Waterloo, Ont. N2L 6H7. All rights reserved
International Standard Book Number: 978-0-8361-9423-4
Library of Congress Catalogue Card Number: 2008929934
Canadiana Entry Number: C2008-903532-1
Printed in Canada
Book design by Joshua Byler
Cover by Judith Rempel Smucker
Cover photo by John Warwick Montgomery

13 12 11 10 09 08   10 9 8 7 6 5 4 3 2 1

To order or request information please call
1-800-245-7894 or visit www.heraldpress.com.

To Heinold Fast

Pastor, scholar, and peace advocate

Contents

Abbreviations

ARG	*Augsburgs Reformationsgeschichte*
CS	*Corpus Schwenckfeldianorum*
Hutterite Chronicle	*Die Älteste Chronik der Hutterischen Brüder*
ME	*The Mennonite Encyclopedia*
MGBl	*Mennonitische Geschichtsblätter*
ML	*Mennonitisches Lexicon*
MQR	*Mennonite Quarterly Review*
TA: Denck 2	Fellmann, Walter (ed.), *Hans Denck: Religiöse Schriften*
TA: Elsass 1	Krebs, Manfred, and George Rott (eds.), *Elsass*
TA: Baden und Pfalz	Krebs, Manfred (ed.), *Baden und Pfalz*
TA: Österreich 2	Mecenseffy, Grete (ed.), *Österreich*, Part 2
TA: Ostschweiz	Fast, Heinold (ed.), *Ostschweiz*
WPM	Klassen, William, and Klaassen, Walter, *The Writings of Pilgram Marpeck*

Foreword

Dissent and conformity are as worthy of critical reflection in the twenty-first century as they ever have been. In societies shaped by the images and messages of mass media, global marketing, and resurgent nationalism, the implications of conformity bear new burdens and the possibility of dissent requires keen rethinking.

Discernment in such a world demands fresh historical and theological perspectives. We find both in the life and witness of Pilgram Marpeck, a sixteenth-century Anabaptist leader who was also a civil engineer and often public servant, at home in the urban worlds of Strasbourg and Augsburg, as well as in underground or marginalized circles of radical religious reformers.

As a Christian thinker in these circumstances, Marpeck sought to articulate a theology that held together concerns for both inner and outer spiritual vitality and faithfulness, a theology mirroring the incarnation of a divine-human Christ present in a blessed and broken world. Marpeck's theology, biographers Walter Klaassen and William Klassen contend, was both traditional and visionary as he grappled with the challenges of dissent and conformity in his own complex religious and political context.

For too many generations after his death, Marpeck's witness was obscured, his writings misplaced or overlooked. In 1958 Harold S. Bender, then a well-established scholar of Anabaptism and vigorous promoter of Anabaptist studies, lamented the fact that Harvard historian George H. Williams had not included Marpeck in a collection of Anabaptist source material Williams had edited. The omission chagrined Bender because he believed Marpeck to be one of the three most important Anabaptist writers, "and probably the best theologian of them all."[1]

Only in recent decades has Marpeck's life fully reemerged from the shadows, and Klaassen and Klassen have been key figures in allowing his witness to speak again. Accomplished scholars in sixteenth-century history and theology, they have translated many of Marpeck's writings into English

---

1. *Mennonite Quarterly Review* (*MQR*) 32 (October 1958), 316.

and have communicated his thought to scholars and lay readers. Now, with this biography, they present Marpeck's message in the context of his life and times, shedding valuable light on his vocation as a mining engineer, his work to foster a viable urban Anabaptism, and his theological effort to find, as they put it, "a middle way between legalism and license."

It is fitting, then, to include this biography of Pilgram Marpeck in Studies in Anabaptist and Mennonite History (SAMH), a series that Bender, who had wanted to raise Marpeck's profile, helped launch in 1929 "to encourage much-needed inquiries into significant source material, and deeper-reaching interpretative work."[2] Through the years SAMH has been a forum for offering new and compelling understandings of the Radical Reformation. Certainly with this readable and deeply informed biography, Klaassen and Klassen continue a tradition of careful, stimulating scholarship.

Editors of SAMH have also hoped that books in the series would strengthen the theological integrity of the church. Again, Klaassen and Klassen prove faithful guides, taking readers on a journey that raises questions, shares insights, and counsels thoughtful reflection. What is more, in keeping with the irenic style of Marpeck himself, their approach is generously wide in its theological invitation to consider faithful dissent and meaningful conformity across the Christian church.

The series Studies in Anabaptist and Mennonite History is pleased to offer *Marpeck: A Life of Dissent and Conformity* as a major contribution to Anabaptist scholarship and to our common task of theological and ethical discernment for the living of these days.

Steven M. Nolt, Series Editor
Studies in Anabaptist and Mennonite History
Goshen College

2. Harold S. Bender, *Conrad Grebel, c. 1498-1526, Founder of the Swiss Brethren* (Scottdale, Pa.: Herald Press, 1950), vii-viii.

Preface

Half a century ago, as graduate students at the University of Zürich and Princeton Seminary, we chanced upon a doctoral topic that would bring us into the turbulence of the Protestant Reformation sweeping across Europe and the heart of the radical religious movement that sprung from it.

It was in the summer of 1958 that Walter Klaassen made his first manual contact with Pilgram Marpeck. Professor Fritz Blanke of the University of Zürich, where he was a student at the time, took him to the city archive and showed him one of the extant handwritten copies of Marpeck's largest work, the *Verantwortung*, as well as a leather-bound book, the *Testamenterleutterung*, prepared by Marpeck and some of his associates. That same summer he was privileged to hold in his hand the *Kunstbuch*, found in the Bern library in 1950 and revealed to the scholarly world in 1955 by Heinold Fast and Gerhard Goeters. Not fully appreciated at first, the collection contained sixteen until-then-unknown letters by Marpeck.[3] Later that fall Walter struggled to read those handwritten letters on an antiquated microfilm reader in the Bodleian Library at the Oxford University.

That same year across the Atlantic, Professor Otto Piper at Princeton Seminary read Heinold Fast's description of the discovery in the Bern Library of a collection of writings from the Marpeck community. With the determination of a wise and seasoned doctoral advisor, he persuaded William Klassen that Pilgram Marpeck had something to say not only to the radical wing of the Reformation but also to all of Christendom. The focus for Bill was the way Marpeck approached the Bible, most specifically, how he found his own way and how he led his people.

During the rest of Walter's academic life in Anabaptist studies and now, after twenty years of retirement, Marpeck has seldom been out of his sight, especially as the corpus of Marpeck works continued to expand, mainly through attribution of previously known works to Marpeck himself. For Bill, Marpeck has been a touchstone to which he has returned again and again during his lifetime of New Testament and peace studies.

3. See Delbert Gratz, "Codicum Bernensium 464" *MQR* 31 (1957), 294-95.

Over the past fifty years, there has been a considerable growth in the number of writings by Marpeck and his colleagues that have been discovered and identified and made available to the world. Virtually all of them have been carefully protected in European libraries, some of them reprinted, but most of them accessible through the modern means of digitization and photocopying.

The two of us first worked together more than thirty years ago, collaborating on the translation and editing of the *Writings of Pilgram Marpeck*, published by Herald Press in 1978. Since then, even more works of Marpeck have been identified and become available.

We have been helped enormously in our research for this book through the publication of the city and court records of many of the chief figures of the time, including the detailed arguments in Strasbourg between Martin Bucer and Pilgram Marpeck, as well as those from Augsburg and various cities in Austria and Switzerland. The efforts of putting together the jigsaw puzzle of Marpeck's life were made more exciting by the clues he left in his writings without ever giving his name, which would have resulted in imprisonment, exile, or death.

⌐

From the start of this venture, there have been four of us involved: the two authors and our wives, Ruth Klaassen and Dona Harvey. Our bonds grew strong during a month-long trip to Europe to retrace the steps of Marpeck, to find his house in Rattenberg, to visit the Schneeberg mines, and to see Moravia (now part of the Czech Republic), St. Gall, Strasbourg, and Augsburg for ourselves. When Marpeck travelled the rivers and roadways, he had to be careful not to be discovered by the agents and spies of Ferdinand. We had no such pressures except for occasionally losing our way in our attempts to avoid the superhighways that slice through the Alps and across the lush countryside.

Thank You to All

Many people have made this book possible. It is our pleasure to acknowledge our profound gratitude to and dependence on the following:

- the Social Sciences and Humanities Research Council of the Canada Council for its generous grant in aid of research and travel;
- the work of predecessors in Marpeck research and writing, whom we name and to whom we pay tribute in the Introduction;
- Heinold Fast, Gottfried Seebass, and Martin Rothkegel, for giving us the critical edition of the *Kunstbuch*;

- Professor James Stayer of Queen's University, a respected colleague who read the manuscript twice, offering warm collegiality and invaluable advice;
- Joe Springer, of the Mennonite Historical Library in Goshen, Indiana, who, like his father, Nelson, never failed in tracking down Pilgram's elusive trail;
- the libraries and archives staffs in Innsbruck, Rattenberg, Vienna, St. Gall, Strasbourg, Augsburg, and at the Universities of Waterloo and Wilfrid Laurier for their kind and helpful assistance;
- Professor Ernst Laubach, for his assistance with Ferdinand research, and Linda Huebert Hecht, for her continuing determination to unearth the illusive details of the life of Helena von Freyberg;
- graduate students Jonathan Seiling, Victor Thiessen, and Nicolai Penner, for their sleuthing, copying, and deciphering archival materials;
- Walter Deller, Principal of the College of Emmanuel and St. Chad at the University of Saskatchewan in Saskatoon, for providing office space for research and writing, and to colleagues at the college who stimulated thought on important theological issues in Marpeck's writings;
- staff of the grants' research offices of the University of Waterloo and the University of Saskatchewan, and of St. Paul's College, University of Waterloo, as well as Graham Brown, principal of St. Paul's, for their support and assistance with complex budgetary matters;
- secretaries Arlene Sleno, for hours of transcribing tapes and her preparation of footnotes and bibliography, and to Pamela Banks, for placing texts on digital data bases;
- Ruth Klaassen, who read the manuscript several times, improving its readability for non-specialists and giving important counsel until completion;
- Dona Harvey, who did major structural work on the manuscript, and who edited and produced it;
- Philip Klaassen of the University of Toronto for preparing the indices.

We also wish to thank the following private donors who so generously supported the research and writing of this book:

John Bender of Waterloo, Shirley Dyck of Toronto, Dorothy Elliott of Waterloo, Jubilee Charitable Trust and Robert Kruse of Halifax and Kitchener, Robert Kreider of North Newton, Kansas, the

Mennonite Historical Society, Mennonite Savings & Credit Union, Mark Stucky of Elkhart, Indiana, John and Margaret Swallow of St. Catharines, David Thiessen of St. Catharines, Al and Marie Yoder of Middlebury, Indiana, and several anonymous donors.

A Lasting Impression

Over the years, Marpeck's theology has made a strong impression on both authors, especially his theology of the incarnation and the consequences he drew from it for the Christian life and the church. We also continue to be intrigued by his skills as a professional engineer. The dialectic between Marpeck's vocations of theology and engineering is one of the more challenging features of our biography. We hope this book will kindle in readers a desire to track down a man who was both a dissenter to injustice and a conformist to the highest human values, especially the right to live according to one's conscience so that all people some day may be free.

With deep appreciation to everyone involved, and most especially to the guiding spirit for this book, Pilgram Marpeck himself.

Walter Klaassen, Saskatoon
William Klassen, Waterloo

Introduction

This narrative explores one man's journey through the religious, social, and political plains, forests, and quicksands of sixteenth-century Europe. The story of Pilgram Marpeck shows what can happen when the lines between church and state become blurred and a ruling power uses force to impose one form of religion upon all its people. It shows especially what can happen when determined individuals hold their ground and stand against the mainstream of society.

Throughout Europe in the sixteenth century, thousands of Anabaptists were imprisoned, tortured, exiled, and executed by authorities in church and state. In the midst of this bloody turbulence, Pilgram Marpeck tried to work from within the power structure—or at least very near to it—to save those at risk. As far as we know, he made no overt efforts to change the system of governance in the places where he worked. He quietly appealed to the authorities to exercise tolerance, for he believed that God endowed rulers with a natural wisdom for the just exercise of their calling. In his mind, one did not have to be a Christian to rule justly.

Marpeck was not a prominent man and therefore was easily and legitimately omitted in most detailed histories of the period. He was briefly visible as a professional engineer in public employment and made a passing but significant appearance in religious debates with the more prominent Martin Bucer, a leading reformer in Strasbourg. Until the twentieth century, all remembrance of Marpeck's life and work as a leader of the Anabaptists in south Germany and Switzerland had been lost, and even his name had vanished.

But it was not gone; it had merely disappeared into the dark, dusty collections of archives and libraries across Europe, from Strasbourg in France to Olomouc in today's Czech Republic. More than three hundred years were to pass before historians saw his name again on sixteenth-century documents and considered it worthwhile to search out this unknown man.

Marpeck's life story was first told and published in 1925 and 1929, along with transcriptions of two of his works (the second of these for the first time). Then in 1956 came an announcement of a discovery of a manuscript in the public library in Bern, Switzerland. The document contained sixteen of Marpeck's letters, shedding more personal light on him. Three years later, two small unsigned books published in Strasbourg in 1531 were shown to have been written by him, and in 1984 a third was added. From these writings, which we examine in this book, we have come to know about Marpeck's interpretation of Christian faith and about his role as a church leader.

His quiet legacy continues to this day. He was one of the first to advocate the separation of church and state. He offered articulate explanations of the theology of adult baptism and Christian commitment to nonviolence. Instead of violence he practised mediation. He believed in a life-transforming baptism for believers who made solemn vows to live in the community of faith and who believed in a practice of church discipline that led to forgiveness, not excommunication.

Marpeck was far more than a sectarian leader and spokesman for a quietist sect determined to separate itself from the world. The Anabaptists began in January 1525, when a group of Swiss adherents to the Reformer Ulrich Zwingli, impatient with his slow progress of change, joined together to baptize each other on confession of faith. Thus, they became known as "anabaptists"—rebaptizers—who formed a community in which Christ was supreme Lord, unqualified by the authoritative claims of religious leaders and governments.

Marpeck very deliberately participated in the public controversy over the nature of religious authority and the meaning of the sacraments of baptism and the Lord's Supper. He was especially vocal about the relationship of the church to government. He refused to obey the state when it required him to report on all religious dissenters in the mines he supervised. Likewise, he saw it as quite improper for the state to demand the baptism of infants, who could not decide for themselves. His Catholic parish priest, a rebel who was soon disciplined, had taught him that the conscience of the believer was more important in these matters than the orders of the monarch.

Quest for the Truth

In the heated religious climate of Catholics against Lutherans and Zwinglians, Lutherans against Catholics and Zwinglians, Zwinglians against Catholics and Lutherans, and all against Anabaptists, where was truth to be found? The issue of truth was of the utmost importance to all the contesting groups. For Catholics and Protestants—at least in their public demands— truth was found primarily in their interpretation of the church creed or in their definition of conforming to church tradition.

Marpeck himself was thoroughly committed to the church's creedal tradition. However, the mark of a truly Christian life for him was not an isolated creedal orthodoxy but a life of conformity to Christ, the revelation of God. For him, that meant a conscious choice to be a disciple of Jesus and to be part of the church of Christ in which neither government nor the state had a determining function. In modern terms, this would be articulated as a total separation of church and state—a radical idea at the time of Marpeck and one he helped introduce and for which he argued passionately throughout his adult life. Marpeck was also adamant that at no time should the church use force to inflict its views on the people. In this matter too, he was a person far ahead of his time. In the company of Jesus, he argued, there could be no use of the sword of coercion.

A passage in *Thinking the Faith*, by Canadian theologian Douglas J. Hall, describes what Marpeck objected to in his time:

> Throughout approximately 1600 years (by far the greater share of its history) the church has consisted of persons who—most of them—were not in the least conscious of wrestling with "the word of the cross" but were pushed into Christendom, generation after generation, by unthinking forces of social custom. Under the conditions of the Constantinian arrangement, the original disciple-community depicted in the Gospels and Epistles assumes a significance that the post-canonical church of the centuries cannot have. The first disciples, elevated to a status of exceptional sanctity, are seen as participants in the story, while all Christians who succeed them are only its recipients.[1]

Marpeck's vision for the reform of the church was to break that pattern and to be a genuine disciple, like the original disciples were, not merely a recipient of the apostolic legacy. But in breaking with that long European tradition, he and his followers also collided with it. The Reformers and the Protestant governments of the time never seriously questioned the rightness of the unified sacred society with religious and secular leadership. In place of the one Christendom before the schism, there were now numerous Christendoms, each with its own way of combining the powers.

Religious liberty and religious pluralism did not exist in the sixteenth century. Whether it was a Christian principality like Bavaria, a city-state like Strasbourg, or a national monarchy like France, the response was the same: anything that challenged the one expression of Christian faith adopted there was forcibly suppressed. Marpeck's understanding of the

---

1. Douglas J. Hall, *Thinking the Faith: Christian Theology in a North American Context* (Minneapolis: Fortress Press, 1991), 60.

church exploded the old confines of parish, city, and country. For him, the church was wherever Christians gathered for Word and sacrament and mutual admonition. To the sixteenth-century Catholic and Protestant guardians of order, this was a recipe for anarchy.

But Marpeck was politically quite traditional. He upheld the legitimate authority of emperors, kings, and councils for the maintenance of social order. He had no vision for a new social or political order such as was held by the Anabaptists of Münster in Westphalia or by John Calvin. But he believed in the autonomy of God's kingdom in the midst of the kingdoms of this world, and he devoted himself to that vision.

Much of his energy, skill, and thought were devoted to the life of the Christian communities he led. The members of these communities were to be not merely the automatic recipients of a tradition but active participants in it. Their calling was to demonstrate to their contemporaries ways of ordering human relationships that characterized the life of the Jesus community as reflected in the earliest records in the New Testament. That kind of community life has been fittingly described by Canadian novelist Rudy Wiebe in the words of one of his characters:

> Jesus says in his society there is a new way for man to live:
>> you show wisdom, by trusting people;
>> you handle leadership, by serving;
>> you handle offenders, by forgiving;
>> you handle money, by sharing;
>> you handle enemies, by loving;
>> you handle violence, by suffering.
>
> In fact you have a new attitude toward everything, toward everybody. Toward nature, toward the state in which you happen to live, toward women, toward slaves, toward all and every single thing. Because this is a Jesus society. And you repent, not by feeling bad, but by *thinking different*.[2]

As we shall see, Marpeck himself did not always measure up to that ideal. But that was the harbour to which he unwaveringly steered. Marpeck was not a modern man. What he would have been, done, and said in another time and place is an idle question. He was what he was and did and said what he did in the context of his time and place. That is the basis of our judgment of him, not whether he fails or meets the test of being relevant to our time. There is, however, a timeless aspect to his theology and to his passionate commitment to living a Christian life. By

---

2. Rudy Wiebe, *The Blue Mountains of China* (Toronto: McClelland and Stewart, 1970), 215-16. Italics in the original.

holding a mirror to the life and times of Pilgram Marpeck, we can capture an image of who we are—and are not—in today's pluralistic, multi-
tasking, highly secular society.

In Search of Marpeck

The two authors of this book became acquainted with Marpeck's professional life as an engineer through letters and reports in archival holdings
in Innsbruck, Strasbourg, Augsburg, and the British Library in London.
Both of us have read all the information about Marpeck known to date. In
1978 we translated into English and published Marpeck's letters, as well
as his confession of 1532 and two of three books published in Strasbourg
in 1531 (the third was published in 1999), and his work the *Admonition*,
first published in 1542.

Only one of Marpeck's writings bears his signature. All his works were
published anonymously, mostly to save them from the Catholics and
Protestants who burned Anabaptist books. Even so, precious few of them
survived. The signed work was the confession that he presented on request
to the city councillors in Strasbourg early in 1532. This work became for
us the "baseline" for identifying the three books of 1531 as Marpeck's. His
letters were attributed to him by the copyist of the manuscript in which
they were preserved and were confirmed to be by him by the German
Mennonite scholar Heinold Fast. The *Admonition* of 1542 was identified
as Marpeck's work by his theological opponent Caspar Schwenckfeld. His
last and largest work, the *Response*, was attributed to him by Magdalena
von Pappenheim, the first owner of one of the three surviving manuscripts,
several decades after Marpeck's death.

We learned a great deal from and depended on previous writers on
Marpeck, among them Johann Loserth, J. C. Wenger, J. J. Kiwiet, Torsten
Bergsten, Stephen Boyd, Harold S. Bender, Neal Blough, and others. Their
works are listed in the bibliography at the back of the book.[3]

Nevertheless, the gaps in our knowledge of Marpeck's life are extensive. Years of his life passed without a trace of his activity. We do know
that he was married, had a daughter, and worked steadily as a professional engineer. Because we know so few other details of Marpeck's day-
to-day life, we have taken the liberty at several points to write about
what he might have done, for instance, how he might have travelled and
what routes he might have taken—careful always not to exceed the prob-

---

3. For a more detailed survey of the many scholars who have written about the
life of Marpeck, see William Klassen, "The Legacy of the Marpeck Community in
Anabaptist Scholarship," *MQR* 78 (January 2004), 7-28.

abilities of time and circumstance. Wherever we have imagined or conjectured undocumented events or courses of action, we have indicated this with terms such as "perhaps," "it seems likely," "it may be," and the like. An example of this is the imaginary description of the journey of Marpeck and his wife Anna from Moravia to Strasbourg in the late summer of 1528.

The Political and Social Backdrop

The backdrop of the Marpeck story is the world of western Europe in the 1500s, a kaleidoscope that was constantly turning, revealing both continuity and change in political, intellectual, religious, and social patterns.

In 1553, three years before Pilgram Marpeck died, Archduke Ferdinand of Austria (who in two years would become emperor) took in hand a project that had been languishing for years: a monument to his grandfather, Emperor Maximilian I, originally begun by Maximilian himself. The original plans called for the monument to be erected in Wiener Neustadt, south of Vienna, the eastern capital of the Holy Roman Empire. But Ferdinand had other plans. He began by building a lavish court chapel (the *Hofkirche*) beside the royal residence in Innsbruck.

At the centre of this chapel is a massive monument to Maximilian. It can be seen there today as a symmetrical arrangement of twenty-eight larger-than-life statues around the emperor's tomb. Among the figures are many male and female members of the Habsburg dynasty, as well as claimed ancestors such as the Ostrogothic king Theodoric (455-526 C.E.) and the mostly mythical king Arthur of Camelot.

The chapel was not only a monument to Maximilian I but also to the ideal of the Holy Roman Empire of the German Nation and the Habsburg dynasty. The Habsburg family held the throne of the empire almost without interruption from 1440 until 1806. The empire stretched 1,200 kilometres (720 miles) from its western border near the French city of Lyons eastward to the border of Poland, and from Hamburg on the North Sea 1,050 kilometres (600 miles) south to the Italian city of Sienna near the Mediterranean Sea.

The French philosopher Voltaire is reported to have said that the Holy Roman Empire was neither holy, nor Roman, nor an empire. Indeed, its claim to be the exercise of a single continuing Roman imperial sovereignty in Europe, succeeding the emperors Augustus, Constantine, and Charlemagne, was a pious fiction. Its claim to be holy was an article of faith derived from the view that the emperor was God's vicar on earth, ruling by the grace and favour of God. Finally, the claim to be an empire had some credibility in that it was a linguistic and ethnic amalgamation of many political units under a single sovereign. But it was never a unitary state like France or England.

Officially, if one travelled from Lyons in France to Cracow in Poland, one traversed the empire from west to east. In fact, one travelled over a patchwork quilt of separate, independent political units: the duchy of Savoy and the county of Burgundy, the duchies of Württemberg, Bavaria, and Silesia, the kingdom of Bohemia, and the county of Moravia. One would also have stopped at perhaps half a dozen independent city-states of the empire, among them Strasbourg, Ulm, and Augsburg. The road might also have taken one through the territories of the bishops of Strasbourg, Augsburg, and Passau. All of these, regardless of name, were then what we would today call independent states.

"The Empire," wrote Reformation historian Thomas A. Brady, "was polyglot but not multinational, for it contained many peoples but no nations."[4]

Unlike the monarchs of England and France, the emperor was not a hereditary ruler. He—it was ever and only a man—was elected to that office by the seven electors of the empire, the dukes of Saxony, Brandenburg, and the Palatinate, the king of Bohemia, and the archbishops of Mainz, Cologne, and Trier. The person chosen as emperor was usually that member of one of the noble houses of Europe who could pay the highest bribes to get the necessary votes. Thus the emperor was at best a coordinator of the powers of the principalities, cities, and church states comprising the empire, but only by their consent. He was dependent on their support and goodwill for the exercise of his power. Still, Charles V, who was emperor for most of Marpeck's active years, was acknowledged by everyone in Europe to be the first prince of Christendom.

When Charles became emperor in 1519, the Holy Roman Empire was composed of 173 secular states (some small, some large), 136 church states ruled by bishops, archbishops, and abbots, and eighty-five imperial cities— a total of 387 political units. All were represented at the regular gathering of the empire, the diet (i.e., "empire day," from the Latin *dies*), which made decisions and laws for the empire and for the individual units only as constituent parts of the empire. This structure is roughly analogous to modern federal governments, which make laws that function in all provinces or states, and provinces or states, which make laws that apply only within their boundaries.

---

4. Thomas A. Brady, *The Politics of Reformation Germany, Jacob Sturm (1489-1553) of Strasbourg* (Atlantic Highlands, N.J.: Humanities Press, 1997), 9.

The duchy of Tirol, ruled by the Habsburg family, was at the strategic geographical centre of the Holy Roman Empire. Innsbruck, its chief city, was one of the administrative centres of the empire in the sixteenth century. Tirol's direct ruler was Ferdinand, archduke and later also king of Bohemia and Moravia, and brother of Emperor Charles V. Ferdinand personally appointed Pilgram Marpeck to be mining superintendent (*Bergrichter*) in Rattenberg in 1525. Tirol was Marpeck's native land, and only recently has he been acknowledged as a prominent native son and influential historical figure.

After the Diet of Augsburg in 1530, when the alienation between Catholic and Protestant began in earnest, a traveller would have had to be alert to the many frontiers to be crossed. Protestants were considered heretics after Martin Luther's excommunication by Pope Leo X in 1519 and therefore in danger in Catholic territories. A case in point was Martin Bucer, known as the Reformer of Strasbourg. On his way back from Bern in 1528, he spent a night at an inn in lower Alsace. The local sheriff said later that if he had known that Bucer was there he would have arrested him and given a hundred guilders to whoever would have betrayed him.[5] Anabaptists like Pilgram Marpeck were in varying degrees of danger in Catholic and Protestant areas alike.

Intellectual Change

Despite its apparent political stability, Europe was changing. Among the intellectuals called humanists there was the conviction that the dark millennium just past—with its unquestioning faith in the divine authority of the church—was yielding to the light of the human mind, reclaimed from the classical heritage of Greece and Rome. Cutting-edge scholars such as Erasmus attempted to vault over that long age of Christian obedience back to the questioning pagan writers of the ancient past. They attacked accepted contemporary guidelines and practices by looking for new prescriptions for thought drawn from the classical writers. The slogan was "Back to the sources!" The new human being invested with dignity and autonomy now became the measure of all things, replacing the old authorities. William Wordsworth's words about the early French Revolution are fitting for the sentiments of the time: "Bliss was it in that dawn to be alive!"

Religious Change

On top of these changes came the religious explosion called the

---

5. Martin Greschat, *Martin Bucer. Ein Reformator und seine Zeit* (Munich: Beck, 1990), 140.

Protestant Reformation, which piggy-backed on the earlier movement of humanism. The Reformers of all varieties sought to bound over the period now called the Middle Ages, back to the beginnings of Christianity. With the Bible, Christianity's written source, they challenged much of the papal church: the papacy itself, the teaching about the intercession of the saints, and the whole penitential system of confession, indulgences, and the like. They disputed the church's claim to be supreme—even over emperors, kings, princes, and city councils. Most of all they proclaimed that salvation was to be had by God's grace through faith alone, and not by obedience to the church's laws and practices.

Many today assume that the various Reformers from the beginning were determined to establish their own sects. This was not the case. The intention of all, including Marpeck, was to reform the one church. But the church was like an old, brittle wineskin; it could not accommodate the new wine of the Reformation. The old skin burst and the unity of church and society was shattered.

That didn't stop traditionalist leaders from attempting to put Humpty Dumpty back together again. During his long reign from 1519 to 1555, Charles V and his brother Ferdinand never relented in their determination to restore all of the Holy Roman Empire of the German Nation to the one Catholic faith; by consent if possible, by force if necessary. Ferdinand especially was driven by a nostalgic vision of what he thought Constantine had achieved in the fourth century and believed it was possible to recover that vision of one faith for the entire empire. Ironically, the harder he tried, the more his goal slipped from his grasp.

One of the most profound changes in Marpeck's life was that he lived his first years in a town where there was only one religious option, while his last years were lived in Augsburg, where virtually all decisions were made in the awareness that there were two major religious options, Catholic and Protestant, as well as a number of illicit smaller sects, including Anabaptists.

Social Change

Martin Luther, the greatest of the church reformers, was a social conservative who cautioned that all should remain in their social place or anarchy would take hold. He especially had no patience with what today is called upward mobility.

But even he could not prevent the changes underway in Europe's social life. The old feudal system, a pyramidal structure with the emperor at the lone peak and the peasants at the broad bottom, was disintegrating. Peasants demanded social and religious rights and the easing of feudal payments and service. A new class of people, what today we would call the middle class, emerged in the cities. These were the merchants and bankers, the *nouveaux riches*, who were fast replacing the old feudal nobility in social position. The nobles' stone castles and armoured war horses were no match for the new technology of destruction, the cannons. There was also a growing class of highly skilled, highly paid professionals. Pilgram Marpeck as a civil engineer was one of them. People's places and roles in society were changing.

These seismic changes in European society created uncertainty and anxiety. Martin Luther's concern with anarchy was prophetic. The year he died, the broken religious unity degenerated still further into open warfare.

Biography and Society

In this milieu Marpeck lived and worked, and in this context we have tried to describe and interpret his life. Writing the biography of a living person is a daunting undertaking, because the subject can repudiate what the biographer has written. Nevertheless, the genie of what has been written can never be put back into the lamp. It is out there for good or ill, and often repudiation cannot change it.

The biographer of a sixteenth-century person is on safer ground. The subject cannot reject the biographer's conclusions and cannot defend himself or herself. But for this reason the biographer of the dead is even more morally obligated to mind the rules that safeguard truth. As Ann Wroe observes:

> [Biographers] have care for souls. We are responsible, sometimes briefly, sometimes for much longer, for the reputation and afterlife of other people. We hold their memorial flame and snuff it out or make it blaze as we please. What we say about these people becomes, for a while at least, the truth of who they were. By writing biography we recast in the world the shadow of a soul that still lives, that cannot defend itself. That soul depends on us.[6]

Wroe's metaphor "the shadow of a soul" suggests that in the outline of the shadow one may recognize the original, but that all else is blacked out. The metaphor warns us to remember that the link between the outward action and the inward motivation is often hidden. We may make inferences from what we know about Marpeck but may well be wide of the mark. In particular, we may never judge sixteenth-century persons by the rules of the twenty-first century. The virtual absence in Marpeck's

---

6. Taken from Ann Wroe's reflections in the Catholic periodical *The Tablet* (London), cited by Michael Higgins in "Biographers have care of the soul of their subject," *Toronto Star,* July 16, 2005, M6.

writings of references to his wife, Anna, for example, should not lead us to the conclusion that he did not love and care for her.

Acquainting the reader with Marpeck's convictions demands thoughtful arrangement of the elements of Marpeck's thought. The danger is that we may be arranging it in patterns Marpeck never thought of. For example, would Marpeck really have agreed with our judgment that because the Bible is a material thing, its authority is not absolute?

The documents themselves can be misleading unless we are alert to the practices of the day. Addressing political authorities as "noble, strong, firm, cautious, honourable, wise, gracious, and respectful lords"[7] should not be understood to be boot-licking obsequiousness or a cover for deception. It was simply part of the convention of the time and was used even if the person addressed was an adversary.

We have tried to be aware of these cautions and many others besides.[8] But the pitfalls have not prevented us from attempting a Marpeck biography, because we believe that the recovery of the past is important for the present.

There is in our culture today a presumption against religion, seeing it as a negative force. Religious people are seen by many as typically prejudiced and bigoted, refusing or incapable of any kind of rigorous thinking. Regrettably, this view has also occasionally infected judgments about people of the sixteenth century, with historians rejecting religious explanations and substituting instead political or economic ones to explain the century's struggles.

In fact, the sixteenth century was a religious century. The dominating arguments of the time were religious even when they touched the worlds of commerce and politics. Atheism was unknown. It should therefore not surprise the reader that Marpeck's mental world was religious, which was true of all his interlocutors as well. Marpeck's memory survived not because he was a competent engineer but because he was a Christian leader and controversialist in his time.

The descendants of the established Roman Catholic and Protestant churches of western Europe and North America find themselves today in a situation radically different from that of their sixteenth-century ancestors. The churches no longer dominate their societies in the northern half

7. *The Writings of Pilgram Marpeck (WPM)*, trans. and eds. William Klassen and Walter Klaassen (Scottdale, Pa.: Herald Press, 1978), 306.
8. David H. Fischer, *Historians' Fallacies* (New York: Harper & Row, 1970).

of the globe. Virtually everywhere they have been ignored or expelled from their assumed role as the conscience of society. The privileges they once enjoyed are gone. They are viewed as tolerated minorities, and in many societies their numbers are shrinking. They need help.

Pilgram Marpeck has long since been part of the church's tradition, even though he was relatively unknown. He and his fellow Anabaptists five and a half centuries ago found themselves wrestling with issues of church-state relations and nonviolent resistance similar to those that face us still today, especially the burning issue of whether Christians can continue to participate in violence against others in the name of Christ.

We are pleased to be able to introduce Pilgram Marpeck to our contemporaries, be they Christian or not, and to Christians of all stripes, since we are today more ready to listen to each other than were our ancestors in that other century, and especially to the community of which he was an early leader and thinker, the Mennonite churches, which today need as much help as everyone else.

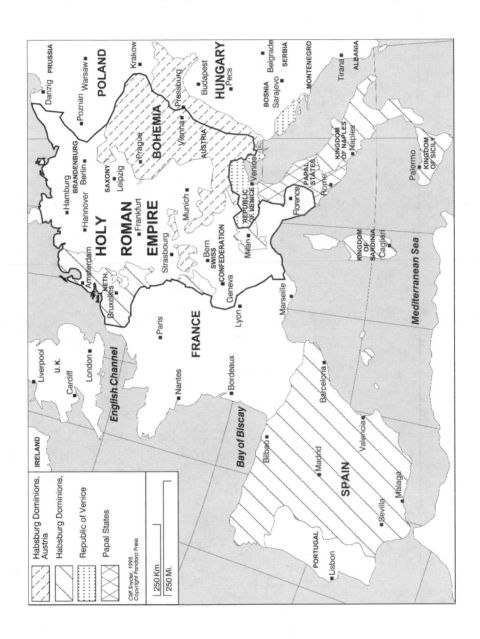

The Holy Roman Empire

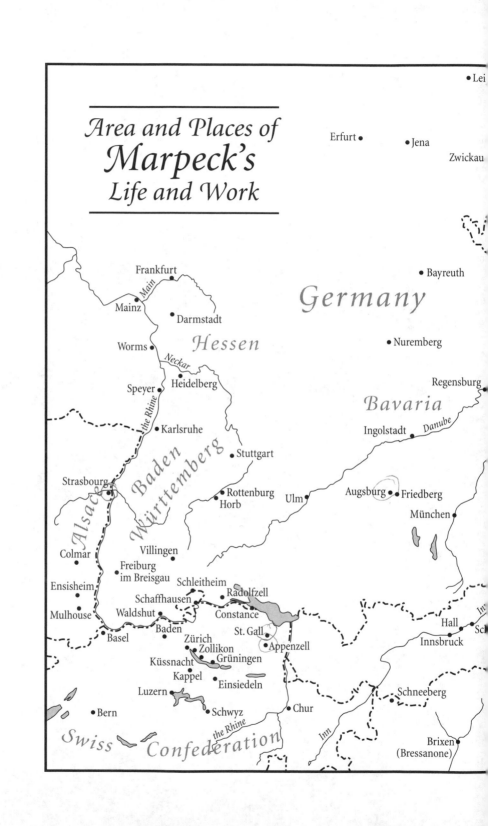

Area and Places of
Marpeck's
Life and Work

Germany

Bavaria

Hessen

Baden

Württemberg

Alsace

Swiss Confederation

• Lei

Erfurt •   • Jena

Zwickau

• Bayreuth

• Nuremberg

Regensburg

Ingolstadt • _Danube_

Augsburg • • Friedberg

München •

Hall

Sc

Innsbruck

Schneeberg •

Brixen •
(Bressanone)

Frankfurt
•   _Main_

Mainz •   • Darmstadt

Worms •   _Neckar_

Speyer •   • Heidelberg

• Karlsruhe

• Stuttgart

Strasbourg •

• Rottenburg
Horb   Ulm •

Colmar   • Villingen
•
Freiburg
• im Breisgau   Schleitheim

Ensisheim •   Schaffhausen • • Radolfzell

Mulhouse •   Waldshut • Constance
•   • Baden
Basel   Zürich •   St. Gall •
• Zollikon   • Appenzell
Küssnacht • • Grüningen
Kappel • • Einsiedeln
Luzern •
• Bern   • Schwyz   • Chur

the Rhine   _Inn_

Dresden •

nnitz

lovy Vary

anske Lazne

Pilsen
(Plzn) •

Bohemia

• Gorlitz

Poland

Prague
(Praha) •

Olmutz
(Olomouc) •

Eibenschitz
(Ivančice)

Brünn
(Brno) •

Austerlitz
(Slavkov) •

Auspitz
(Hustopeče) •

Znajim
(Znojmo) •

Nikolsburg
(Mikulov) •

Moravia

Budwies •
(CeskeBudejovice)

Krumau •
(Česky Krumlov)

Kreuzenstein •

Pressburg
(Bratislava)

Passau •

Inn

Danube

Vienna •

Danube

Linz •

Eisenstadt •

Neusiedlersee

Wiener Neustadt •

Chiemsee

Salzburg •

Austria

rf •

Kitzbühel

Brück an
der Mür •

Szombathely •

Hungary

ol

• Badgastein

Graz •

Klagenfurt •

Villach •

N

W ⊕ E

S

For easier reference, contemporary borders are shown.

Pilgram Marpeck, engineer. Portrait by Ivan Moon, town of Rattenberg by Jan Gleysteen.

-1-

Turmoil in Tirol

The people in the courtroom of Horb in what is today southwest Germany could scarcely believe what they had heard from the prisoner. A former priest named Michael Sattler was accused of heresy.

"If waging war were proper," he was reported to have said, "I would rather take the field against the so-called Christians who persecute, take captive, and kill true Christians, than against the Turks."

The year was 1527 and Europe was in political, religious, and economic turmoil. Adding to the climate of fear and uncertainty, the Holy Roman Empire was engaged in a life-and-death struggle with the Ottoman Turks, who since 1453 had created a vast empire that would last for the next four centuries.

For the court, Sattler's words and actions were beyond comprehension. A former prior of the Benedictine monastery in Freiburg, Sattler had recently left the monastery to become the pastor of a fledgling Anabaptist congregation at Horb. Speaking in clear and measured tones, Sattler minced no words in defending what he was accused of saying.

"The Turk is a genuine Turk and knows nothing of the Christian faith," he declared. "He is a Turk according to the flesh. But you claim to be Christians, boast of Christ, and still persecute the faithful witnesses of Christ. Thus you are Turks according to the spirit."[1]

Such provocative words could only result in condemnation. The sentence of the court was as harsh as one could imagine: "In the matter of the prosecutor of the imperial majesty versus Michael Sattler, it has been found that Michael Sattler should be given into the hands of the hangman, who shall lead him to the square and cut off his tongue, then chain him to a

---

1. John H. Yoder (ed. and trans.), "The Legacy of Michael Sattler" 1, in *Classics of the Radical Reformation* (Scottdale, Pa.: Herald Press, 1973), 72-73.

wagon, there tear his body twice with red hot tongs, and again when he is brought before the gate, five more times. When this is done to be burned to powder as a heretic."[2]

The sentence was carried out beside the Neckar River, outside of the town of Rottenburg in the principality of Württemberg. It was a spring day in May, the stone buildings and tile roofs of the picturesque town reflected in the quiet water in contrast to the agony that was playing itself out nearby. Two days later, Sattler's wife, Margareta, was executed by drowning in the same river after she, like her husband, steadfastly refused to recant.[3]

News of the Sattler executions reverberated throughout the empire. Printed accounts flew across the country and caused widespread revulsion. Strasbourg's leading Reform clergyman, Martin Bucer, referred to Sattler as "a dear friend of God." Capito, another Reformer from Strasbourg, in a letter urged city councillors in Horb to defend their prisoners from the Austrian government. The prisoners may have erred, he wrote, but they were not blasphemers.[4] At the opposite end of the spectrum, Archduke Ferdinand, in Innsbruck, doubtless felt grimly vindicated by Sattler's harsh sentence, which he had himself counselled. In his mind, Sattler was one of the chief figures in a new and dangerous conspiracy against the holy church and empire.

Adherents of this so-called "conspiracy" were present even in the Austrian Tirol. In Rattenberg, a charming town nestled at the foot of a mountain beside the Inn River, a young mining superintendent named Pilgram Marpeck had become acquainted with some of Sattler's co-believers among his miners and felt a magnetic attraction to what they taught. The news of Sattler's execution must have haunted him that summer of 1527. For several years, Marpeck had met every three months with Ferdinand to report on his mining operations. Did the archduke ever share

2. Ibid., 74-75.

3. C. Arnold Snyder, *Anabaptist History and Theology* (Kitchener, Ont.: Pandora Press and Scottdale, Pa.: Herald Press, 1995), 62. For a full account of Sattler's life and trial, see "Michael Sattler" by G. Bossert and H. S. Bender, in *Mennonite Encyclopedia (ME)* 4, 427-34.

4. His letter is dated May 31, 1527. Capito also wrote to the prisoners, urging them to desist from their errors of rejecting force, declining to hold public office, and refusing to swear oaths (i.e., a loyalty oath to the city or state). He encouraged them to pray for their enemies and to lose all hate for them. These letters by Capito are moving testimonials of the Christian spirit. They can be found in the *ME* 2: 811, "Horb," by Bossert. Compare with Neff's "Capito" in *ME* 3. For original, see Baum, Capito, 371, and Abraham Hulshof, *Geschiedenis van de Doopsgezinden te Straatsburg van 1525 to 1557* (Amsterdam: J. Clausen, 1905), 66-68.

with Marpeck his satisfaction that Sattler had received what he considered the full justice of the kingdom? Sattler's fate would make Marpeck cautious about his own future, which professionally looked very bright. He would wait and see. Unprecedented changes were in the air.

A Decade of Tumult

The decade preceding Pilgram Marpeck's turn toward Anabaptism in 1528 were among the most tumultuous and stressful periods in early modern history. They were the chaotic years of the emergence of the movement to reform "the church" (which later became known as the Roman Catholic Church), the only church in Europe at the time except for the Orthodox churches in Greece, the Balkans, and Russia. The Reform movement had its immediate roots in the revolution of the inner life of Martin Luther. Driven by personal agony to find "a gracious God," the Augustinian monk finally found him in the assurance of forgiveness and acceptance based not on reward for spiritual performance but on the totally unmerited grace of God.

Thousands, it seems, had been waiting to hear this proclamation, which pealed like church bells across the lands of the Holy Roman Empire. It was a voice that spoke with authority, not like the weak and self-serving voices of many clergy of the time. There was a hunger for a word from God, a word that most clergy in the towns and villages could not provide. Untrained and ill-equipped, many could neither care for the souls of their people nor speak effectively about God's Word.

It was the New Testament book of Romans that had become the means of Luther's liberation. Luther was plagued by guilt bordering on obsessive scrupulosity. In the book of Romans, he found solace and the confidence to embrace the free mercy of God. He was inspired in reading the first chapter that "the just shall live by faith." He treated this insight as a vision from God, and no argument (especially a few years later from the emerging Anabaptist community) that the text might mean "the just shall live by their faithfulness" would deter him.[5] Luther also boldly rejected the divine authority claimed by pope, clergy, and church council. The Bible, he declared, was the sole and ultimate authority for all Christians.

From October 1518 when Luther first defended his teaching before Cardinal Cajetan in Augsburg until his return to Saxony early in 1522, he was in mortal danger. "With the emperor, the pope, and the cardinal against him Luther had but slender hope of escaping the stake," wrote church his-

5. See George Forell's perceptive reading of Luther's social ethic in *Faith Active in Love: An Investigation of the Principles Underlying Luther's Social Ethics*, reviewed by William Klassen, *MQR*, July 29, 1955, 244-47.

torian Roland H. Bainton.[6] But he survived, thanks in part to the calculating protection of the prince of Saxony, the wily Frederick the Wise.

The brilliant young Luther served as a professor at Wittenberg University, which Frederick had endowed in 1502 as the first university in Germany to be founded without the permission of church authorities and which historian Diarmaid MacCulloch refers to as a "rather brash little institution."[7] Frederick, a strong supporter of such artists as Albrecht Dürer, held the influential position of elector of Saxony. There were only seven electors in the Holy Roman Empire, and it was they who had the power to elect (hence their title) the emperor. Thus, the influence of Frederick and other electors was substantial, and Frederick—although a religious traditionalist—was able to protect Luther from religious and imperial authorities that sought to do him in.[8]

Luther had been prepared to suffer the fate of Jan Hus, who had been burned at the stake in Constance in 1415 for his call to reform the church in Bohemia. Instead, Luther went on to set the theological and even political agenda for centuries to come.

Even before Luther had been heard from, the call for reform had come from the humanist scholar Erasmus of Rotterdam, who in 1516 published the first modern text of the New Testament in Latin and Greek as an alternative to the Vulgate, the church's authoritative text. His intention was to get back to the purified source of the church's life and thought by means of the most accurate possible text of the New Testament. It was to be the best available baseline from which the present state of the church could be judged and reformed. Erasmus's work turned out to be one of the most important catalysts of the Reformation, especially as it sparked other translations that were soon available all over the empire in German, Dutch, and other languages of the people.

The church for centuries had relied upon the Latin Vulgate, which had been prepared mainly by St. Jerome in the late fourth century, as the only "authorized" version of the Bible. New translations in languages that even ordinary people could understand sparked radical new insights to the biblical text. In the Vulgate, for example, Matthew 4:17 referred to *penitentiam agite*, "do penance," but the Greek New Testament of Erasmus read *metanoeite*, "repent," a difference that Martin Luther noticed and that became for him a weapon against the church's system of penance. According to Luther, no

6. Roland H. Bainton, *Here I Stand* (New York: Mentor, 1950), 70.

7. Diarmaid MacCulloch, *The Reformation* (New York: Penguin Books, 2003), 116-17.

8. Ibid.

longer should people be required to perform penances imposed by the clergy. Luther's call, based on Scripture, was to take responsibility for one's sin by repenting of it and accepting God's gracious offer of forgiveness. The popular writer and poet Hans Sachs called this message the song of the Wittenberg nightingale.

The city of Zürich became another centre of church reform. In 1519 Ulrich Zwingli, a devoted parish priest now serving the main church in the city, the *Grossmünster*, also began with the centrality of Scripture as the authority for church reform. He believed the Word of God to be as clear as Swiss mountain spring water flowing from its source in God. He was a disciple of Erasmus, not of Luther, and so were his young supporters Andreas Castelberger, Conrad Grebel, and Felix Mantz. They were the first representatives of a movement that came to be known as Anabaptism and charter members of what ultimately became the Mennonite church.

These three impulses for reform should not be mistaken for what later became the Lutheran, Zwinglian (Reformed), and Mennonite denominations, which separated from the Roman Catholic Church. Denominations were a much later invention of Christians in the United States, evolving in the nineteenth century. In the sixteenth century, these three movements as well as the Catholic Church were all devoted to reforming the One Church, each with special emphases, but all of which were present in the history and tradition of the church.

Forerunners of Reform

The religious crisis that had convulsed Europe for 150 years and peaked in the sixteenth century was predominantly a crisis of authority. The Great Schism of the church began in 1378 with the death of Pope Gregory XI and a new papal election. The papacy had become the religious and political football of opposing power blocks in Europe. When agreement became impossible, both blocks elected a new pope. Both claimed apostolic legitimacy: theirs was the only real pope. The crisis became worse in 1409 when, after another election, there were actually three popes, none of whom would surrender their claims to legitimacy. How could the faithful know which of the popes spoke with the voice of God?

This breakup of divine order was so serious that many expected the world to end. Travelling preachers announced the coming of the antichrist. Church councils attempted to resolve the crisis by claiming the authority traditionally held by the popes. Reform was attempted but failed because many of the "reformers" benefited from the abuses they were trying to correct. Even when a single pope was elected in 1417, the crisis was not resolved. Most of the popes of the fifteenth century had little concern for the plight of the church. The demand for reform of the church "in head and members" grew in volume as the question of where religious authority was to be found still appeared to many to go begging. Now the sudden appearance of Martin Luther and his slogan of "the Scriptures only" (*sola scriptura*) was the ringing answer to the question of where religious authority lay.

The Impact of Bankers and Miners

These large dislocations in European society were also at work in the smaller world of Pilgram Marpeck in Rattenberg and other towns in the lush hills and valleys of Austria's Inn River Valley. The roots of discontent had their origins not just in religion but also in the economic pressures that increasingly bedevilled the Habsburg Empire. As the emperor sank deeper into debt, he became increasingly beholden to the bankers who granted him the funds he needed and to the miners whose exhausting, dangerous work produced the wealth in the first place.

Primary among the bankers was the extremely wealthy Fugger family of Augsburg, whose financial dealings stretched across large segments of the empire and beyond. Just 20 kilometres (12 miles) east of Innsbruck, a five-storey building known as the *Fuggerhaus* had stood in Schwaz since early in the sixteenth century. It was one of the largest buildings in this little city on the Inn River and a close neighbour of Rattenberg. The building with the prominent corner turrets was the most visible symbol of the success of the Fugger family, as well as of the insolvency of Tirol, which was a crown possession of the royal house of Habsburg.

Dynastic wars with France and Hungary, conducted with mercenary armies in the previous century, had resulted in a chronic shortage of money in the emperor's coffers. Jakob Fugger, the rich banker from Augsburg, became the money lender to Emperor Maximilian I. It was Fugger who also provided the money to finance the enormous bribe of various electors needed to make his nineteen-year-old grandson, Charles, emperor after Maximilian died in 1519. To accomplish all this, much of the rich mining industry in Tirol had been mortgaged by the Habsburg family to the Fuggers well before the year 1500.

In 1522, the Fuggers bought out a competitor, and the mines in Schwaz and Rattenberg came under their control. Two years later the Fuggers took over seventeen of the richly successful mines at the Schneeberg, located high above the Brenner Pass, where the Alps of Italy, Austria, and Switzerland come together. In 1525, against strong local opposition, the royal government sold the smeltery of Rattenberg to the Fuggers for forty-seven thousand guilders to pay for suppression of rebellious peasants in Württemberg.[9] It is calculated that in 1522 the Habsburgs owed a total of more than one million guilders, about three hundred million in today's dollars. About half of this amount was owed to Jakob Fugger, and became payable upon his death in 1525.[10] Throughout Tirol, people were increasingly outraged that the new owners of the mines and smelters were outsiders who cared little for the residents of Tirol, or, in particular, for their employees in the mines and smelters.

Schwaz was the largest mining centre in the Inn Valley. In 1526, there were an astounding 142 mine shafts west of the city, employing nearly five thousand miners. Many of them and their families had left Germany, Hungary, and Bohemia to work there.[11] By 1556, there were 111 kilometres (68 miles) of tunnels worked by more than seven thousand miners.[12] Rattenberg was second only to Schwaz in order of importance as a mining centre in the Inn Valley.[13]

Sowing Seeds of Rebellion

Miners were migrant workers moving from place to place, depending upon where work was to be found. Wherever they were, miners represented a socially and religiously unstable population. They did not integrate with local residents because they had no social or ethnic roots in common. Wages of the miners were normally paid partially in currency, and the rest in staples such as grain, flour, cheese, nuts, wine, shoes, and cloth. All these had to be bought in company stores, which acquired the goods below cost.

In a pattern that was to become prevalent in mining and forestry communities around the world, miners often had to buy on credit, and because of their low wages they usually sank into debt. Thus they became dependent on the mining company and could not leave their employment until their debt was paid. The goods to sustain the mining community had to be imported, since local production was not sufficient to feed the huge number of mine workers and their families. So the workers were frequently the victims of manipulated pricing on the part of the company. To make matters worse, wages were often scandalously in arrears, causing repeated outbursts of anger and revolt.[14]

9. Josef Macek, *Der Tiroler Bauernkrieg und Michael Gaismair* (Berlin: VEB Deutscher Verlag der Wissenschaften, 1965), 47-48.

10. Max Steinmetz, "Die dritte Etappe der frühbürgerlichen Revolution. Der Deutsche Bauernkrieg 1524 bis 1526," in *Der Deutsche Bauernkrieg 1524-1526*, ed. Rainer Wohlfeil (Nymphenburger Verlagshandlung, 1975), 84.

11. Macek, *Der Tiroler Bauernkrieg*, 44.

12. Eduard Widmoser, *Tirol A bis Z* (Innsbruck: Südtirol-Verlag, 1970), 856.

13. Macek, *Der Tiroler Bauernkrieg*, 43.

14. Georg Mutschlechner, *Erzbergbau und Bergwesen im Berggericht Rattenberg*

Because of their social rootlessness and economic vulnerability, as well as their feisty, independent streak, the mining communities in Tirol in the 1520s also became centres of religious agitation. The miners often were the first to accept the message of the new evangelical preachers. They participated in the popular piety of the day. In fact, their religious faith may have been more important to them than it was to people in the settled communities. In Rattenberg, the wariness of local people to these boisterous outsiders and the solidarity of the miners among themselves became manifest in the parish church where the mine workers were allocated their own place of worship: the right-hand nave of the church. The sanctuary was divided into two parts: the miners on one side and the townspeople on the other. We don't know if they regularly held separate services, but we do know that at times they had their own preachers.

Among the miners as among the peasants, religious and economic grievances tended to flow together. The miners were very aware of their economic importance because of their irreplaceable skills. They were the ones who held the secrets of mining technology and were conscious of the power that gave them.[15] They also knew how to enforce their demands. There were at least six uprisings of miners in Schwaz during the sixteenth century.[16] For all these reasons, the miners were often feared by the authorities in Innsbruck as well as by the indigenous population.

Early in 1525, the first of these revolts occurred when six thousand miners in Schwaz stopped work, refused obedience to the city authorities and elected their own officers. They then set out for Innsbruck to appeal directly to Ferdinand, who, at the behest of his brother, Emperor Charles V, ruled over that section of Austria as archduke. Ferdinand met the miners at Hall, just east of Innsbruck, where a delegation presented a list of grievances to him. They wanted exploitation by investors to cease and the mining superintendent to be replaced. They also demanded the right to elect a representative body to look after their interests as miners. This time and again shortly thereafter, Ferdinand mollified the miners by promising that their ancient rights would be restored and their grievances would be rectified, especially offering more saints' days as holidays and an end to having to buy their staple food at company stores.

But Ferdinand's generosity extended only so far. A few weeks later, in February 1525, the revolt ended with a threat of force by the gov-

---

(Im Selbstverlag der Gemeinden Alpbach, Brixlegg, Rattenberg, Reith im Alpbachtal, 1984), 33-34.

15. Rudolf Palme, "Zur Täuferbewegung in Tirol," in *Mennonitische Geschichtsblätter (MGBl)*, 43-44, 1986-87, 50.

16. Widmoser, *Tirol A bis Z*, 856.

ernment.[17] Nevertheless, a few months later Ferdinand proved he was still listening to the miners' concerns.

In April he reached into the ranks of the city council in Rattenberg and appointed thirty-year-old Pilgram Marpeck as superintendent of mining in Rattenberg. Five years earlier, Marpeck had been elected to city council and in 1522 had served a one-year term as mayor. Despite his youth and relative inexperience, word of his skills as a community leader and pragmatic problem-solver must have spread. Ferdinand evidently saw in Marpeck an official able to deal with the challenges of this volatile but essential component of the Tirolean economy. Marpeck became a trusted official, but it was a trust that would be shattered in just a few years.

The Voice of the Nightingale

At the same time as the miners of Schwaz and Rattenberg became increasingly restless, the rising call for church reform in Wittenberg and Zürich echoed through the valleys of Tirol. The freedom song of Martin Luther, "the Wittenberg nightingale," was brought to Tirol by itinerant preachers who arrived from Germany in 1520 and 1521. Many of them were priests and monks who were absent-without-leave, representing what has been called "the reformation of the common man." But among them were also well-educated clergy.

A preacher of considerable eloquence arrived in the large mining centre of Schwaz early in June 1521. Jakob Strauss, a former Dominican friar who for fifteen years had been an outspoken partisan of thorough church reform, preached to large assemblies of the miners who had invited him. In 1526, he wrote that he had been working for reform for nineteen years against much opposition.[18] Perhaps this explains his insistence that Martin Luther had not taught him the gospel.[19]

On June 24, 1521, Strauss proceeded to Hall, east of Innsbruck, where he began his work by instructing local priests in the Latin text of the Gospel of Matthew. Before long he was asked by members of the city council to preach publicly, first in local churches and then in the open air to large assemblies. His popularity grew as he attacked the immorality of the clergy and the errors of the theologians. Before the end of the year, the bishop of Brixen, in whose diocese Hall lay, was determined to get rid of Strauss as a dangerous agitator. He ordered the council of Hall to

17. Macek, *Der Deutsche Bauernkrieg*, 122-25; Stephen Boyd, *Pilgram Marpeck, His Life and Social Theology* (Durham, N.C.: Duke University Press, 1992), 20, n119.

18. Jacob Strauss, *Christenlich vnd wolgegrundet antwurt . . .* D. Johannis Coclei, n.d., E4r.

19. Ibid., C2r.

dismiss him and demanded that Strauss appear before him. But the people and the council supported their preacher and ignored the bishop.

The struggle to get rid of Strauss continued through the early months of 1522, involving the bishop, his aides, Hall's city council, the secular government in Innsbruck, Archbishop Lang in Salzburg, and even the emperor. Citizens provided Strauss with a bodyguard and even stationed guards for protection at his lodgings. Although his preaching was especially popular with the city's salt miners, it was very unpopular with a stormy, wrathful Dominican friar from Schwaz named Michael.[20] Strauss soon realized that he could not remain in Hall. To prepare the people for his absence, he preached sixteen sermons on confession during Lent, ending on Maundy Thursday. Thousands came to hear him.[21] Strauss preached his last sermon in Hall on May 4, 1522. At that point, the city council reluctantly yielded to threats from Brixen and Innsbruck for his expulsion. However, the councillors' sympathies were evident when they provided Strauss with money and food for his journey to Wittenberg. On May 10, he quietly left Hall after promising to provide its residents with printed versions of his teaching.[22]

By Pentecost at the end of May, his first printed sermon was available in Hall. He had been forced out, he wrote to his friends, by the followers of Pilate and Herod—a reference to Luke 23:12, where it is reported that Pilate and Herod became friends when they conspired to get rid of Jesus.[23] We don't have the actual text of the sermons Strauss preached in Hall, but the published versions record that he preached against the immorality and greed of the clergy, against the abuses of the confessional system, and against usury. He comforted the people with the message that God required only one work for salvation and that was faith, trusting in the forgiveness of sins offered in the cross of Christ. That faith would, if genuine, produce the works of love toward others.

With Strauss's departure, the people of Hall refused to give up. Late that summer they engaged Urbanus Rhegius from Augsburg, a rising clerical star who had just joined the Reform movement. Rhegius was amazed at the commitment of the people to the new evangelical doctrine.[24] He wasted no time tackling the sacred precepts of the established church,

20. Hermann Barge, *Jakob Strauss: Ein Kämpfer für das Evangelium in Tirol, Thüringen und Süddeutschland* (Leipzig: M. Heinsius Nachfolger, 1937), 8-14; [Jakob Strauss, *Ein new wunderbarich Beychtbuechlin*, 1523, A2v, B2r.].

21. Barge, *Jakob Strauss*, 15, 21; [Jakob Strauss, *Eyn verstendig trostlich leer . . .*, 1522, A2r; Strauss, *Beychbuechlin*, C2r.].

22. Barge, *Jakob Strauss*, 22-23; Strauss, *Eyn verstendig* C2r.

23. Strauss, *Eyn verstendig*, A2r.

24. Barge, *Jakob Strauss*, 26.

directing most of his ecclesiastical fire against indulgences. These were pledges given by the church to any who could pay that their time in purgatory would be reduced for them and their deceased parents. The money collected was used for everything from supporting church-run hospitals and other institutions to building the massively expensive St. Peter's Basilica in Rome.[25] Rhegius also demanded that German replace Latin as the language of worship and attacked the greed of the church hierarchy. Before long, however, there was a replay of the expulsion of Strauss. By year-end, Rhegius was also gone, despite courageous support for him by the council and citizens of Hall.[26]

The Ferment Spreads

All of these events constituted the news of the day, which spread to farms, towns, and cities across the Tirol, including to the small city of Rattenberg, where Pilgram Marpeck in 1522 was serving his one-year term as mayor. Rattenberg at that time had its own popular, independent-minded preacher. Stefan Castenbaur had been appointed prior of the Augustinian monastery in Rattenberg early in 1520 and almost immediately created a sensation. Scripture, not the pope or church hierarchy, was the final authority for the church, he declared. Then, echoing Martin Luther, he proclaimed that salvation came by faith alone. He said later that he paid no attention to an official order of the pope (known as a "papal bull") excommunicating Martin Luther because he was himself not a follower of Luther. Besides, he said, with some cheekiness, the bull had not been read in Rattenberg.

The sweeping valleys and mountains of Tirol were a hotbed of religious ferment at the time. Strauss, Rhegius, and Castenbaur as educated monks and priests were only the most visible spokesmen for reform. Everywhere along the valley of the Inn River another kind of religious agitator appeared, all the way from the point of entry to Tirol at Reutte and Fuessen in the Alps northwest of Innsbruck to the great monastery of Stams in Imst, west of Innsbruck, and on to Hall and Schwaz, Rattenberg, Kitzbühel, and Kufstein.

Little is known about these preachers, some of whom were renegade monks. When appearing in public at Schwaz became too dangerous, the monk preachers became miners who literally and figuratively went underground. We hear of a preacher named Eustachus who preached in the Zillertal, not far from Rattenberg in the summer of 1525. When he

25. MacCulloch, *The Reformation*, 120.
26. Macek, *Der Tiroler Bauernkrieg*, 80.

was imprisoned, the local people attempted to liberate him by force.[27] The Innsbruck authorities conducted constant searches for books and pamphlets that were circulating everywhere promoting church reform.

Early in 1526, clerical agitators who followed Michael Gaismair (the leader of a peasant revolt whom we shall meet later in this chapter) preached in Sterzing, Brixen, and Meran. Everywhere they challenged church doctrine, some going so far as to call for the complete destruction of ecclesiastical authority. Ferdinand called for immediate harsh measures against these disturbers of the peace, but government officials in Innsbruck were more cautious. The surly mood of the people, they warned, made the situation too tense for strong measures.[28]

An itinerant preacher named Wölfl, a goatherd by trade, became an important link between the widespread evangelical agitation and the rise of Anabaptism a few years later. He left his goats in the Sarn Valley and first appeared as a preacher in nearby Bozen in 1525, where he was given a copy of the New Testament. He made his way north over the Brenner Pass into the Inn Valley west of Innsbruck, where he preached at a number of places as well as at Hall. In Innsbruck a schoolmaster taught him to read after he had heard him preach. After Easter 1526, Wölfl travelled south of the Brenner Pass again and preached to large crowds at Klausen among the miners of the area. From there he went to the Puster Valley east of Brixen and preached in the area of St. Lorentz. Not only did peasants, artisans, and miners go to hear him, but several public officials and priests did as well. He was even invited into their castles and houses.

When the sheriff threatened to arrest him, Wölfl said: "Even if they drowned or killed me, five others would arise in my place and preach the word of God."[29] It was in one of Wölfl's meetings in this area that the young Jakob Hutter was persuaded by his teaching to begin his meteoric rise as an Anabaptist leader. Wölfl was arrested early in 1527 and interrogated at Brixen, after which we hear nothing of him. He was likely the Wölfl who was executed as an Anabaptist at Gufidaun near Klausen in 1533.[30]

From the answers he gave to his interrogators, we can get a good summary of Wölfl's views and also, no doubt, those of other Reform

27. Macek, *Der Tiroler Bauernkrieg*, 81-85; Barge, *Jakob Strauss*, 26.

28. Walter Klaassen, *Michael Gaismair: Revolutionary and Reformer* (Leiden: Brill, 1978), 58-59.

29. Matthias Schmelzer, "Jakob Hutters Wirken im Lichte von Bekenntnissen gefangener Täufer," in *Der Schlern* 63 (1989), 598.

30. Werner O. Packull, *Hutterite Beginnings: Communitarian Experiments during the Reformation* (Baltimore and London: Johns Hopkins University Press, 1995), 183, 212.

preachers. Several times he mentioned tracts by Luther that he and his followers read and discussed. To the religious and secular establishment, Wölfl's comments were outrageous and inflammatory. The pope, monks, and priests led the people astray, he declared. Oral confession was unnecessary. The Lord had instituted the Lord's Supper but not the mass, which he said was nothing more than a street vendor's stand. What's more, God was not physically present in the bread, and the holy water in the font wasn't holy. Fasting had no value. The crucifix along the roadside was simply a piece of wood for the fire or for beating a dog. Only Christ should be followed and only Christ, not the church hierarchy, was the sole intercessor to God.

The appeal to the Bible as the authority, and especially to the example of Jesus in the Gospels, had a long history in the one church. Moreover, a fierce anti-clericalism, in particular drawing attention to the immoral lives of the clergy, was standard anti-church polemic since the twelfth century. The teaching of justification by faith rather than by works was well-known, especially in the Augustinian order to which Luther belonged.

Luther appears to have had the role of opening the floodgates of discontent with—and a longing for—a church more conformed to God's mercy and grace and less to a pervasive legalism that created fear and guilt. The water of liberation had flowed over the dam before Luther's time, but he did away with the dam. There were many more like Strauss and Castenbaur who were preachers of reform inspired by Luther but did not necessarily share all his views. Many others, like Wölfl, knew little about Luther. They most likely depended on the existing Jesus piety for what they knew, a piety that was prevalent especially among the socially marginalized. But all of them, it needs to be said emphatically, were part of the movement for the reform of the one church in head and members. None of them, however, took this passion for reform to such radical lengths as the secretary to the bishop of Brixen, a fiery layman by the name of Michael Gaismair.

Gaismair's Uprising

In the fall of 1524, a peasant uprising began in the Black Forest of Württemberg, in the crook of the Rhine River north of Switzerland. Peasants and people of the towns had greeted the message of Luther about the free grace of God with enthusiasm. They agitated for changes in church and society that they believed were implied in Luther's message. When he wrote about "the freedom of the Christian," the peasants thought in the first instance of their liberation from the demands of their feudal masters and from the power of the priests. They wanted to be respected as human beings. They demanded the right to choose their own priests so they could hear the pure Word of God and not the fabrications of the papal church.

The peasant movement initially was an ordinary peoples' movement for the reform of society and church. During the course of the winter 1524-25, the movement became radicalized because of the slow and devious response of the authorities. By March 1525, armed bands of peasants began to loot and burn castles and monasteries. Martin Luther himself turned against the peasants, declaring that his message had nothing to do with economic liberation. Eventually he urged the governing authorities to use soldiers to suppress the movement and announced that anyone who died in this "crusade" against the agitators would immediately earn a place in heaven.

The movement for change in Luther's neighbourhood in central Germany came to a violent end when its ragtag army was massacred by the cavalry of the princes of Saxony and Hesse at the town of Frankenhausen in Thuringia on May 14, 1525. On May 10, perhaps a week before the news of this disaster reached Tirol, peasants seized control of the bishop's city of Brixen. Three days later they elected Michael Gaismair, the bishop's secretary, as their leader.

Their aim was to return the Tirol "purged of the perversion of injustice and oppression by prelates and nobles" to Ferdinand, archduke of Austrian lands. Ferdinand responded immediately. A truce was arranged with the peasant representatives and a general diet was called to begin on June 12, 1525. Ferdinand promised that all social and religious grievances would be dealt with. Sadly, it was a ruse. Ferdinand and his advisor and supporters played for time and totally out-manoeuvred the peasants, who had no negotiating experience. All present agreed to a new constitution that dealt with some grievances and promised to deal with others.

But Gaismair and the other peasant leaders soon realized that Ferdinand was negotiating in bad faith in order to gain time to brutally suppress the renegades, which occurred months later. In August Gaismair, who was still in charge in Brixen, was summoned to Innsbruck ostensibly to deal with the continuing unrest. Instead, he was forcibly imprisoned. Two months later he escaped and fled to Zürich and the protection of the Swiss Confederacy. There in 1526 with the support of Ulrich Zwingli, the Zürich reformer, he drew up a war plan to invade Tirol and wrest it from the ruling Habsburgs. That plan was frustrated by a betrayal involving Gaismair's own brother, but Gaismair remained undeterred. From Switzerland, he led his army into Tirol, hoping to gain the people's support as he moved through the valleys.

But the peasant rebellion of the previous summer had been so brutally suppressed in the fall and winter that Gaismair's hopes to rally the people met with disappointment. Still he did not give up. He took his army through Tirol into the archbishopric of Salzburg to support yet another peasant uprising there. After some initial successes, that too failed. To escape capture by the soldiers of the Swabian League sent against him, Gaismair led his army south into Italy to the Republic of Venice. From there he kept plotting to invade Tirol until he was assassinated by one of Ferdinand's henchmen in Padua in 1532.

Through these turbulent years, Gaismair imagined himself a Moses preparing to lead his people into the promised land. His vision for Tirol foresaw a social order with equality for all and extensive religious reform. Soon after the beginning of the revolt, he brought an evangelical preacher to Brixen, and others soon followed in support of his resistance and vision for change. Even after Gaismair's flight to Zürich, his followers among the clergy kept resistance alive, challenging the traditional doctrines and practices of the church. Evangelical books circulated throughout Tirol. On one occasion, Gaismair even met with Anabaptists with the aim of enlisting them in his cause.[31]

Thus, three years after the departure of Strauss, Rhegius, and Castenbaur, the whole land was convulsed by an attempt to abolish the existing authorities and put new ones in their place. There is no longer any doubt that the military protest of the Gaismair movement was revived a year or two later in Tirol with the rise of weaponless Anabaptism.

Preparing the Ground

There were four figures—Strauss, Castenbaur, Wölfl, and Gaismair—who did much to prepare the ground for the revolution in Pilgram Marpeck's life in Rattenberg in late 1527. The work of Strauss and Wölfl certainly had its effect in Rattenberg, although indirectly. Stefan Castenbaur may be credited with instructing Marpeck in the teaching of Martin Luther, which we will discuss in more detail in chapter 3. Gaismair's movement was almost totally confined to Tirol south of the Brenner Pass. But his line of retreat to Venice was along the Puster Valley toward Sterzing, one of the most important areas of Anabaptist life a year or two later. Marpeck knew about Gaismair because Tirolean communities, including Rattenberg, were required to help pay for the military suppression of Gaismair's movement and to contribute armed men.

Of the four, however, only Castenbaur had a direct influence on Marpeck. But we can be certain that the climate of religious ferment

31. For this story see Klaassen, *Michael Gaismair*, 110-11.

would have stimulated questions in Marpeck's lively mind and awakened his critical faculties. As we will see in chapters 2 and 3, Marpeck exercised his engineering and political professions during these tumultuous years, and he was certainly well aware of what has been described above, even though his writings contain no hint of any of these events except general references to the peasant uprising.

Anabaptism Comes to Tirol

Anabaptist emissaries had arrived in the Inn Valley by May 1526, but no particulars are known about this. They most likely came from Zürich, where the movement had begun a year earlier. Anabaptists were reported first among the miners in Rattenberg in March 1527.[32] Their presence in the area is confirmed in April by a letter of Ferdinand. At about the same time Georg Blaurock, one of the charter members of the Anabaptist beginnings in Zürich, entered Tirol and preached along the Etsch Valley in South Tirol as far as Bozen and then north to Klausen. Many of his converts had been followers of the evangelical preachers.[33] In November 1527 Lienhart Schiemer, a Franciscan monk who had left the monastery and had become a tailor, and who recently had been rebaptized in Vienna, arrived in Rattenberg. He was arrested a day after his arrival, a victim of the success of Ferdinand's organized policy of suppression.

Ferdinand's repressive policies were motivated partly by the very public cases of Balthasar Hubmaier and Michael Sattler. Hubmaier was the leading Anabaptist reformer of Waldshut. He had made common cause with the insurgent peasants in 1525, thus creating the link made by Ferdinand between Anabaptism and rebellion. Sattler was associated with the refusal to fight against the Turks who threatened the empire militarily. Early in 1528 there was a rumour that four thousand Anabaptists in Tirol were plotting rebellion. Sometime during the final weeks of 1527 and early 1528, Pilgram Marpeck himself joined the feared movement.

What could have persuaded this successful, wealthy, intelligent, civically influential man to embrace an outlaw religious movement? As we shall see in the next two chapters, his change from a believer in the Roman church and trusted employee of Ferdinand to passionate reformer was directly the result of the ferment that swirled around him. As he wrote in 1531 in *A Clear and Useful Instruction,* "I was born blind through my former unbelief, the reason for which blindness you may ask of my parents, but the desire has always been in me to be able to see."[34]

32. Palme, "Zur Täuferbewegung in Tirol," 53.
33. Boyd, *Pilgram Marpeck,* 21-22; Packull, *Hutterite Beginnings,* 181.
34. Klassen and Klaassen, *WPM,* 98.

-2-

Entrepreneur and Imperial Official

Pilgram Marpeck's birth date and place are not known, but most likely he was born in 1495 in Rattenberg,[1] a little city nestled between the mountain and the Inn River in one of the most scenic valleys of the Austrian Tirol. The city was so narrow that the public road went through the grounds of the castle belonging to the guardian of Rattenberg,[2] which loomed over the town on the mountainside above the houses of the wealthier citizens. While Rattenberg's history as a town goes back to the year 1000 as a toll station, it became part of Tirol (as did the cities of Kitzbühel and Kufstein) only in 1504 after two centuries of Bavarian control. The area had been part of the church diocese of Salzburg since the year 739.

Tirol was considered the heart of the Holy Roman Empire because it was one of the long-time holdings of the ruling Habsburg family, and because Innsbruck, its chief city, was one of the administrative centres of the empire in the sixteenth century.[3] Tirol's direct ruler was Archduke Ferdinand, who also became king of Moravia and Bohemia and who personally appointed Pilgram Marpeck to be mining superintendent in Rattenberg in April 1525.

Marpeck's father and mother had come to Rattenberg in the early 1490s from Rosenheim, a Bavarian city about 40 kilometres (25 miles) north of Kufstein. His father, Heinrich, apparently was serving as sheriff in

---

1. Evidence suggests that he was born around the time of the adoption of the family coat of arms.

2. Boyd, *Pilgram Marpeck*, 17.

3. Marpeck visited Innsbruck many times to confer with governmental officials on mining matters and during his mediation of the Stefan Castenbaur case (see chapter 3).

Rattenberg, on the Inn River, Marpeck's birthplace as seen from the castle above the town.

Rattenberg by 1494. A year later, on October 18, 1495, a family seal or coat of arms was issued in the name of Heinrich Marpeck, sheriff (*Landrichter*) of Rattenberg. The coat of arms depicted a shield with a helmet above the shield, and a bird perched on mountains atop the helmet. Since the Marpecks were not members of the nobility, the coat of arms does not bear the family name. A copy of it is on record and can be seen at the Ferdinandeum library in Innsbruck.[4] It is quite possible that Heinrich applied for this coat of arms soon after Pilgram was born. It would be logical for a leading, wealthy citizen to establish a coat of arms in celebration and recognition of the birth of a first-born, especially a son.

Heinrich continued to be prominent in the civic life of Rattenberg, becoming mayor in 1511 and representing the city at the Tirolean Diet in Innsbruck. The diet was the annual meeting of the estates, which were privileged groups such as aristocracy, clergy, senior officials of specific towns, and well-to-do peasantry. Because of his involvement in some way with mining, Heinrich in 1509 became a member of the Brotherhood of Mine Workers (*Bergwerksbrüderschaft*). The brotherhood was not, as

4. The name Heinrich Marpeck does not appear in Johannes Siebmacher's standard work on coats of arms, *Grosses Wappenbuch* 28, *Die Wappen des Adels in Salzburg, Steiermark und Tirol* (Neustadt an der Aisch: Bauer and Raspe, 1979). However, the Marpeck name does appear as "Marbeck" in the special index to Siebmacher's work, *General-Index zu den Siebmacherischen Wappenbücher, 1605-1964* (Graz, Austria: Akademischer Drucker, 1964), 363 (Tirol), Bgl 28.

one might imagine, an association of those who worked in the black depths, but rather was "a small corporation of middle-class investors and older propertied miners."[5]

The Marpecks were evidently upright and pious people. In a public document of 1531, Pilgram Marpeck is recorded as saying that he "was brought to the faith by . . . God-fearing parents in Catholicism."[6] His comment is an acknowledgment of the piety and faith of his parents and, for an Anabaptist, a relatively positive statement of religious origins. It testifies to a personal appropriation of Christian faith. Thus he was without doubt baptized in the parish church of Rattenberg. No evidence suggests that his childhood was anything but happy. Indeed, the emotional maturity which characterized his adult life was undoubtedly rooted in a secure and orderly upbringing by his parents.

We may assume that he learned to read and write as a child, given the secure social and economic status of the Marpeck family. Although there is no record anywhere about his education, he must have enjoyed the best that was available in Rattenberg. His writings reveal some knowledge of Latin, enough that Johann Loserth, one of the first historians to give careful attention to Marpeck, suggested that his knowledge of humanist Latin is clearly visible in the sentence structure of his German writings[7]—for example, his long, run-on sentences, his piling up of adjectives and adverbs, and use of the Latin term "Item" in his frequent listings of many points. Whether he learned Latin in Rattenberg or was enrolled in a Latin school in Innsbruck is not known.

The Marpeck family was very well-to-do, so much so that their house became a landmark in Rattenberg. One of the city gates was identified as the Marpeck Gate, located close to the family house. Was this the house that later belonged to Pilgram that still graces the city centre of Rattenberg? If so, it was likely the house that today bears the number 28, located near the western entrance to the city, where the road from Innsbruck in Marpeck's time turned to the right and passed through the grounds of the castle.

Pilgram Marpeck was about eighteen years old when he was appointed by Rattenberg's city council in 1513 to work in the city hospital.[8] Soon there-

5. Boyd, *Pilgram Marpeck*, 7.

6. *TA: Elsass* 1, *Strassburg* 1522-1532, ed. Krebs and Rott (Gütersloh: Gerd Mohn, 1959), 352. In English see Klassen and Klaassen, WPM, 22.

7. *Quellen und Forschungen zur Geschichte der oberdeutschen Taufgesinnten im 16. Jahrhundert. Pilgram Marbecks Antwort auf Kaspar Schwenckfelds Beurteilung des Buches der Bundesbezeugung von 1542*, ed. Johann Loserth (Wien: Kommissionsverlag der Verlagsbuchhandlung Carl Fromme, 1929), 1-2.

8. Apparently he also organized Rattenberg's crossbow competition. See Stephen Boyd, "Pilgrim Marpeck," in *ME* 5 (Scottdale, Pa.: Herald Press), 1990, 538.

after he was working in the *Brüderhaus*, a hospice for disabled and aged miners established by the Brotherhood of Mine Workers and supported with monthly contributions by all miners. This appointment brought him into direct contact with the most important industry in Rattenberg, the mining of silver and copper.

It also may have brought him into contact at some point during the next fifteen years with Paracelsus, the noted holistic physician who spent considerable time with the Tirolean miners studying their illnesses, visiting their homes and going into the mines with them.[9] Paracelsus worked in the Tirol during the years that Marpeck was associated with mining, and it is logical to assume that they would have come to know each other. The poor health of miners thoroughly mystified Paracelsus, who had developed a medical theory that the closer one lived to the earth, the healthier one would be. The theory may have worked for farmers and shepherds, but it fell apart when miners were included. According to the early thinking of Paracelsus, miners who worked deep in the earth should have been the healthiest of any people anywhere. Instead, they were among the most sickly.

The mining industry began in Rattenberg in the early fifteenth century and contributed much to the prosperity of the city. We may assume that it was at the hospice for miners that Marpeck began or continued his informal education toward his later professional life. At the same time, he also in some way acquired engineering skills in mining, forestry, and weaving, all of which later enabled him to earn his living and secure his life. His publicly acknowledged skill as a civil engineer and machine builder strongly suggests a period of apprenticeship.

On February 26, 1520, Pilgram was received into the Brotherhood of Mine Workers. By this time he had married Sophia Harrer, about whom few details are known. She and Pilgram had one daughter, Margareth. They also adopted three foster children who may have lost their mothers to childbirth or the plague, and whose fathers probably died in the mines.

Rattenberg was one of the most important mining centres in Tirol, second only to Schwaz. A sixteenth-century sketch of the city shows the entrances of many mine-shafts in the mountain above the city. With Pilgram's father a member of the miners' brotherhood, the boy must have been introduced to the chief economic occupation of the area early in his

9. Paracelsus believed that in order to help cure illness, a physician should listen to his patients' stories. It was a practice he recommended to his medical students at the University of Basel. See Franz Hartman, *Paracelsus. His Life and Prophecies* (New York: Rudolf Steiner Publications, 1973), 12-13.

Mine buildings in the area of the Italian Alps that Marpeck supervised.

life. No wonder that in 1520, when Marpeck was about twenty-five years old, he and his associate Melchior Stuntz started an ambitious, independent business of transporting ore.

The Challenges of Mining

Young Marpeck's venture coincided that year with the high point of the production of silver and copper in Tirol.[10] Lead sulphide ore, essential for copper smelting, had to be moved from the ancient mines in the Schneeberg region of the Italian Alps, high above the Brenner Pass that now separates Austria from Italy, down to the smelters at Kitzbühel.[11] When we consider that the Schneeberg mines were located at an elevation of 2,400 metres (7,800 feet), it immediately becomes evident that the transport of ore in that extreme mountain region was a supreme challenge. One can still get a sense of this today. It's still possible to travel to an ancient mine site in the Schneeberg by climbing a steep mountain road northwest of the Italian town of Brixen. At the end of miles of switchbacks and stunning scenery is a museum located at the base of a mining site that operated from the thirteenth century until it closed in 1985. Would this have been the site of Marpeck's operations? We don't know, but it's certainly possible.

Illustrations from the sixteenth century give us some idea of how the ore was brought out of the mine to its destination.[12] Once out of the mine-shaft, the ore was taken to a yard where pack-horses were gathered. Georg

10. Brady, *The Politics of the Reformation in Germany. Jacob Sturm (1489-1553) of Strasbourg*, 12.

11. Kopialbuch, *Missiven und Befelch 1520* (Tiroler Landesarchiv Innsbruck), fol. 3r.

12. See Georgius Agricola, *De re metallica*, trans. H. C. and L. H. Hoover (New York: Dover, 1950).

Agricola, in a wonderfully descriptive sixteenth-century manual on mining, tells us that the ore was put in sacks "bound with thongs, and fastened to a rope." Then "a man, winding the rope around his arm or breast, drags them down through the snow to a place where horses, mules, and asses bearing pack-saddles can climb."[13]

Marpeck's transport company presumably took over at this point. The ore was transferred from pigskin bags to strong linen bags carrying approximately 75 kilograms (165 pounds) each. Two bags were joined and placed across the pack-saddle of a horse or a mule, each animal carrying 150 kilograms (330 pounds) of ore. This transport could be done only in the summer months, since from September to June the depth of snow on the mountain made it impossible.

Once the pack train was assembled, the trek began to Kitzbühel, a distance of at least 150 kilometres (90 miles). The route first took the pack train over the Schneeberg Pass at 2,700 metres (8,775 feet), then northeast down the rocky stone-surfaced trail of the Lazzacher Valley to the more easily passable Ridnaun Valley. At the junction of the valleys was a rest area where the saddles were removed for the horses to recover. Then the pack train descended to Sterzing. The horses carefully made their way down 1,700 metres (5,525 feet) over a distance of about 30 kilometres (18 miles), a precipitous trek requiring carefully shod horses and men skilled in guiding them. Sterzing was a major rest stop. From there the route continued north on the difficult 1,000 metres (3,250 feet) ascent to the Brenner Pass and then down through Matrei to Hall on the Inn River.

At Hall, the ore was deposited in special storage containers until it could be loaded on barges to be floated down the Inn to the Kitzbühel landing, most likely located at the town of Wörgl.[14] Hall had been a shipping centre for various goods including ore since 1442. The Inn River was much deeper in 1520 than it is today and its cold, blue-green water could accommodate heavy shipping. It is not hard to imagine Marpeck as a boy standing on the bridge at Rattenberg as a barge loaded with ore stopped to report at the customs house, getting the idea that he himself might become part of that adventurous life. The last leg of the transport to Kitzbühel, after unloading the barges at Wörgl, was not as difficult as the earlier part of the journey, but here too the ore was likely carried by pack-horses or mules.[15]

13. Ibid., 169.
14. G. Mutschlechner, "Die Verwendung der Schneeberger und Gossensasser Erze," in *Der Schlern* 67, Mai 1993, Heft 5, 339.
15. Jean-Jacques Bergier, "Wachstum, Energie, Verkehr vor der industriellen Revolution im Raume der heutigen Schweiz und der Zentralalpen," in *Wirtschaftliches*

From Businessman to Civic Official

We don't know how long Marpeck's entrepreneurial undertaking lasted. In 1520, the same year that he was received into the mining brotherhood, he followed in his father's political footsteps by becoming a member of the Rattenberg Lower Council. The city government consisted of two councils, upper and lower. The upper council was what we would call the executive part of the government and was composed of aristocratic and prominent persons of the town. The lower council was elected primarily from the craft guilds such as millers, weavers, and chimney sweeps.

The following year Marpeck trav-

Marpeck home in the centre of Rattenberg, Austria.

elled to Hopfgarten, a town near Kitzbühel, where he assisted in settling a resource claim.[16] One of the estate owners in Hopfgarten was Leupold Scharnschlager, who later became a close associate of Marpeck and co-author of many of his Anabaptist writings. We shall learn much more about Scharnschlager as the story of Marpeck unfolds. Two years later, in 1522, Marpeck was fully occupied with the affairs of Rattenberg, having been elected mayor for a standard one-year term.

Financially Marpeck's situation continued to improve. He now owned two houses; the surviving one at number 28 on Rattenberg's main west-east street testifies to his wealth. Four storeys tall with a gracious half-moon entrance of inset stone, window boxes, and a small balcony, the building today is an elegant row-house structure rising above a trendy main-floor glass shop.

Between 1521 and 1524, Marpeck represented the city council to the Tirol administration in Innsbruck regarding a dispute over the rights of non-resident artisans to work near Rattenberg. Since 1521, these artisans had been prohibited from working within a seven-kilometre (4.2 miles) radius of the city in order to protect the city's craftsmen. This prohibition was breached by artisans in Reith, a little southwest of Rattenberg. The dispute dragged on from August 1521 to August 1524, when the original

Wachstum, Energie und Verkehr vom Mittelalter bis ins 19. Jahrhundert. Bericht über die 6. Arbeitstagung der Gesellschaft für Sozial-und Wirtschaftsgeschichte. ed. Hermann Kellenbenz (Stuttgart: Gustav Fischer Verlag, 1978), 21-22.

16. Boyd, *Pilgram Marpeck*, 6-8.

order was again enforced. During those three years, Marpeck travelled to Innsbruck seven times to represent the interests of Rattenberg's craftsmen. Perhaps this was the "school" in which he acquired his skill to negotiate disputes, a skill he used many times in the conflict-ridden years ahead.

During 1524 and 1525, Marpeck was a member of the city's upper council. By age twenty-four, he had become a highly visible and respected member of the city elite. His prominence increased when he represented Rattenberg at three sessions of the Tirolean Diet called by Archduke Ferdinand during 1524. In 1525, Marpeck was also given the important task of supervising firewood distribution in the city.[17]

On February 1, 1525, Marpeck was assessed a special imperial tax— one of the highest assessments (presumably based on equity) in the city. Several months later he made a loan of one thousand guilders to Ferdinand, charging the archduke 5 percent interest plus twenty guilders against the principal. This was a large sum of money considering that a skilled carpenter earned about thirty-two guilders per annum. (It was not uncommon for wealthy entrepreneurs to loan significant amounts of money to the Habsburg royalty, whose resources were stretched to the limit by the combined effects of inflation, massive building projects, and above all, war with the Turks.)

On April 20, 1525, Marpeck was appointed mining superintendent (*Bergrichter*) by Archduke Ferdinand,[18] a position he held until January 29, 1528.[19] Evidently Ferdinand or some of his advisors had come to know Marpeck during his frequent visits to Innsbruck on official assignments. It is possible that Marpeck was regarded as a good candidate for the position of mining superintendent because of his abilities at mediation and conflict resolution, skills that would be called on regularly in the community for which he was responsible. His acceptance of the position and its conditions is dated April 21, 1525. The letter bore the family seal of the shield: helmet, mountains, and bird.[20] Marpeck's term began on June 7, 1525.[21]

The appointment confirmed his command of the whole mining enterprise, a recognition of the administrative skills he had acquired as mayor of Rattenberg in 1522 and as a member of the upper council in

17. Ibid., 5-9.

18. Kopialbuch, *Bekennen 1525*, TRA, fol. 81v-82r.

19. Georg Mutschlechner, *Erzbergbau und Bergwesen im Berggericht Rattenberg* (Im Selbstverlag der Gemeinden Alpbach, Brixlegg, Rattenberg, Reit im Alpbachtal, 1984), 42.

20. There is a sketch of this coat-of-arms in the *Wappen* file at the Ferdinandeum in Innsbruck.

21. Boyd, *Pilgram Marpeck*, 12.

1524 and 1525.[22] The appointment did not imply that he was a trained lawyer, as the term *Richter* (judge) might suggest. Georg Agricola identified the office as *praefectus metallorum*, literally mining prefect, the German rendering being *Bergamtmann*[23] (mining official). The term *Bergrichter* (mining superintendent) used in the notice of appointment therefore describes the one who makes the final decisions, on whose desk the buck stops. His salary was set at sixty-five marks annually plus three marks for a formal professional gown, a respectable professional salary (a mark was equal to two guilders).

The appointment came at a critical time. Jakob Fugger, head of the hugely wealthy Fugger financial empire and known as "the Rich One," died that year. Therefore new people would be representing the Fuggers in negotiations with Ferdinand and Charles, a change that in turn would affect their demands upon the mining industry. Figures show that under Marpeck's term, the revenues from the mines grew incrementally. At the same time, however, Ferdinand's need for cash was growing as he struggled to finance the defence of the Holy Roman Empire and contend with growing conflict at home.

As mining superintendent, Marpeck was part of a larger administrative structure. He was responsible directly to the Royal Accounting Office (*Rechnungsbehörde*) based in Innsbruck, as were his counterparts in all the mining centres. At the top was the sovereign, Ferdinand, who was the mining governor (*Bergherr*). In each mining jurisdiction (*Bergrecht*), the mining superintendent had full authority by virtue of his appointment.

The document appointing Marpeck included a job description and summary outline of his duties. He was made responsible for the whole mining enterprise from Brixlegg to Kufstein, a roughly triangular area with each side about 20 kilometres (12 miles) long. He was responsible for overseeing the wood lots and timber needs of the mines and smelters. Wood was the only material available for securing mine shafts and especially as fuel for smelting. Long-term supply contracts had to be made because timber could comprise as much as 70 percent of the cost of mining ore.[24] Marpeck purchased ore and supervised the refining of copper and silver. He oversaw the structure of the eight-hour shifts of those working the mines. He also had to see to it that the monarch received his royalties, plus collect all local fines and forward the monies annually to the financial office (*Raitkammer*). The document obligated him to make

22. Ibid., 8.
23. Agricola, *De re metallica*, 78.
24. Kellenbenz, *Wirtschaftliches Wachstum*, 257.

his decisions without favour to either poor or rich, and to guard the whole enterprise for the sovereign.[25] Beyond that he also leased mines, smelters, water, and wood supplies to entrepreneurs on behalf of the monarchy. It was his duty to ensure that every such lease was unencumbered by checking the records of leases. The miners under his care swore an oath to abide by the decisions of the mining superintendent.

Assigned to him were two or more officials who were sworn to assist and advise him in his wide-ranging responsibilities and especially to help deal with the cases that came before him at the assizes (civil courts) held four times a year. In addition, three other senior administrators were appointed to work under Marpeck: the *Markscheider* (surveyor), the *Bergmeister* (the technical overseer of the mines), and the *Schichtmeister* (shift boss),[26] who regulated the shifts. Finally, a woman was assigned to carry messages for him to all the others who served under him. Marpeck was required to report periodically to the authorities in Innsbruck on his work. He lived and worked in Rattenberg, which was the administrative centre of his jurisdiction.

As mining superintendent, Marpeck also was the keeper of the peace in the mining community and was required to report all dissension to the authorities.[27] It was this responsibility, more than any other, that two years later led Marpeck to thwart a direct order of Ferdinand to report to authorities the names of any and all Anabaptists about which he knew. Anabaptism—an outgrowth of church reform that advocated nonviolence and believers baptism (i.e., baptism of those old enough to offer informed consent)—was just beginning to take hold in scattered parts of the empire. Ferdinand viewed Anabaptists as dangerous heretics that had to be converted or killed. Marpeck refused to provide names, and, as we will see in chapter 3, soon after began his life on the run.

Marpeck was directly responsible for the welfare of all the people in the mining enterprise, including the miners and the smelter workers, a responsibility it appears he took very seriously. Smiths, wood supply workers, charcoal burners, and all others indirectly related to the industry, plus their families and servants, were Marpeck's obligation. All of these, referred to as *Bergwerksverwonten* (persons related to mining) were subject to his care "*im Leben und im Tode*" (in life and death). In

25. TLA Kopialbuch, *Bekennen*, 81v.
26. The original German technical terms translated in the foregoing pages are accounting office = *Rechnungsbehörde*; mining governor = *Bergherr*; mining jurisdiction = *Bergrecht*; financial office = *Raitkammer*; surveyor = *Markscheider*; technical overseer of the mines = *Bergmeister*; shift boss = *Schichtmeister*.
27. Boyd, *Pilgram Marpeck*, 11.

A—Kindled logs.   B—Sticks shaved down fan-shaped.   C—Tunnel.

Illustration of a sixteenth-century mine tunnel.

civil matters he was the primary official, affecting the lives of thousands of people. The one area where he had no jurisdiction was on matters involving capital crimes.

Mining Dangers and Demons

To say "in life and death" was no trivial rhetorical flourish. Mining was an occupation in which danger was faced every day. Mines were notorious for bad air and humidity. Miners prepared the rock-face by heating it with large wood fires, producing smoke in the tunnels even though every effort was made to prevent this by venting. Dust and noxious gases were a constant hazard. Water could not always be pumped out, so miners often found themselves working with their feet and legs in cold water. Many were injured by falling rocks or by falling off long ladders while entering or leaving a mineshaft. For those who were weakened by dust and gas, the long climb in and out of the shafts was especially perilous.

Life expectancy for miners was low, in particular, because of the prevalence of fatal lung diseases. Miners themselves were responsible for wearing adequate protective clothing like leather boots and elbow-length leather gloves. Some miners could not afford these protections and were therefore doubly at risk. And it was the miners, not the companies, who contributed a fixed amount every month to support their colleagues who were injured. The companies assumed no responsibility for them.

As dark, dank places of smoke, dust, illness, and injury, the mines were regarded as the haunts of ferocious, malicious demons. For centuries new mines had been opened with religious ceremonies and rites, especially prayer and fasting.[28] In fact, the writer Agricola reported that demons could be expelled *only* by prayer and fasting.[29] Five centuries later, Lewis Mumford aptly wrote about mining: "In its destruction of the environment and its indifference to the risks to human life, mining closely resembled warfare—though likewise it often, through its confrontation of danger and death, brings into existence a tough, self-respecting personality."[30] These were the people for whom Marpeck was responsible. It is no wonder that they were a particularly volatile constituency, especially conscious of their mortality and therefore more bellicose in their demands for domestic security.

Marpeck's work as mining superintendent was especially difficult because he was responsible for a community of people who were not indigenous. There were often jurisdictional disputes between mining superintendent and sheriff because geographically their jurisdictions over-lapped. Thus, for example, the government in Innsbruck appropriated common land for the houses and gardens of miners. This caused anger among the permanent residents because common land, by long-standing custom, was available for use by everyone. The miners lived apart from the social life in city and country. There was little cooperation between the civic and mining communities. To the contrary, there were all kinds of frictions.[31]

Soon after his appointment in 1525, Marpeck and the sheriff Bartlme Anngst were ordered to hire three armed men for the suppression of insur-rection.[32] It is likely that this was a response to the peasant uprising in Brixen

28. Morris Berman, *The Reenchantment of the World* (Ithaca, N.Y.: Cornell University Press, 1981), 88.

29. See Georg Mutschlechner, *Erzbergbau und Bergwesen im Berggericht Rattenberg*. Im Selbstverlag der Gemeinden Alpbach, Brixlegg, Rattenberg, Reith im Alpbachtal 32 (1984), 32, and Agricola, *De re metallica*, 214-18.

30. Quoted by Ivan Illich, *Tools of Conviviality* (New York: Harper & Row, 1973), 29-30.

31. Ibid., 50-51.

32. Mutschlechner, *Erzbergbau*, 42.

in May of that year. The authorities in Innsbruck were always apprehensive about a possible revolt among the miners and were afraid that they would now make common cause with the peasants. In 1526 Marpeck had custody of an arrested smith and in 1527 of an ironworker arrested for disturbing the peace. In the spring of 1526, Rattenberg was assessed five hundred guilders to help finance the defeat of Michael Gaismair, whose peasant uprising had spread throughout Tirol. City council paid the assessment under protest.[33]

For all his skills as an administrator and mediator, Marpeck also had a short fuse for certain people and situations. In late 1526, we have our first glimpse of Marpeck's temper at work. On December 14, the royal council in Innsbruck issued a kind of cease-and-desist order to Marpeck as mining superintendent and to his civic counterpart, Sheriff Bartlme Anngst. Mutual charges of jurisdictional infringement had been made, with intemperate language on both sides. The case illustrates confusion regarding overlapping jurisdictions in Tirol, much like overlapping federal and provincial or state jurisdictions in modern Canada or the United States in such services as police. In such systems, occasional conflict is inevitable.

Marpeck and Anngst were called to Innsbruck to state their grievances before the royal council. The order then issued by the council suggests that the dispute involved the assistants of both officials. Marpeck and Anngst were ordered to respect each other because their dispute endangered public order. They were threatened with punishment should there be any recurrence of their feud. The record indicates that both men accepted the royal judgment.[34]

Charting a Different Path

In addition to civic and mining matters, the religious issues of Rattenberg were also close to Marpeck's heart. The welfare of the parish church and the integrity of its ministry were a concern of his for more than a decade. In the sixteenth century this would have been seen as entirely appropriate because the modern view that church and state are separate would then have been met with incomprehension. The authorities, for example, had made special provision for the spiritual welfare of the miners, in addition to the ceremonies to cleanse the mines of demons.

The same year that Marpeck joined the Brotherhood of Mine Workers and began serving on Rattenberg's city council (1520), Stefan Castenbaur

---

33. Josef Macek, *Der Tiroler Bauernkrieg und Michael Gaismair* (Berlin: VEB Deutscher Verlag der Wissenschaften, 1965), 329.

34. "Endscheid zwischen denn Perckh-und Lanndgericht zu Ratemberg," in *Rattenberger Bergbuch*, HS 6248.

was called to Rattenberg to become prior of the Augustinian community there. Soon after, he was called to serve the parish church. A gifted preacher and scholar, Castenbaur charted his own spiritual path with such passion and eloquence that miners and townsfolk flocked to the church to hear him.

One could imagine that the parish church in Rattenberg was likely filled to capacity on the Sunday morning early in 1521 when Castenbaur gave his first homily there. After many months of searching and considering candidates,[35] leaders of the parish selected him as the primary preacher at the *Pfarrkirche*, the Church of St. Vigil.[36] As the leading church in town, the *Pfarrkirche* placed much more emphasis on good preaching than did other churches, which may have emphasized pastoral needs or liturgy. When Marpeck was a young boy, the church was constructed with two naves: the north nave reserved for the civic community of the city and the south nave for the miners and the auxiliary trades, the *Bergwerksverwonten*. The two communities did not mix much, and the day-to-day concerns of the miners were different from those of the townspeople. Many rich and influential people attended there, but so did many of the miners who had been drawn to Rattenberg by its robust mining industry. As migrant workers, they generally cherished their participation in a vibrant congregation.

The churches of Rattenberg operated under a special arrangement forged in 1378 in which the people of the parish helped select their own priest. Through private endowments, parishioners also paid all expenses of the clergy.[37] This appointment process was in sharp contrast to that of most churches, whose clergy were assigned to them by a local bishop, a monastery, or a prominent layperson. Excellent preachers were hard to find. In fact, there were widespread complaints throughout Europe about the lack of educated, articulate clergy. It sometimes took several years for the people of Rattenberg to find the preacher they wanted, but on the whole their system worked fairly well. The parishioners became devoted to their priests and generally were able to get exceptionally talented people to serve them.[38]

Castenbaur was no exception. From the beginning, all people—rich

35. The church did not begin to keep thorough records until two hundred years later. However, the length of time between a number of the appointments during this time period indicates that outstanding preachers were hard to come by.

36. Some Tirolean sources such as Eduard Widmoser in *Tirol A bis Z*, refer to St. Vigil, but a local pamphlet on Rattenberg refers to St. Vergil. St. Vigil was Bishop of Trent in the fifth century, while St. Vergil (or Virgil) was Bishop of Salzburg in the ninth century.

37. From *Rattenberg*, a tourist brochure in the *Pfarrkirche*. It provides a detailed history of the churches of Rattenberg. From 1378 onward, they endowed their preachers, and after 1786, their selection was totally independent of church authorities in Salzburg.

38. The support for Castenbaur and Jakob Strauss, where parishioners literally fought with authorities to protect and retain their priest, are just two examples.

and poor, miners, and wealthy patrons of the church—apparently were inspired and uplifted by his preaching. As the congregation listened to him, there probably were whispers of admiration. To be sure, there had been some confusion over whether his name was Stefan Castenbaur or Boius Agricola, the Latin name he apparently had chosen when a doctorate was conferred on him in 1518 by the head of the Augustinian order. Being an Augustinian, he knew the writings of the church fathers, especially those of the founder of the order, St. Augustine. From him, Castenbaur had learned that books of the Bible could open up rich spiritual nourishment to the people if the books were treated as a complete, literary entity. Lectionary readings had their place, but Castenbaur enjoyed teaching from Romans and other books such as Isaiah.

From the start of his preaching in Rattenberg, he chose not to follow the established lectionary but took his people through the whole book of Romans in an extended series of sermons. Castenbaur claimed he had learned this approach from Augustine himself, but church and secular authorities were not impressed.

Castenbaur's sermons dealt specifically with current problems such as the abuses of the church. He led the people to think about the message of the Bible and its call to serve God, so that parishioners often had new things to think about when they left the service regarding the meaning of *Gottesdienst* or serving God.[39] He sensed the spiritual hunger among his people, and he fed them, stressing especially the central command that God required of the people: Love God with all your being and love your neighbour as yourself.[40] He had been to Italy and to the Vatican and did not hesitate to say the church should risk all its property and adornment if diminishing its assets would help to serve God better. While in Venice he had been asked to serve his order in the highly respected position of *definitor*, separating essential theological questions from peripheral ones. This is where his knowledge of the church fathers and the Scriptures particularly came to his aid.

---

39. Augustine has been criticized for avoiding some of the technical issues in the Bible. He left that to specialists and allowed the Bible spiritually to feed the people. See P. Philipp Platz, *Der Roemerbrief in St. Augustin's Gnadenbegriff* (Würzburg: 1937), and also Gerhard Strauss, *Schriftgebrauch, Schriftbeweis und Schriftauslegung bei Augustin* (Tuebingen: Mohr, 1959).

40. Stefan Castenbaur, *Ain köstlicher guter Sermon vom Sterben* (Augsburg: Steiner, 1523), written in prison. Also, *Ein Bedencken des agricola Boius wie der wahrhaftig Gottesdienst von Gott selbst gebotten möcht wiederumb auffgericht werden* [A Consideration by Agricola Boius on How the Divine Service as God himself instituted it can again be Restored] (Leipzig: Stoeckl, 1520). First edition and reprinted several times. This is his most important book and one in which he outlined from the Bible itself his program of reform.

Sitting in church on Sunday mornings, and doubtless in conversations with him, Marpeck on many occasions would have heard Castenbaur emphasize the central theme of Romans,[41] "the obedience of faith" (Rom. 1:5; 16:26). Those who live by faith are renewed by the resurrection of Christ (Rom. 6) into newness of life. The parishioners who helped select Castenbaur were familiar with the priest's passionate theology because they undoubtedly had read a widely circulated book on church reform that he had published in 1520 before coming to Rattenberg.[42] It is quite likely that either Pilgram or his father was part of the selection group.

For Castenbaur, the church had only one goal: to help people deepen their love for God and their neighbour, and purify their obedience of faith. He insisted that if the order of God were to be achieved on the earth, it would take the action of cardinals, bishops, emperors, and kings, who saw themselves as accountable servants of God.[43] He rejected all violence and acts of vengeance and did not hesitate to say that people must obey kings and emperors, but that they in turn were accountable to God. If the monarch ordered something in contradiction to God's law, the people were not bound to obey. Such a message would not have pleased Ferdinand, who did not yet sit very securely on his throne.

Luther's Defence Is Rejected

Castenbaur's arrival in Rattenberg came during a time of considerable tension between the Habsburg monarchy and those who sought religious and secular reforms. The Diet of Worms, the first parliament for Charles and Ferdinand,[44] was summoned on November 1, 1520. Charles had been elected emperor a year earlier at the age of nineteen. Ferdinand, just seventeen when the diet was called, was yet to be married and be made archduke.

The emperor arrived in Worms on November 28 and the diet opened without "undue delay" on January 17, 1521. During the next three months

41. Paul describes his call as "to call all people in all nations to faith and obedience" (Rom. 1:5-6).
42. He had published his fundamental convictions about church reform in 1520 and also, in the midst of his court case, the booklet *Articles Against S. Castenbaur and his Answers to them (Artickel Wider S. Castenbaur auch was er darauf geantwortet hat)* (Augsburg: Steiner, 1523).
43. He cited Isaiah 11:4: "[W]ith righteousness he shall judge the poor, and decide with equity for the meek of the earth; he shall strike the earth with the rod of his mouth, and with the breath of his lips he shall kill the wicked."
44. Concise description by Pieter C. Bietenholz, *The Correspondence of Erasmus* (Toronto: University of Toronto Press, 1988), 194-95. See also articles on "Diet of Worms," in *Encyclopedia of the Reformation* and "Edict of Worms," in *Encyclopedia of Protestantism*.

the diet tackled constitutional, juridical, fiscal, and military matters. Religious turbulence was a primary concern.

On December 20, 1520, Martin Luther had publicly burned a statement of censure from the pope, along with volumes of canon law establishing the papal administration. The embers of his bonfire at the gates of Wittenberg had barely cooled before a papal bull was issued on January 3, 1521, pronouncing Luther's excommunication. But Luther's works continued to circulate. In his popular book, *Address to the Christian Nobility of the German Nation*, Luther called the pope a threat to the good government of the empire and urged that he be overthrown. He appealed to the emperor and his nobles to punish the crimes of the pope and the clergy. The young emperor—a strong opponent of radical church reform yet possibly flattered by Luther's seeming support—decided to give Luther a hearing.

On April 17, 1521, Luther stood before the members of the diet, including the twenty-year-old emperor and eighteen-year-old archduke. Ordered to say yes or no to the question, "Will you recant?" Luther asked for a day's grace to contemplate his answer. The next day in a long speech, he declared that he would recant nothing. Thus, Charles and Ferdinand saw early in their reign the stubborn, passionate articulation of faith with which the authorities would have to contend wherever Luther's influence and the monarchy might collide.

The result is well known. The emperor did not equivocate. Charles issued an edict declaring Luther a heretic but honoured his pledge of safe conduct for Luther to the Saxon territory of Frederick the Wise, Luther's benefactor and protector. While Luther lay low for ten months, rioting and other challenges to the authority of church and state swept across the empire.

A Community Divided

It was no surprise that amid this turmoil, Castenbaur's preaching should speak to the religious yearnings of many people while horrifying others. The first recorded complaints against Castenbaur arose from his public sermon on All Souls' Day, November 2, 1521. Yet no official action was taken as a result of these complaints, and Castenbaur's popularity (as well as notoriety) continued to grow. Feelings were so strong among those who supported and opposed Castenbaur that when he and Jakob Strauss had preached together on Easter Sunday 1521 to thousands of people in Schwaz and Hall, they had to be protected by a large number of miners so that the crowd's enthusiasm didn't get out of hand.

In 1522, authorities once again issued a formal protest against Castenbaur, this time for a sermon he preached on Ascension Day, May 29.

In the months that followed, he was accused of heresy and rebellion. His crimes: reading from Luther's *Babylonian Captivity* and *Abolition of the Mass*, slandering the Roman See, bishops, and clerics, and advocating the violent abolition of religious ceremonies.[45] The climate was already supercharged, with other evangelical preachers in the Tirol drawing large crowds, much to the dismay of the church and secular establishment.

Castenbaur consistently maintained that his views were drawn from the authority of Scripture and St. Augustine. As we shall see in chapter 3, his protests of innocence didn't matter. Complaints against him finally captured the attention of Ferdinand, who issued an order addressed to Marpeck as mayor and the Rattenberg city council to arrest Castenbaur immediately. On November 17, 1522, Castenbaur was placed under house arrest.

Such an intervention on the part of Ferdinand in local parish matters was a complete breach of normal procedures. All spiritual leaders in the church, whether monks, priests or nuns, were accountable to their own church legal authorities, not to the reigning monarch. The arrest undoubtedly shocked the parishioners of the *Pfarrkirche* and placed Marpeck, as mayor, in the centre of the struggle between the accused Augustinian priest and the archduke. Moreover, city councillors were in an especially difficult position because they were not sure at this point whether they had authority to arrest a priest.

The arrival of Castenbaur in Rattenberg and his subsequent arrest proved to be a defining time in the life of Pilgram Marpeck. He was a city councillor and member of the Brotherhood of Mine Workers when the priest arrived in town and then served as mayor during the turbulent year that led to Castenbaur's arrest. It is possible, indeed likely, that Castenbaur first introduced Marpeck to the writings of Martin Luther,[46] thus helping to shape a new faith direction for Marpeck. It was a life change that would ignite within the young civic leader a passion for church reform and a commitment to justice that increasingly brought him into conflict with the ruling powers.

During the years following Castenbaur's arrest, Marpeck struggled to serve as a bridge between Ferdinand and church authorities on one side and Castenbaur and his enthusiastic followers on the other. Neither they

45. Boyd, *Pilgram Marpeck*, 16. Castenbaur's writings indicate these charges are without foundation. Marpeck himself followed Castenbaur in affirming all the ceremonies of the church, although administered differently than by the Roman method.

46. See Johann Sallaberger, *Kardinal Matthäus Lang von Wellenburg (1468-1540)* (Salzburg: Verlag Anton Pustet, 1997), chap. 8, and Castenbaur, *Schlussreden* and *Artickel wider Doctor Steffan Castenpaur*, 1523.

nor Ferdinand could separate themselves from growing religious and secular turbulence. Dark clouds of violence loomed on the horizon and soon swirled around them, covering more and more people with their ominous shadows.

-3-

The Hammer Descends

In the summer of 1522, an event that undoubtedly had an unsettling impact on Pilgram Marpeck and other mayors and civic officials throughout the Austrian lands occurred hundreds of miles from Rattenberg while the Castenbaur mediation process was about midpoint. Seventeen civic leaders—including the mayor of Vienna, nobles, judges, city councillors, and a distinguished professor—were executed on August 9 and 11 in the town square of Wiener Neustadt, fifty kilometres south of Vienna.[1]

A grim depiction of this event was captured in a large mural in the entrance hall of the Wiener Neustadt Museum as part of a 2003-2004 exhibit on the life of Ferdinand.[2] In the mural, hundreds of townsfolk jam the city square and peer from the windows of nearby buildings to view the executions. The front rows are occupied by the wealthy in fine attire, standing close enough to the hapless victims to be able to reach out and touch them. The rest of the townsfolk jostle for positions behind them or struggle for space at the many windows overlooking the square. According to one account, the condemned men were led into the square at six-thirty

---

1. There are conflicting accounts regarding the number of men who were executed. The best-known account, which claims that seventeen leaders were killed, is that of Alfred Kohler, *Ferdinand I* (Munich: C. H. Beck, 2003), 78-82 and numerous other passages later in the book.

2. The exhibit at the Museum Wiener Neustadt ran from September 26, 2003, to January 4, 2004. The museum also displayed the original painting *Hinrichtung der Wiener Ratsherren auf dem Hautptplatz von Wiener Neustadt*, by Josef Ferdinand Waßhuber (1698-1765). The mural was featured on the cover of the museum catalogue, *Ferdinand I Herrscher zwischen Blutgericht und Türkenkriegen*, 2003. A photograph of a section of the painting by Waßhuber is featured on p. 26 of the catalogue. A photograph of the full painting is published in *Kaiser Ferdinand I. 1503-1564, Das Werden der Habsburgermonarchie* (Vienna: Kunsthistorisches Museum, 2003), 341.

in the morning.[3] They knelt unbound and without blindfolds to receive their fate while the morning sun glinted off the swords of the executioners. One by one, the swords slashed through the air. In the mural, the bodies lie sprawled against each other, blood dripping from the open necks, with each of the severed heads lying at awkward angles a short distance away.

The civic officials were executed for the crime of rebellion. In fact, what they had attempted to do was regain the rights that had been granted to their cities a few years earlier by Emperor Maximilian, Ferdinand's grandfather. At the centre of the dispute was the nature of the relationship between the various estates and the monarch.

Since the late Middle Ages, there had been a delicate—though not always peaceful—balance between the ruler of the land and the leaders of the four estates: the clergy, the nobility, the cities, and the business community. There was no constitution stipulating how the land was to be governed. However, upon assuming power the monarch would swear to rule in a manner that benefited the land and maintained the rights and freedoms granted to the estates. The leaders of the estates would then pledge to be faithful and obedient to the ruler, while offering him wisdom and help. They would pay taxes and tariffs and uphold certain trade monopolies, all to the benefit of the government. Tellingly, this did not happen when Ferdinand became archduke. For whatever reason, he did not offer his pledge to the estates, so they in turn felt no obligation to swear fealty to him.[4] The issue of whose rights and duties held sway was a continuing, albeit periodic, source of tension.

In 1513, the estates had been granted freedom to establish their own governmental house in Vienna. But the gains they made soon crumbled under the burden of increasingly heavy taxation brought about by the empire's burgeoning debt. In 1518, Maximilian promised to ease their financial burdens and grant them even greater local autonomy. But in January 1519 Maximilian died, leaving a staggering debt of more than 6.5 million guilders, equal to the emperor's operating budget for the next five years. (Ferdinand, upon his death in 1564, left an even greater debt, 12.5 million guilders owed to the Fuggers of Augsburg.)[5]

3. A graphic account of the execution and the reasons for it is provided by Norbert Koppensteiner in "Das Neustädter 'Blutgericht' und die Folgen für die Niederösterreichischen Stände," a chapter in Museum Wiener Neustadt catalogue, *Ferdinand I Herrscher zwischen Blutgericht und Türkenkriegen*, 2003, 26-33.
4. Alphons Lhotsky, *Das Zeitalter des Hauses Österreich: die ersten Jahre der Regierung Ferdinand I in Österreich 1520-1527* (Vienna: In Kommission bei H. Böhlaus Nachf, 1971), 95.
5. Kohler, *Ferdinand I*, op. cit., 182-83. Kohler states, "It is probably no exaggeration to say that upon the death of Maximilian I, the political, administrative and

Normally when an emperor died, the estates ruled during the interim period until a new emperor was chosen by the seven electors. But this time, normal practice was pre-empted by Maximilian himself. Just one day before he died, he added a codicil to his will specifying that all officers of his regime were to remain in place until his grandsons, Charles and Ferdinand, entered into their respective offices as emperor and archduke. Although some nobles and senior clerics, including the bishop of Vienna, agreed to recognize the continuing authority of the old regime, most of the leaders of the estates challenged Maximilian's hand-picked interim government as fraudulent and incompetent.[6]

Leadership of the opposition to the old regime coalesced around three individuals: Dr. Martin Siebenbürger, formerly mayor of Vienna and a distinguished professor at the University of Vienna, nobleman Michael Eitzing, and the Viennese mayor, Wolfgang Kirchhofer. Yielding to pressure from the masses and the radical reform movement, the estates soon called for a new constitution. The Lower Austrian Provincial Diet decided by majority vote in Vienna in January 1519 not to recognize the bureaucrats and nobles who remained in power after Maximilian's death.

In May 1521, eighteen-year-old Ferdinand arrived in Austria for the first time. Physically, he was by no means an imposing figure. Neither tall nor handsome, he had a homely face with big nose, fleshy mouth, and a slightly protruding lower lip. Portraits of the young archduke invariably show him with his mouth slightly open, as if he had trouble breathing through his nose. Born and raised in Spain, at this point he spoke no German—a handicap that doubtless added to his difficulties as he attempted to assert his authority over the Austrian lands.

Very shortly after his arrival, on May 26, 1521, he married Anna of Bohemia and Hungary, who Maximilian had decided should wed either him or his brother, Charles.[7] Maximilian had decreed that once Ferdinand married, he could then rise to the position of archduke. It is relevant to note that Ferdinand's marriage to Anna, which was agreed to by Charles, worked out well in many ways. She was an accomplished dancer who enlivened many a palace party. She travelled everywhere with Ferdinand and from all accounts was a fine mother and

---

financial life of the Habsburg empire suffered a total collapse" (total *zusammengebrochen*). The "mountain of debt" and "forest of debt" are ably treated by Kohler, 72-74.

6. Koppensteiner, "Das Neustädter 'Blutgericht,'" 26. See also Lhotsky, *Des Zeitalter des Hauses Österreich*.

7. Matthias Pfaffendichler, "Ferdinand I der Aufstieg eines Kaisers," in *Ferdinand I*, Museum Wiener Neustadt Catalogue, 19-24.

bore him abundant heirs.[8] Most important, she apparently did not hesitate to advise her husband to incline toward leniency.[9]

When Ferdinand was asked by officials of the estates to judge between them and the old regime, Ferdinand demurred and postponed a decision to a later, unspecified date. After some time in Nuremberg, he returned to the Austrian lands in June 1522 to confer with supporters of the old regime who had retreated from Vienna and had gathered in Ferdinand's official city of residence, Wiener Neustadt. The city was long known for its loyalty to the monarchy. Once a place of refuge for Ferdinand's great grandfather, Frederick III, against a 1452 rebellion of the estates, it was also the city where Maximilian I was born and where he died.

According to the Austrian historian Alfred Kohler,[10] Ferdinand's interest in Wiener Neustadt went beyond sentimental family ties. The town possessed a spacious central square well-suited to the process of a court proceeding. Ferdinand was determined to take the issue of governmental authority to the courts and to break the power of the estates' opposition. On June 17, 1522, the order went out to the estates in the lands south of the Enns River requesting all persons who had attended the Vienna Diet of January 1519 to come to Wiener Neustadt. The estate leaders apparently had no premonition of the peril that awaited them.[11] They saw themselves as being completely justified in the actions they had taken, and expected to be warmly welcomed by Ferdinand and his court.

They could not have been more wrong. Ferdinand had been raised with a typically Spanish royal understanding that it was only by divine graciousness that the estates were accorded even the most minimal rights. The archduke had little interest in protecting the reforms that benefited the various estates.

Ferdinand himself presided over the trial, which began on July 10, 1522.[12] To help ensure the independence of the court, he excluded local judges who might be knowledgeable about Austrian politics and sympa-

8. Ferdinand's biographer, Alfred Kohler, concluded that they had a "happy marriage," in part because they had fifteen children! See Kohler, *Ferdinand I*, 96. Part of Ferdinand's agreement with Charles was that Charles would pay Ferdinand a dowry of 400 guilders. On December 23, 1523, it was agreed that it would be paid on April 7, 1524, see *Die Korrespondenzen Ferdinands 2*, family correspondence until 1526 (Kern reprint 1970). According to the correspondence, it took Charles some time to pay that amount. Ferdinand did not hesitate to call in the debt.
9. Kohler, *Ferdinand I*, 88-129.
10. For a fuller treatment of the estates' opposition to Ferdinand, see Kohler, *Ferdinand I*, 61-88.
11. Koppensteiner, "Das Neustädter 'Blutgericht,'" 30, and Kohler, *Ferdinand I*, 78.
12. Koppensteiner, "Das Neustädter 'Blutgericht,'" 30, and Kohler, *Ferdinand I*, 79.

thetic to one side or the other. Instead, he brought in a slate of foreigners from Holland and south Germany, such as the bishop of Trieste and the chief chancellor of Württemberg. All developments since the death of Maximilian were to be investigated.

The archduke, his entourage, and twelve judges arrived at the city square promptly at seven o'clock in the morning and took their places on a tribunal draped with tapestries. Ferdinand occupied a gold throne.[13] Over the next several days, the case was presented for and against the advocates of the new constitution. On July 23 at seven o'clock in the morning, Ferdinand returned to the civic square throne and the court was asked to read the verdict and the reasons for the decision.

According to Hans Oder, the court secretary, the adherents of the new constitution did not have the right to take to themselves the power to govern using those rights that had been introduced by the king and thus could not be taken away from him.[14] It was contrary to law, the secretary declared, for the accused to establish a new constitution and through its implementation to confiscate goods from the treasury. It was further inappropriate for the estates to establish their own rules regarding capital punishment, to mint their own coins, and to install their own custodians and government officials.

At this point, Chancellor Dr. Wilkenhofer rose to tell the group that Archduke Ferdinand was opposed to the idea of punishing all those on trial. Only the leaders should be held responsible for the attempted rebellion and should pay for their deeds. With that, guilty verdicts were issued for the first eight men, including the mayor of Vienna and the university professor who led the movement for a new constitution. They were sentenced to death by beheading.[15] The accused were never granted an opportunity to defend their actions on the basis of past agreements with Maximilian. Furthermore, they were convicted on the basis of laws that were not yet enacted. The minting of coins, for example, was specifically provided for, as were some of the other actions the group took.

Three weeks later the convicted men were marched from a nearby dungeon to the civic square of Wiener Neustadt, where their heads were sliced off while hundreds of townspeople watched. Several days later

13. According to Koppensteiner and Kohler, adherents of the new constitution had hoped to be the first presenters, levelling charges at the old regime. Instead, the court chose to hear first from the old establishment, delivering a severe tactical and psychological blow to the estate leaders. Instead of being the accusers, they were now the accused.

14. Koppensteiner, "Das Neustädter 'Blutgericht,'" 31.

15. Ibid., 27.

Memorial in the Wiener Neustadt town square to eleven mayors and notables executed by Ferdinand in 1522.

Ferdinand withdrew virtually all privileges and traditional rights from the city of Vienna.

The trial at Wiener Neustadt brought to an abrupt end the battle between those who wished to protect and expand the rights of the people and those who supported the near-absolute power of the monarch.[16] Maximilian's practice of calling upon the estates to take decisive action or speak as representatives of the people had come to an end. Power now moved firmly back to the House of the Habsburgs. As Ferdinand chillingly declared at Wiener Neustadt, perhaps with more prescience than he himself realized, "Justice must run its course, even if the world is destroyed through it."[17]

16. Visible opposition to the 1522 trial remains to this day. In Wiener Neustadt, a simple memorial to the fallen officials known locally as "*Kreis im Pflaster*" (circle in pavement) is embedded in the pavement of the town square. Placed there during the nineteenth century, the memorial forms an iron circle roughly the size of a manhole divided by eleven pie-shaped segments, each bearing a cross. In Vienna, the city in 1922 erected a monument to Martin Siebenbürger at the entrance to its new city hall. In recognition of the four-hundredth anniversary of his execution, the inscription pays tribute to the mayor's early struggle for the "freedom of Vienna" and the "rights of the Estates over against the ruler's capriciousness." One could argue that the University of Vienna (and, one might say, the city itself) never did fully recover its status and intellectual vigour after Ferdinand imposed his restrictions on freedom of speech and action.

17. Matthias Pfaffenbichler, "'Fiat iustitia aut pereat mundus,' Ferdinand und das 'Wiener Neustadt Blutgericht,'" *Kaiser Ferdinand I, 1503–1564*, 85-88. Kohler, although

The Chill Spreads

The events at Wiener Neustadt reverberated throughout the empire, and sent a chill through all town councils that allowed reformers to be active in their communities. The lengths to which the young archduke would go were further made clear in the city of Kentzingen. The city was part of the archdiocese of Johan Faber, who about this time became a key advisor to Ferdinand and therefore was surely involved in the latter part of the Castenbaur case.

Early in July 1522, troops of the Catholic prince marched into town, if not on Ferdinand's orders certainly on his wishes. However, the parish priest, who presumably had dared to stray from traditional church teachings, and many of the men of the town had already fled.[18] When it was learned that the secretary of the town was carrying a German-language Bible, he was immediately hauled into the town square and beheaded in the presence of his wife and small children. As final punishment, the troops then raped the women of the town.[19]

Two years earlier, Johan Faber, one of Europe's most brilliant Catholic theologians, had issued a manual to crack down on heretics. The document was based on a manual first issued in 1487 in Strasbourg by two Dominican inquisitors on how to deal with witches, sorcerers, and possessed people. Known as the *Malleus maleficarum* (the Witches' Hammer), the earlier volume came on the heels of one of the first waves of systematic witch persecutions in the Tirol. Neither the *Malleus* nor the witch hunts had garnered much public support,[20] but Faber saw an opportunity to transform the *Malleus* into a tool with which to hammer dangerous reformers of his own time. In 1520 in Rome, he issued a new document, the *Malleus in haeresim Lutheranam*, a manual for staunch believers to rid their communities of Lutherans and other heretics.[21]

---

favouring the action taken by Ferdinand, admits that on two points the trial was flawed. The defendants were not allowed to state their case or outline their past agreements with the emperor, so that the court never looked at the endorsement they had received. More importantly, Kohler notes that the fundamental rule of law was not observed. One could be accused and tried only on the basis of the law in effect at the time one committed an act. One could not be judged on the basis of laws enacted after one's deed. See Kohler, *Ferdinand I*, op. cit., 76-84.

18. Elsie Anne McKee, *Katharina Schütz Zell* 2 (Leiden: Brill, 1999), 1-3.

19. Ibid., 1-14. McKee presents the letter written by Katharina Schütz Zell, a model of sensitivity to their experience. An analogous situation is the way Hutterite women were treated after they were raped by Turkish soldiers. See Marlene Epp, *Profiles of Anabaptist Women* (Waterloo: Wilfrid Laurier University Press, 1996), 215-17.

20. MacCulloch, *The Reformation*, 565-68.

21. Denis Janz, "Johannes Fabri," in *Contemporaries of Erasmus* 2, eds. P. Bietenholz and T. Deutscher (Toronto: University of Toronto Press), 5-8. The *Malleus in haeresim*

Ferdinand apparently was impressed by the mind and zeal of Faber. In mid-year 1523, Faber was invited to join Ferdinand's court to counsel the archduke on all matters related to the faith. Thus Faber, who renamed himself Johan Fabri (the Latin form of his name), became one of the most powerful clerics in Europe. He was certainly a key figure in the writing of Ferdinand's mandates against the Anabaptists, orders with which Pilgram Marpeck would have to contend for the rest of his adult life.[22]

Another senior cleric who was intimately involved with the Castenbaur case was Cardinal Matthew Lang von Wellenberg, who oversaw the Salzburg diocese, which included the Tirol in Austria and extended into Bavaria in southeast Germany.[23] Cardinal Lang had a hand in virtually every major decision pertaining to Castenbaur.

A Delicate Balance

The house arrest of Castenbaur was ordered by Ferdinand himself in November 1522, three months after the beheadings in Wiener Neustadt. Mayor Marpeck and his city council were in a most precarious situation. With only eighteen months experience as a head of state, Ferdinand had demonstrated a taste for the dramatic and gory when dealing with those who defied his authority or that of the established church.[24] On the other hand, for the Rattenberg city council to ignore the sympathies of the miners, who had been gathering in large numbers in front of the building where Castenbaur was detained under house arrest, could also prove disastrous.

It's clear that as soon as Castenbaur was arrested, Marpeck and two councilmen hastily left for Nuremberg, where they hoped to meet with

---

Lutheranam is Faber's revision of an earlier book against Luther. The title "Malleus" is his. Available in the original Latin (Cologne, 1524) in the series Corpus Catholicorum #25\26 (Münster: Aschendorff, 1952).

22. Kohler, *Ferdinand I*, 130-51. Kohler gives a fine description of the make-up of Ferdinand's advisors. It is clear that after 1526, Bernard Cles, a powerful bishop from the Tirol, became chair of the advisory council to Ferdinand, thus freeing Fabri to spend more time preaching against the Anabaptists and drafting mandates against them. In 1530 he became bishop of Vienna and was commissioned to renew the university there (an endeavour which some would say failed). Fabri returned to his first love, preaching, which he did until his death in 1541.

23. A detailed profile of Cardinal Lang is offered by Johann Sallaberger, *Kardinal Matthäus Lang von Wellenburg (1468-1540), Staatsmann und Kirchenfürst im Zeitalter von Renaissance, Reformation und Bauernkriegen* (Salzburg: Verlag Anton Pustet, 1997). Castenbaur's arrest and trial are dealt with at length in chap. 8, 269-78.

24. It is likely that Ferdinand was still feeling insecure in his new position and, according to his own mandates, expressed impatience with the lack of enforcement by his brother Charles of the Edict of Worms against Luther and his followers.

Ferdinand to clarify who had jurisdiction in the Castenbaur case.[25] They obviously met with some success, because Marpeck then travelled directly to Innsbruck, carrying orders from Ferdinand himself. On November 27, Marpeck met with the administrative council of nobles in Innsbruck. The content of the orders is not known, but a December 4 letter from Ferdinand to the Innsbruck council says that Marpeck and the other city officials argued they had no jurisdiction to hold Castenbaur. Citing the strong public feelings in Rattenberg, the delegation suggested that Castenbaur should either be freed or should be turned over to Rattenberg's city council to decide his case.[26] Their plea fell on deaf ears. Ferdinand was concerned that giving a city council such unprecedented jurisdiction would lead to a backlash against him by the Innsbruck council. Having just squelched what he perceived as a rebellion among officials in Vienna, he was of no mind to risk unrest within the administrative centre of Innsbruck.

While these discussions were unfolding and Rattenberg's officials had not yet returned home, Castenbaur was allowed to preach to a throng of miners from the window of his upstairs room. It was a week after his arrest. Two days later, on November 29, (All Souls' Sunday), the miners again agitated for Castenbaur's release. In an apparent effort to talk with the workers, Castenbaur leapt from his upper-storey window into their midst and broke his leg in the fall. The miners hurriedly carried him to one of their houses, where he convinced them to return him to his home and the custody of city council. Its protective custody was short-lived.

On December 13, 1522, orders were sent from Ferdinand to Rattenberg through the Innsbruck council that Castenbaur should be sent for trial to the religious authorities in Salzburg at the earliest opportunity.[27] However, on December 24, Ferdinand told the Rattenberg city council to postpone this order until further notice. This time, pressure came from a delegation from the Rattenberg mining works.

The miners' purpose was apparently two-fold. Their primary objective was a renewal of an agreement outlining their freedom to operate the mines, which they had received in previous years from the duke of Bavaria and Emperor Maximilian. The miners had failed to get a renewal of the agreement from the administrative council, so they decided to appeal directly to Ferdinand. They appear to have painted a graphic picture of

25. The case was very complicated, mainly because jurisdictions and responsibilities were not clearly defined. See Boyd, *Pilgram Marpeck*, 16.

26. Ibid., 16-17. See for a detailed description of these events. They are also recounted by Johann Sallaberger in chap. 8 of his biography of Cardinal Lang.

27. Boyd, *Pilgram Marpeck*, 16, and Sallaberger, *Kardinal Matthäus Lang*, 271.

what might happen if the agreement was not continued. Ferdinand dispatched a letter to the Innsbruck council ordering its officials to renew the agreement, citing "a disadvantage or danger to us" if they refused.[28]

The miners' second objective apparently was to change Ferdinand's mind about sending Castenbaur to Salzburg. On December 27, Ferdinand told the Rattenberg council to have Christoph von Liechtenstein, the guardian of Rattenberg, incarcerate Castenbaur in the prison on the lower portion of his castle grounds on the hill just above the rooftops of the city.[29]

As historian Stephen Boyd describes it, this was not an easy decision for Ferdinand. "If he sent Castenbaur to Salzburg, he risked the wrath of the miners. But if the monk was released and continued preaching, Ferdinand feared that he would incite rebellion among the burghers as well as the miners."[30] Confining Castenbaur to the hillside prison would have mollified the miners by keeping him in Rattenberg and addressed the city council concerns that it had no legal jurisdiction to arrest him.[31]

For the next two months, the anxious city councillors of Rattenberg received no word as to Castenbaur's fate. During this time, both Ferdinand and Cardinal Lang were in Nuremberg, attending the diet. According to historian Johann Sallaberger, it is during this period Ferdinand and Lang made a decision to send Castenbaur via the Inn River to the prison in Mühldorf, an area under the jurisdiction of Cardinal Lang. Since the way to this location went through Bavarian territory, the order to give Castenbaur free passage was sent to the officials of Bavaria. The order came from Ferdinand himself in the name of the emperor, who at that time was in Spain.[32]

Unaware of this decision, the Rattenberg city council sent two emissaries to the church authorities in Salzburg to seek a solution. None was forthcoming. Alarmed at the rising tensions in Rattenberg, the council selected Marpeck, who had completed his one-year term as mayor, and another councillor to take a letter to the archbishop warning of the threat of violence by angry miners and asking for Castenbaur's release. Marpeck apparently met with the archbishop, who refused to comply despite Marpeck's appeal.

The miners responded with fury. According to Boyd, their protests reached such a pitch that Rattenberg's council frantically asked the admin-

28. Boyd, *Pilgram Marpeck*, 17.
29. Sallaberger, *Kardinal Matthäus Lang*, 271.
30. Boyd, *Pilgram Marpeck*, 17.
31. Ibid.
32. Sallaberger, *Kardinal Matthäus Lang*, 273.

istrative council of Innsbruck for armed help.[33] At this point, Ferdinand could no longer dither. On March 10, he sent word to Rattenberg that Castenbaur was to be sent to the religious authorities in Mühldorf in Salzburg territory. The news was delivered to the mayor and council at von Lichtenstein's castle overlooking the prison and the city below.

There is disagreement between historians Boyd and Sallaberger regarding where Castenbaur was sent and when. Sallaberger indicates he was sent briefly to Salzburg, and then to Mühldorf for the greater part of his imprisonment. Boyd mentions only the Salzburg part of his incarceration.

According to Sallaberger, Castenbaur was taken immediately by boat from Rattenberg to the Augustinian enclave in Salzburg. At midnight on March 11 he entered the city accompanied by three guards and four men who piloted the boat. The day after he arrived in Salzburg, the Innsbruck council was informed of his successful transfer, and Ferdinand issued a mandate that placed a ban on all of Luther's writings, books, and teachings, which were forbidden "at the highest penalty."[34]

When Cardinal Lang returned from the diet in Nuremberg, he found a written request from Castenbaur asking for an audience with the cardinal to defend his case.[35] On March 16, consultations between the church hierarchy and prisoner began in Salzburg, after which Castenbaur apparently was transferred back to the Mühldorf prison. Meantime, Castenbaur had asked for help from Marpeck and the Rattenberg city council. On March 21, Marpeck and a fellow citizen of Rattenberg travelled to Salzburg to intervene with church authorities on Castenbaur's behalf.[36] They had little success.

Castenbaur continued to languish in the dank, dark Mühldorf prison, a move that would cause him much personal hardship[37] and created tension throughout the land. It also was a source of sharp disagreement between state and religious authorities over which jurisdiction would pay the thirty-two Rhine guilders needed to house him and guard him in the facility. William IV, the duke of Bavaria, was not pleased to have this new prisoner

---

33. Boyd, *Pilgram Marpeck*, 17.
34. Sallaberger, *Kardinal Matthäus Lang*, 271.
35. Ibid., 272.
36. Boyd, *Pilgram Marpeck*, 17.
37. It was during this period that Castenbaur wrote an eloquent meditation on death, which was published immediately. See *Ain köstlicher guter Sermon vom Sterben* (Augsburg: Steiner, 1523). He also wrote his own "transcript" of his interrogation by authorities, since the notary did not do so. See *Artickel wider S. Castenbaur auch was er darauf geantwortet hat* (Augsburg: Steiner, 1523).

in his domain. To add to his displeasure, in April he received a communication that Castenbaur's imprisonment was creating all kinds of problems in many parts of Bavaria and beyond. There were fears of revolution unless his case was dealt with soon (presumably resulting in his release). Authorities begged William to deal with the matter quickly so that the furore in the land and the cry of the farmers could be stilled.

According to Sallaberger, William wrote to Cardinal Lang that he would have nothing to do with deciding the fate of the imprisoned monk. Sympathetic to Luther, William was quite happy to allow Ferdinand and the church find their own way out of the mess they had made.[38]

On April 20, 1523, the Augustinians stepped into the fray when the head of the order in the Salzburg region issued a directive that Castenbaur should be taken back to Salzburg.[39] This was an attempt to move Castenbaur's case back into the jurisdiction of the church and out of the control of the duke of Bavaria. Three days later the Salzburg council of advisors to Cardinal Lang declared that it had a mandate to deliver a verdict to Ferdinand and that a decision should be made as quickly as possible. The council's plan was to have a representative (Dr. Eberhard Englemar, an expert on canon law) interview Castenbaur in Mühldorf and then pre-sent an analysis of his answers. The prisoner was not to be brought to Salzburg until the interview process was finished and he was given an opportunity to recant.

Castenbaur offered a passionate defence.

"Whoever calls me Lutheran does violence to me," he said in a written statement to the head of his religious order.[40] "I proclaim and preach God's Word daily out of the book according to the text of the Holy Scriptures. For three years now, I have studied very diligently the church fathers. I follow Luther only when he is in harmony or in unison with the Holy Scripture. I have never attacked the Church fathers, the Church leaders or the clergy, but only the abuses that are present and which have begun here. I have never attempted to teach Luther's writings or his teachings for I do not understand them all."

In May 1523, Marpeck reported back to Rattenberg city council regarding the accusations against Castenbaur and his defence. Sallaberger states that twice during 1523, the city of Rattenberg commissioned Marpeck to work on behalf of Castenbaur and to intervene for him.[41]

---

38. Sallaberger, *Kardinal Matthäus Lang*, 273.
39. Ibid.
40. Ibid., 274-75. See especially n38.
41. Ibid., 276.

The wheels of justice are known to grind slowly, and this certainly was the case in Marpeck's time. Not until December 1523 was Castenbaur moved from the city hall prison in Mühldorf to a cell in the cardinal's detention centre in the same city where he could be watched more closely. During his time in the city's dungeon he was starved, tortured, and exposed to cold weather in an effort to get him to recant. In January 1524 a number of counsellors of the cardinal met to discuss whether Castenbaur should be turned over to the church authorities in Salzburg or to the Augustinians, his own religious order. He wrote on May 4, 1524, that "by now for six hundred days I have suffered greatly."[42] Meanwhile, a leading cleric in the Vatican let it be known that the delay in resolving the Castenbaur case was quite inexcusable.[43]

Freedom at Last

Despite this rebuke, the procrastination by religious authorities, most especially Cardinal Lang, continued. During this period Castenbaur twice asked for help from Rattenberg's city council.[44] It's not clear whether or how the council responded. What is clear is that Castenbaur continued to languish in the cardinal's cell until the summer of 1524, when finally he was set free. There is considerable speculation regarding the reasons for his release. One version—intriguing to be sure, but for which little evidence exists—is that Ferdinand's wife, Anna, had intervened in support of his release because, so the tale goes, Castenbaur used to be Anna's confessor.[45] Sallaberger says that fourteen officials, including jurists and officers of the court, met in February to discuss whether to take Castenbaur to Salzburg under Bavarian protection, but no decision was made. Ferdinand apparently met with Cardinal Lang in Regensburg, and it may have been at this meeting that Anna's plea for Castenbaur's release was discussed. It is also possible that she convinced her husband that since Ferdinand was in Regensburg to discuss reforms for the church, he had already conceded Castenbaur's main point: The church needs renewal and change.

Cardinal Lang and Ferdinand helped to draft the Regensburg Accord, which, had it been drafted four years earlier, might have prevented the whole Castenbaur affair. The accord was the only major platform designed by Ferdinand and Fabri to reform the Catholic Church from within. It called for

42. Ibid., 270, n8.
43. The comment was made by Dr. Theologicus Johan Eck of Rome. See Sallaberger, *Kardinal Matthäus Lang*, 277, n56.
44. Boyd, *Pilgram Marpeck*, 18.
45. Sallaberger, *Kardinal Matthäus Lang*, 277.

more education and supervision of parish priests and provided for three-person teams to arbitrate problems at the parish level.[46]

Several senior clerics had recommended varying degrees of punishment for Castenbaur. In the end, the verdict was a compromise on all sides. Castenbaur acknowledged that perhaps he had been too flippant and caustic. He denied that he had intended to incite rebellion and said that he always preached unity and peace. Walking a fairly fine line, he affirmed that the pope and emperor received their power from God—if they did not oppose God's will. He accepted that disobedience should be punished with force but maintained that spiritual and civil power should be distinguished one from the other.[47]

In May 1524, Castenbaur finally was released. A key figure in this release was Abbot Johann Staupitz, a trusted associate of Cardinal Lang, who half a year earlier had concluded that Castenbaur's most serious failure was his "lack of considerateness." The preacher, he wrote, "is above all to be edifying, not tearing things down. He is to rebuke but never to provoke, comfort but never to condemn. None of the above is found in the teaching of the accused. To be sure, Agricola (i.e., Castenbaur) has spoken much truth but little for encouragement and comfort."[48]

In the end, after a year and a half in prison, the Augustinian monk was released to the superintendent of his order to be disciplined as the superintendent saw fit. After all that had happened, there is no evidence that he received any punishment whatsoever. But Castenbaur didn't last long in the cloister. In a matter of months he left for Augsburg in south Germany, where he was also using his Latin name, Boius Agricola.[49] There he married and became pastor of St. Anna Lutheran Church. The renegade monk had fully joined the movement for reform.

⁓

It is ironic that, as an Augustinian, Castenbaur very likely helped sow the seeds of Marpeck's eventual move to Anabaptism. It is highly probable that Marpeck read all or most of what Castenbaur published and most certainly would have read his first work, *Reflections on How the Church Can Be Renewed*, which was published as early as 1520. The

46. See Christian Hege and J. Loserth, "Regensburger Ordnung," in *ME* 4, 272.

47. The assessment of Castenbaur by Johann Staupitz, Nikolaus Paulus, "Gutachten von Staupitz aus dem Jahre 1523," in *Historisches Jahrbuch der Görresgesellschaft* 12, written in November 1523. N. Paulus, 1891: 773-77.

48. Ibid., 273.

49. Even in his earlier years he had used this name when he published a book, but its usage was inconsistent.

booklet of twenty-two pages laid out Castenbaur's strong conviction that change cannot be brought about by violence or pressure. He built a case that neither coercion nor war can cause people to change their views. He argued that his thesis could not be deflected by examples drawn from the Old Testament, for they did not apply in the kingdom of God as founded by Jesus. His writings were so strong in their affirmation of nonviolence that whatever threats of violence were coming from the miners probably did not emanate from Castenbaur.

It is reasonable to conclude that Marpeck not only read Castenbaur but must have had many occasions to discuss these matters with him. Some of the themes of Castenbaur reappear in later Marpeck writings, such as the central role of divine "order" and a strong commitment to retaining ceremonies of the church, even though they needed to be reviewed in order to strengthen people's love for God and for their fellow human beings. Castenbaur and Marpeck also placed a strong emphasis on justice. They could have derived this commitment to justice from Romans or Isaiah, from their exposure to the plight of the miners, and possibly from the life example of the Rattenberg heroine, Notburga.

Born in Rattenberg in 1265, Notburga was a cook in the family of Count Henry of Rothenburg.[50] She routinely gave leftover food to the poor until her mistress found out. Ordered to feed all leftovers to the swine, Notburga then gave her own food to the poor. She was elevated to sainthood in 1862. As patroness of servants and peasants, Notburga would have been a legendary figure and role model for the people of Rattenberg during the time of Marpeck.

Whatever the various influences upon Marpeck and Castenbaur, they built a strong commitment in Marpeck to a community created by divine love, made up of people who responded to God's call.

As for Castenbaur, once he became a Lutheran, he turned with fury both on the church he had left and on the growing movement of Anabaptism. His "lack of considerateness" that had been observed by Staupitz moved to a new level of intensity. Staupitz's vision of a preacher as someone of "encouragement and comfort" was lost in the relentless zeal that characterized Castenbaur for the rest of his life.

In Search of Another Priest

During the time that Castenbaur was imprisoned, the parish of Rattenberg struggled on without a cleric. Marpeck's concern that the city have competent religious leadership persuaded him to support an invitation

---

50. Michael T. Ott, "St. Notburga," in *The Catholic Encyclopedia* 11 (New York: Robert Appleton Company, 1911).

by the city council to Wilhelm Kern to become the permanent priest. Little is known about Kern except that he asked for more money than Rattenberg offered, as well as an assurance from the council that it would support him if opposition to his preaching arose from among the princes.[51] It's not clear whether the city fathers were aware of Kern's reformist theology, but it's hard to imagine they were unaware of it. His request for security indicates that he sensed his evangelical views would put him on a collision course with Innsbruck.

Negotiations dragged on for more than a year until Kern finally accepted the invitation, perhaps at Marpeck's urging. By October 1524, Kern was under suspicion of teaching the new evangelical doctrines. He appealed to the city council to shield him from arrest by the Innsbruck administration, but the council refused. As a result, he began to preach only in the miners' nave of the *Pfarrkirche* and not in the adjacent community nave as he had been doing. The mining community now paid most of his salary.

During this time Kern is reported to have abolished the mass, following in the steps of a number of other church reformers. Rattenberg itself was beset by violent incidents of people attacking or defacing statues and icons of the saints and other traditional symbols of the church. The tense situation continued for a year, with the city council unwilling to infuriate Innsbruck and Ferdinand by returning Kern to the community nave or to antagonize the miners by asking him to leave his role as their preacher.

In January 1526, Kern was summoned to Innsbruck to give an account of his activities. Marpeck accompanied him as mining superintendent but possibly also as a secret friend and supporter. Kern was interrogated and dismissed from his position—interestingly, not because of his heretical views, which for some may have been an issue of debate, but because of a much more clear-cut infraction of church law. Kern had recently married, and marriage of a priest was considered a legitimate reason for dismissal on the basis of church law. Priests who underwent formal marriage vows in those years were judged to be supporters of Martin Luther, who had very publicly and provocatively married on June 27, 1525, as he said, "to spite the pope and the devil."[52] Authorities in Innsbruck were now sufficiently concerned about the situation in Rattenberg that they were prepared to deal with whatever unrest might develop among the miners as a result of Kern's dismissal.

---

51. Boyd, *Pilgram Marpeck*, 19.
52. Bainton, *Here I Stand*, 225.

His departure once again left the citizens of Rattenberg, including Marpeck, without a priest. City councillors then demanded that a priest named Christoph, who was serving the nearby town of Reith and who was responsible for general oversight of Rattenberg, supply them with the religious services for which they were paying. The priest at Reith was responsible for the spiritual welfare of Rattenberg but did not properly fulfil his obligations of providing the necessary leadership there. A young inexperienced vicar was eventually sent, but he became ill. The city council was persuaded to increase the stipend for a local priest, which Marpeck and others agreed to provide. Clearly, the church situation in Rattenberg was a pressing issue for Marpeck. One could imagine that he was deeply concerned for the peace of his city and for the spiritual welfare of his people. The troubles continued until 1527, when the city finally was able to hire its own priest.

A Change in Marpeck

What happened in Rattenberg religiously between 1520 and 1527 was a reflection of what was happening publicly elsewhere in the German-speaking lands. But what was happening privately in the soul of Pilgram Marpeck, who was such a prominent public official and professional?

Although we hear nothing specific from him in answer to this question, we know that he was close to both Castenbaur and Kern. He likely read the tracts of Jakob Strauss, which were readily available in the Inn Valley in 1523. He read Castenbaur's writings and no doubt also the early works of Martin Luther, which were circulating widely. When did he become persuaded by the new gospel of reform? Did he, like the priest Menno Simons in Witmarsum, far to the north in the Netherlands, continue to conform at least outwardly for a few years? It seems that he did. Did he experience a conflict of loyalties like that of Sir Thomas More, lord chancellor of England, between his faith and loyalty to his sovereign? Marpeck almost certainly did. Did he consider the cost to himself, professionally, and to his family should he change his religious allegiance? Did he discuss these inner conflicts over his changing convictions with anyone? Regrettably, we don't know.

Early in 1526, about the time of Kern's dismissal, the Innsbruck administration was frantic in its fear of Michael Gaismair, who was then in Zürich and plotting to invade Tirol to turn it into an evangelical agrarian republic. Was Marpeck sympathetic to Gaismair's goal or was he already persuaded—perhaps from observing the violence of the Peasant Revolt and the bloody fury of its aftermath—that the gospel could not be promoted and protected by violence? None of these public events could have escaped the notice of this lively imperial official, especially because all these commotions produced sympathy among his miners, among whom were the first converts to Anabaptism.

Marpeck's 1531 tract the *Exposé of the Babylonian Whore* contains one of the few autobiographical passages available to us. The tract was a critique of the evangelical (i.e., Lutheran) argument for opposing the emperor by military means. Without telling us when it happened, he relates that he came to the conviction that he "was deeply possessed and imprisoned by the laws of the papacy." This must be a reference to what happened during 1523-27. Observing that his tract was written against the followers of Luther, he acknowledged that it was in fact these very people, now his opponents, who had helped him to a liberating faith.

> I was set free to the liberty of the flesh. Where before I had been bound and had suffered in conscience, I was now free. I ate and drank with those teachers before the Lord . . . and thought that they preached a splendid Christ. In this new freedom I vigorously opposed the papacy with all the writings that helped me in that task so long as they agreed with the understanding, which was true, that it is not what goes into a man that makes him unclean, but what comes out of his heart. [What evangelical preachers said about] confession and other papist rules and human inventions, which were not so easy to fulfil but did not have the true spirit of Christ, I readily accepted.[53]

This passage is evidence that sometime between 1523 and 1527, he had thrown his lot in with the evangelical reform as presented by Strauss, Castenbaur, and Kern, although apparently with some misgivings. Some of those misgivings must have come as he read the Bible for himself. We notice, for example, that in later life he repeatedly turned to the book of Romans, but what he found there was not the same as Luther did. No doubt this change in Marpeck's convictions took place through a process of listening, discussion, and careful reflection. The stakes were high for a man in his position, but they were to rise even higher.

53. *Later Writings by Pilgram Marpeck and his Circle* 1, ed. John D. Rempel (Kitchener: Pandora Press, 1999), 28.

-4-

Years of Transformation

We have already sketched the arrival of Anabaptism in Tirol and its connection to earlier evangelical agitation, especially identifying the goatherd Wölfl as an important link between the two. In chapter 1 we saw how the peasant resistance of the Gaismair revolt mutated into Anabaptism in the Tirolean valleys. Finally, we also noted the arrival of a young, former Franciscan monk, Lienhart Schiemer, in Rattenberg on November 27, 1527. He was arrested and imprisoned that same evening.

But another person was also critical to this story: a man named Hans Schlaffer, who, like Schiemer, made his appearance in the Inn Valley late in 1527. Schlaffer had been ordained a priest in 1511 in the "country above the Enns River," which meant the area between the Enns and Inn Rivers in Upper Austria. Assuming that he was at least twenty years old at his ordination, he was now about forty. Like Schiemer, he had been with early Anabaptist leaders Balthasar Hubmaier and Hans Hut in Nikolsburg and had travelled west through Nuremberg, Augsburg, and Regensburg before turning south with a companion to the Inn River and down to Rattenberg. Although he was certainly rebaptized by this time, he said that he had not been sent to Tirol by anyone but had come of his own decision. This means that Schlaffer was not commissioned by a congregation, as Schiemer had said about himself. Since the destinations of Schlaffer and his companion were Rattenberg and Schwaz, we may assume that they made contact with the mining communities there. Thus it is likely that Marpeck knew about him and likely met him.

Schlaffer stayed with a relative in Brixlegg, just west of Rattenberg. Stephen Boyd suggests credibly that perhaps Schlaffer was responsible for the beginning of the Anabaptist congregation in Rattenberg. We don't know exactly when he came to Rattenberg or how long he stayed there. He decided to leave his lodgings when he noticed that his presence was an annoyance for his cousin. The reason for this could certainly have been the events in Rattenberg that led to the arrest of Lienhart Schiemer on November 27. Schlaffer left the town, briefly stopped over in Schwaz and then went on to Hall, intending to get employment there for the winter. Perhaps, like other clergy before him, he was hoping for work in the mines. The next day, December 6, 1527, as he walked back to Schwaz with a companion, he was arrested and imprisoned. This means that he probably left Brixlegg on December 3, from which we may gather that he spent perhaps as much as two weeks with Anabaptists in Rattenberg. Schlaffer was tried and executed in Schwaz on February 10, 1528.[1]

Schlaffer's writings breathe the same mysticism of the cross as Schiemer's, both of them having received it from Hans Hut; if indeed all of them did not get it from the Catholic mystical tradition. Whatever the roots of this theology, Schlaffer left a legacy of five separate epistles: the last, a deeply moving prayer and confession of sin written the night before his execution.[2] This last epistle was also included in the *Kunstbuch* (see appendix B), which was a collection of letters, epistles, and theological statements by members of the Marpeck community and others whom they admired.

In the weeks before his arrival in Rattenberg, Lienhart Schiemer had evangelized along a route from Steyr in Upper Austria through Salzburg to Augsburg and baptized well over two hundred people, according to his own confession. From Augsburg he travelled to Hall in the Inn Valley and on to Schwaz, where he planned to baptize many. He had been commissioned by the congregation at Steyr to preach and baptize, but because of the danger of betrayal by a monk named Reichert, whom Schiemer knew, he left for Rattenberg. Word of the thriving community of believers in Rattenberg must have reached him earlier, and he had likely been invited to come there. The night after his arrival he was arrested and imprisoned in von Liechenstein's castle. Three others found with him were also arrested.

Bartlme Anngst, the sheriff of Rattenberg, appears to have been a mild jailor at the beginning of Schiemer's imprisonment. Schiemer tells us in his epistle *Vom Fläschlen*, dated December 5, 1527 (*Pfinztag nach Andrea,* Thursday after St. Andrew's Day), that he left the prison at night several times, presumably to meet with the Anabaptist congregation, of which he was the bishop. Once he actually tried to escape but was caught. The Lord

1. *Glaubenszeugnisse oberdeutscher Taufgesinnter,* ed. Lydia Müller (New York: Johnson Reprint Corp., 1971), 120, 123; also Boyd, *Pilgram Marpeck,* 36-37.
2. Müller, *Glaubenszeugnisse,* 120, 123. For the texts in English, see *Spiritual Life in Anabaptism,* ed. C. J. Dyck (Scottdale, Pa.: Herald Press, 1999), 194-209.

would not allow him to escape, he wrote. These visits could have taken place over the course of a week and would help to explain his close ties to the people of Rattenberg reflected in his epistles. Moreover, upon Schiemer's request, Anngst provided him with pen, ink, and paper.

Schiemer wrote his extant epistles during the days and nights between November 27 and December 6, the date of the last one. In it, he wrote that he desired to write more but that physically he could no longer do so.[3] Imprisonment in the sixteenth century was always dangerous to life and limb, but it was doubly so in the Tirolean winter. He knew the end was near, for he wrote that the beast with the seven heads already had him in its claws and was ready to devour him. One can sense his alarm and dread at his approaching death as he wrote sentence after sentence as though he believed that, as long as he was addressing his co-believers, the darkness would be held at bay.[4] He signed himself "their unworthy bishop." He was the first Anabaptist bishop in Upper Austria and by virtue of that, also bishop of Rattenberg.[5]

On December 14, 1527, the Innsbruck government received his confession[6] and sent it on to Augsburg and Salzburg to alert the authorities there. That confession was extracted under torture (probably done by Sheriff Anngst under orders that likely originated with Ferdinand) and contains the biographical information on Schiemer that we have today.

Schiemer Stands Trial

The same day that Schiemer's confession arrived in Innsbruck, Pilgram Marpeck was ordered by the officials there to assist the sheriff in prosecuting Anabaptists. In his position as mining superintendent, he was responsible for the harmonious function of the mining community, which was known to be hospitable to new religious ideas. This prosecution was designed by Ferdinand not merely to stamp out unapproved religious beliefs, but also to eradicate in its beginning stages what he believed to be the invariable consequence of anti-church belief: insurrection and revolt. In 1526, Ferdinand had become king of Moravia and Hungary, but still remained archduke of the Austrian lands. It will be remembered that in

---

3. His "Letter to the Church of God at Rattenberg" is available in English in *Sources of South German/Austrian Anabaptism*, W. Klaassen, ed. (Kitchener, Ont.: Pandora Press, 2001), 64-80. The critical text is found in *Quellen zur Geschichte der Täufer* 17, *Briefe und Schriften oberdeutscher Täufer 1527-1555. Das "Kunstbuch" des Jörg Probst Rotenfelder gen. Maler*, ed. Heinold Fast and Martin Rothkegel, Gütersloher Verlagshaus, 2007, 242-97. Hereafter Fast and Rothkegel, *Kunstbuch*.

4. Ibid., 290-94.

5. Ibid., 48.

6. *TA: Österreich* 2, ed. G. Mecenseffy (Gütersloh: Gerd Mohn, 1972), 53-58.

1525 Marpeck and Anngst were ordered to equip three men with weapons to deal with local unrest if necessary. Marpeck by virtue of his position was obligated to help Anngst in this new emergency. On December 18, 1527, Anngst was ordered by Innsbruck to suspend any further actions and decisions regarding Schiemer but also to make sure that he was securely held in prison.

Rumours about Anngst's initial leniency must have reached Innsbruck because he was now admonished that Schiemer be allowed no visitors, which he had requested, in order to deny him the opportunity to defend his convictions to church and university authorities. The suspension of the prosecution provided time for Innsbruck to assemble judges from all over Tirol for Schiemer's trial. They did not trust local officials to carry out Ferdinand's orders. The reason for this is transparent, since as late as January 10, 1528, Rattenberg's city council discussed the Schiemer case and agreed that an attempt should be made to persuade Schiemer to change his mind—and if this was successful, to acquit him. If he did not change his mind, he would be allowed to leave the country.[7] Innsbruck frequently had to deal with local administrations that were unwilling to prosecute fellow citizens, or even preachers from the outside like Schiemer, sending them to their death by fire and sword.

While all this was happening, Ferdinand's attitude toward the Anabaptists was made vividly clear when he issued a mandate in Vienna on December 23, 1527,[8] written to all imperial officials in the archduke's name by Johan Fabri:

> Our public mandate and warnings have recently been published in our kingdoms, dukedoms and lands, and have under threat of the most severe punishment forbidden everyone to embrace the seductive new, heretical sects and teaching, especially rebaptism. All these are totally contrary to our traditional Christian faith . . . . Some, who have become adherents despite our gracious warning . . . flee from their homes and go to other places in our kingdoms . . . and lands . . . and perhaps persuade others also to join. This has greatly burdened our spirit and aroused our extreme displeasure. For if this heretical, seductive teaching and trend and especially rebaptism were to take root, there would surely follow general rebellion against all government, as some who were arrested and executed have stated in their sworn testimony. In this matter we charge all of you and each one in particular.

7. Mecenseffy, *TA: Österreich* 2, 52-53.
8. Ibid., 37-39.

He then urged his subjects not to give Anabaptists any lodging and not to help them on their way. If any people declared themselves to be Anabaptist, the mandate asserted, they should take them into captivity immediately and punish them. If the people failed to do this, the punishment of the monarch himself would be visited upon those who failed to obey this order.

This mandate came on the heels of an earlier one issued in August 1527, which warned that Ferdinand expected his mandates to be heeded, for the threat that sects posed to both the church and the Austrian lands was very grave indeed.

These were among the sharpest, strongest mandates of Ferdinand. There is little doubt that Fabri was behind them, and they must have come to Marpeck's attention, probably at the very time he was weighing whether to remain in the archduke's employ. Ferdinand was a devout Catholic who displayed no doubt about the course of action he felt he needed to take. He was haunted by the brash determination that Martin Luther had displayed at the Diet of Worms and was determined to meet resolve with resolve. His mandates do not hesitate to criticize his brother, Emperor Charles V, for his "mildness" toward Luther. He seems to have tried to make up for the lack of enforcement of the Edict of Worms by enforcing it more strictly himself. The massacre at Wiener Neustadt and similar actions were justified by Ferdinand because they dealt swiftly and decisively with rebels who challenged the monarch's authority and threatened to establish their own domains.

Taking a Stand

As Marpeck deliberated over his response to the latest mandate, the lives of Schiemer and Marpeck became more entwined, although not visibly. On January 1, 1528, Marpeck requested that he not be forced to prosecute Anabaptists because that was not part of his job description as mining superintendent. To Marpeck, Ferdinand's order must have seemed like a noose tightening around his neck. If it was not to throttle him, he would need to walk very carefully.

That same day Ferdinand, then in Hungary, reported to his officials in Innsbruck that he had received Schiemer's written confession. He immediately demanded with alarm that Schiemer be dealt with according to the provisions of the August 20 mandate as a bloody warning to all others not to become involved with insurrection and revolt against the established imperial and church authorities.[9] The messenger service between Innsbruck

---

9. Mecenseffy, *TA: Österreich* 2, 42-43.

and Rattenberg was fast and efficient in these crucial days, no doubt reflecting the gravity of the events in the view of the government.

On January 3, 1528, a letter went from Innsbruck to Sheriff Anngst insisting that Marpeck must give his active support to these measures.[10] A week later, a further letter reported that Marpeck had agreed to act as requested, according to the mandate. He had been summoned to Schwaz to meet with the regents of the government concerning his request not to be involved in the prosecution of suspects among his miners. Instead, according to the letter of January 10, 1528, the regents had persuaded Marpeck to take action, especially to warn the families of the miners not to get involved with Anabaptism. The same letter also sharply reproved Anngst for having given pen and paper to Schiemer in prison. He was now to see to it that everything Schiemer had written in prison be passed on to the judges for their information.[11] He was not able to do so because these writings by that time were secretly dispatched out of prison to Anabaptist hands, where they have been passed along and preserved until today.

On January 12 Schiemer was tried before a provincial court made up of two representatives of cities from all over Tirol. He refused to recant and was sentenced to death. Two days later Schiemer, just twenty-seven years old, was delivered to the executioner to be burned at the stake to ashes.[12] It appears, however, that in spite of threats, local authorities asserted a small measure of independence. On January 14 Schiemer was granted the clemency of a beheading in the castle yard. Only then was his body incinerated in the lower grounds of the castle, adjacent to the tower on the mountainside a short distance above the roof of Marpeck's house. Was the merciful change to beheading instead of being burned to death made possible by the intervention of Marpeck to the Rattenberg city council? We will never know.

These were dark days in Rattenberg, symbolized by the absence of the sun. In these winter days the mountain that loomed over Rattenberg shut

10. Ibid., 48.

11. Ibid., 51-52.

12. Ibid., 58. This "cruel and unusual punishment" seems to have emerged in the early eleventh century, first applied to a group of religious who claimed they were being inspired by God. Burning at the stake was then applied to sorcerers and witches but especially to heretics. Because so many praised God even as they burned, they often had their tongues cut out first. Where the idea came from apparently has never been determined, although some would argue it was copied from the Romans, who burned Christians at the stake during the first three centuries of Christianity before it became a powerful and respectable religion under Constantine. For a detailed look at this subject, see Brad Gregory, *Salvation at Stake: Christian Martyrdom in Early Modern Europe* (Cambridge, Mass.: Harvard University Press, 1999).

Prison grounds in Rattenberg, where Lienhart Scheimer was incarcerated and his body burned to ashes.

out the sunlight, making the town cold and dark. Warnings were issued by Innsbruck that a plague was on its way. To make matters worse, the town also lay under the dark shadow of persecution. Lienhart Schiemer was the first of Rattenberg's seventy-one recorded martyr-victims over the course of fifteen years,[13] testimony to Ferdinand's grim determination to exterminate heresy and insurrection. The Chronicle of the Bishopric of Brixen, perhaps with a desire to produce impressive statistics, reported that one thousand heretic martyrs were recorded in the Inn Valley prior to 1530.[14]

A Time of Inner Turmoil

Marpeck was fully aware of what transpired in Rattenberg by virtue of his public office. With hindsight, we know where his religious sympathies lay and therefore we know that he must have endured extreme inner turmoil beginning at least with Schiemer's arrest on November 27, 1527.

Evidently he was able to hide the real reason for his request that he not be required to assist in the prosecution of those charged with Anabaptism. Even after his meeting with the regents in Schwaz on December 10, and after what we may assume were frequent meetings with Sheriff Anngst, there appears not to have been the slightest suspicion that Marpeck was

13. See Robert Friedmann, "Rattenberg," in *ME* 4, 254-55.
14. Ibid.

anything but a faithful official of the government and supporter of its religious policies. He was walking a perilous tightrope between his real religious convictions and his public loyalty. During the past two years he had become aware of what could come of Ferdinand's efforts to pursue the "heretic" in seeing what happened with his own parish priest, Stefan Castenbaur. The reason Marpeck gave for not wanting to assist the sheriff was a technical point, namely that such assistance was not required of him by the terms of his appointment as mining superintendent. How fervently he must have hoped that this technicality would protect him!

What may have been the nature of Marpeck's relationship to Lienhart Schiemer? Did he know Schiemer personally? Did he attend night meetings with Schiemer and other Anabaptists in the town before December 10? Not likely. Now that the authorities were alerted to their presence, attending Anabaptist meetings and being discovered would have been very risky. He was being extremely careful. His public agreement to assist Anngst as late as four days before Schiemer's execution indicates that he probably was not yet himself an Anabaptist.

Did he want to be excused from turning in Anabaptists, perhaps because of a personal sense of the injustice of prosecuting people for their religious views? Or perhaps it was his humane concern and sense of obligation to the mining community that was committed to his charge, many of whose members were at least Lutheran evangelical, if not Anabaptist. Perhaps he truly was on the verge of throwing in his lot with the Anabaptists, but hesitating because of his loyalty to Ferdinand (to whom he had sworn an oath of fealty) and the security of his position and reputation, as

Rattenberg as seen from the prison yard above the town.

well as his own personal wealth. One wonders if he was the person about whom Schiemer wrote who would not say anything evil about the followers of Christ, but also nothing good, and who says: "I don't like doing this, but I am not guilty. I cannot afford to risk the wrath of the sovereign."[15]

Could it be that the tracts Schiemer wrote in prison, which we may safely assume were in the hands of the congregation at Rattenberg, also came into the hands of Marpeck? It is possible. If we assume that Marpeck knew these writings and gave close attention to them during the last two weeks in December 1527, we may be on the trail of the shift in his convictions from a partisan of Luther (influenced in part by Castenbaur) to an adherent of Anabaptism as Schiemer presented it.

Marpeck cannot but have been impressed by the kind of person Schiemer was. Despite his youth, Schiemer evidently had some formal theological education because his writings reveal that he wrote with understanding about both philosophy and theology. He was able within six days to write three theologically informed, eloquent treatises that critiqued Catholic and evangelical interpretations of Scripture but, more importantly, offered a coherent biblical alternative interpretation as firmly rooted in the best of the church's traditions as the other two. All of this was done by the light of the fire that certainly awaited him.

By reading and by personal acquaintance with followers of Luther, Marpeck had by this time gained a layperson's theological education. He must have been brought up short by Schiemer's critical words about Luther's teaching. Perhaps it was Schiemer who first made him aware of what he was able to say later, that "wherever the Gospel was preached according to the Lutheran manner one could also sense a fleshly freedom which made [Marpeck] somewhat reticent so that he could not be at peace in it."[16]

This was the complaint about the Lutheran way made frequently in these years, such that, because of the doctrine of *sola gratia* (by grace alone), Christians did not need to be overmuch concerned about their ethical behaviour. Schiemer knew Lutherans from personal experience in Augsburg as well as in Nuremberg during his tailoring apprenticeship there after he left the monastery. In his treatise *Von dreierlei Gnad*, Schiemer especially went after Luther and Lutheran formulations of belief. He did this in all probability because the members of the Rattenberg Anabaptist congregation most likely were, like Marpeck, former Lutheran evangelicals and were now being taught the difference between Lutheran and Anabaptist beliefs.

15. Fast and Rothkegel, *Kunstbuch*, 273.
16. *TA: Elsass* 1, *Strassburg 1522-1532*, ed. Krebs and Rott (1959), 352. In English, Klassen and Klaassen, *WPM*, 22.

But the matter went deeper than that.

In 1531, Marpeck wrote: "Then as now the evangelical teachers said nothing about the mystery of the cross of Christ, the narrow gate through which the flesh and the one who has been liberated from the Babylonian captivity could once again be led into the liberty of Jerusalem. . . . They teach the truth and the gospel partially. . . . What is missing in their teaching is the cross of Christ."[17] The refusal of the cross, of adopting the Christlike life, was specifically linked by Schiemer with the Lutherans.[18] Just as Marpeck did later in his writings, Schiemer became very concrete.

When in the creed we confess that "He was crucified also for us," this means not only Christ's crucifixion, central as that is, Schiemer wrote. It also means direct participation in the cross by his followers. "Christ must not be separated from his brothers."[19] Marpeck was to return again and again in his own writings to this interpretation of the cross. Schiemer's writings had other important themes that also emerged in Marpeck's works: that Lutherans wanted both Christ's kingdom and the kingdoms of this world, and the emphasis that the material always witnesses to the spiritual.

A Decision Is Made

It appears likely that Marpeck received this particular Anabaptist interpretation of the gospel from reading Schiemer's prison epistles during the last weeks of December 1527. If that is what happened, Marpeck's internal agitation would only have increased. The struggle was not yet over. He too still wanted both kingdoms. As late as January 10, 1528, there is no evidence that he refused to assist the sheriff in enforcing Ferdinand's decree. But the trial of Schiemer on January 12, which Marpeck quite possibly witnessed, and his execution two days later must be regarded as the turning point for Marpeck. He had to choose one kingdom or the other, and he did.

A day or two later he resigned his office of mining superintendent. His resignation was acknowledged and accepted by Innsbruck on January 18. Ten days later came Ferdinand's formal acceptance, in which he still refers to Marpeck as "our faithful Pilgram Marpeck." It is quite likely that only Marpeck, his family, and perhaps some among the local Anabaptists knew what had taken place. Only the cover of Marpeck's public position and reputation and his determination to use it could have kept his true

17. "The Exposé of the Babylonian Whore," trans. Walter Klaassen, in Rempel, *Later Writings by Pilgram Marpeck*, 28.
18. Müller, *Glaubenszeugnisse*, 53.
19. Ibid., 51-52, 55, 66, 78.

decision—not just to resign his position as mining superintendent but to begin a new life as an Anabaptist—hidden from public view.

To judge from Ferdinand's letter to Marpeck dated January 28, 1528, the archduke suspected nothing. He requested that Marpeck turn over the work of mining superintendent, including his books, to Wolfgang Schönman, his successor. Providing that Marpeck was clear of all financial obligations, he was released from his vow, duty, and oath "with which you are joined to us." Ferdinand probably thought that the young, successful Marpeck was simply moving on to another job.

In fact, Marpeck's life was in turmoil on many fronts. In the midst of the swirling public events surrounding Schiemer's fate, Marpeck's wife, Sophia, died. This must have happened shortly before the end of 1527 and may have been a result of the plague about which Innsbruck authorities had warned the citizens of Rattenberg in the late summer of 1527. Marpeck himself made no reference to his wife's death. We know about it because on January 14, 1528, Sophia's brothers-in-law Hans Stetner and Lienhart Berndarffer arranged with Marpeck's consent to appoint Hans Stetner and Erhart Guglweit as guardians for Pilgram and Sophia's daughter, Margareth.[20]

Why would this be necessary if the girl's mother were still alive? And why would his daughter not simply remain under his care? One possibility may be that it was not uncommon for Anabaptists fleeing for their safety to other lands to leave their children behind, in the care of specified guardians.[21] To help pay for her support, Marpeck asked that Margareth receive the fifty guilders from the yearly interest of Marpeck's loan to Ferdinand.[22] Many Anabaptist parents were able to send for their children later when they were settled in their new home. There is no indication, however, that this occurred with Margareth Marpeck.

There is no evidence at all about the relationship between Marpeck and his wife during that stressful December. Sophia may have been the daughter of Lienhart Harrer, a Rattenberg city councillor from 1512 to 1514. Boyd cites sources indicating Pilgram and Sophia may have been married as early as 1514 when Marpeck was perhaps nineteen or twenty years old.[23] (Men who became citizens usually were required to be married.

20. Boyd, *Pilgram Marpeck*, 7, n15.
21. Wolfgang Kunigl, a crown prosecutor in Austria, urged Ferdinand to lessen the "Horb formula" for recantation because it was too demeaning. Kunigl sought to lower the number of fugitives and people leaving their families behind. Ferdinand was not convinced. See Johann Loserth, "Wolfgang Künigl"(sic), in *ME* 3, 258.
22. Boyd, *Pilgram Marpeck*, 7.
23. Ibid., 6, n14.

Pilgram confirmed his father's oath of citizenship in 1514.) If so, Sophia likely would have been in her late twenties or early thirties when she died, and their child between six and twelve years old. Was Sophia privy to his struggles? Did she resist the direction in which he was moving religiously? Without a doubt, her death would have made it much easier for him to move toward Anabaptism, considering the cost of giving up his home, his position, and virtually assured financial security for the life of a fugitive heretic.

A Man on the Run

After Marpeck left Rattenberg, his property was confiscated in 1530. He now owned nothing except his personal effects and perhaps some furnishings for the homes he later made in Strasbourg, Appenzell, and Augsburg. His use of the word *Eigentum* in his 1531 work, the *Exposé of the Babylonian Whore*, gives us a clue to his thinking about all this.[24] In contrasting the earthly and heavenly kingdoms, Marpeck cited the story in Matthew 8:28-34 of the two men from Gadara possessed by demons who were set free of their affliction when the demons moved to a herd of pigs. The owners of the pigs were seized by love of their possessions and asked Jesus to leave.

Where physical and fleshly matters rule, Marpeck wrote, Christ has to leave. "He who looks for Christ anywhere except under the cross in patience will not find him." But those who bear the cross and resist the enemies of Christ, said Marpeck, will easily win the eternal, not the earthly, victory. For Marpeck the word *Eigentum* actually had a wider meaning than its standard English translation, property. For him, *Eigentum* was everything pertaining to a person in this earthly life, both material and spiritual, personal and social: one's self-appraisal, reputation, training, social position, money, and things, and the attitude of possessiveness that went with them. All of these, insofar as they put self and the concerns of self at the centre, were a barrier to following Christ in his humility.

Marpeck used the term *Gelassenheit*,[25] an important concept for mystics and Anabaptists used to describe the nature of the regenerate life. *Gelassenheit* is a term notoriously difficult to translate, but means total yieldedness to God and detachment or disengagement from all "creatures," that is, all created things that a person may depend on as of ultimate value instead of depending on God. The creatures belong to this world and to this

24. Rempel, *Later Writings of Pilgram Marpeck*, 29-30.
25. He wrote a tract on the concept, which unfortunately has been lost. Klassen and Klaassen, *WPM*, 549.

age. In the process of coming to depend on God alone, unless these creatures become material pointers to divine reality, they are barriers that separate us from God. Like the apostle Paul, Marpeck was prepared to lose wealth, position, and reputation in order to "gain Christ."[26]

There is total silence regarding what happened to Marpeck during the next five months. We have no date for his departure from Rattenberg, but it may have been soon after January 28, 1528, assuming that he himself received Ferdinand's letter of that date. His departure happened under the cover of his position of mining superintendent, which did not expire until January 29. He must have made some provision for the uncertainty of his new life, but he could not dispose of his property for fear of betraying his intention to leave and the questions that would raise. His considerable property was later confiscated, with some of the proceeds going to provide for the care of the orphans he had adopted. His daughter, Margareth, also stayed behind in the care of her guardians. Is she the Gretel Marbeck, living somewhere in the Adige valley, to whom Jakob Hutter sent greetings in 1533? We don't know.

We can only imagine that it must have been agonizing for Marpeck to leave behind not only his daughter and his wife's grave but also his extended family and many associates and friends. But Marpeck was forced to make a choice: either to remain in the physical security of his profession and live a lie or to leave for the spiritual freedom and inner security of his newfound faith. He chose to strike out into the unknown.

Historians may ponder whether Pilgram ever longed for the Tirolese mountains and valleys. Did he ever look back to what had been his earlier life?[27] He probably did not. While his early days began with great promise, after Ferdinand began to issue his damning mandates, Marpeck must have become increasingly uneasy. During the months he spent trying to free Castenbaur from unproved accusations, Marpeck saw first-hand the slow grind of trying to honour both church and state. The decision to break with his mother church was surely the most difficult he had ever made in his life. He knew that leaving the church would brand him as a heretic and would make burning at the stake a likely fate for him. If Schiemer could not escape the wrath of Ferdinand, why should Marpeck be spared?

---

26. Philippians 3:8—"I regard everything as loss because of the surpassing value of knowing Christ Jesus my Lord. For his sake I have suffered the loss of all things, and I regard them as rubbish, in order that I may gain Christ."

27. Cf. Hans Guderian, *Die Täufer in Augsburg: ihre Geschichte und ihr Erbe: ein Beitrag zur 2000-Jahr-Feier der Stadt Augsburg* (Pfaffenhofen: W. Ludwig, 1984), 101-6.

Marpeck was probably well-acquainted with the biblical stories of Abraham, the man of faith who followed God's call to "a land that I will show you" (Gen. 12:1). So too Marpeck would do what he could to bring into existence a community to be governed by the living Christ. Every time Marpeck wrote about these years of transformation, he stressed that he was led by the Holy Spirit. Later writings indicate that the Jewish heroine Judith also made a strong impression upon him. The book of Judith is included in the Apocrypha and is a tale that in some respects goes entirely against Anabaptist theology and ethics. According to the story, Judith seduced the pagan general and beheaded him while he slept. Marpeck's interest, however, focused on the fact that she was a woman who felt called to save her people, holding the leaders to account for their lack of faith and inability to believe that God could save them (see Judith 8). Although she defied the commitment to nonviolence that Marpeck had learned from Castenbaur, she became a divine instrument who saved her people.

For Marpeck, there was enough evidence that God was calling a new community into existence that he chose to side with Schiemer and Schlaffer. He put his shoulder to the wheel, gathering what he began to call the community of suffering in Christ. That community would survive by God's grace, without state subsidy or ecclesiastical structure. To Marpeck's credit, he did not waver in that faith, but pressed resolutely forward.

-5-

Baptism and Commission

When Marpeck left Rattenberg, it appears that his destination was Krumau (now Česky Krumlov, in the southwest corner of the Czech Republic), a small city in Bohemia about 60 kilometres (40 miles) to the north of Linz. Marpeck was probably alone when he boarded a boat on the Inn River, heading from Rattenberg 160 kilometres (100 miles) north and east toward Passau. Travelling as a professional person and dressed according to his station, he would not have created any suspicion. At Passau he would have transferred to a boat going down the Danube as far as Linz and then travelled overland to Krumau.

No doubt Marpeck had learned via the believers' grapevine of the growing numbers of Anabaptists who had settled in communities in Moravia and Bohemia, including Krumau, because of the relative religious toleration there. So many had fled, leaving their children behind until it was safe to bring them to rejoin their families, that some areas of Austria were officially asking the Innsbruck government to lessen the persecution.[1] The fiery persecution of Anabaptists in the Inn Valley had forced considerable numbers of them to make their way to Krumau, where they could hope for employment in the mines. Krumau was a silver mining centre, so it is likely that Marpeck too was hoping for an opportunity to pursue his

1. Wolfgang Kunigl as royal prosecutor filed such a request with Innsbruck authorities on November 1, 1527 (see p. 103 n21). But on January 4, 1528, Ferdinand issued a mandate from Steyr making a link between insurrection and Anabaptism and declaring that rebaptism was so horrendous that it should be rewarded only with severe punishment. On January 12, 1528, the estates of Steyr sent a letter to Ferdinand noting that his frequent mandates were not being heeded, partly because the traditional freedoms vouchsafed them by royal agreement had not been provided. They called for a diet to deal with the grievances of the nobles and landowners, saying that such a meeting should be preceded by some "genuine heartfelt compassion." See Mecenseffy, *TA: Österreich* 1, 59-61.

Tower where Hans Hut was imprisoned in Nikolsburg, Moravia, prior to his death in Augsburg.

professional life there. The earliest record of an Anabaptist gathering in the city comes from June 1528,[2] and we can assume that it had begun there perhaps early in 1528.

Krumau was a small, picturesque city nestled in a loop of the Vlatava (Moldau) River on a main trading route between Trieste and Bavaria. With a mixed population of Czech and German, Krumau was a prosperous centre when Marpeck lived there. This prosperity can be seen even today in the beautiful and substantial buildings that have survived from the sixteenth century, including a massive castle on a high hill on the south side of the town. With the city's size controlled by the river and the castle mount, the town must have reminded Marpeck of Rattenberg.

In his new residence, Marpeck must have thought long and hard about how he could maintain both his newfound illegal faith and his profession as an engineer actively engaged in public life. At the very least, his ability to perform this dual role would depend on whether the Bohemian nobility of Krumau would be able to hold on to sufficient independence from Ferdinand to protect Anabaptists from persecution. As king of Moravia and Bohemia as well as archduke of Austrian lands,[3] Ferdinand never lost his determination to carry out the decrees that he and his brother, the emperor, had both issued against the Anabaptists.[4]

2. J. K. Zeman, *The Anabaptists and the Czech Brethren in Moravia 1526-1628. A Study of Origins and Contacts* (The Hague: Mouton, 1969), 199.

3. Ferdinand became ruling monarch of Moravia and Bohemia after the death of King Ludwig, husband of his sister Maria. One of Ferdinand's first moves was to melt down much of the silver in the royal household and use it to help finance his battles with the Turks. See Paula Sutter Fichtner, *Ferdinand I of Austria: The Politics of Dynasticism in the Age of the Reformation* (Boulder, Colo.: Columbia University Press, 1982), 70-75.

4. A total of thirty-one mandates were issued or reissued by Ferdinand during the period 1521-66. See T. A. Bossert and "Mandates" by Christian Hege and N. van der Zjipp in *ME* 3, 445-53.

Indeed, his desire to crush the heretical Anabaptists seemed to intensify after one of their most successful leaders, Hans Hut, died in a fire in his prison cell in Augsburg on December 7, 1527. Hut had travelled widely and baptized possibly as many as several thousand people prior to his arrest. As we have seen, Ferdinand was determined to stop the spread of the heresies that Hut and others were promulgating. It was during the three months after Hut's death that he decreed the executions of Lienhart Schiemer and Hans Schlaffer (see chapter 4). Ferdinand was determined to consolidate his own power in the Moravian lands. The cooperation of the leadership there was critical to his success.

In the following decades there was a long struggle between Ferdinand and the nobility as the latter attempted to maintain their autonomy. The year-by-year and location-by-location results of this struggle were crucial to the well-being of Anabaptists. Peaceful development of the Anabaptist communities in Moravia happened whenever the nobility could assert their autonomy in exchange for supporting Ferdinand's various wars. Whenever Ferdinand did not need their support, he asserted his prerogative as king and persecuted the Anabaptists. Ironically, attacks by the expanding Ottoman Empire helped provide a few years of stability for Anabaptists. Between 1526 and 1532, the Habsburg Empire was at war with the Turks. Since Ferdinand depended on the nobility to help finance his huge military expenditures, he was forced to postpone dealing with the religious nonconformity of the Anabaptists in Moravia and Bohemia.

Marpeck was an astute political observer. He would have calculated that political events were in his favour and that he could work professionally at Krumau while being part of the Anabaptist gathering there. Nowhere is there a hint that he even considered giving up his profession. Perhaps he had adopted for himself Luther's teaching that every Christian should continue in the station to which God had assigned him or her, and he therefore should continue to work as an engineer. Perhaps he also remembered the example of Schiemer who, although he was an Anabaptist leader, made his living as a tailor, and of the apostle Paul, who remained a tent-maker throughout his ministry.

Marpeck Marries Anna

It is likely that soon after his arrival in Krumau, Marpeck met a woman named Anna among the Tirolean refugees, and they married. Regrettably, we know nothing about Anna's background. What we do know is that Pilgram and Anna appear to have established an enduring, close relationship as evidenced by the number of times he mentions her endearingly as "my sister Anna" and "my Andle" in his letters to Anabaptist associates, and their references to Anna in their letters to Pilgram.[5] (For a detailed description of Pilgram and Anna's relationship and the role of the wife in Anabaptist marriages, see chapter 13). Pilgram and Anna took up residence on the estate of Jan of Lipé, the lord of Krumau and one of the Czech nobles who later initiated gatherings to discuss a merger between the Czech Brethren and the Anabaptists. An Anabaptist community was established on his estate at Eibenschitz (Ivançiece) in 1526.[6] Whether the Marpecks were personal guests of the lord of Krumau or whether they were living in the Anabaptist community located on the estate cannot be established.

On July 2, 1528, Ferdinand wrote a letter from Prague to officials in Krumau in which he mentioned reports that Pilgram Marpeck and his wife were staying at the lord's estate.[7] It is likely that Ferdinand's officials in Bohemia, who kept a close watch on what was happening on the estates of the reform-friendly nobility, spotted Marpeck and reported the sighting to Ferdinand. Unfortunately, we know nothing about Marpeck's stay in Krumau, whether he found employment or what his relations were with the Anabaptist gathering there. We certainly may conjecture that Ferdinand's letter made life uncomfortable for Marpeck. We may also speculate that he used this time to concentrate on learning to know what it meant to be an Anabaptist and considering how to use his own gifts for the future.

It is intriguing to think that Marpeck brought with him copies of the writings of Schiemer and Schlaffer. His journey to Krumau would have taken a number of days and he would have had time to read their work with more care than during the crowded and dangerous final weeks of his time in Rattenberg.

Schiemer's teachings on the relationship between the Old and New Testaments and of the "gospel of the creatures" are found later in Marpeck's writings. They also shared a commitment to obey government in matters of the body and God in matters of the soul, as well as the correlation of the outer and inner in God's witness to humankind.[8] Hans Schlaffer's discussion of the "gospel of all the creatures" is found again in Marpeck as well as specific expressions like "the gruesome desert of this world."[9] Several sets of copies would have been made of these writings to ensure their survival. Schlaffer knew about Schiemer's writings during his

5. Klassen and Klaassen, *WPM*, see examples 416 and 482.
6. Zeman, *The Anabaptists and the Czech Brethren*, 222, 238.
7. Ibid., 256, n57.
8. Fast and Rothkegel, *Kunstbuch*, 310; Müller, *Glaubenszeugnisse*, 78.
9. W. Klaassen, ed., *Sources of German-Austrian Anabaptism* (Kitchener, Ont.: Pandora Press, 2001), 85-8.

imprisonment, for he refers to Schiemer's tract *Vom Fläschlen* in his last epistle written early in February 1528. Schiemer's tracts must already have been circulating in the Anabaptist communities in the lower Inn Valley. They survived in handwritten copies preserved for centuries in East European archives. The writings of both Schiemer and Schlaffer are referred to in the *Hutterite Chronicle*. Marpeck must have had copies made for his own use. These later passed into the hands of the congregation in Augsburg and thus found their way into the *Kunstbuch*.[10]

'Buried by Baptism'

It seems likely that Marpeck was rebaptized in Krumau. He refers to this rebaptism in his early writings: "I have been baptized precisely because it is written that one should do so and I have been baptized because it is written that the Lord Christ died for our sakes. . . . Therefore upon the foundation of the strong belief and trust in the resurrection, I allowed myself to be buried by baptism into the death of Christ. This faith is the living letter in my heart."[11]

Marpeck undertook the most important step of his life when he allowed himself to be rebaptized. Combining the passion for church renewal, which he had learned from Castenbaur, and his passion for the proclamation of the gospel, which he had learned from both Schiemer and Hans Hut, Marpeck undertook this step in full awareness that it had already cost other Anabaptists their lives and could well cost him the same.

What shines forth from Marpeck's writings is that baptism was no pro forma act carried out simply because Christ had commanded it. For Marpeck, it was a reenactment of the death and resurrection of Christ, a throwing off of the sin that had dragged him down and a reemergence in the newness of life with Christ.[12] Marpeck wrote often about the power of resurrection and tried to help his fellow brothers and sisters in Christ to experience it in their own lives. He wrote about his own baptism twice anonymously, but once—while under oath before the city council of Strasbourg—he fiercely and calmly proclaimed that he had been baptized. He knew that such a statement was self-incriminating and could possibly result in arrest and death. But he also knew that he was being drawn forward by his belief in Jesus, who beckoned him to join the church of conscious believers without any reservations. The invitation of Jesus was not

10. See Fast and Rothkegel, *Kunstbuch*, 242-43, 344.
11. Klassen and Klaassen, *WPM*, 94.
12. "The Exposé of the Babylonian Whore, 1531," in Rempel, *The Later Writings of Pilgram Marpeck*, trans. Walter Klaassen, 28.

just to live for his faith but to die for it as well. In this act, more than any other, the faith of Abraham was manifest and became the guiding star throughout the rest of Marpeck's life.

Commissioned into Leadership

After his baptism, sometime during the early summer of 1528, Marpeck was commissioned into Anabaptist church leadership. The commissioning must have taken place in Austerlitz because it was the main Anabaptist centre in Moravia. The church in Moravia was by now the stable anchor for Anabaptist communities everywhere.[13] It is reported that when he arrived in Strasbourg in September 1528, he came as a commissioned Anabaptist elder.[14]

The ties that developed between Marpeck and Austerlitz were very strong. From a letter written by Wilhelm Reublin to Marpeck in January 1531, it is clear that Marpeck continued to maintain a deep interest in Austerlitz and that his ties with others in the community, apart from Reublin, are apparent in the correspondence that flowed between them.[15] In terms of his commissioning, Marpeck would have been selected and led in his commissioning vows by other church leaders who laid hands on him. We can assume that commissioning involved preaching, baptizing, and overseeing the Lord's Supper, as well as dealing with disciplinary matters in the congregation and ensuring that the poor were attended to and that the church treasury was not depleted.[16]

No doubt Marpeck reported to the church in Austerlitz (Slavkov) about the martyrdom of Schiemer and Schlaffer. Perhaps it was these reports that found their way into the *Hutterite Chronicle*.[17] Marpeck's link to Schiemer and Schlaffer and his acknowledgment of Schiemer's part in

---

13. See Robert Friedmann, "Moravia," in *ME* 3, 747-750. Ferdinand had special concerns and limited success in ruling Moravia and paid several visits there to shore up support for his policies. According to Friedmann, in Moravia in 1528 there is only one recorded Anabaptist martyr, whose execution took place in Brünn (Brno), 748. However, Johann Loserth, citing the *Hutterite Chronicle*, says that seven Anabaptists were killed in Znaim (Znojmo) in 1528. "Znaim," in *ME* 4, 1034.

14. *TA: Baden und Pfalz* 4, ed. Manfred Krebs (Gütersloh: Bertelsmann Verlag, 1951), 422.

15. Note the letters, nos. 17 and 18 in Fast and Rothkegel, *Kunstbuch*, 418-27, and the note describing the relationship between Marpeck and these churches in Klassen and Klaassen, *WPM*, 549.

16. See Leupold Scharnschlager, the "Church Order," Fast and Rothkegel, *Kunstbuch*, 440-45. Edited with English trans. by William Klassen, "'A Church Order for Members of Christ's Body,' by Leupold Scharnschlager," *MQR* 36 (1964), 354-56.

17. *Die Älteste Chronik der Hutterischen Brüder*, ed. A. J. F. Zieglschmid (Ithaca, n.p., 1943), hereafter referred to as *Hutterite Chronicle*, 55-58.

his conversion would have been an especially high recommendation for him. For Marpeck, Schiemer's violent martyrdom had been the equivalent of the abrupt revelation to Saul on the Damascus road: an epiphany that altered his life course. It enabled him, like Paul, to count wealth, position, reputation, and human acclaim as loss in order to gain Christ. From a physical standpoint alone, it must have been difficult for Marpeck to overcome the memory of the odour of Schiemer's remains burning on the hill just above his house in Rattenberg. Was Marpeck's vacillation, his struggle to surrender the security of his life in Rattenberg for the insecurity of the cross of Christ, also known to the church? On these matters, which must have been very important to Marpeck and the church, there is now total silence.

Archduke Ferdinand must have been grimly surprised when he learned that Marpeck had left Rattenberg and the imperial service because he had become an Anabaptist. It was the basest form of betrayal of the royal confidence, and his surprise would have quickly turned to wrath. How could a trusted servant turn so totally against his lord? Did he not know of Ferdinand's policy regarding Anabaptism? Surely he had read or heard the edict of August 20, 1527, renewed on January 16, 1528, both of which (like all of Ferdinand's many mandates) would have been proclaimed in full from the pulpits of the land. "Whoever teaches against the twelve articles of the Christian faith and the seven sacraments, and in so doing proves himself to be a heretic, the same will . . . be punished in life and limb, has no right to buy or sell, to work or to pursue a profession, may not will or inherit property."

Ferdinand's written inquiry about Marpeck on July 2, 1528, was the first move in his attempt to capture his former trusted employee and to quickly prevent anything Marpeck might do to further the spread of this dangerous insubordination. Ferdinand knew Marpeck. He was fully aware of his managerial and intellectual strength and correctly surmised that Marpeck would now turn all of his ability against his sovereign in the service of this rebellious heresy. It was very important that he should be made harmless without delay.

For his part, Marpeck knew that he was in danger anywhere in Ferdinand's domains. A sober reminder of that came to him on Palm Sunday in April 1528 when three men were burned at the stake in Brünn (Brno). One of them was Thomas Waldhauser, an Anabaptist who had a faith pilgrimage similar to Marpeck's.[18] The Bohemian and Moravian nobles had been protecting Anabaptists for several years, so Marpeck had travelled from

18. Wilhelm Wiswedel, "Thomas Waldhauser," in *ME* 4, 876.

Krumau to Austerlitz in relative safety. If he returned to Krumau after his commissioning as an elder, he may have been warned by the lord of Krumau that Ferdinand had made inquiries concerning him and his wife. He must have concluded immediately that staying on at the estate not only jeopardized his and Anna's life but also put his hosts at risk. He was fully aware of the extreme danger to his own life.

Almost exactly a year earlier Count Leonhard von Liechtenstein had been unable to resist pressure from Ferdinand and finally surrendered Balthasar Hubmaier for trial for heresy and insurrection. Hubmaier had made common cause with the rebellious peasants of Waldshut in 1525. In chapter 2 we saw how the estate leaders were invited by Ferdinand to Wiener Neustadt to discuss their rights and freedoms but then found themselves on trial. So too Hubmaier was invited by the cleric Johan Fabri, a former classmate of his and Ferdinand's leading counsel on church matters, to join him in Vienna for a leisurely colloquy on the nature of the church. To underscore the relaxed nature of the exchange, Hubmaier was moved from his jail cell to a castle. After a week of meetings with Fabri, Hubmaier on the final day refused to yield to Fabri's arguments regarding baptism and several other contentious issues. The next day, on March 10, 1528, Hubmaier was burned alive. The next month in Znaim, Fabri preached against what he perceived as the many weaknesses of Anabaptism in a series of six sermons during the sessions of the Moravian Diet. These were immediately published in German to help the common people understand why Ferdinand had to stop this pest from spreading.

Thus, while most Anabaptists in Bohemia and Moravia were still enjoying immunity from prosecution, the same did not hold for their leaders in the Austrian lands. Hubmaier's execution occurred just weeks after Schlaffer had been executed and shortly after Marpeck's departure from Rattenberg. Would Jan of Lipé, like Count von Liechtenstein, now be forced to deliver Marpeck to a fate similar to that of Hubmaier?

Fleeing to Strasbourg

No wonder Pilgram and Anna decided to leave for a safer place. Marpeck's Anabaptist contacts while still in Rattenberg (and also in Austerlitz) had doubtless assured him that since the imperial city of Strasbourg had embraced the Reformation, the authorities there held to a policy of religious toleration. Although Strasbourg was part of the Holy Roman Empire, Ferdinand's decree that no Anabaptist could pursue a profession in the empire had no force there. The people of Strasbourg were especially proud of an imperial *privilegium* (a special legal privilege given only to Strasbourg) that guaranteed the city's virtually unrestricted readiness to receive strangers. Sebastian Franck wrote in his *Weltbuch* (1542) that "they care not whence a person comes. As long as they promise to be upright in conduct they are carelessly accepted without recommendation as citizens or residents. Especially in Strassburg they do not ask where one comes from or about the circumstances that prompted him to leave his city."[19]

Because Marpeck had been commissioned as an elder, he also had the authority to assist in strengthening the Anabaptist community that already existed there. It is entirely possible that he was commissioned by the Anabaptist churches of Moravia to go to Strasbourg to attempt to unify the Anabaptist groups there because Strasbourg had been—and promised to be in the future—an important centre of Anabaptist life.

The first Anabaptists in Strasbourg were Wilhelm Reublin, one of the original Anabaptist leaders in the Zürich area, and Michael Sattler, a former Benedictine prior, both of whom arrived there early in 1526. Hans Denck had come for a short stay before New Year 1527. At the end of that year Jakob Kautz arrived. Reublin and Sattler had left a group of followers, as had Denck and Kautz. The first two represented a biblicistic form of Anabaptism based on a literal, as opposed to literalistic, reading of the New Testament. It was strongly influenced by the Christian humanist call to return to the biblical sources as guide for church reform. It also carried forward the medieval monastic, specifically Franciscan, call to follow Jesus. The Anabaptism presented by Denck and Kautz was also influenced by humanism but more importantly by the Dominican tradition of Rhenish mysticism, which concentrated on the inner spiritual life of the believer and less on external church reform. Marpeck was to struggle with the extreme forms of these two types of Anabaptism for the rest of his life. If he was sent to Strasbourg to try to unite these two groups, he did not succeed. We will see why as the story unfolds.

By Land and Water

Sometime, then, after July 2, 1528, and before the end of August, Pilgram and Anna set out for Strasbourg, located in the Alsace border area of Germany and France. Marpeck had good reason to think he might find employment in such a large and prosperous city. It is also quite likely that Marpeck knew of a call from the Black Forest region just east of Strasbourg to workers of the Tirol who knew the forestry regulations

19. Quoted in Klaus Deppermann, *Melchior Hoffman. Soziale Unruhen und apokalyptische Visionen im Zeitalter der Reformation*, trans. W. Klaassen (Göttingen: Vandenhoeck und Ruprecht, 1979), 143.

established by Maximilian and who also had the skills needed for opening mines in the region of Strasbourg.[20] Work opportunities were abundant for a person of Marpeck's skills and experience.

As they headed west Pilgram and Anna may have taken a coach overland to Linz and then transferred to a transport vessel, going by sail and oar up the Danube as far as Ulm, where navigation on the Danube ended. River travel was safer than journeying overland because shipping crews rarely betrayed their passengers, despite official threats. We have no record of further attempts by Ferdinand to apprehend Marpeck, but it is hard to imagine they did not take place. We know from Gaismair's story that Ferdinand had spies everywhere who reported on the movements of people hostile to him.[21] For this reason it is virtually certain that the Marpecks travelled by water. Besides, water travel was not subject to the highway robbery so prevalent at the time.

From Krumau to Linz the fugitives probably travelled at night. All major imperial roads had coach stops with rested horses at set intervals. There were Anabaptists in Linz following Hans Hut's stay there in the summer of 1527. The notable Anabaptist leader Wolfgang Brandhuber was in Linz at the time, but Marpeck and his wife likely did not tarry there. If they travelled westward on a river boat, they would have travelled during the day, as navigating the river was safe only in daylight. Once aboard they would have enjoyed relative safety with leisure to relish the beauty of the river flowing between wooded hills. After about a day's travel they would have passed out of Austria into Bavaria.

Passau was the first major city on that route. As they approached Passau they would have seen the Inn River entering the Danube on the left, while to their right was the looming Trutzburg, the fortress residence of the prince-bishops of Passau.[22] The confluence of the Inn and Danube rivers made the city an important transfer point for travellers. They could have had some anxious hours there. Although they had left Ferdinand's Anabaptist hunters behind, Bavaria was no safer than the Austrian lands. At least twenty Anabaptists had been executed by order of the dukes of Bavaria between December 23, 1527, and May 15, 1528. Anyone who

---

20. William Klassen, *Covenant and Community. The Life, Writings and Hermeneutics of Pilgram Marpeck* (Grand Rapids, Mich.: Eerdmans, 1968), 26, n56. Otto Stolz points to the dependence of mining procedures and operations on miners from the Tirol in his essay "Zur Geschichte des Bergbaues im Elsass im 15. und 16. Jahrhundert," in *Elsass-Lothringisches Jahrbuch* 18 (1939), 116-71, especially 122.

21. Walter Klaassen, *Michael Gaismair: Revolutionary and Reformer* (Leiden: Brill, 1978), 59.

22. These were church bishops who were also secular rulers.

assisted in the capture of an Anabaptist was rewarded with thirty-two guilders (a year's salary for a carpenter). An imperial order declared "all Anabaptists are to be punished with death. Whoever recants will be beheaded. Whoever does not recant will be burned." At the very time the Marpecks travelled through Passau, the Anabaptist evangelist Augustin Würzlburger lay in prison there and was executed on October 10, shortly after they arrived in Strasbourg. Would Pilgram and Anna have dared to look up any Anabaptists remaining in Passau? Hardly. It would have endangered everyone.

One hundred and twenty kilometres upriver from Passau lay the imperial city of Regensburg, with its great cathedral where Balthasar Hubmaier had been preacher twelve years earlier. Anabaptists Hans Hut, Oswald Glaidt, and Hans Schlaffer had passed through there in 1527. After another two days of travel, the Marpecks would have passed Ingolstadt, with its old university, and then after a further 115 kilometres (69 miles) they would have come to Ulm. There they probably stayed at the inn Zur Sonne, which lay near the bridge over the Danube and was a favourite stopping place for Anabaptists. Ulm was an imperial free city and would not likely have interfered with travellers passing through, even though the Duchy of Württemberg, which surrounded the city, was then under the control of Ferdinand.

From Ulm their journey would have continued overland through the free city of Reutlingen, where Wilhelm Reublin had evangelized a year earlier. The next city in direct line to Strasbourg was Rottenburg, which lay in Ferdinand's territory of Hither Austria, the most western part of the kingdom. It was here that the brutal torture and execution of Michael Sattler had taken place in May 1527. For Ferdinand, Sattler and Balthasar Hubmaier were prime examples of heretical rebellion. As we saw in chapter 1, Sattler had said at his trial that he would not fight for Ferdinand against the Turks, who posed a very real threat to Christian Europe. If Marpeck and Anna travelled according to the route just described, they would certainly have turned north now to avoid anyone hunting Anabaptists in the king's domains.

But even if they successfully avoided Ferdinand's agents, cross-country travel in the 1520s was often dangerous as a result of deserting or unemployed mercenary soldiers and other fugitives from the law who lived by robbing travellers. Total silence about this journey suggests that they completed it without incident. Their relief must have been great.

Thus, after perhaps a fortnight of travel overland and by water, Pilgram and Anna would have arrived at Kehl on the east bank of the Rhine. Strasbourg, one of the largest of the free cities of the empire, was situated across the river. They would have crossed the wooden bridge and most likely entered via the Butchers Gate (*Metzgertor*). The city was a bustling centre of business and trade, a transportation hub with roads converging from all directions. Riverboat traffic on the Rhine extended north to the Netherlands and south to Switzerland. Strasbourg was a well-protected city. Even so, fortifications were being strengthened on the side facing the Rhine, especially a new bastion called the Turkish Bulwark.

All of Europe was preparing for an attack by the Turks, now led by Suleiman the Magnificent, whose military campaigns were dramatically expanding the Ottoman Empire. The visions that the Anabaptist clairvoyant Ursula Jost saw in Strasbourg between 1524 and 1530 testify to the fear of a Turkish invasion.[23] In one vision, she saw a large and spreading heath. "On it I saw a big horrible black man riding toward me in gloomy darkness. A bright light preceded him. I wondered what this could mean when the glory of the Lord revealed to my heart that this man was the leader of the Turks and the light which preceded him the power of God. He will commit great violence and distress before he will bring about his own end."[24] In another vision, she described "how the people were walking up to their ankles in blood." And in another, "Then I saw in the sky many guns, large and small. . . . And I also saw clouds, which were entirely the colour of blood."[25]

The mood of crisis could only have been intensified in 1528 when thousands of refugees were added to the city's population of between twenty thousand and thirty thousand people. The refugees fled religious oppression by Protestants and Catholics alike, both near and far away, as well as a severe crop failure in various parts of Europe. However, because of Marpeck's professional appearance, he and Anna would not have been regarded as refugees. Upon arriving in Strasbourg, they would have entered an inn for shelter and food.

23. *Prophetische gesicht vnd Offenbarung, der götlichen würckung zu diser letsten zeit, die vom xxiiij. jar biss in dz xxx. Einer gottes liebhaberin durch den heiligen geist geoffenbart seind, welcher hie in disem büchlin lxxvij verzeichnet seind.* n.p., 1530 [published with an introduction by Melchior Hoffman].

24. Walter Klaassen, unpublished manuscript, vision 74.

25. See Lois Barrett, "Ursula Jost and Barbara Rebstock of Strasbourg," in *Profiles of Anabaptist Women* 3, eds. C. Arnold Snyder and Linda A. Huebert Hecht (Waterloo, Ont.: Wilfrid Laurier University Press, 1996), 277, 283.

-6-

Citizen of Strasbourg

When Pilgram and Anna Marpeck entered Strasbourg in early September 1528, there were some two hundred fifty Anabaptists in the city, representing about 1 percent of the population. Even with this small number, the struggle between the authorities and Anabaptists had begun heating up a year before the Marpecks arrived. The leading evangelical preachers were especially concerned with the followers of Hans Denck, the brilliant Anabaptist leader who, along with Ludwig Haetzer, in 1527 had translated parts of the Hebrew Bible into German. Both a humanist and spiritualist, Denck leaned strongly toward a more spiritualistic interpretation of Christianity and thus became a major force among those known as Spiritualizers.

Strasbourg's leaders had not forgotten the disaster of their loss of face in their public debate with Denck in December 1526. The debate was widely reported as having been won hands down by the Anabaptists, who ably handled the Scriptures and showed humility in spite of their confidence that they were right. As a result, no public dialogue was ever again allowed between city preachers and the Anabaptists. The leading preacher, Martin Bucer, especially found it difficult to argue with Anabaptists because they refused to accept his scholarly exegesis and insisted on taking the biblical text literally. Although a confirmed biblical literalist, Bucer drew extensively from the Old Testament, thus opening a number of battle fronts with the Anabaptists. "They read nothing but the New Testament," he complained, "and that almost exclusively in the German language."[1] In his mind, Anabaptists did not respect the authority of the Old Testament or that of Latin, the scholarly language.

Strasbourg's first government decree against the Anabaptists was issued

---

1. Krebs and Rott, *TA: Elsass* 1, *Stadt Strassburg, 1522-1532*, 79.

The imperial free city of Strasbourg, "the city of hope."

on July 27, 1527. The text was likely prepared by Jakob Sturm, the *stettmeister* (chief magistrate). The decree contained nothing about baptism or other points of theology. It concentrated solely on Anabaptists as "schismatics and offenders against [Strasbourg's] Christian and harmonious order."[2] Viewing Anabaptists primarily as troublemakers who disturbed the order of society, Sturm regarded quarrels over baptism and the eucharist as disagreements over trifles. There were some arrests and imprisonments in 1528, but the authorities continued to believe that Anabaptists could be won over by persuasion.

Like most of the imperial free cities, Strasbourg by 1528 had a long history of internal stability and faithfulness to the emperor. Its civic stability had been assured when, in the fifteenth century, the patriciate (the old hereditary nobility) had joined with the merchant guilds to control and promote the welfare of the city. In the free cities of southern Germany, a vision had developed of the city as a "sacral corporation," a tightly knit miniature Christian society.

In Strasbourg the traditional tensions that had characterized medieval Europe—tensions between the spiritual and temporal authorities, and between clergy and laity—were largely overcome. In all important respects the city was in control of its own religious affairs, the non-resident bishop having only limited ecclesiastical power and no political authority. It was a

2. Ibid., 122.

politically independent corporation within the Holy Roman Empire, although it acknowledged the far-away emperor as overlord. Stras-bourgeois saw themselves as a community ruled by God.[3]

Although the craft guilds annually elected representatives to Strasbourg's city council, called the senate, and its executive, called the Council of XXI, the real power lay in the hands of the merchant guilds. Many of their members lived primarily from the income of extending loans at usurious rates of interest. The Catholic clergy, monastic and secular (in other words, those who were parish or diocesan priests), were also in the high-interest loan

Martin Bucer, a leader in the Strasbourg reformation and Marpeck debating partner.

business. They did not pay taxes but instead paid what James Kittelson called protection money to the city for their privileged position.[4]

In Strasbourg, as in Zürich since 1520, the earlier ideal of the sacral corporation was found to be compatible with the new expression of evangelical theology. Church life was brought under the supervision of the government, and the interpretation of Scripture was placed in the hands of educated interpreters, the Reformers.[5] The government had literally taken over the role of the bishop for the institutional welfare of the church, while the new evangelical clergy were responsible for its spiritual life. This was not a separation of church and state but rather a distinction of governmental and church functions.

The Reformation had come to Strasbourg gradually. It began with the

3. This is also what the Catholics thought, and it made for interesting exchanges between the Strasbourg clergy and Johan Fabri, who had a deep commitment to returning the city to the Catholic fold. For a general picture of Strasbourg, see Thomas A. Brady, *Ruling Class, Regime and Reformation at Strasbourg 1520-1555* (Leiden: Brill, 1978), 18. For Fabri correspondence, see Letter 286: 23 May 1526, Strasbourg, The Strasbourg Preachers to Johannes Fabri, *Epistola v. Fabritii Capitonis ad Hulderichum Zuinglium* (Strasbourg: W. Köpfel, 1526), ff. A3v-A5v; printed in Bucer Corr. 2, 114-7, Ep. 127.

4. James M. Kittelson, "Strasbourg," in *The Oxford Encyclopedia of the Reformation* 4, ed. Hans J. Hillerbrand (New York: Oxford University Press, 1996), 115.

5. Brady, *Ruling Class*, 238-39.

preaching of Matthias Zell, who had come to Strasbourg in 1518 as the cathedral preacher. By 1521, he was preaching a message of God's free grace to large, enthusiastic crowds in the cathedral. Because of his popularity, the politicians ignored the bishop's call to put him on trial for heresy.

Martin Bucer arrived in Strasbourg in 1523. A former Dominican monk and scholar with a doctorate from the University of Heidelberg, he had committed himself to the Reformation through Luther's influence. When the Strasbourg council refused him permission to preach because he was married, the parishioners of St. Aurelian, who were members of the gardeners' guild, unilaterally appointed Bucer as their preacher. With Bucer also came Wolfgang Capito, a humanist biblical scholar with a doctorate from the University of Freiburg who had been won over to the cause of reform by Martin Luther. Capito's high regard for Christian moral standards and, above all, his strong intervention on behalf of Anabaptists who were imprisoned at Horb[6] endeared him to the Anabaptists, even though he steadfastly refused to support believers baptism.

Pushed by an aggressive citizenry, Strasbourg's city council took over the appointment of new preachers, who in August 1524 took the oath of citizenship and swore loyalty to the city and its council. The councillors acted not out of evangelical conviction but from political prudence, keeping religious affairs firmly in their own hands to preserve the freedom of Strasbourg within the Holy Roman Empire.[7]

The most important and influential politician in Strasbourg was the chief magistrate, Jakob Sturm. He had studied arts and theology at the University of Freiburg to prepare for the priesthood, but in 1523 was converted to the evangelical faith after he had already espoused the Christian humanism of Erasmus. In 1524 he entered the political life of Strasbourg as a member of the council and, as chief magistrate, became the architect of Strasbourg's life as an evangelical city.

Marpeck Becomes a Citizen

For the three years after his arrival in September 1528, Marpeck became part of the corporate and multi-faceted life of Strasbourg. He knew and interacted with great and small in the city and was personally acquainted with

6. Capito's letters dated May 31, 1527, try to persuade the authorities at Horb to disobey Ferdinand's severe orders by eschewing torture and seeking to convince the prisoners to change their minds. These extraordinary letters were written on behalf of himself and several of his colleagues. See John Howard Yoder, *The Legacy of Michael Sattler* (Scottdale, Pa.: Herald Press, 1973), 86-99.

7. Miriam Usher Chrisman, *Strasbourg and the Reform* (New Haven, Conn.: Yale University Press, 1967), 108-16.

Jacobus Sturmius von Sturmeck/
Stadtmeister/und erster Cantzler der Univesität
zu Strasburg.

Jakob Sturm, chief magistrate of Strasbourg.

Bucer, Capito, and Sturm. As well, he got to know many Anabaptist refugees in Strasbourg, most of whose names we don't know but who made an impression on Marpeck. Here he also met Christian Entfelder, Hans Bünderlin, Caspar Schwenckfeld, and Melchior Hoffman, all prominent figures in Strasbourg's dissenting community. Marpeck had major disagreements with each of them, debating about baptism, the Lord's Supper, bearing arms, and the role of government in matters of faith. More than most other Anabaptist leaders, he was always ready to learn from his opponents without surrendering his own distinctive views.

Unfortunately for the Anabaptists, the evangelical Reformers in Strasbourg soon became as intolerant of new expressions of faith as the Catholic hierarchy was. Over the years 1526-27, the Strasbourg authorities became more and more concerned that the continued presence of Anabaptists would shatter the unity of the Christian society they were seeking to establish. They were particularly concerned about the divisive potential of the Anabaptist refusal to baptize infants. In 1524 neither Bucer nor Capito was prepared to force parents to baptize children against their will. But Bucer changed his mind after the Zürich reformer Ulrich Zwingli demonstrated to him the inherent danger to the corporate Christian society of not baptizing infants. Until 1527 the Strasbourg Reformers were concerned about the Anabaptist teaching that baptism participated in the process of salvation. Later they rejected Anabaptist baptism not so much on theological grounds, but because of its threat to the internal unity and peace of the city.[8]

On September 19, 1528, Marpeck purchased Strasbourg citizenship. Official records include the following statement: "Pilgram Marpeck from Rattenberg in the Inn Valley purchased his citizenship and is a member of

8. The laymen Clemens Ziegler and Hans Wolff had loudly raised the question of the biblical legitimacy of infant baptism in 1524 and 1525 and claimed that evangelical preaching had not led to the improvement of Christian life.

the wagoners section of the gardeners' guild."[9] That document also confirms that Anna was with him, but we hear only one other reference about her during the Strasbourg years, a compliment that Bucer pays her when he describes Pilgram and his wife as having unblamable character.[10]

The conditions of citizenship were strict. According to Stephen Boyd, an applicant had to reside in the city, be registered with a guild, pay a citizenship tax, and swear an oath of loyalty and obedience that had to be made annually to each new city council.[11] Furthermore, a citizen was responsible for payment of taxes and for military defence of the city, which usually consisted of sentry duty on the walls. Finally, a citizen was responsible for aiding fellow citizens, especially in case of fire. We shall examine his approach to oaths and the demands of citizenship in chapter 12.

Marpeck apparently met the conditions of citizenship and assented to the requirements (although it appears he did not swear an oath to defend the city; see also chapters 9 and 12). Thus, he must already have had a place of residence. We are not told specifically where his house stood; only that it was on the Staden, next to one of the waterways. It must have been roomy, for Anabaptists very soon began to meet there.[12] He clearly also had the financial means to get established.

It is intriguing that, given his engineering and civic background, Marpeck decided to join the gardeners' guild. Given his professional qualifications, it is curious that he didn't aim higher. Of the twenty guilds in Strasbourg, the gardeners were the largest and poorest. They were market gardeners producing for the urban market and were concentrated in the parish of St. Aurelian in the western part of Strasbourg, near the White Gate—well outside the centre of the city but within the outer wall. The gathering place of the wagoners, a subsection of the gardeners, was the tavern Zur Art. It is likely that Marpeck joined this guild because he had made an inner surrender of the social position and professional prestige he had enjoyed until earlier that year. However, it is also true that members of this guild, which had been so prominent in the early course of the Reformation in the city, were the most likely to give him a hearing.

By joining the gardeners' guild, whatever his motive may have been, Marpeck deliberately identified himself with the labouring people of the

9. The official statement is dated October 22, 1528, when Marpeck was briefly imprisoned. See Krebs and Rott, *TA: Elsass* 1, 185.

10. Letter to Blaurer, cited in Klassen, *Covenant and Community*, 27, n55. Cf. Krebs and Rott, *TA: Elsass* 1, 338-39, 342, 350. The letter states, "Sonst ist er und sein Weib eines feinen unsträflichen Tuns." (He and his wife have otherwise a fine irreproachable behaviour.)

11. Boyd, *Pilgram Marpeck*, 53.

12. Krebs and Rott, *TA: Elsass* 1, 185.

city. Guild membership and annual dues provided for periodic banquets and the strengthening of the life of the guild. It was likely that here Marpeck picked up his first impressions of the social and religious currents in Strasbourg.

It was among the parishioners of St. Aurelian that the reform movement in Strasbourg first made major gains. They had unilaterally chosen Martin Bucer as their preacher in 1523. The gardeners were "moved so full and hard by the gospel" that in 1525 they had petitioned the authorities to take over all the monastic properties in the parish to be sold to citizens or distributed by lottery.[13] Clemens Ziegler, a citizen of Strasbourg and one of the most prominent lay leaders of the reform, was a gardener and a theologically articulate layman. He wrote and published books on the current theological issues of baptism and the Lord's Supper, and believed that the Bible should guide Christians in contentious social issues like the tithe. Although he claimed the right to preach under the direct inspiration of the Holy Spirit, Ziegler was a moderate man who in 1525 exerted himself to persuade rebellious peasants to avoid violence. The sword, he wrote, should never be used to defend the gospel.[14] Ziegler, however, was never an Anabaptist. And in spite of his non-traditional theology, he was committed to the Christian commonwealth of Strasbourg.

In the Thick of Politics

Marpeck was about thirty-three years old when he and his wife settled into life in Strasbourg. By the standards of the day, he was already nearing middle age. Since the beginning of 1528 he had been a fugitive, moving from one town to the next. Yet a month after he took out citizenship, we find him in the thick of Strasbourg politics and in trouble once again.

Together with Fridolin Meyger, Wilhelm Reublin, Jakob Kautz, and several other Anabaptists, Marpeck was arrested on October 22, 1528, and briefly imprisoned. The house of Meyger, a contract notary, was a prominent gathering place for Anabaptists. An interrogation of Anabaptists on April 22, 1528, revealed that twenty-five people met in Meyger's house every Sunday. However, the charge on October 22 was apparently that they had gathered illegally in Marpeck's house on the Staden.

At his interrogation, Marpeck explained that they had met to discuss

13. Chrisman, *Strasbourg*, 145.
14. Boyd, *Pilgram Marpeck*, 47-48; Krebs and Rott, *TA: Elsass* 1, 38. In his views regarding the sword, he agreed with Erasmus, the early Luther, Castenbaur, and Marpeck.

financial support for the many refugees that had come into the city.[15] These refugees were mainly Anabaptists who had been expelled from Augsburg and other centres.[16] There were so many, reported Marpeck, that the city social support system could not meet the need. So the Anabaptists collected funds, intending to turn them over to Lukas (Lux) Hackfurt, the city almoner, to distribute or put them directly into the city alms chest. Their action, he insisted, had been taken with the prior knowledge and presumably the blessing of the preachers Bucer and Capito.[17] He also stated that he and Meyger had given shelter to refugees and had gathered with others in his house to agree on an "order" to help their brothers and to sustain their fellowship.[18]

Most of the Anabaptists in the city were immigrants. While there had been much public interest in what leaders like Denck and Reublin had to say, the Anabaptist message did not produce an indigenous following. The people of Strasbourg were not averse to radical change, but they preferred the leadership of non-Anabaptists. It was therefore doubly important for the immigrant Anabaptists to develop a community discipline. Not surprisingly Marpeck, himself an immigrant, was quickly thrust into leadership.[19] In that role and also because he was financially able, he covered the debt of two refugees from Salzburg so that they qualified for treatment at the syphilis hospital that stood outside the western wall of the city. Strasbourg was one of a number of cities in the Holy Roman Empire that had built specialist hospitals to deal with this new and terrifying disease that swept through Europe in the late fifteenth and early sixteenth century. At times syphilis seemed to be almost as lethal as the plague.[20]

We have no official response to Marpeck's explanation for the Anabaptist meeting that had occurred in his house. It therefore seems likely that his comments were accepted and that he was released. It is possible that Marpeck's case was helped by support from the Reform preacher Capito, who not only authorized the meeting at Marpeck's house but also visited him while he was in prison. Marpeck reported later that he and Capito had a

15. Krebs and Rott, *TA: Elsass* 1, 185.

16. Ibid., 137-38, 180-82.

17. Ibid., 185.

18. They were reading a booklet of John Bünderlin in early March 1529 to help them establish the order by which their community could be organized. See Klassen, *Covenant and Community*, 31, n70.

19. On the "order," see Packull, *Hutterite Beginnings*, chap. 2 and especially 49-50.

20. An Italian doctor, Girolamo Fracastoro, bestowed the term "the French pox" on syphilis in a poem published in 1531. For the devastating impact of the disease on Europe, see MacCulloch, *The Reformation*, 94-95, 630-34.

friendly but unfruitful discussion. (It is unfortunate that during Marpeck's difficult final weeks in Strasbourg, when he might have benefited from Capito's involvement, the preacher was away from the city on an extended trip, beset by depression after the death of his wife.)[21] Despite Marpeck's release, the city council concerned itself with Anabaptists repeatedly after this series of arrests and struggled to arrive at a policy that would do justice to the Anabaptists while at the same time securing the welfare of the city. In all the deliberations that continued throughout 1529, Marpeck's name never came up.

On October 26, 1528—four days after the arrest—the city council decided that all Anabaptists who were prepared to be obedient were to be released upon swearing an oath of truce and a promise not to meet again. Fridolin Meyger accepted these terms and was released. Jakob Kautz and Wilhelm Reublin were imprisoned in a tower for a period of religious instruction. They were finally expelled from Strasbourg in 1529. But Marpeck was absent from the list. Members of the Council of XXI repeatedly referred to Kautz and Reublin "and other principals," but Marpeck was not one of them. Perhaps because he was relatively new in the city, he had not yet been identified as a principal. After Marpeck's release from prison, more arrests took place. These prisoners were required to swear the oath of truce. Marpeck met with them and comforted them in their distress. He was officially censured for this but he does not say by whom. Several times thereafter he requested a friendly discussion with the leading Reform preachers. He had come to Strasbourg, he explained, because the gospel was preached there and he expected that there could be conversation about it.[22]

Two Well-Placed Instructors

Whether or not the authorities were fully aware of Marpeck as a principal, he most assuredly was one. He was a leader not simply of an immigrant group that was socially and ethnically distinct from the city's population; from the beginning he was a link between the two. Marpeck was accustomed to associating with public officials. He had been one himself, and he understood their interests and priorities. Two men, especially, introduced him to the public life of Strasbourg. They were Fridolin Meyger and Lukas Hackfurt.

Meyger was a notary in the administration of the bishop who, while he did not live in Strasbourg, had many financial interests there. Meyger's

21. Boyd, *Pilgram Marpeck*, 55-56.
22. Krebs and Rott, *TA: Elsass* 1, 351-52.

work was to draw up contracts for various kinds of loans for borrowers—
often the poor, who routinely bore high rates of interest. He had become
an Anabaptist perhaps under the influence of Hans Denck, and as mentioned, his house was a regular meeting place for Anabaptists. From his
office he could see the social and economic injustice inflicted on the poor
by the wealthy in church and civic society. He complained that the new
evangelical regime in Strasbourg had done little to alleviate social distress.
He believed that because Anabaptism required that one's confession of
faith should be accompanied by a changed life of love to God and the
neighbour, it also had the potential for dealing with the injustices in the
city.

Near the end of 1528 Martin Bucer commissioned Meyger to write a
report for him on the effects of the excessive interest that was commonly
charged on loans. Meyger wrote a passionate condemnation of the heart-
less treatment of the poor, who were required to pay up to 100 percent
interest even when hail or drought destroyed their harvest. I know about
this, he wrote, because it all comes across my desk.[23]

Regardless of his friendly relationship with Bucer, Meyger was again
arrested in March 1529. He was sentenced to exile with his family, but
pardoned once more. Another arrest followed later that summer. This
time his employer, the bishop, demanded an explanation from the council for his incarceration.[24] But in 1533 it was reported that meetings were
again being held in his house.

Marpeck's other influential acquaintance was Lukas Hackfurt, who
had been appointed the city's chief administrator of welfare in 1523. He
had been a priest but had been won over to the evangelical cause, becoming a crusader for justice in the city and calling on the wealthy to aid the
poor. He identified high inflation, increasing immigration, dispossessed
peasants coming into the city for work, and unemployed youth as the reasons for the social distress in the city.[25] He was never an Anabaptist but
attended their meetings occasionally. Hackfurt had been excommunicated
from the Reform church because of his view that no government could be
Christian. He recanted that view in 1531 and continued as almoner dis-
tributing aid to the poor.[26]

Marpeck spent time in the company of these two educated and devoted
men, and through them gained insight into the social, economic, and reli-

23. Ibid., 218-24.
24. Ibid., 246.
25. Boyd, *Pilgram Marpeck*, 55.
26. Krebs and Rott, *TA: Elsass* 1, 334.

gious milieu of Strasbourg. The two worked hard at being responsible civil servants yet also highly visible religious dissenters. One can imagine their numerous conversations with Marpeck, from which he learned many lessons to guide his own actions in similar situations. When later he engaged in public debate with Bucer, he could speak on public issues with assurance.

Marpeck left no visible footprints in Strasbourg during the whole of 1529. It is possible that during this time he was engaged in mining in the Lebertal (which runs west of Schlettstadt about 40 kilometres southwest of Strasbourg), and thus had moved his residence there.[27] There were mining links between Rattenberg and the Leber Valley. It is likely that Marpeck took advantage of these links to gain employment. He also established an Anabaptist fellowship there and he addressed letters to Anabaptists in the area in 1540, 1544, 1547, and 1555.[28] All of that points to a stay of some time, long enough to establish firm relations with people whom he names in his letters over a period of twenty-five years. This and the later examples in the Kinzig Valley and Augsburg demonstrate that while he worked professionally, he was also an effective evangelist.

Marpeck Begins to Write

Meanwhile some important political and religious developments occurred in Strasbourg in 1529. Up to this point we have known Marpeck only in the third person. We have had reports about him, but not a word from him personally. That is about to change.

Early in 1530 Marpeck began working for the city of Strasbourg, so we may presume that he took up residence there again after the time he spent mining in the Lebertal. By 1531 he had begun publishing his own reflections about the changes in Strasbourg. Among the most significant developments was the abolition of the mass on February 20, 1529. The gardeners' guild had been agitating for its abolition since 1526. Once the central rite representing the old church order was gone, a new order had to be established, which is what the clergy together with the Strasbourg city council tried to do.

This joint effort marked a change from confrontation to cooperation between civic and religious authorities. It also reflected the subordination of the clergy to the government. Equally important, the new order represented a united front against the Anabaptists. As Emmett McLaughlin

27. This may be one reason that the Strasbourg city council did not identify Marpeck as a "principal" among Anabaptists in 1529. He likely was not living in the city at the time.

28. Heinold Fast, "Pilgram Marbeck und das oberdeutsche Täufertum. Ein neuer Handschriftenfund," *Archiv für Reformationsgeschichte* 47 (1956), 214-15.

writes, it was the "transition from *Gemeinde* to *Obrigkeit*" (from Christian community to political community).[29] The abolition of the mass was also a daring political move, given Strasbourg's place in the empire at a time when dark clouds of confrontation between Catholics and evangelicals were mounting.

Being familiar with city politics, whether he was in the Leber Valley or in Strasbourg, Marpeck must have followed these developments with apprehension. He began formulating the responses that were to appear in his books of 1531. Among them in a new form was the old debate about the relationship between civic and faith communities.

During the second week of March 1529, an Anabaptist meeting of forty-five people was raided at the house of Claus Bruch, a riverboat sailor. Several abusive letters had been written about the abolition of the mass and publicly posted. It was immediately assumed that the authors were Anabaptists. Handwriting samples were extracted from a number of the arrested Anabaptists in order to determine the culprits.[30] The writer turned out later to have been the sixteen-year-old son of a Catholic artisan. The youth was executed for his crime.[31] This incident provides evidence for the increasing apprehension of the authorities about the possibility of an uprising in the city. At the interrogation of Meyger and Bruch, the authorities heard that there were at least one hundred Anabaptists newly arrived from Augsburg.[32]

The reformers Martin Bucer and Matthias Zell approached the city council and appealed for permission to have a public disputation with Anabaptists. They were confident that they could help avert any trouble by publicly exposing the views of the Anabaptists as false and dangerous. The council refused. Civic officials were now determined to clip the wings of the clergy by refusing to give them undue influence on public affairs.

Five Radicals Arrive

The evangelical clergy were obviously worried about the arrival in Strasbourg of five prominent radical figures during 1529. Hans Bünderlin arrived from Nikolsburg (Mikulov) in Moravia early in the year, as did Christian Entfelder from Eibenschitz (Ivančiece), also in Moravia, where he had been an Anabaptist elder. It is very likely that Marpeck knew Entfelder, since their time in Eibenschitz overlapped. The third was

29. R. E. McLaughlin, *Caspar Schwenckfeld Reluctant Radical: His Life to 1540* (New Haven, Conn.: Yale University Press, 1986), 132. Italics are added.

30. Krebs and Rott, *TA: Elsass* 1, 226-33.

31. Ibid, 232, n1.

32. Ibid., 232.

Caspar Schwenckfeld, an aristocrat from Silesia. The fourth was Melchior Hoffman, who came from East Friesland about the end of June and continued his writing and publication on the end times. The fifth was Sebastian Franck, a Lutheran chaplain who was now confessionally unattached and who arrived late in the fall.[33] All of these men, who were welcomed perhaps because of their opposition to Luther, represented a threat to the theology of the Strasbourg Reformers.

But the radicals also became a threat to the Anabaptists in the city, a threat that was not immediately evident. By the time of the arrests of Anabaptists in March 1529 over the abusive letters about abolishing the mass, Bünderlin had already published two works, both printed in Strasbourg. The first of these, *A Simple Consideration of the Content of Holy Scripture*, was probably the work from which Meyger read at the meeting on March 16, 1529, at Claus Bruch's house.[34] At this point Bünderlin was actively involved with the Anabaptist group in a leadership capacity. The second book he published had the potential to destroy any effectiveness of the work of Marpeck and Reublin. The title was as long as some titles composed by Marpeck, a common style of the day, and clearly announced its content: *Explanation through comparing the biblical Scriptures, that water baptism as well as other external ceremonies used in the church are currently being reintroduced without God's command or the testimony of Scripture.*

Bünderlin was moving more and more into a private piety of mystical communion with God for which the external ceremonies of baptism and the Lord's Supper were not essential.

Some months later Christian Entfelder wrote in similar vein in his book, *On the many divisions in the faith* (1530), about the divisions among Christians over the bread and wine and baptism. No doubt Entfelder had in mind the politicizing of Christian ceremonies (making them part of city law) by Lutherans and Zwinglians during the negotiations of 1529 and early 1530, as well as the intramural quarrels among Anabaptists. Drawing especially from his experience in Moravia, he contended that the splits resulted from excessive zeal in interpreting the Bible, with each group seeking to outdo the other in carrying out its commands. He argued that Christians should suspend their use of baptism and the Lord's Supper while waiting for new revelation on these issues, much as the church in Antioch had to wait until the command came for Paul and Barnabas to carry out the

33. The careers of Hoffman and Franck in Strasbourg do not merit discussion at this point because they do not appear to have had dealings with Marpeck.
34. Krebs and Rott, *TA: Elsass* 1, 231-32.

mission to the Gentiles, and in Acts 10, where Peter had to wait until he was sent to the house of Cornelius to baptize him.

It was in response to the work of Bünderlin, Entfelder, and Schwenck-feld that Marpeck became a writer for the church. For the rest of his life, writing would become the predominant means for Marpeck to explain the breadth and depth of Anabaptist theology. With burning intensity, he passionately put mind and soul to paper as he sought to nurture and instruct his fledgling, beleaguered community of believers.

7

Defender of the Faith

Although Pilgram Marpeck had written no theological tracts up to this point, it was logical that he should turn to publishing to both lead and evangelize. In just a few years after the start of the Reformation, the printed word had become a primary means of witnessing to the nature of faith. Just as email and the internet have transformed communication in today's world, so too did technological developments in printing and the production of paper change the way the people of Europe shared ideas and engaged in public debate. In fact, in the decade prior to Marpeck's arrival in Strasbourg, the Lutheran Reformation availed itself in a remarkable way of publications in the vernacular in order to get its message across. Lutherans and Lutheran sympathizers, men and women, wrote prolifically in both Latin and in German. Publishers and printers were only too eager to distribute what they had to say.

From 1518 to 1546 the presses of the German-speaking lands produced more than six million tracts either supporting or opposing the Reformation. As historian Mark Edwards reminds us, that works out to about one tract for every two people living in the Holy Roman Empire at that time![1] Among the printers who eagerly published and then distributed these materials were a number who were quite friendly toward the Anabaptists. It appears that Augsburg, where Marpeck spent the last years of his life, was an important centre for publishing Anabaptist material, as was Nikolsburg as early as 1526.[2] These documents were openly

1. Mark U. Edwards Jr., *Printing, Propaganda and Martin Luther* (Berkeley: University of California Press, 1994), 108-10. For Marpeck's role as a "writer," publisher or editor, see the intriguing article by Werner O. Packull, "Preliminary Report on Pilgram Marpeck's Sponsorship of Anabaptist Flugschriften," *MQR* 75 (2001), 75-88.

2. Sigmund Sorg at Nikolsburg as early as 1526 openly published some twenty-

published, even though Ferdinand issued several mandates prohibiting their publication, sale, and distribution. They provided a veritable flood of information for anyone who cared to read about the Anabaptists' position.

As an example, Philip Uhlhart of Augsburg printed nine Anabaptist tracts, seven of them in 1526 and 1527. In 1529 he also printed one thousand copies of the second edition of Christof Freisleben's classic book on baptism, first published in 1528.[3] The 1528 publication coincided with a note that he sent to the congregations at Esslingen and Augsburg that they could buy his book at a discount of two pfennig. Many Anabaptist booksellers were arrested for selling such books. When Anabaptist books appeared in Schwaz and Hall, the authorities closed the shops and searched them.[4] Undeterred, determined writers, publishers, and booksellers continued their work. In 1544 in Bern, for example, some 1,500 copies of an Anabaptist book were printed. With so much happening across Europe, it is clear that the pamphlet could be a powerful weapon in the hands of people like Marpeck who were committed to the struggle for truth and justice in the free church and to using reason to convince people to follow the way of Jesus.

The first fruits of Marpeck's writing were two relatively short books published in 1531 that we explore in more detail later in this chapter. These books appeared on the censor's list of July 1531, but because the authorship was anonymous the censors could only surmise that they were written by Marpeck.[5] His writing was neither an academic argument nor a disputation over the fine points of scriptural interpretation, although both of these were present. It was rather a passionate defence of the doctrine of the incarnation and of his understanding of the nature of the Christian communion, the church.

The year 1531 was tumultuous for the immigrant Anabaptist commu-

---

seven Anabaptist books. Similarly, Philip Vollandt at Neumühl also openly printed Anabaptist books in 1565.

3. See Christian Neff and Robert Friedman, "Eleutherobius," in *ME* 2, 183-84, and A. Nicoladoni, *Johannes Bünderlin von Linz . . . 1525-1531* (Berlin, 1893), in Packull, *Mysticism and the Early South German Austrian Anabaptist Movement, 1525-1531* (Scottdale, Pa.: Herald Press, 1977), an excellent and extensive examination of this topic and especially of Freisleben. See also Jonathan Seiling, ed. and trans., "Christoph Freisleben's 'On the Genuine Baptism of John, Christ and the Apostles,'" *MQR* 81 (2007), 623-54.

4. See Claus-Peter Clasen, *Anabaptism, A Social History, 1525-1618* (Ithaca, N.Y.: Cornell University Press, 1972), 354-56; here Clasen, 355.

5. These books did not become a part of Marpeck research until 1959; see William Klassen, "Pilgram Marpeck's Two Books of 1531," *MQR* 33 (1959), 18-30.

nity of Strasbourg, with growing pressure from the government policy of suppressing dissent and from the arrival of the radicals Bünderlin, Entfelder, and Schwenckfeld. Anabaptists had been listening to these recent arrivals, all of whom counselled the suspension of external rites and ceremonies of their churches, especially of believers baptism, in order to escape the threat of imprisonment or worse.[6] We may be sure that Marpeck was aware of the developments in Strasbourg during his absence in the Lebertal. It may be that the crisis brewing for his people there motivated him to arrange for employment in Strasbourg and therefore his return to the city.

Marpeck responded with considerable alarm to what Hans Bünderlin had been teaching. Bünderlin was a university-educated man who became an Anabaptist under the influence of Hans Denck and Hans Hut. In 1526 he was leader of the Anabaptist group in Linz, but persecution forced him to move from Linz to Nikolsburg. There he began to move away from Anabaptism into a mystical spiritualism, concerned more and more that Anabaptist biblicism was creating divisions among Christians. When his stay at Nikolsburg became impossible, he fled to Strasbourg late in 1528. There he apparently saw an opportunity to refashion Anabaptism into his spiritual vision. A year later he left Strasbourg for Constance.

Bünderlin's work *Explanation Through Comparison of Biblical Scripture* (*Erklerung durch vergleichung der Biblischen geschrifft*) was published in 1530. It was a long, rambling journey through biblical and church history, designed to prove that the time of the institutional form of the church was over and that "the age of the Spirit" was unfolding. The title page announced that through careful examination of Scripture it would be shown that water baptism and other external church usages that had been practised in the apostolic church were now being mimicked by some without any divine authority.

There were two ways to know God, Bünderlin wrote. One was through external, visible things according to the letter, which was able to appeal to the physical senses. The other was the inner way in which God taught the soul through the Holy Spirit, without external means. It was by the first way that God had made himself known to the ancients through institutions and laws as recorded in the Old Testament. The inner teaching was always there as well, but it was hidden under the external. The ancients sensed it, but they were unable to throw off the external because they could not do without it. But God was always pushing his people from the outer to the inner, and John the Baptist was the pivotal figure. He pointed away from water

6. Klassen and Klaassen, *WPM*, 71.

baptism to Christ and the baptism of the Spirit. That is where the transition happened from the letter to the Spirit. What had been hidden to the ancients, but sensed by them, was now made clear in Christ. He transformed everything to Spirit.

The apostolic church still had to work with externals like baptism, the Lord's Supper, and the laying on of hands. They were needed, said Bünderlin, for the sake of the Jews, who continued to cling to the letter of the law and the external forms of faith. Moreover, these externals were accompanied by signs and miracles specifically to persuade the Gentiles of the truth of the gospel. However—and here we come to the heart of his argument—there was never any divine command to continue the practice of the apostles to baptize, to observe the Lord's Supper, or to consecrate bishops. Nevertheless, these practices continued. The new life of the Spirit declined in the church after the apostolic age by reverting to and concentrating on external forms. The life of the Spirit was ruined by the antichrist to the present day, and this would continue to the end.

Still, there were many in the church who participated in these externals through ignorance. But there were Christians like Bünderlin among whom the true state of affairs had now been recognized once again. At the same time there were those who were again beginning a new church with water baptism. Baptism, they taught, would show the difference between Christ's own church and the world. This was a direct attack by Bünderlin on the Reublin-Marpeck group of Anabaptists. Despite the fact that the transition from the outer to the inner was now taking place, Bünderlin argued, they again appealed to the letter of Scripture as their authority to justify what should be left behind. They were thus opposing the new way of the Spirit, like the people who opposed Paul by defending circumcision (Gal. 5:2-6).

But Christians no longer needed anything external because it no longer had any legitimacy. Unlike the past, when God had patience with human ignorance, there could no longer be any compromise with externals out of consideration for the weak or stubborn, since the Holy Spirit had given no such command. Especially, there was no longer any need for the apostolic office (i.e., the pope and even clergy). And as for the loud appeal to Scripture by the Anabaptists, announced Bünderlin, Scripture could be twisted any way at all to support the view one desired to prove. Scripture, being one of the externals, was no final authority and therefore any appeal to it was futile. It only pointed to God, as a sign outside the inn pointed to the wine inside. He went further: The antichrist himself has his seat in Scripture, and receiving water baptism was receiving the sign of the beast.

Toward the end, Bünderlin came to the logical outcome of his argument. Christians did not need to be held together in a community by baptism as the Israelites were by circumcision. They were no longer a community; each Christian was a solitary bearer of the Spirit without the urging of the Spirit through someone else. Faith was not tied to time, place, person, or congregation. The internal work of the Spirit concerned only the individual, because that was where the kingdom of God began.

Marpeck Steps Forward

Appalled at such individualistic theology, Marpeck felt compelled to respond.[7] His first venture into public debate on matters of Christian faith was a direct reply to Bünderlin's *Comparison of Biblical Scripture*. Marpeck's 1531 work was entitled *A Clear Refutation (Clare Verantwurtung)*,[8] a short book directed at the specific arguments advanced by Bünderlin. Marpeck began by refuting Bünderlin's central claim that the ceremonies of the New Testament—baptism and the Lord's Supper—and Scripture should no longer be used by God's children. Bünderlin had argued that they were to be avoided because the antichrist had ruined them and polluted their use. This condition, he said, would continue to the End.

Marpeck responded that the ceremonies were legitimate and that their abuse did not invalidate them. In the Old Testament, he argued, the ceremonies were not abolished because they were abused; rather, they were restored by prophets or kings. In the same way, Christ was now restoring the spiritual Jerusalem. When this king returns, he wrote, the true leap (*übersprung*) from outer to inner will happen. All externals will then disappear for they will no longer be needed.

Marpeck refuted Bünderlin's claim that since the time of the apostles no command had been given to continue the ceremonies, and thus, they were suspended until Christians were given a new, explicit command to use them again. Marpeck's response was that the ceremonies were to remain in place until the end of history. The command to baptize was given not only to the apostles but to all Christians, and the Lord's Supper was to be kept until his coming again (1 Cor. 11:26). As for the claim that the purification of the ceremonies had to be accompanied by signs and miracles, none were required in the Old Testament, and none were

---

7. In fact, throughout his life Marpeck warned his readers of the threat posed by the theology of Bünderlin and his followers. See Loserth, *Quellen und Forschungen*, 25, 149.

8. The translators of this work, Klaassen and Klassen, now believe that *Verantwurtung* could more appropriately be translated as "defence" or "account," but for consistency, have opted to continue to use the title as originally translated.

required now. If ceremonies were to be suspended, he demanded a clear command from Scripture to do so, even as there was scriptural warrant for discontinuing the Old Testament ceremonies.

Marpeck rejected Bünderlin's view that Christ through the apostles had instituted special, temporary bishops to look after the flock. He argued for the orthodox view that the apostles appointed successors who in turn appointed others to the office. For Marpeck, every Christian who has Christ's Spirit could be called an apostle. Indeed all creatures are revealers of the gospel. Humans are led to the invisible, to God, by that which is visible. But whoever uses the visible ceremonies without faith, no matter how perfectly they are done, is going astray.

Marpeck also responded to Bünderlin's extreme individualism. It was clear, he wrote, that Bünderlin and others like him lacked the Holy Spirit because the gifts of the Spirit are given for mutual up-building and for service. Marpeck saw quickly that there would be no church if the path that Bünderlin espoused was taken. No Christian can ignore fellow believers, he argued, for the fruit of the Spirit is love and faithfulness. There can be no purely private faith. And how could all that be if, as Bünderlin maintained, the Holy Spirit had been poured out once at Pentecost and no further outpouring was possible? Rather, the Spirit is given to each believer when faith is born, until the end of time.

Toward the end of his work, Marpeck raised a penetrating question for Bünderlin. The reasons for the abolition of baptism and the Lord's Supper would also apply to Scripture, teaching, prayer, and the example of other believers—indeed to all ceremonies established for the improvement and benefit of believers. If everything external was suspended, he asked, who had sent Bünderlin to write books, using proofs from Scripture that had no authority? The fact is, he wrote, the suspension of the external would entail the destruction of the internal as well. For Marpeck, Scripture was crucial and central. Without Scripture it would be impossible to know about Christ's death, burial, and resurrection, a faith Bünderlin also shared.

Marpeck employed similar arguments in his response to Christian Entfelder's work, *About the Manifold Divisions* (*Von den mannigfaltigen Zerspaltungen*), which appeared in print soon after Marpeck's return to Strasbourg. Entfelder came from Upper Austria. He was well-educated, had studied law, and was drawn into Anabaptism by Balthasar Hubmaier in Nikolsburg in 1526. That year Entfelder became leader of an Anabaptist group at Eibenschitz, Moravia. He had contacts both with the Bohemian Brethren and the followers of Caspar Schwenckfeld in the area. In order to promote relations with these groups, he allowed both infant and adult baptism. By the fall of 1528, stricter Anabaptists gained control at Eibenschitz, disrupting these peaceful ecumenical relations. Entfelder lamented that concerns over the externals of baptism caused the divisions.[9] He came to Strasbourg with the manuscript of his work, *About the Manifold Divisions*, which was published soon after his arrival. Although this work was more radical and was likely published before Bünderlin's, Bünderlin got Marpeck's attention first because he was active in Anabaptist life in Strasbourg, while Entfelder was not.

Entfelder's writing was addressed primarily to the brothers in Eibenschitz, whom he had led before leaving for Strasbourg. He had lain sick in hospital, he wrote, "and although through my own fault I have not yet recovered, I have full confidence that death will be vanquished by life." He referred to his "sickness" as the conviction he had held of his divine calling as a church leader. But the Lord had taught him, he wrote, that he had long been an unreliable (ignorant) leader and that henceforth he should bring up the rear with understanding. He had been demoted from the teacher's lectern to the least of the students sitting below. It was a hard lesson for him, as for his Anabaptist people. Because of all this, he (who had come to his people by human decision) had to leave Eibenschitz abruptly without any human call to do so. He did not know, he wrote, what would now happen to him, but he prayed God not to lead him into temptation.[10]

In a long, complex opus that is often hard to follow, Entfelder explained the cause of his "illness." The problem lying at the heart of all the schism that he observed among Christians was a central principle of the Reformation: the place and use of Scripture. The Scriptures, he wrote, everywhere were being read literally. The "mere letter" of Scripture was being elevated into the supreme authority for faith. Scripture was the source of all the material ceremonies such as baptism, the Lord's Supper, and the laying on of hands in calling people to church leadership. The problem was that there were a lot of contradictions in Scripture.[11] This led one leader to claim one truth based on Scripture, and another to claim truth for its opposite. Obviously they could not both be literally true. That, insisted Entfelder, was the cause of all the schisms.

People need to recognize the difference between Scripture and the Word of God, written in the heart by the Holy Spirit. Scripture witnesses to the living Word of God and is its servant. The living Word is not con-

9. Packull, *Hutterite Beginnings*, 139. "Von den mannigfaltigen Zerspaltungen im Glauben, die in diesen Jahren enstanden sind," in *Flugschriften vom Bauernkrieg zum Täuferreich*, (1526-1535), ed. Adolf Laube (Berlin: Akademie Verlag, 2002), 939.
10. Ibid., 971.
11. This view probably goes to Hans Denck's work, *Wer die Wahrheit wahrlich*

trary to Scripture but only to mistaken interpretation of Scripture and its
use. Christians misused it as a child might misuse a sharp knife, with similar disastrous results. Clinging to Scripture and at the same time leading
an unholy life created more harm than good. Looking for a godly life in
Scripture without the Spirit was like dipping water out of a dry well.[12]
Few books were required for living a godly life. Christians were much
better off in the early years of Christianity, Entfelder wrote, when they
had few Scriptures and listened instead to the inner Word. In his book on
Gottseligkeit (being blessed in God), he mocked the flood of Christian
tracts—as if Christianity could be built up by an edifice of publications,
he wryly observed. The Christian divisions over baptism, the Lord's
Supper, and other ceremonies were due to reading Scripture literally.

One might have expected Entfelder to argue that a way out of these
divisions was to get guidance from the true authority, the Inner Word. But
he knew that would only move the problem to another level. His proposal
for a solution was to allow individuals (rather than the church as a whole)
to decide whether to suspend the ceremonies for the time being.[13] The ceremonies indeed had apostolic authority, but as then instituted they were valid
only for the apostolic period as visible supports for the fledgling church.
When disputes arose over baptism, he noted, the apostle Paul renounced for
himself the calling to baptize (see 1 Cor. 1:14-17). This passage became for
Entfelder the legitimation for his solution, the temporary suspension of all
ceremonies until a specific command came from God to reinstate them.
However, unlike Bünderlin, he did not devalue the sacraments; indeed, he
believed them to be very important.[14] "The command of Jesus [to baptize]
remains eternally," wrote Entfelder. "Once established it cannot be revoked;
God does not repent of his gifts."[15]

Entfelder devoted many pages to the description and importance of
baptism, what it is, what has happened to it in the church, and what is
now to be done. In God's time, he insisted, baptism and the Lord's Supper
would be restored,[16] but no one knew when that would be. When the time
came, the reinstatement would be done by the return of Elijah, for he was

---

lieb hat (1526), a discussion of forty paradoxes or contradictions in the Bible. It
was a favourite argument in the attempt to replace the outer word of Scripture
with the inner word of God's voice. It was also used by Sebastian Franck's
Paradoxa, 1534.

12. "Von den mannigfaltigen Zerspaltungen," 938.
13. Ibid., 957.
14. Ibid., 943, 960-61.
15. Ibid., 963. See also 968, 970.
16. Ibid., 948.

the leader of all who had not surrendered to the idolatry of the ceremonies (see 1 Kings 19:18).

This approach was also taken by John the Baptist, whose baptism was one of repentance only, and this repentance was now the proper condition of the truly godly. Elijah's coming would be accompanied and confirmed by signs. Because that had not yet happened, the suspension (*Stillstand*: an important term in Spiritualist-Anabaptist debate) remained in force. Meanwhile the faithful were called to watch over the inward mansion (see Matt. 24:43) of understanding the present state of God's intention, do deeds of mercy, and live in daily repentance. "This will be our divine service, ceremony, offering, and mass until God has mercy on us, the Son sets us free, and the Holy Spirit liberates us."[17]

Entfelder's book was completed on January 24, 1530. It belongs to the mystical literature of the Reformation period. With its emphasis on inwardness, it is rooted in late medieval mystical piety. For Entfelder the baptism with water was important only if the inner baptism was also present. He departed from Marpeck significantly only by his insistence on the temporary suspension of the ceremonies. The suspension of church ceremonies because of the controversy over them was first initiated by Schwenckfeld (as we will see later in this chapter), when he applied it to the Lord's Supper in Silesia in 1525. After he arrived in Strasbourg in 1528, he extended it to baptism as well.

According to some scholars, Entfelder's book constituted the most serious internal challenge to Marpeck's Anabaptists. Marpeck noted with alarm that many of them had apostatized and had been persuaded by the arguments for suspension of baptism and the Lord's Supper.[18] There can be no doubt that Marpeck was convinced that he had to refute "these false prophets," as he called Entfelder and others like him. Perhaps because of his lengthy absences from the city in 1530 and 1531, he decided to put his refutations to writing. The written word would give him a voice across time and space.

Challenging False Prophets

Marpeck's refutation, printed early in 1531, was *A Clear and Useful Instruction* (*Ein Klarer vast nützlicher Unterricht*). Most leading scholars see this as a point-by-point refutation of the arguments advanced by Entfelder. Like its predecessor, it was a small book, easily portable and easily concealed. Only one copy has survived.

17. Ibid., 967.
18. Klassen and Klaassen, *WPM*, 71.

Marpeck began by stating the purpose of the book: to oppose many prophets who led believers astray. Some of them were once with us, he wrote, but were evidently not of the same mind as us; otherwise they would have remained with us. While the arguments refuted were those of Entfelder, he was not the only "prophet" Marpeck opposed. Entfelder had been an Anabaptist, but Marpeck also aimed his arrows at Caspar Schwenckfeld and perhaps even Sebastian Franck. These prophets came with the message that no Christian had the authority to use church ceremonies, and that those who did, did so without permission.

Where, Marpeck asked, did these prophets receive the authority to suspend the ceremonies and persuade others to do it? They charged others with being preoccupied with the letter of Scripture, but they themselves taught from the dead letter of Jewish commentaries and figurative interpretations of the Old Testament. How, he asked, was it possible to dispel present darkness with the shadow of the Old Testament? There is not a trace of a command from Christ to live in repentance as a permanent condition, to expect a prophet whose work was confirmed by signs, and only then to baptize and use the bread and wine. Had they not read in the Gospel about how people disregarded signs (Luke 16:31)? If Entfelder did not believe the visible signs of the ceremonies, how could he believe what was invisible? Marpeck simulated surprise that the eleven disciples chose a replacement for Judas before the Holy Spirit came when they had no special command to act. In fact they acted according to the command of Scripture. Why then can overseers not be elected now? The Holy Spirit did not come to Cornelius (Acts 10)[19] without external preaching and faith. He did not need to stand still and wait in ignorance. Finally, Marpeck, like Entfelder, argued that the apostle Paul did not counsel suspension of the Lord's Supper to the Christians of Corinth because of its abuse and the divisions in that church. Rather, he counselled how it should be properly observed.

Marpeck then described the importance and function of the external ceremonies of the church.

> The secrets of God lie hidden under the outward speech, words, deeds, and ceremonies of the humanity of Christ; as Christ himself says in Matthew 13 [:35]: "I will open my mouth in parables and utter that which has been hidden from the beginning of the world."

19. Cornelius is introduced by Schwenckfeld and becomes one of Marpeck's favourite examples (Klassen and Klaassen, *WPM*, 101-3). He often appears again in *The Response*, and, together with the image of the Ethiopian eunuch (Acts 8), is proof for Marpeck that God needs humans to carry out the Christian mission.

He has physically fulfilled this prophecy, and commanded His apostles and all His disciples who possess His spirit to "preach the gospel of all the creatures" (Mark 16:15). For the secrets of the kingdom of Christ can be neither expressed nor understood without parables, as it plainly became evident when Christ spoke to His disciples (John 16:25) and to Nicodemus (John 3:12); without parables, they still could not understand Him.

Therefore, whoever presumes to discover the secrets of God, or presumes to be taught by God, without the outward, that is, the exterior or visible, casts away, as did the Jews, the very means by which he could be taught, could learn, or discover the divine secrets. It is precisely the humanity of Christ which is our mediator [Entfelder uses the term *Mittel*] before the Godhead (1 Tim. 2 [:5]), and not the Godhead before the humanity.[20]

Through his humanity, through his physical life of teaching, word, ceremonies, and deeds, Christ himself leads the way to the inner, spiritual Christ. Thus forgiveness of sins comes through faith, and water baptism is its external sign. Marpeck would not have physical baptism devalued. "Precisely because it is written," he wrote, "I submitted to baptism." His faith, his hope for resurrection because he was buried in baptism into Christ's death, "is a living letter in my heart."

To be sure, he wrote, the world will tolerate those who stand still because they will no longer be an offence. He pleaded with his readers not to allow their freedom to be compromised through splendiferous (*hochprächtige*) words, a clear reference to the academic style of both Entfelder and Schwenckfeld.

The notable scholar of Anabaptism, Heinold Fast, drew attention to another possible link between the works of Entfelder and Marpeck. On the title page of Entfelder's book can be seen the motto "Not who, but what" (*Nicht wer sondern was*). On the title page of Marpeck's work the motto is "Not what, but that" (*Nit was sondern das*). Fast deftly unravels the mystery and relationship of these mystifying mottos.[21] Entfelder's motto meant that what is important is not who wrote something but *what* was written. The content speaks for itself. Marpeck's motto, wrote Fast, was a direct contradiction of Entfelder's. Marpeck's "what" ("not what, but that") pointed to Entfelder's uncertainty, while Marpeck's "that" pointed to the answer he was providing. From all this Fast concluded that the real

20. Klassen and Klaassen, *WPM*, 81-82.

21. "'*Nicht was sondern das*,' Marpeck's Motto wider den Spiritualismus," in *Evangelischer Glaube und Geschichte*, ed. A. Raddatz and K. Lüthi (Vienna: Peter Karner, 1984), 66-74. See also Klassen, *Covenant and Community*, 37-39. Fast's reference is to Fast and Rothkegel, *Kunstbuch*, 130-31.

target of Marpeck's *Clear Instruction* was Entfelder. That said, in a more recent observation, Fast admits that the motto, "Not who, but what," appears frequently among the Anabaptists and Spiritualists, and so cannot suggest a special link to Entfelder. Apparently it goes back to Thomas à Kempis (Thomas of Kempen), an early fourteenth-century Dutch priest who wrote the spiritual classic *The Imitation of Christ* (chapter 1: 5-6).

Marpeck's Main Theological Opponent

Marpeck's motto also sparked comment from another person against whom Marpeck's two books were directed: Caspar Schwenckfeld. A much more prominent Reformation figure than either Bünderlin or Entfelder, Schwenckfeld was Marpeck's major theological opponent for the rest of his life.

Caspar Schwenckfeld was born into an aristocratic family in Silesia in 1489. He enjoyed a broad education at several universities. Like Marpeck, he never studied systematic theology and he never took a university degree. He was converted to Luther's reform in 1518 and worked for church reform in Silesia. His method was to call many small groups of pastors and lay people who had accepted Reformation ideas to nurture and fellowship.

But Schwenckfeld's views on the Lord's Supper were abrasively rejected by Luther. After observing the conflicting interpretations of Catholics, Lutherans, and Zwinglians, on April 21, 1525, Schwenckfeld and a group of like-minded people announced their strategy of *Stillstand*, a moratorium of observing the Lord's Supper until all Christians could arrive at a peaceful agreement and leave behind the bitter divisions that had developed. This announcement was not a rejection of the importance of the Lord's Supper, but in fact quite the opposite. Their conviction that the Lord's Supper was at its heart an inward matter rather than an external experience made the moratorium easier to live with.[22] It was intended to be provisional, not permanent.

Pressure by Archduke Ferdinand on Duke Frederick of Liegnitz in Silesia soon led to the suppression of Schwenckfeld's work. When this happened Schwenckfeld, like Bünderlin and Entfelder, turned his steps toward Strasbourg, arriving there in May 1529. Not only did he seek refuge in Strasbourg, but he hoped that the Strasbourg Reformers would accept his theology of the Lord's Supper.

He was received by them in friendship, and for a while he lived in the house of Wolfgang Capito, co-worker of Martin Bucer. But Bucer became

22. George H. Williams, *The Radical Reformation*, 3rd ed., Sixteenth Century Essays and Studies 15 (Kirksville, Mo.: Sixteenth Century Journal Publishers, Inc., 1992), 205-8.

more and more concerned about the presence of so many religious nonconformists in the city and soon successfully isolated Schwenckfeld from Capito. Schwenckfeld also had contacts with various groups of Anabaptists, especially those associated with Marpeck and Jakob Kautz, a young Lutheran preacher turned Anabaptist. He also met with Wilhelm Reublin, a close friend of Marpeck. He very much wanted to work with and have the support of the Reformers, but he was also attracted to the Anabaptists with whom he had much in common, especially his emphasis on holy living and his rejection of coercion in matters of faith. But he was

Portrait of Caspar Schwenckfeld von Ossig, dated 1556. Oil on panel.

apparently also "an official agent of the church and the ruling regime" in the city.[23]

It has been suggested that Schwenckfeld's judgment of the Anabaptists (*Judicium de Anabaptistis*)[24] was prepared in July 1530 at the request of the city government. Some scholars also suggest the Diet of Speyer drew Schwenckfeld into this attack against the Anabaptists. Despite its irenic tone, the six-page *Judicium* clearly revealed that Schwenckfeld shared with Bünderlin the conviction that the external ministrations of the church were relatively unimportant compared to the centrality of the inner spiritual experience. Yet in this document Schwenckfeld was very gentle in his criticism, noting that among the Anabaptists there was "a great zeal for God and the living of the Christian life. Because of this many of them bear the cross of Christ." Schwenckfeld used the *Judicium* to urge Anabaptists to spell out their sense of mission.[25]

23. McLaughlin, *Caspar Schwenckfeld, Reluctant Radical*, 275.

24. *Corpus Schwenckfeldianorum* (CS) 3, eds. C. D. Hartranft and J. E. Schultz (Leipzig: 1907–1961), 830-34.

25. Daniel Husser wryly observed that Schwenckfeld's critiques of the Anabaptists usually "lacked subtlety." See Husser, 514-15 in "Caspar Schwenckfeld et ses adeptes

His main disagreement with them was that they put far too much emphasis on externals, such as the water in baptism, and their inability to distinguish carefully between the inner and the outer, the spiritual and the material. They were "ministers of the letter and not the Spirit." They went forward without having been called and without having the spiritual knowledge given by God. He warned that without a specific command from God, action on externals would be dangerous and should not be taken. As for the Lord's Supper, the believers did not truly know the meaning of the words "this is my body." If these words were not properly understood, the sacrament could not be taken without harm. Schwenckfeld's moratorium on the observance of the Last Supper did not, however, prevent him from participating in its observance in Strasbourg.

Schwenckfeld's Influence Grows

By the time Marpeck returned to Strasbourg in 1530, both Bünderlin and Entfelder had left the city, leaving Schwenckfeld as the spokesman for the inner as opposed to the outer. Even those Anabaptists who could read would have had difficulty wading through the heavily academic books by Bünderlin and Entfelder.

By contrast, the more plain-spoken Schwenckfeld remained in the city, teaching and gaining followers. His peaceable presence and his friendliness and tolerance attracted everyone, including Anabaptists. The fact that he had rejected infant baptism, that he argued that baptism had to be accompanied by faith, and that he abhorred religious coercion and gathered his followers in small groups must have created the impression for many Anabaptists that he was one of them.[26] He wasn't. Although he rejected infant baptism, he also did not advocate believers baptism. Similarly, although he had a vision of a voluntary church, he did not believe that such a church now existed. He "awaited God's intervention and the re-institution of the apostolic forms."[27] He thus suggested that whoever had doubts about the importance of baptism should do without the sacraments until God provided more help.[28] "God," he wrote in 1528, "needs no external thing or means to give his inner grace and for his spiritual purpose."[29] The apostles, he wrote in another place, never insisted on externals nor urged

---

entre l'Église et les sectes à Strasbourg," eds. G. Livet and F. Rapp, *Strasbourg au coeur réligieux du XVI siècle* (Strasbourg: Librarie Istra, 1977), 511-35.

26. Although Schwenckfeld was much more moderate in his views than either Bünderlin or Entfelder, his views during this time are on record.

27. McLaughlin, *Caspar Schwenckfeld, Reluctant Radical*, 138-39.

28. CS 3, 124.

29. Ibid., 97.

anyone to their use. Nor were they required for salvation. What they did urge was a godly life and knowledge of Christ.[30]

The precise relationship of Schwenckfeld to the Anabaptists in Strasbourg has been much debated because the evidence is so sketchy. The few hints of information left to us raise as many questions as answers. There is no hard evidence that during 1530 and 1531 the relationship between Schwenckfeld and Marpeck was one of controversy. Nevertheless, statements by both of them suggest that they were active opponents during this period. Soon after arriving in Strasbourg, Schwenckfeld began writing harsh, judgmental statements about the Anabaptists, dismissing their ministers as uneducated, inexperienced and, above all, addicted to the letter of the Bible. His own deafness made person-to-person communication difficult. As well, having noble blood and apparently a haughty air did not always make it easy for him to be accepted by the non-nobility, nor for him to accept them.

We know that Schwenckfeld was teaching crucial elements found in the books of Bünderlin and Entfelder that were opposed to the views of Marpeck and his group. Since Schwenckfeld had so much to say about Cornelius and Philip the Evangelist, and Marpeck devoted his longest single section of the *Clear Instruction* to these figures, one can well imagine that his comments were directed at Schwenckfeld.[31]

It is therefore hard to avoid the conclusion that there was controversy between the two men, or at least considerable distance between them, and that Marpeck in his two books was writing against Schwenckfeld, as well as the others. The difference was that Schwenckfeld had not written a book to refute, as the other two had done.

Twelve years after Marpeck's departure from Strasbourg on New Year's Day 1544, he expressed in a letter to Schwenckfeld his surprise that the Silesian attacked him behind his back without first discussing matters with him, "especially since in the past you often discussed matters of faith with me."[32] Schwenckfeld for his part is reported to have written in 1560 that Pilgram was a dear friend of his until he began to warn others against his teaching.[33] These statements suggest that the two enjoyed friendly relations and amicably discussed matters of faith in the early months of 1530. In fact some historians contend that the two agreed on many issues.[34] And,

30. Ibid., 369.

31. Packull notes this connection and provides an English summary of Schwenckfeld's call to Anabaptists to write more about their apostolic sense of mission. See *Hutterite Beginnings*, 145.

32. Loserth, *Quellen und Forschungen*, 57-58.

33. Ibid., 176.

34. Neal Blough, "Pilgram Marpeck and Caspar Schwenckfeld: The Strasbourg Years," in *Bibliotheca Dissidentum: 16th Century Anabaptism and Radical Reformation*

as shown above, Schwenckfeld's judgment about Anabaptists in Strasbourg was not entirely hostile. Still, he stated in 1533 that the Anabaptists hated him and regarded him as an outsider because he would not be baptized.[35]

Thus it seems legitimate to conclude that the Anabaptist ill will toward Schwenckfeld, resulting from his refusal to undergo believers baptism, marked the end of friendly relations toward the end of 1530. It also appears likely that Schwenckfeld first saw the *Clear Instruction* in the summer of 1531, when he was asked to review a number of confiscated books. After examining it, he came across the words, "Not what, but that" (as suggested earlier in this chapter, words that many identify as Marpeck's 'motto'—"*Nit was sondern das*"), and wrote an angry note assigning the book to Marpeck, chiding him for his devotion to externals and for sharing the intolerance of papists, Lutherans, and others.[36]

In 1542 Marpeck wrote: "We have been subjected to the terrible errors of many sects. . . . What hindrance, insults, apostasy have taken place because of the poison and stealth of the serpent, now into the twelfth year."[37] That takes us back to 1530. In 1531, Schwenckfeld wrote that the Anabaptists had published a book against him, and he referred to the Anabaptist leadership as wrong-headed (*irrig*),[38] clearly a reference to one of Marpeck's books of 1531. One of the authors of this book has argued that the *Clear Instruction* was directed at Schwenckfeld, given the frequency of Marpeck's use (twelve times) of Schwenckfeld's watchword "*Stillstand*," and especially his treatment of Cornelius.[39] Schwenckfeld himself seems to have been certain of it. In September 1531, Schwenckfeld wrote to John Bader that "the Anabaptists have allowed a book to go out against me."

The irreconcilable positions of Marpeck and Schwenckfeld on the relationship and order of inner and outer in the manner of God's working developed in Strasbourg and were the central feature of the long-running controversy between them, a struggle that resumed in 1542.

Baden-Baden: Koerner, 1987), 371; Walter Klaassen, "Schwenckfeld and the Anabaptists," in *Schwenckfeld and Early Schwenkfeldianism*, ed. Peter C. Erb (Pennsburg, Pa.: Schwenkfelder Library, 1986), 394.

35. *CS* 4, 776, 834.

36. A number of historians have recorded these comments, which find a permanent resting place in Krebs and Rott as well as in the *Corpus Schwenckfeldianorum*. They may represent the last word on the question of the relationship of Marpeck and Schwenckfeld in 1531.

37. Klaassen and Klaassen, *WPM*, 163.

38. *CS* 4, 259.

39. Klaassen, "Pilgram Marpeck's Two Books of 1531," *MQR* 33 (1959b), 21.

-8-

Redefining Church and State

Despite all the energy that Marpeck poured into his theological writing and debates, he seems to have been able to lead a full professional life. In fact, it may have been because of his skills as an engineer that he was able to continue his activities in the church without interference, even while the government's attitude toward Anabaptists was hardening. Intriguingly, his public standing in the city actually improved.

Strasbourg authorities had become aware of his technical competence, and early in 1530 hired him as city *Holzmeister*, the city's manager of timber resources. Since good timber was unavailable near the city, Marpeck began his work by advising the officials responsible for procuring timber to purchase a woodlot and transportation rights in the Black Forest, southeast of the Rhine, which flowed north past Strasbourg. This was done on April 2, 1530, some eighteen months after his arrival in the city. The woodlot was located on the left slope of the Einbach River. To get to that site, Marpeck needed to travel southeast along the Kinzig River, which flowed into the Rhine at Strasbourg, past several towns to Hausach, and then left and north up the valley of the Einbach past Doebishof, where the Neuenbach River flows into the Einbach.

In early spring when the snowpack was thawing and the streams and rivers were in flood, Marpeck travelled to the site to assess its potential for the city's needs and then proposed its purchase. He needed to assess not only the extent and quality of timber resources, but also the rights to transport. He had to decide whether it would be possible to convey the timber to Strasbourg via these waterways—and if so, how to do it. Marpeck had some previous experience finding and transporting timber when, as mining superintendent at Rattenberg, he had also been responsible for the extensive timber needs of the mines under his care. It is likely that his work was also influenced by the guidelines for forestry development mandated

Feldberg in the Black Forest, where Marpeck worked, looking south to the Swiss Alps.

by Emperor Maximilian during the early years of the sixteenth century. The Strasbourg contract was for thirty years of unlimited cutting and floating of timber down the Kinzig without paying tolls.

We are fortunate to have a glimpse into the work and character of Marpeck provided by Johannes Walch, a Lutheran deacon who resided in Strasbourg at the end of the sixteenth century, many years after Marpeck had died. Despite religious tensions in the community, Walch had close association with Anabaptists who apparently told him about a certain Pilgram Marpeck and his work many years earlier.[1] Walch referred to him as "a pious and admirable man and avid patriot," distinguished and very skilled.

Based on what he was told, Walch described how Marpeck had called for many large fir trees to be felled and their trunks cut into sections. These were trussed together into floats or rafts, and then rolled one on top of the other into the deep gorge of the Einbach. Spring runoff accumulated behind this makeshift dam until the whole structure was dislodged by the force of the water and the logs tumbled into the Kinzig "with a deafening roar."[2]

---

1. There is some evidence that Walch for some time was himself an Anabaptist. The complete text of his comments on Marpeck is available in English in William Klassen, *Covenant and Community*, 25, and in Latin in Krebs and Rott, *TA: Elsass* 1, 186. For details on Walch's fascinating life and affiliation with the Anabaptists, see Gustav Bossert, "Johannes Walch," in *ME* 4, 872-73.

2. Krebs and Rott, *TA: Elsass* 1, 186; John C. Wenger, "The Life and Work of Pilgram Marpeck," *MQR* 12 (1938), 140.

Another description based on contemporary accounts was that Marpeck supervised the building of a series of dams which collected water from the winter snows. According to Boyd,

> When the dams were opened, the [Einbach] swelled large enough to carry the logs down to the Kinzig. Once at the Kinzig, the logs were bound together to form rafts, which ranged in width from about seven to twenty feet. These rafts were then connected front-to-back in a large flotilla, reaching up to six hundred yards in length. Raftmen, standing on these great floats, navigated them with long poles down to the city lumber yard at Kehl on the Rhine. . . . At the stockyard at Kehl, by the Rhine bridge leading to Strassburg, the building lumber was divided by a tariff agent and sold, with private burghers receiving priority over carpenters and auctioneers. The firewood was transported by carts into the city woodmarket on the *Barfuesser Platz* [today Place Kleber].[3]

These wood-rafts were referred to as *Pilgerholz* (i.e., Pilgram's timber) until well into the seventeenth century and were precursors to today's log booms that dot the Canadian and American coastal waters. It may well be that Marpeck's fellow-wagoners were employed with their carts in transporting the wood to its destination in the city.

Marpeck's own participation in the enterprise was short-lived. Assuming that the dams were built in the summer of 1530 following the purchase of the woodlot, the first allocation of wood would have been cut during the fall and winter of 1530. The logs would have been floated into Strasbourg beginning in the spring and summer of 1531. No floating was allowed between November 12 and February 24, presumably until spring runoff.

Marpeck's work as *Holzmeister* must have kept him in the Black Forest for extended periods of time during 1530 and 1531. He would have been most occupied in the spring of the year when, after trees had been felled in the winter, they could be floated down his waterway to the Kinzig and then down to the Rhine.

However, we now know that he was occupied not only with cutting and transporting timber, but also with gathering together groups of people

3. Boyd, *Pilgram Marpeck*, 57-58, based on Ludwig Barth, *Die Geschichte der Flösserei im Flussgebiet der oberen Kinzig* (Karlsruhe, 1895), 53, Georg Sölch, "Die Holzbringung im oberen Kinzigtal," in *Der Forstmann in Baden-Württemberg* 7 (1957), 158-63, and U. Cramer, "Die Verfassung und Verwaltung Strassburgs von der Reformationszeit bis zum Fall der Reichsstadt (1521-1681)," in *Schriften des Wissenschaftlichen Instituts der Elsass-Lothringer im Reich*, N.S. 3 (Frankfurt, 1931), 116.

Channel dams on the Kinzig River, similar to those used by Marpeck for floating lumber from the Black Forest.

into Anabaptist fellowships in the Kinzig Valley. Large numbers of miners from Schwaz in Tirol came into the valley in 1525 to work in the mines there.[4] It is entirely likely that his name and reputation were known among them. Perhaps there were even personal acquaintances. Some of the miners were apparently drawn to this skilled professional who could talk to them in their own dialect about God and following Christ. They accepted his message, and a disciplined community life began. An Anabaptist group also came into being at Langnau, about 55 kilometres (33 miles) south of the Kinzig. Historian Heinold Fast identified the place as being near Schopfheim but belonging to the Kinzig district.[5] Nothing is known about how a Marpeck community came into being there. We know about these Black Forest fellowships only because Marpeck addressed letters to them in 1540 and 1555.

4. Boyd, *Pilgram Marpeck*, 56, n68.
5. Heinold Fast, "Pilgram Marbeck und das oberdeutsche Täufertum. Ein neuer Handschriftenfund," in *Archiv für Reformationsgeschichte* 47 (1956), 224. Reprinted in Fast and Rothkegel, *Kunstbuch*, 13-41.

Anabaptists Flood into the City

Near the end of 1530, the city authorities of Strasbourg called on a number of citizens to provide them with information on Anabaptists. Interrogation sessions with them took place just before October 22 and again on November 2. The reports of those days reveal the presence of Anabaptists and their gatherings in virtually every quarter of the city. There appear to have been concentrations near the Franciscan monastery next to what is today the Place Kleber, and farther northwest along the Steinstrasse (today's Rue du Faubourg de Pierre), with the taverns Grauer Mann and Zum Plug as gathering places. The Steinstrasse was one of the areas of the gardeners' guild, as was the Krautenau in the eastern section where the Gärtnerstub (Gardeners Hall) was located. A little to the south was the Metzgertor (Butchers Gate), one of the main city gates, next to which was another gathering place for Anabaptists. Finally, in the west end was the Finkweiler area, and across the canal the parish of St. Aurelian, the main area of the gardeners. No fewer than nineteen meeting places and street names were mentioned, most of which can still be identified.

Interrogation reports also provide the names of many Anabaptists, but they give us no certain clue as to which Anabaptist group they belonged. The priest at Old St. Peters on the Oberstrass (today's Grande Rue) reported that the number of people bringing their children for baptism had declined sharply and that there was a drop in church attendance, but he said that he knew no names of those involved. It appears that he was protecting his parishioners. Several informants reported hearing conversations in which clergy were dismissed as liars and barking dogs. Commenting on the renewal on September 24 of the royal mandate of July 27, 1527, against the Anabaptists, some Strasbourg Anabaptists were heard to say: "Now it comes! Keep a stiff upper lip!"[6]

Anabaptists apparently met in considerable numbers, sometimes for days at a time. Reports said that they read and discussed the Bible, prayed together, gave shelter to refugees, and cared for their brothers and sisters in prison. Anabaptists had come into the city from Horb and Rottenburg in Württemberg, from Zabern, Schlettstadt, Lauterburg, and Rossheim in Alsace, from Augsburg and Lauingen in Bavaria, and from Landau in the Palatinate. They were clockmakers, cutlers, locksmiths, butchers, bakers, gardeners, weavers' apprentices, goldsmiths, tailors, woodworkers, and a swordsmith, all artisans who could find employment in a large city.

One person, not an Anabaptist, reported a rumour that there were

---

6. This is a colloquial rendering of *"Secht . . . der Kuntz kombt itzt, seit nur keck!"* See Krebs and Rott, *TA: Elsass* 1, 272.

at least two thousand Anabaptists in the city.[7] His figure, which was based on hearsay, was wildly exaggerated. A tally of the number of known Anabaptists in the city comes to about one hundred, according to information given by non-Anabaptists interrogated on October 22-23, 1530. Some informants told of "many" gathering at different locations.[8] Thus a figure of two hundred would appear to be nearer the truth. Some of these Anabaptists were members of the Marpeck group, but we don't know how many.

At this time there were three major groups of Anabaptists associated with the names of Jakob Kautz, Melchior Hoffman, and Wilhelm Reublin. Kautz had been an associate of Hans Denck and thought much like Bünderlin, Entfelder, and Sebastian Franck, all of whom held to a mystical piety that tended to disparage baptism, the Lord's Supper, and the visible fellowship of believers. Hoffman was preoccupied with the early end of history and saw faithful Christians as the community of the Last Days, chosen by God to occupy a central place in history's final events.[9] Reublin was expelled in 1529, after which the leadership of the Anabaptists with ideas and practices similar to the Swiss Brethren of the late 1520s gradually passed to Pilgram Marpeck.

By 1531 Marpeck was an acknowledged leader who more and more distinguished himself by his writing and his intense interaction with the leading Reform preacher of Strasbourg, Martin Bucer, whom we will meet in greater detail later in this chapter. Anabaptist scholar George Williams notes that between 1531 and 1533, the most significant development in the interreligious dialogue in Strasbourg lay in the emergence of Marpeck as the major spokesperson and theorist in support of what he termed a "responsible, pacifist, evangelical Anabaptism unencumbered by any marked differences from Protestant orthodoxy with respect to the Trinity, christology and eschatology."[10]

Marpeck had a vision of the loving, responsible, disciplined community of faith. Its liberator and model was Christ, who had been man-

7. Ibid., 268-78.

8. Ibid.

9. Hoffman also wrote commentaries on the Apocalypse and on Romans. His writings were in German, so they could be understood by the common people. His work on Romans was one of only two written in German. According to T. H. Parker, the commentaries on Romans were mostly written in Latin as part of a war of words between Protestants and Catholics; see T. H. Parker, *Commentaries on the Epistle to the Romans 1532-1542* (Edinburgh: T. & T. Clark, 1986). Hoffman, whom Parker does not mention, believed that Romans was intended to be spiritual food for the people and made sure they had access to it by providing his commentaries in the vernacular.

10. Williams, *The Radical Reformation*, 404-8.

ifested in the world in deep humility and then exalted by God to the highest place as the Christians' Lord. He could not agree with the polity of the Reformers, which supported an undisciplined church that spelled out few guidelines or restrictions regarding the behaviour of believers and deferred to civil, not church, authorities on the enforcement of moral standards. Marpeck felt he had no choice but to separate his group from the mainstream of the Reformation. In fact he was simply doing what Martin Bucer later hoped to do, that is, forming smaller disciplined groups of believers within the larger church structure of Strasbourg. Bucer later became convinced about the necessity of a form of church discipline. Perhaps his life in a Dominican community had made him receptive to Marpeck's critique.[11] However, Marpeck's group, having been designated heretics, did not have any formal link to the larger church structure.

The year 1531 must have been the busiest of Marpeck's life. In addition to having a full-time professional position as a city employee working in the Black Forest, he also did evangelistic work in the Forest. At the same time, he completed the writing and publishing of *A Clear Refutation* and *A Clear and Useful Instruction*[12] (discussed in chapter 7), and a major work, the *Exposé of the Babylonian Whore*. In these three books, he engaged his opponents among the Anabaptists as well as Lutheran scholars in Wittenberg, and the clergy and council in Strasbourg.

Marpeck must have had considerable physical stamina to be able to maintain such a hectic pace. He may also have had the assistance of a stenographer to help record his reflections. Whatever his circumstance, his books show marks of hurry and lack of concentration. For example, following the completion of the *Exposé of the Babylonian Whore* but before the printing was finished, he hurriedly added two notes at the end after it was too late to integrate them into the body of the text.[13] In this work, likely published before the end of 1531, Marpeck addressed the decision of the Lutherans to defend the Reformation faith by militarily opposing the emperor if he decided to attack them to force them to turn away from their confession.

11. We do know that Marpeck and Bucer listened to each other with respect, even though they continued to disagree.

12. Both books, unsigned by Marpeck, ended up on the censor's list of July 1531.

13. See Rempel, *Later Writings of Pilgram Marpeck*, 42-43.

No Pardon for Anabaptists

Before examining the *Exposé of the Babylonian Whore* in detail, it is first necessary to sketch out the political developments that led to the Lutherans' decision to oppose the emperor militarily if circumstances required them to do so. It is also relevant to describe the foreign policy of Strasbourg, since the city eventually allied itself with the Lutheran princes in their confrontation with Emperor Charles V.

An important event affecting nonconformists all over Europe was the decree against Anabaptists passed at the Diet of Speyer in April 1529.[14] This was not a new law but a reactivation of provisions against rebaptism in the Code of Justinian[15] from the sixth century, which still constituted the basis of imperial law.[16] The decree provided the death penalty for Anabaptists. Normally cases of heresy were tried in church courts, but that rule was now bypassed in the case of Anabaptists. The instructions were severe. The "rebellious agitators of this vice of Anabaptism" were not to be pardoned under any circumstances. Only those who confessed their error and were willing to accept the death penalty could appeal for clemency. Exile was forbidden so that the authorities could keep an eye on any who might revert to Anabaptism.[17] Whoever gave shelter or showed kindness to Anabaptists would likewise be subject to the penalties of the decree.[18] The Lutheran princes agreed to honour the decree even

---

14. Sermons were preached at this diet at the main cathedral by Johan Fabri. He chose to speak on the Beatitudes and offered a brilliant analysis of the reasons Christians should be "peacemakers" and thus be called the sons of God. He spoke at length on the themes of compassion and loving your enemies. Fabri's sermons were published immediately after the diet, but there is no evidence that the sermons had any influence tempering the harsh measures against Anabaptists. For Fabri's sermons, see Johan Fabri, *Several Sermons on the Eight Beatitudes Preached at the Stift Church during the Diet of Speyer* [*Etlich Sermon von den Acht seligkeiten: gepredigt in der hohen Stift, zu Speyer auff dem Reichstag*] (Vienna: Hans Singrietter, 1528).

15. The Roman emperor Justinian I issued his famous law code in 529. It was of first-rate importance for jurisprudence throughout medieval times into the sixteenth century.

16. H. J. Goertz, "Ketzer, Aufrührer und Märtyrer. Der zweite Speyerer Reichstag und die Täufer," in *MGBl* 36, N.F. 31 (1979), 8.

17. The way the decree was enacted varied considerably according to different jurisdictions. For details, see Horst W. Schraepler, *Die Rechtliche Behandlung der Täufer in Deutschen Schweiz, Südwestdeutschland und Hessen 1525-1618* (Tübingen: Mennonitischer Geschichtsverein, 1957), and Claus-Peter Clasen, *Anabaptism, A Social History*, 370-86, who stressed the much greater mildness of Protestant implementation of anti-Anabaptist decrees.

18. Johann Loserth, "Reichsgesetze gegen die 'Wiedertäufer,'" in *MGBl* 1 (1936), 27-8.

as they protested against the threatened compulsion of the emperor against themselves.

The elector John of Saxony had managed to get all the evangelical governments in the empire to agree to form a military alliance to oppose the aggressive policies of the emperor. At the same time the evangelicals still hoped for an accommodation with Charles, as was evident from the Schwabach Articles of June 1529, in which the Lutherans distanced themselves from the Swiss evangelicals, who could not accept the Lutheran view of the Lord's Supper, the heart of which was Christ's real presence in the bread and wine. Strasbourg at this point took the side of the Swiss and would not sign the articles. An attempt to save an evangelical alliance was made by bringing Luther and Zwingli together at Marburg in October to forge an agreement on this matter. Martin Bucer worked hard to mediate consent on a common statement but failed miserably due to Luther's stubborn refusal to compromise.

This failure led to the formation of a third religious party of the Swiss and the South German imperial cities, including Strasbourg. When Jakob Sturm returned to Strasbourg from the Diet of Speyer in December 1529, he told the city council that Strasbourg would have to choose from three alternatives: They could await God's pleasure, appease the emperor, or prepare for Charles's wrath.[19] They opted to risk the wrath of the emperor. Strasbourg then proceeded to form a military alliance with Zürich, Basel, and Bern because they feared that John, the elector of Saxony, would make a deal with the emperor that left them vulnerable to attack. As for the Lutherans, Philip Melanchthon, Luther's right-hand man, worked feverishly to prove to Charles that they were not heretics.

Scarcely had the Swiss alliance been concluded when Sturm began to see that Strasbourg and the Zwinglians could not hope to successfully oppose a Lutheran-Catholic union. As a result, from February 1530 onward, Sturm worked quietly to move Strasbourg in a Lutheran direction and away from the more radical reformers of Switzerland.

At the heart of the negotiations among Protestants was always the interpretation of the bread and wine of the eucharist: whether Christ is truly present in the elements, as the Lutherans believed, or whether he is only spiritually present, which was the position of the Swiss Reformers. The ongoing battle over this issue had so sickened Sturm that he had absented himself from the eucharist for years. He was not interested in being Lutheran, but only in the security of Strasbourg. He regarded the whole

---

19. Thomas A. Brady, "Jacob Sturm of Strasbourg and the Lutherans at the Diet of Augsburg, 1530," *Church History* 42 (1973), 184.

eucharist debate as quarrelling over trifles, and therefore did not hesitate to make compromises.

At the Diet of Augsburg in the summer of 1530, the *Confessio Tetrapolitana* (Confession of the Four Cities) composed by Bucer was submitted as the doctrinal position of a new group of cities: Strasbourg, Constance, Memmingen, and Lindau. The confession leaned toward the Lutherans in eucharistic doctrine. Elector John now tried again with more success for a defensive league. Melanchthon and Bucer reached a compromise on eucharistic teaching in August, and in February 1531, Strasbourg joined the Schmalcald League of Lutheran princes.[20] From Strasbourg's side, all of this was stage-managed by Sturm—once again, not out of theological conviction but solely for the security of Strasbourg.

An immediate consequence of this was a much more repressive policy against Anabaptists in the city because Strasbourg had accepted in principle the draconian decree of the Diet of Speyer. Even Capito, who for so long served as a brake upon the suppression of dissent, now turned toward a Lutheran view. The religious climate for dissent was rapidly deteriorating, not because Strasbourg authorities were becoming more bloody-minded but because they feared for their city. "Prudent religious experimentation"[21] in Strasbourg had ended.

Exposing the Babylonian Whore

The central theme of Marpeck's third work, the *Exposé of the Babylonian Whore*, related directly to the developments we've just described. The work was effectively lost soon after Marpeck's time and not rediscovered until 1958.[22] The *Exposé* offered a brilliant use of the Leviathan image taken originally from Isaiah 27, where Leviathan represented the superpower of the day, and then used to great effectiveness as the whore in the Apocalypse of John in Revelation 17. Marpeck used the two terms Leviathan and the whore interchangeably. With a passionate yet reasoned appeal to the common people, Marpeck spelled out his indictment against those who had bedded down with the whore of Babylon by seeking to establish a union between church and state.

20. Brady, *Ruling Class, Regime and Reformation at Strasbourg*, 244-47.
21. McLaughlin, *Caspar Schwenckfeld, Reluctant Radical*, 133.
22. "Exposé of the Babylonian Whore," in *Later Writings of Pilgram Marpeck and His Circle* 1, trans. Walter Klaassen, 24-44. The text was re-discovered by Hans Hillerbrand and photographically reproduced in *MQR* 32 (1958), 34-47. It was identified as Marpeck's work by Walter Klaassen in 1987. See Klaassen, "Investigation into the Authorship and the Historical Background of the Anabaptist Tract, *Aufdeckung der babylonischen Hurn*," *MQR* 61 (1987), 251-61.

From the context of his own life experience and the society in which he lived, Marpeck had long been concerned with the functioning of public affairs, about how governments ruled, and how political authorities—the princes and the councils in the imperial cities—related to their common overlord, Charles V. The charge made by their detractors in Reformation times and by modern writers that Anabaptists consigned all government to the realm of Satan and therefore did not need to obey it is generally inaccurate and applies not at all to Marpeck. His years of participation in government made him a sympathetic defender of governments and of their legitimate place in God's economy. But Marpeck had his own unique understanding about how the worldly and spiritual powers—i.e., government and church—should relate to each other.

In the late medieval church, the dominant view was that governments were appointed by God to be responsible for the sphere of material life. They were the servants of the church, not its master, so that the church could carry out its spiritual mission to preserve and strengthen divine sovereignty in the world.

Marpeck believed that Christians have no mandate from Christ to use the sword for Christian purposes; in other words, no mandate to defend the gospel militarily or to suppress dissent within the church. Martin Luther boasted that he had been the first to liberate government to carry out *with* the sword its secular mandate to preserve civil order without the interference of the church. The church's task, said Luther, was to preach the gospel and to wield only the spiritual sword, the Word of God, for the spiritual liberation of the subjects.

At first blush, Marpeck's separation of the spiritual and secular powers into independent spheres looks very Lutheran. There is every reason to believe that to a considerable degree Luther was his teacher. He was almost certainly deeply influenced by his Rattenberg priest, Stefan Castenbaur, who for several years promulgated Luther's early views on the separation of church and state (see chapter 2). But the difference between Marpeck and Luther was as important as the similarity. Luther taught that in the best case, God gave the authority of the sword to believing Christians and that in this capacity they were authorized—indeed mandated—to kill with the sword should the necessity arise. Marpeck argued in the *Exposé* that no Christian has been given a killing sword because it is contrary to the command and example of Christ.

Marpeck, along with most Christians from New Testament days to more modern times, acknowledged and taught that government is divinely instituted. Government has been given authority over all temporal things except vengeance, he noted, which the Lord has reserved for himself. Christians are obligated on the authority of Jesus himself to obey government and pay taxes. If governments ignore their divine mandate and oppress people, Christians should follow the example of Christ and suffer the wrong without resisting. More than that, Christians are taught by the gospel to love their enemies.

Marpeck was offering far more than an abstract theological discussion. He pointed to what was happening in the world around him and named names. The supreme authority in the Holy Roman Empire was Charles V, to whom all lower authorities had pledged obedience. To oppose the emperor by force of arms, therefore, was rebellion. Luther had taught that rebellion against government was rebellion against God. By now resisting, the Lutherans were abandoning their own teaching. Marpeck reminded them of the horrors of the Peasant Uprising six years earlier and predicted that if the Lutherans pursued their confrontation with the emperor, what was coming would be even worse.

The Sword-Wielding Antichrist

But Marpeck's real objection to the Lutheran reformers ran deeper than this political judgment. These "so-called evangelicals," he wrote, propose to use the sword against the divinely appointed authority, and then they go on to argue that such action has the sanction of Christ himself. It is this claim that most offended Marpeck, and it is this that he called the "Babylonian whore," the antichrist. "Everyone," he wrote, "should completely depart from these prophets who betroth the patient loving Christ to the secular authority under the pretence that it is spiritual, to ensure that a new Antichrist is born or fashioned."[23]

For Marpeck, this union of Christ and the secular is a hopeless confusion of the distinct and independent functions of spiritual and secular authority. There is no biblical warrant for it. First of all, Marpeck argued, the appeal that rulers in the Old Testament used the sword at the command of God is misplaced, because the whole of the Jewish law had been abrogated by Christ. "Christ is the end of the law" (Rom. 10:4), he reminded readers. More importantly, he said, there is no record whatsoever that Christ ever committed the sword of steel to his followers. The only sword he gave them was the sword of the Spirit. And Christ's own example totally negated their argument. He subjected himself to the authority of Pilate and Caiaphas and did not resist. Never did he dominate or coerce anyone. His is the example that Christians are called to follow.

Unlike some Anabaptist leaders, Marpeck did not deny that the Lutherans were Christians. He stated specifically that it was Lutherans

23. Rempel, *Later Writings by Pilgram Marpeck*, 39.

who led him to the truth. But they were halfway Christians, he said; they refused to enter through the narrow gate of following Christ without the sword. They would not accept a king who did not wield the sword.

It is entirely likely that this passionate admonition was aimed as much at the authorities of Strasbourg as it was at the Lutheran theologians of Wittenberg who had developed the doctrine of resistance and at the princes who were ready to resist. As noted earlier, Marpeck specifically addressed "the so-called evangelicals and their teachers and preachers."[24] He did so within a context of mounting tension. The government was not prepared to tolerate dissent and punished it with imprisonment and exile, using the sword in the name of Christ to punish believing Christians.

It may well be that Marpeck had read Luther's *Warning to his Dear German People,* which was published in Strasbourg in April 1531. Luther had written: "He is called a rebel who will not tolerate Authority and law, but attacks and fights against them to suppress them, to be lord himself and make his own law."[25] Marpeck used almost identical words to describe the behaviour of the evangelicals. When Marpeck wrote that "these people demand only protection and security," he was putting his finger directly on Sturm's determination to protect the city of Strasbourg whatever the cost. It was also an allusion to the suspicion widespread among Anabaptists of the sinfulness of private property.[26] He linked the use of the sword with the protection of property. The sword, he wrote, encouraged self-centred acquisitiveness, and "governments and their subjects have their source in this generation preoccupied with" property.[27] The church has its source in Christ, not in property, and can therefore never condone the use of the sword for either coercing faith or protecting property.[28]

The gravity of this issue for Marpeck was underscored by his use of apocalyptic language. This language carried with it the weight of divine judgment, drawn as it was from the book of Revelation. Marpeck did not invent its use to describe contemporary events. Luther had done it before him by calling the papacy the antichrist and the papal church the Babylon-

24. Ibid., 27. This conclusion represents a considerable refocusing of the argument made in Klaassen, "Investigation into the Authorship and the Historical Background of the Anabaptist Tract *Aufdeckung der babylonischen Hurn*," *MQR* 61 (1987), 251-55.

25. Translation by Walter Klaassen of the modern German in the *Martin Luther Studienausgabe*, Fischer Bücherei, 1970, 232.

26. See James M. Stayer, *The German Peasants' War and Anabaptist Community of Goods* (Montreal: McGill-Queen's, 1991), chapters 4, 5, 7.

27. Rempel, *Later Writings by Pilgram Marpeck*, 31.

28. James M. Stayer, *Anabaptists and the Sword* (Lawrence, Kan.: Coronado Press, 1972), 172.

ian whore. In April 1530, the Strasbourg Anabaptist Melchior Hoffman published his commentary on Revelation at the printery of Balthasar Beck. On the title page was the by-now familiar woodcut image of the whore of Babylon riding on the seven-headed monster of Revelation, chapter 17. Perhaps it was this woodcut, also used by Luther in his German New Testament of 1522, that prompted Marpeck now to identify the whore. But whereas both Luther and Hoffman had identified the whore with the papal church, Marpeck identified her simply as the antichrist-like teaching and action of evangelical Christians, the term he and others used for Christians who were neither Catholic nor Anabaptist.

The sixteenth century was a time when the apocalyptic imagination was in full flower. Scholar J. J. Collins observes that the legacy of such apocalyptic literature includes "a powerful rhetoric for denouncing the deficiencies of this world" and a conviction that the world as now consti-tuted is not the end.[29] Above all, he says, apocalypses show the strength of the human imagination "to construct a symbolic world where the integri-ty of values can be maintained in the face of social and political powerless-ness and even of the threat of death." Marpeck's *Exposé of the Babylonian Whore* in all these respects was a classic expression of the literature of end times.[30]

In the *Exposé*, Marpeck was not simply employing the various apoca-lyptic motifs and vocabulary. As in Michael Sattler's letter to his followers at Horb, Marpeck in this work offered a sense that the events of the end times were unfolding. He did not present a complete scenario, as Hoffman did. Nor did he offer a specific date for the second coming. Perhaps he had been sobered by the rebuke given to Hans Hut by other Anabaptists at the so-called Martyrs' Synod, a meeting of Anabaptist leaders in Augsburg in 1527. Hut had predicted the second coming would take place in 1528.

Marpeck's writing was more typical of the late medieval response to contemporary events, which was that events were moving toward the final climax. There was no sign here of an expectation that this world could be renewed. It was part of a call to faithfulness in the interval between now and the End. Because the judgment was coming, faithfulness in the details of Christian life was imperative.

It is possible that Marpeck and his colleagues built on a manuscript of

29. John J. Collins, *The Apocalyptic Imagination: An Introduction to the Jewish Apocalyptic Literature* (Grand Rapids, Mich.: Eerdmans, 1998), 215.

30. For further details, see Walter Klaassen, *Living at the End of the Ages: Apocalyptic Expectation in the Radical Reformation* (Lanham, Md.: University Press of America, 1992), and *Armageddon and the Peaceable Kingdom* (Kitchener, Ont.: Herald Press, 1999).

Clemens Adler, who, while imprisoned in Moravia, in 1529 wrote a tract on the kingdom of nonviolence established by Christ. Although it was never published by a commercial printer, Adler's work circulated widely among Hutterites and Moravian Anabaptists and has been lauded by historians as one of the most significant Anabaptist statements on nonresistance of the sixteenth century.[31] It is worth noting that Adler's writing on Jesus as king of justice or righteousness is similar to Marpeck's treatment of that theme in the *Exposé*. They shared a commitment to Jesus as the suffering and conquering Lamb who, by his own sacrifice, is able to establish a kingdom of justice and peace.[32]

Marpeck's view of life as a struggle is seen in many of his writings. He drew heavily from 2 Corinthians 10:4-5: "for the weapons of our warfare are not merely human, but they have divine power to destroy strongholds. We destroy arguments and every proud obstacle raised up against the knowledge of God, and we take every thought captive to obey Christ." This passage empowered his drive to seek justice but also formed the manner in which he confronted the world.

By the time the *Exposé* was published, Marpeck himself had been served with an order of banishment. One cannot help but wonder if Marpeck's declaration that evangelical teachings and action were the antichrist (a term once reserved by the evangelicals for the papal church and now turned against them in Strasbourg) contributed to Pilgram's expulsion. Whatever the various factors, it was clearly the collusion of city politics and the clergy—the combined retribution of state and church—that led to the decision to expel Pilgram Marpeck from what was known as "the city of hope."

31. For more on Adler, see H. S. Bender, "Clemens Adler," in *ME* 4, Suppl 1056; Samuel Geiser, "An Ancient Anabaptist Witness to Nonresistance," *MQR* 25, 1951, 66-69, 72; Packull, *Hutterite Beginnings*, 130-32.

32. Adler says, "Christ has given his people a new commandment, also a new calling, that they should be children of peace and not servants of vengeance." See Packull, *Hutterite Beginnings*, 130.

-9-

A Very Public Confrontation

Pilgram Marpeck's expulsion from Strasbourg was preceded by a series of remarkable debates between him and Martin Bucer, one of Strasbourg's leading reform theologians. We have seen that during the course of 1531, many civic and religious officials were alarmed by the disruptive potential of the growing number of Anabaptists in the city. They feared for Strasbourg's safety and independence as threats of war, invasion, and internal strife afflicted the Holy Roman Empire. The emergence of Marpeck as the leader of a major Anabaptist faction, a leader equipped with both theological and organizational skills, led to an open confrontation between Marpeck and Bucer, as well as with the Strasbourg city council.

Many Anabaptists criticized Bucer and other reform clergy for making no distinction between those who were serious about following the example of Christ in daily living and those who were not. They argued that at the root of this disorder was the baptism of infants. Infant baptism was fundamental to Bucer's developing view that the whole community of Strasbourg—citizens, clergy, government, businesses, and the guilds—comprised the church. In 1530, Bucer was persuaded that civil authorities should be responsible for assuring that citizens lived a Christian life, while the clergy should be responsible for stating clearly what the Christian life was and how it was to be lived. Bucer and the other clergy wanted a system of church governance in which they were equal partners with the government. Government officials, however, saw the clerical position as a new version of what had been the medieval church's view of the relationship of the spiritual and secular powers—that the secular was subject to the spiritual—and they would have none of it.

Chief Magistrate Jakob Sturm rejected clerical meddling in politics and the Reformers' image of themselves as the real leaders of the community. Instead, he imposed what historian Tom Brady calls "a thoroughgoing system of lay government of the church." According to Brady, parish life at Strasbourg was brought under the regime's direct control, beginning with the institution of parish boards (*Kirchenpfleger*) in 1531.[1] The seven parish boards were lay committees of three members each. A major function of these boards was actually supervision of the clergy to make sure that they preached correctly.[2]

Although Bucer, like Luther, believed that the whole community was the church, within that whole were those elected by God for salvation, who represented only a segment of those calling themselves Christian. Those so elected were to be yeast to the bread of faith, to penetrate the whole body with a personal appropriation of faith in Christ. Bucer suffered all his life under the contradiction of what the church ought to be and what it was. He agreed with his Anabaptist critics that the church must discipline itself and eventually concluded that the organs of government were incapable of such discipline. But, as Heinrich Bornkamm wrote, "in Strassburg his hands were shackled." From 1530 until 1549, the year of his exile, every suggestion that Bucer brought forward for the church to discipline itself was rejected by the city council. Bucer's last such proposal was that small groups of committed believers within the church would elect their own elders who, together with the members of the parish boards, would carry out a voluntary regime of discipline. Yet even this suggestion avoided any idea of separation from the whole church. This concept of separation was Bucer's quarrel with the Anabaptists, who rejected infant baptism (which to Bucer was the sign of the whole church) and formed separate groups of believers.[3]

Trading Accusations

Bucer was well aware that Marpeck was a formidable opponent. Marpeck's books published in 1531 were persuasive evidence of that. Marpeck's followers, wrote Bucer, regarded him as a god (*numinus instar*).[4] We have evidence of this from an exchange of letters between

1. Brady, *Ruling Class*, 246-47.
2. Miriam Usher Chrisman, *Strasbourg and the Reform* (New Haven, Conn.: Yale University Press, 1967), 209.
3. Heinrich Bornkamm, *Martin Bucer's Bedeutung für die europäische Reformationsgeschichte* (Bertelsmann Verlag Gütersloh, 1952), 13-15. For a good analysis in English, see John S. Oyer, "Bucer and the Anabaptists," in *Martin Bucer and Sixteenth Century Europe* 2, eds. Christian Krieger and Marc Lienhard (New York: E. J. Brill, 1993), 603-13. An expanded form appears as John Oyer, "Bucer Opposes the Anabaptists," *MQR* 64 (1994), 24-50.
4. Klassen, *Covenant and Community*, 27.

Bucer and Margaret Blaurer, sister of the Constance Reformer Ambrose Blaurer, who must have read one or both of Marpeck's booklets published in 1531.[5] In fact, Bucer wrote prolifically to both Margaret and Ambrose Blaurer. The collected writings of these exchanges constitute one of the richest sources for our modern understanding of how the Reformation was built in part by people who were not part of either the Lutheran or Zwinglian reformation—people such as Bucer, Blaurer, and Marpeck.[6]

Margaret Blaurer must have written to Bucer asking about Marpeck and making positive observations about what she had read in his booklets. On August 19, 1531, Bucer replied. He was making an effort to be fair to Marpeck and to give reasons for Margaret's favourable impression. He has given up much, wrote Bucer, but he cannot surrender his own ego. Marpeck is free from obvious vices, but the spiritual ones are that much worse. He and his wife live a good and blameless life, but that is the lure by which people are deceived. In fact, he wrote, Marpeck is a stubborn heretic, much like the heretics of earlier times who made impossible moral demands, in particular the surrender of all personal property in support of the community of goods. Moreover, said Bucer, Marpeck is inordinately impressed with his own knowledge.[7]

A second letter from Margaret to Bucer expressed her respect for Marpeck, eliciting a much stronger response from her good friend. Bucer confided that Marpeck would not be in the city much longer, since he had acted against the mandate and baptized several people. Bucer was deeply offended that Marpeck, by seeking his own version of a godly life, was destroying the godly life of Strasbourg by creating division and thereby bringing the gospel into disrepute.

How, he asked, could Marpeck be so certain in his understanding of the gospel? How could he so trivially send to the devil all who did not agree with him? Is this Christian love?[8]

The Blaurers had had their own experiences with Anabaptists. Margaret's brother, Ambrose, at this point was ambivalent about them. On the one hand he wrote about "the evil of the Anabaptists." On the other, writing in November and December 1531, he said he was persuaded that they were not heretics and that his own insistence on purity of life had won most of them over to Blaurer's evangelical faith. At this point Ambrose

5. Marpeck's two booklets appeared on the censor's list that same month.
6. For an astute analysis of this part of the Reformation and Bucer's own relation to the Blaurers, see Bernd Moeller, "Bucer und die Geschwister Blarer in *Martin Bucer and Sixteenth Century Europe* 1 (Leiden: Brill, 1993), 441-50.
7. Krebs and Rott, *TA: Elsass* 1, *Stadt Strassburg, 1522-1532*, 338-39.
8. Ibid., 342.

was not ready to adopt Bucer's method of fighting Anabaptists. He later hardened his position, suggesting that Anabaptists be imprisoned and then be visited in jail in an effort to get them to recant.[9] Blaurer's sister was not persuaded by Bucer. She chided him for his treatment of Marpeck and refused to believe that Marpeck was a heretic or a hypocrite.[10]

The letters between Margaret Blaurer and Bucer are testimony to Marpeck's persuasive ability and to his irreproachable, although sometimes stubborn and perhaps arrogant, public persona. He clearly was emerging as the strongest Anabaptist leader in Strasbourg. Bucer's frustration with Marpeck must also be seen as a function of Bucer's struggle for his vision of reform: first with the government of Strasbourg, second with the Lutherans over the eucharist, and third with Marpeck about the nature of the church in Strasbourg. Fighting on three fronts for a high prize did not leave Bucer much room for generosity.

In his letters he expressed satisfaction that Marpeck could be "got rid of" (i.e., banished from Strasbourg) on the technicality that he had acted against the imperial mandate by baptizing. One would have expected Bucer to highlight Marpeck's faults, which he did. But Bucer was not at heart a persecutor. A former Dominican who early in his priesthood became an enthusiastic disciple of Luther and then married a former nun, he was very much a Christian of his time, sharing an almost universal assumption that coercion in the cause of truth was right and proper. It was part of the holy war against error, first articulated by Constantine the Great and St. Augustine, two important founders of the medieval church. As a sixteenth-century person, he believed there could be only one Christian church in place. His vision for the church in Strasbourg, therefore, was of one church built on the traditional model of close cooperation between clergy and magistrate, both servants appointed by God, albeit with different functions. Anabaptists were heretics to him because they would not accept this unitary vision. He charged Marpeck with heresy— that is, breaking the unity of the church,[11] although one might wryly observe that Bucer himself had left the mother church—and with making

---

9. Christian Hege, "Blaurer, Ambrosius," in *ME* 1, 353-54. Hege traces his change toward the Anabaptists and his discussions with Bucer on this point. After the debacle at Münster while Blaurer was a professor at Tübingen, he hardened his position, drawing from both the Old Testament and Augustine.

10. Boyd, *Pilgram Marpeck*, 64. Curiously, Margaret Blaurer is not mentioned in either the *ML* or the *ME*.

11. Bucer's charge that breaking the unity of the Christian commonwealth was heresy had an important precedent. Emperor Frederick II (1194-1250) identified the Lombard cities of northern Italy as heretical because they resisted Frederick's vision

harsh judgments, the offence against love. But, wrote Bucer, I say before the Lord that I have no animus against him personally, seeing I am also a sinner.

Bucer and Marpeck were close on many important issues such as the need for justification and sanctification. These agreements made Bucer doubly frustrated by the differences they had on other matters. Bucer's colleagues at the synod of 1533 described him as "quick to judge, intolerant, obstinate and inclined to attack individuals from the pulpit."[12]

Bucer's vision was that of one overarching divine covenant, according to which the distinction made by Marpeck between the Old and New Testaments was totally wrong. Moreover, Diarmaid MacCulloch suggests that Bucer may have held the view that Strasbourg could be the New Rome, the new centre for a renewed Christendom mediating between Lutherans and papists.[13] This kind of hope provided energy and rationale for the suppression of opposition.

Bucer's third letter to Margaret Blaurer, dated late November 1531, repeated that Marpeck would not abstain from baptizing. Not only that, but Marpeck was attempting to persuade people that it was wrong to swear the oath of allegiance to the emperor and to protect the city of Strasbourg. Marpeck also taught that bearing weapons was wrong for a Christian. Yet three years earlier Marpeck had sworn several oaths when he became a citizen and guild member (see chapter 6). Had he changed his mind? It is possible that, as a result of the influence of Musculus, a learned and compassionate man who served as Bucer's secretary, Marpeck began to see the New Testament treatment of oaths with fresh eyes, hardening his position on certain kinds of oaths but relaxing on others. The apostle Paul, for example, several times swore an oath (2 Cor. 1:23, Gal. 1:20, Phil. 1:8, 2 Tim. 4:1-2), thus opening possible options for Marpeck. It may well be that Marpeck served as an unnamed dialogue partner in a booklet by Musculus on the oath published in 1533.[14]

Stephen Boyd is undoubtedly correct when he argued that Marpeck counselled other Anabaptists not to swear the oath of truce (*Urfehde*), which would call for them to desist from attending Anabaptist meetings.[15] Curiously, he did not reject the oath of citizenship, pledging to be a loyal citizen. But on the issue of swearing an oath to bear weapons in

---

of a single divinely willed universal kingdom of peace. See Ernst Kantorowicz, *Kaiser Friedrich der Zweite*, 3rd ed. (Stuttgart: Klett-Cotta, 1992), 421.

12. Krebs and Rott, *TA: Elsass, Stadt Strassburg 1533-1535*, 49, 50, 52, and McLaughlin, op. cit., 60 n5.

13. MacCulloch, *The Reformation*, 175.

14. See William Klassen, "Oath," in *ME* 4, 4-8.

15. Boyd, *Pilgram Marpeck*, 72.

defence of the city, Marpeck was uncompromising. Thus, at a time when Strasbourg was moving toward joining the Schmalcald League, the refusal of a citizen to bear arms became a serious concern for the government. Bucer told Margaret that (because of Marpeck's exhortations) he expected that Marpeck would be expelled.[16]

The frustration of the Strasbourg clergy was clearly revealed in a letter to the city council around December 16, 1531. In the letter, they petitioned the council to take action against the malicious defamation of their teaching, about which they had heard from other clergy and townspeople alike.[17] There were no signatures on the petition as we have it, only a reference to "Martin Bucer and the other clergy." They had not been prepared to speak publicly about this, the clergy wrote, since they would need to be specific about the slurs used against them, and they had no desire to provide grounds for further soiling Strasbourg's already doubtful reputation in the empire. People are saying that "no gospel is being preached here," the petitioners lamented, and that the holy sacrament is not the teaching and sacrament of Christ. "They call us murderers of souls, and that no one should listen to us." Some are saying that everyone will be saved and the human nature of Christ is denied. We are tired, the clergy wrote, of being the only ones in the city who can be maligned with impunity.

This complaint was not a broadside against Anabaptists. But the implication was that in Strasbourg any views, including those of the Anabaptists, were officially allowed to flourish.[18] No specific names of defamers were mentioned, but the clergy may have had Melchior Hoffman, Sebastian Franck, and Michael Servetus in mind, because all three were acted against by the council on December 11 and 18, 1531.[19]

The Case Against Marpeck

The case against Marpeck, which had been gathering steam, continued. Here the tone of the clergy was much more reserved, although the issues were equally serious. The events of the next ten days soon led to the end of his stay in Strasbourg. At a meeting with Bucer on Saturday, December 9, in the presence of the council, Marpeck began by saying that he wanted to have a discussion on theological issues with all Christians, not just with the clergy. He had come to Strasbourg, he said, because he believed that such an open discussion could happen there.

16. Krebs and Rott, *TA: Elsass* 1, 350.
17. Ibid., 358.
18. Ibid., 357-58.
19. Ibid., 355, 358-59.

"Such a discussion should if possible take place without any respect of special position or party," said Marpeck. "If it could take place good results could come from it; if not things will get much worse."

If all spoke as Christians rather than as papists, evangelicals, or Anabaptists, he suggested, agreement could more easily be achieved on issues. It was a call for Christians to go beyond their separate sets of convictions, and pointed a way to reconciliation. Unless this was done, Marpeck warned, the tensions among them would only get worse. He also urged that the same rules of debate be applied to all. "For my part, if I am convinced by Bucer or anyone else to be truly shown my error, I will gladly desist from it. At the same time, I would expect the same of them."[20] There could be no fruitful conversation where one party could threaten the other with sanctions unless he agreed.

Marpeck charged that the "clergy had hatefully fulminated against" the Anabaptist view of baptism. He said he had first spoken to "Master Zimprian"[21] and then to Capito, "but had accomplished nothing." Despite that failure, and despite his own imprisonment and being scolded for comforting Anabaptists in prison, he still wanted to converse with them. But Strasbourg had no established rules or Christian order for dealing with differences in conviction, he observed. When the Anabaptists requested discussion, they got threats. Part of the lack of "order" was that the clergy had not been free in their preaching. Either they took refuge behind the "common man" (in other words, they felt the public wasn't ready for such a step forward) or behind princes and cities, a reference to the adjustment in doctrine for the sake of Strasbourg's security.

Bucer responded that "the clergy had made constant efforts to have discussions with him and others of his faith to avoid schism" and had called on the government to allow this to happen. Bucer's comment wasn't good enough for Marpeck. In frustration, he shot back that whoever calls on government is cursed.

This was totally unfair, because Marpeck knew that the freedom of the clergy was being restricted by the council. One might wonder why Marpeck lost his temper here. One possible explanation is that since his early days with Castenbaur, Marpeck had profoundly respected people who observed the separation of church and state. Now that Castenbaur had abandoned this idea and was hunting down Anabaptists in Augsburg,[22]

---

20. Ibid., 351, December 9, 1531.
21. Symphorian Altbiesser, one of the city clergy.
22. Castenbaur diligently pursued the routing of Anabaptists in Augsburg. He and other Lutheran preachers in Augsburg were also apparently paid extra for preaching against Anabaptists. See Maximilian Liebmann, *Urbanus Rhegius und die Anfänge der Reformation* (Münster: Aschendorffer Verlag, 1979), 194-97.

Marpeck probably found it infuriating that Bucer also viewed the state and church as one. The discrepancy between Bucer's words about Strasbourg's treatment of dissenters and Marpeck's own experience may have lit his fuse. Or perhaps, like Paul in Galatians 1, he felt justified in using the same curse words as Paul did to condemn those who lived under the unholy alliance of church and state. Whatever Marpeck's motivation, Bucer paid back in kind, goading Marpeck by defending the government's right to punish those who would not listen.

After a short interval they moved to the subject of baptism, putting forward opposing views. The issues of baptism, church order, and the role of government in matters of faith were central to the exchanges between Marpeck and Bucer that followed during the next few weeks. But neither got the public hearing that they both wanted. The council was determined to allow no public expression of dissident views. Anabaptists would not be allowed publicly to express their views, which the council considered a threat to public order and to foreign policy negotiations. Furthermore, the clergy would not be given a public platform that might create the impression that they—and not the council—were in charge. Despite these rulings, neither Marpeck nor Bucer gave up.

On Monday, December 11, 1531, the council decided to permit further conversation in private. Marpeck was allowed to bring two associates with him to speak with four of the reform clergy. The council's abrupt order was that they were to be heard, but if they had nothing new to say, they were to shut up. Nothing was accomplished that day although the clergy again requested a public debate for the sake of the people of the city.

Marpeck also asked to defend his views publicly against the clergy. But the council again rejected his request. In the clergy's submission to council, they admitted that Marpeck had many notable gifts and in many respects commendable zeal.[23] This was why, along with his aggressive (according to the clergy) and impetuous manner, he led many astray. He was a danger to the city, they warned, and that was precisely why it was imperative that he be refuted in public.

On December 18, 1531, the council ruled that Marpeck intended to create a schism in the Christian community. In a decision formulated by Jakob Sturm, city council said that this goal to foster division, as well as Marpeck's advice to others not to swear oaths or bear arms, represented a threat to Strasbourg that could not be tolerated. Unless he abandoned his disruptive ideas and ways, he could not remain in the city. He was given leave to put his views in writing and the clergy to respond.

---

23. Krebs and Rott, *TA: Elsass* 1, 359-60.

The next day Marpeck requested three or four weeks to sell the few belongings of his household and collect the wages he'd earned for his work in the mines and the Black Forest. Marpeck stated that "my lords of the council" had always treated him "in a fatherly manner" and that he did not expect special favours. But, he said, he had received the decision of the council and agreed to live by it "subject only to the prompting of the Spirit [who may determine otherwise]." He was granted two more weeks.[24] The expulsion of Marpeck by the council was the first formal doctrinal decision on its own assumed authority, action that was set in place by Sturm.[25]

Records indicate the clergy were inclined to ask council to give Marpeck even more time. Marpeck had come to the clergy and once again asked for a discussion with them on the basis of the articles he had written in order for the truth to be established. They had responded that he should bring with him whomever he wished. But Marpeck insisted that this discussion should not be done behind the backs of the city council. He asked the clergy to clear it with the council, which they did, emphasizing that they were anxious for such a meeting and that Marpeck did not have much time. The council agreed and allowed Marpeck some extra time. But it did not relent in its judgment that Marpeck must leave the city permanently.

In response to the council's instruction, before the end of December Bucer wrote a defence of infant baptism, and Marpeck in reply submitted to the council his *Confession of Faith*. Several weeks later Bucer wrote a line-by-line refutation of the confession. The December-January debates between Marpeck and Bucer are among the most extensive of recorded exchanges between any Anabaptist and Reform leaders, debates which, when published several decades ago, extended to several hundred pages.

In Bucer's summation, he tabulated what he considered to be Marpeck's errors. Marpeck denied plain Scripture, Bucer declared, and made a historical event of the eternal achievement of Christ. Of equal gravity, Bucer said, was that Marpeck made a sacrifice of Moloch out of the innocent, faithful practice of infant baptism—a reference to the sacrifice of children to the god Moloch, as in 2 Kings 23:10—and robbed the office of government of its place in the kingdom of Christ.[26]

---

24. References to the events taking place from December 9 to 19 in Krebs and Rott, *TA: Elsass* 1, 351-563.

25. Thomas A. Brady, "Architect of Persecution: Jacob Sturm and the Fall of the Sects at Strasbourg," *Archiv für Reformationsgeschichte* 79 (1988), 273.

26. This whole discussion is found in Krebs and Rott, *TA: Elsass* 1, 395-530.

Marpeck's Contentious Confession

In his *Confession of Faith*, Marpeck sounded again at greater length and volume the themes he had presented in his book *Exposé of the Babylonian Whore*. In particular, he dealt with the contentious issue of the relationship between the Old and New Testaments. The nature of this relationship was probably the central theological issue in Strasbourg during Marpeck's time there.

Over the centuries, the Christian Scriptures generally gave rise to two interpretations, both of which attempted to reconcile the obvious differences between the two testaments. The Reformers, including Bucer, followed the traditional interpretation formulated after the emergence of the Christian empire in the fourth century. That interpretation held that the Old Testament provided a model for the ordering of society in which spiritual and secular power—the priestly and the royal—were established as a unit to be responsible for the spiritual and material life of God's people. The spiritual assisted the secular—and the secular the spiritual—in performing their joint divine mandate.

A good example was the papal encyclical *Unam sanctam* issued by Pope Boniface VIII in 1302. In it he said: "We are told by the gospel that in this His fold there are two swords, a spiritual, namely, and a temporal. . . . Both swords, the spiritual and the material, therefore, are in the power of the church; the one, indeed, to be wielded for the church, the other by the church; the one in the hand of the priest, the other by the hand of kings."[27] All of this was possible because both priest and king, preacher and magistrate, were believing Christians. Both were gifted with the Spirit of God to discharge their mandate according to the divine-human covenant. It was a seamless construct in which the two testaments were really a single entity.

The Anabaptists came with a different, and in some senses an opposing, interpretation. Marpeck was the Anabaptist who most extensively described their view, the longest treatment of it in the *Testamentserleutterung*, (*Testament Explanation*), which was the collective work of Leupold Scharnschlager, Marpeck, and several others. In the *Confession* we hear only Marpeck's voice.

In earlier chapters we noted that Marpeck had been exposed to a clear differentiation between Old and New Testaments, especially by his parish priest Stefan Castenbaur, reinforced by the theology of Lienhart Schiemer and Hans Schlaffer. It is also possible that Marpeck built on

27. Anne Fremantle, *The Papal Encyclicals in their Historical Context* (New York: Mentor Book, 1956), 73.

sixteenth-century versions of the three-age scheme of Joachim of Fiore, the twelfth-century Cistercian visionary (ca. 1132-1202). Joachim saw history divided into the ages of the Father, the Son, and the Holy Spirit: the first two roughly being the Old and New Testaments.[28]

Marpeck argued that Old and New Testaments relate to each other as promise and fulfilment. He then expanded and clarified the meaning of those two words with other word pairs such as law-liberty, death-life, desire-performance, fear-love, and coercion-voluntary spirit. It was this approach that is reminiscent of Joachim, who, instead of doubles, used word triplets like knowledge-wisdom-complete understanding, fear-faith-love, starlight-dawn-full daylight, water-wine-oil to correspond to the three ages of the Father, the Son, and the Holy Spirit. Marpeck repeatedly emphasized that in the Old Testament, there was only the promise of salvation; in the New, full salvation came in Jesus. The coming of Jesus had abrogated the Old Testament law. The old had passed away and everything had become new.

The apocalyptic interpretation of Scripture that flowed from Joachim also included the view that there was development—in other words, forward movement—in divine history from one age to the next. That is certainly also true for Marpeck who, with Joachim, held to a dynamic view of history with movement from the Old to New Testament. The Reformers stood in the Augustinian tradition, which held to a static view of history—hence their view of Scripture as describing a single covenant. There was no bridge over the interpretive gulf that separated the Reformers from Marpeck.

On this basis, then, the question of baptism was raised. Marpeck rejected the old view that the baptism of infants, which had become the norm in the church, was the New Testament equivalent of Old Testament circumcision. Circumcision, he wrote, was the seal of the old covenant, whereas baptism was the *sign* of the new. For a sign to do its work, it had to be consciously appropriated. This called for baptism of adults who voluntarily submitted to it. Only with conscious faith could there be love, even for the enemy; only with the Spirit given after Jesus' resurrection could there be free performance of what was pleasing to God. Because of Jesus' voluntary, unresisting submission to crucifixion, there could now be human relations without coercion and domination.

This led directly to the other main point made by Marpeck: the new ordering of the relationship between the spiritual and secular powers.

---

28. Contemporaries of Marpeck who held this view were Thomas Müntzer, Hans Hergot, and also, interestingly enough, Christian Entfelder. See *Gottselkigkeit*, 1533.

Throughout his working days, Marpeck had long conceded that the earthly, secular government had its role, which he spelled out concisely in his *Confession of Faith*. Drawing from Romans 13, he saw government as a God-ordained construct. However, he also insisted on a distinction between the earthy realm and the "Kingdom of God, which consists of justice, peace and joy" (alluding to Romans 14). This, he said, is the realm in which Christians have their primary responsibility.[29] "When, however, such governmental officials become Christians, which I would certainly wish for them," he said, "they cannot use the worldly accoutrements of power in the Kingdom of Christ, nor can it be supported by any Scripture."

Marpeck pointed out that Jesus, the initiator of the new age, had refused to be a secular king. He had rejected the use of earthly power to coerce and dominate, which he demonstrated by not resisting the tyrants that killed him. His resurrection was the beginning of a king and a kingdom in which all violence, all vengeance, and all forceful coercion are forbidden. Rulers, even Christian ones, have no role whatsoever in *this* kingdom as rulers. Their role is now limited to keeping order among the unregenerate who are not yet directed by the free Spirit of Christ. Members of Christ's kingdom are to obey the government, pay taxes, and support it in its God-given task. "Where the governmental authority is used, as it was in the Old Testament, to root out the false prophets, Christ's Word and Spirit are weakened, and are turned into a servile spirit, designed to uphold insufficient and weak laws."[30]

He then offered words that inflamed the powers of his age and have remained an issue to modern times: If rulers use the power of the sword to defend the gospel, he said, they are perverting and exceeding their mandate. They are never permitted to coerce anyone in matters of faith.

This interpretation of the relationship between the two powers directly challenged the concept of the Christian commonwealth, the union of state-church, the final touches to which were even then being put in place in Strasbourg. The two interpretations ruled each other out, especially with respect to the role of secular government. Marpeck's bold confession provided the Strasbourg authorities with more than enough evidence that he could not be allowed to stay.

On January 12, 1532, Marpeck wrote that it was God's will that "in constraint of conscience I have agreed to be expelled." In the same letter he gently admonished members of the council that, for their own sake and not for his, they should carefully consider what they had done.

29. Krebs and Rott, *TA: Elsass* 1, 505-6.
30. Klassen and Klaassen, *WPM*, 150.

But, beyond that, he wrote, "I hope that, God giving his grace, you will cease to persecute the wretched people who flee to you because they have no other place in the whole world . . . and that you will give them refuge in their misery without forcing their consciences."

⏤

Marpeck's *Confession of Faith* [31] was written during the final weeks of his residence in Strasbourg while he was winding down the affairs relating to his employment and disposing of what little property he had. The dissolution of the household no doubt fell to Anna, although she is not mentioned. Marpeck was still meeting with the clergy to discuss the issues that separated them. It is no wonder, therefore, that his *Confession* appears to be written in a hurry. Suffering from repeated interruptions, it is both poorly organized and tiresomely repetitive. In defence of Marpeck the writer, it's important to acknowledge that he was not a trained theologian and did not have the academic discipline for a terse, systematic presentation of the issues that exercised him.

Despite these shortcomings, Marpeck garnered respect among those with whom he debated. Williams calls Marpeck "the master craftsman of a rough, toughly woven sectarianism." He says Bucer felt obligated to come to terms point by point with "Marpeckian Anabaptism" in order to vindicate the magisterial Reformation[32] and try to halt the numerous defections to spiritualism.[33] In the whole of Bucer's long refutation of the *Confession*, he never put down Marpeck as an opponent. To be sure, there are instances of impatience and outrage. Bucer pointed out contradictions in Marpeck's argument, saying that Marpeck misunderstood Scripture, and called on him to prove his assertions.

Bucer's strong reaction to Marpeck's *Confession* should not surprise us, for Marpeck expressed his fundamental disagreement with the central pillars of Bucer's theology and demonstrated his readiness to act on his convictions. Yet never did Bucer disqualify Marpeck's arguments because they were not scholarly. Bucer never claimed to know more than Marpeck because he was a doctor of Scripture. These two contenders demonstrated respect for each other even though one had the power of the state behind him and the other had only the power of persuasion.

31. Krebs and Rott, *TA: Elsass* 1, 416-518, 529-30; Klassen and Klaassen, *WPM*, 107-57.

32. The magisterial Reformation is a term used for the mainstream Reformation theology of Luther, Calvin, Bucer, Zwingli, and others.

33. Williams, *The Radical Reformation*, 158-68.

Their exchange had none of the scatological *ad hominem* aggression that marked, for instance, Martin Luther's attack of 1524 upon Andreas Karlstadt in his polemic *Against the Heavenly Prophets*, in which he called Karlstadt a presumptuous ass, devil-possessed, and a liar and rogue who spreads around his own dung. Similarly, when Schwenckfeld wrote to Luther about his view of the Lord's Supper, Luther in his response called him "Stenkfeld" (stinking field), which actually was one of the milder of Luther's epithets directed to Schwenckfeld.[34]

The Bucer-Marpeck exchange shows that opponents could be respectful of each other even in the midst of controversy during the Reformation, when disagreement so easily developed into legal coercion and even bloodshed. The subsequent histories of both Bucer and Marpeck show them to have been, each in his place, defenders of generous tolerance. Both of them went on to demonstrate their peaceable spirit as reconcilers in a violent time.

A Lasting Influence

Both Marpeck and Bucer also left a lasting imprint on their respective church communities with the introduction of distinctive practices related to children and the church, practices that may well have arisen, at least in part, from the discussions that Marpeck and Bucer had with each other. Marpeck learned from his encounter with Bucer the importance of welcoming infants into a community in a spiritual way.

Many critics during Marpeck's time accused Anabaptists of according little status to children. Perhaps because of these accusations and because of the thought that he gave to this issue during his discussions with Bucer, Marpeck introduced a ceremony of infant dedication or blessing that is practised in many Mennonite churches today.[35] The dedication ceremony helped congregations focus on the new life that God had given them. It brought them to their knees in thanksgiving and intercession that they might help the little ones grow into faith when they became mature

34. G. H. Williams and Angel Mergal, *Spiritual and Anabaptist Writers* (Philadelphia: Westminster, 1957), 163. The hurling of epithets was quite common among opposing church leaders, although Marpeck himself generally refrained from this practice. Sebastian Franck filled his letter to John Campanus, an Anabaptist detractor in Strasbourg, with maledictions against the church fathers—something one wouldn't expect from a leader who advocated tolerance and free thinking. See Williams and Mergal, *Spiritual and Anabaptist Writers*, 145-60.

35. See "Child Dedication" by Neff and Bender in the website Global Anabaptist Mennonite Encyclopedia Online (www.gameo.org). For more analysis, see William Klassen, "The Role of the Child in Anabaptism," in *Mennonite Images*, ed. Harry Loewen (Winnipeg, Man.: Hyperion Press Limited, 1980).

"Let the children come to me" – Jesus

enough to make such a commitment. In dedicating their children to God, parents and the church together affirmed their belief that children belong to the kingdom. They committed themselves to the loving care of bringing up children in the nurture and admonition of the Lord, so that when the children reached the age of full accountability, they would, through faith in Christ, be baptized for the forgiveness of sins.

Marpeck also said that infants should be named before the congregation (in his time, the child's name was not uttered publicly until the dedication service) and that God shall be praised for them.[36] Most modern Mennonite congregations are unaware that they owe this ceremony to Pilgram Marpeck.

For his part, Bucer reintroduced an old rite involving children that is practised by many Protestant churches to this day: confirmation. Bucer first introduced it in Hesse, where he served as a consultant to Philip of Hesse on how to deal with Anabaptists.[37] Interestingly, Bucer found that confirmation was the single most effective way to get Anabaptists to leave their community and return to Lutheranism—presumably, because their desire for responsible church membership could now be obtained within Lutheranism itself. Nevertheless, he was never able to introduce confirmation to Strasbourg.[38] Years later, after the military victory of the Catholic emperor Charles V forced him to leave Strasbourg, Bucer was exiled to England and introduced the rite of confirmation to the Anglican church in Cambridge as a living symbol of the commitment of young people to the gospel and the church. The rite continues among Anglicans and many Protestant churches to this day.

In addition to the church practices that could well have come from the Marpeck-Bucer discussions, these debates also give us a glimpse into the humanity of both men. Bucer's wife gave birth almost annually, but lost most of her children at birth or later due to illness such as the plague. She and her husband must have wondered about the state of children who died, whether or not they were baptized, and may have drawn some consolation from Marpeck's theology. One also wonders if Marpeck, who fathered only one child, offered comfort to the Bucers when their children

---

36. Klassen and Klaassen, *WPM*, 147.

37. See Rhoda A. Schuler, "Confirmation," in *Encyclopedia of Protestantism* 1, ed. H. J. Hillerbrand (New York: Routledge, 2004), 501-6. Martin Rothkegel explores the complexity of the origins of confirmation possibly coming from the Bohemian Brethren or perhaps Erasmus in Martin Rothkegel, "Beneš Optàt on Baptism and the Lord's Supper," *MQR* 79 (2005), 372, n48 passim.

38. Amy Nelson Burnett has demonstrated this debt of Bucer's to Marpeck, as well as Bucer's deep commitment to church discipline, in "Martin Bucer and the Anabaptist Context of Evangelical Confirmation," *MQR* 68 (1994), 95-122.

died. We can never know, but we can presume that both men were influenced by their life experience and also learned from each other.

Departing in Peace

After more than a month of back-and-forth discussions, the Strasbourg council issued its final judgment on January 12, 1532. Pilgram Marpeck was deemed a *Winkelprediger*, a clandestine preacher, meaning that he worked underground to create division in Strasbourg.[39] Despite this judgment, it is clear that all the parties involved—the clergy, Marpeck, and the council—acted in a remarkably peaceful and generous manner toward each other in spite of their fundamental disagreements and the harsh sentence of exile passed on Marpeck. Although the clergy were relieved that Marpeck was leaving, they seemed genuinely regretful. His writings and discussion points may not have changed their views, but they certainly clarified important theological and church issues both for Marpeck and for his unpersuaded opponents, especially those holding political power in Strasbourg.

As for Marpeck, he seems never to have been resentful at his expulsion, although he never again engaged in a public theological debate with civic leaders and Reform or Catholic clergy. So far as we know, he appears to have honoured the terms of his forced departure. After his dismissal from his position as *Holzmeister* (manager of timber resources), the council appointed Christian Steiger and Gilg Brenner to replace him. Both were Anabaptists whom Marpeck himself had trained.[40] Thus the city continued to benefit directly from his work.

Marpeck left the leadership of the small Anabaptist community in the capable hands of Leupold Scharnschlager, his co-worker and closest associate, whom we shall meet in more detail in chapter 10. A man with notable mental and spiritual gifts, Scharnschlager was a well-read schoolteacher who had come to Strasbourg in 1530. One could be sure that, insofar as the fortunes of the little fellowship depended on him, things would go well.

And so, sometime early in January 1532, Pilgram and Anna left Strasbourg, never to return. It is likely that they departed by the Butchers Gate, through which they had entered three years and four months earlier. We may assume that they left with luggage containing what they would need for the journey and for starting again somewhere else.

Once more they were fugitives. What may have occupied their minds

39. Klassen and Klaassen, *WPM*, 530-32.
40. Krebs and Rott, *TA: Elsass* 1, 361.

as they left behind the achievements and failures of those years? How would life unfold for the Anabaptist community they had gathered together now that the political situation made its existence increasingly difficult? One thing was virtually certain. Political and religious turmoil would continue throughout the vast Holy Roman Empire.

-10-

Retreat to the Hills

At the midpoint of Marpeck's life, a book emerged that had a profound influence on the European society in which he lived. *The Prince* by Niccolo Machiavelli was published in 1532, five years after Machiavelli's death. Written in 1513 and circulating privately for nineteen years before publication, *The Prince* would soon become one of western civilization's most important analyses on the theory of statecraft and the use of power by the state.

As a statesman and political philosopher from Florence, Machiavelli argued the case for acquiring and holding on to political power by any means for the sake of public order. To achieve this end, a ruler would have to be ready to adjust his moral principles. In order to maintain his state, Machiavelli wrote, a ruler "is often forced to act in defiance of good faith, of charity, of kindness, of religion. And so he should have a flexible disposition, varying as fortune and circumstances dictate. . . . He should not deviate from what is good, if that is possible, but he should know how to do evil, if that is necessary."[1]

It has been noted that Machiavelli did not invent this manner of state-craft but was accurately describing what even then was being done all over Europe. Nevertheless, *The Prince* became a professional handbook for both Emperor Charles V and King Francis I of France. One may be certain that Ferdinand I also used it, and that Jakob Sturm, humanist that he was, would also have been acquainted with this important Renaissance work. Certainly one can see Sturm working with Machiavelli's theory of state-craft when he betrayed the Swiss cities with whom he had so recently been allied by negotiating with the Lutherans behind their backs. It was also vis-

---

1. Niccolo Machiavelli, *The Prince*, trans. George Bull (Harmondsworth: Penguin U.K., 1961), 90-91.

ible in his treatment of Anabaptists in Strasbourg. Sturm's religious views suggest that under other circumstances he easily could have been their friend and supporter. But they were a threat to the order and security of Strasbourg and therefore had to be suppressed.

One of the great disappointments of the Reform movement both for sympathizers in the Catholic Church as well as for Anabaptists and other dissenters was that its initiator, Martin Luther, in their view had not completed what he had begun. Not the least of the specific issues involved was the relationship of the church to secular government. The term *secular* in sixteenth-century usage did not mean "nonreligious" as it does today. Rather, it meant Christian government run by lay people, as distinct from church government run by clergy.

Luther prided himself on having returned "secular" government to its rightful place and function, free from the tutelage of the church. In 1520 he called on the governing authorities in the empire to make themselves responsible for the reform of the church, thus giving them at least a partial church function.[2] Although he was concerned with church order (note, for example, his reworking of the liturgy in *The German Mass* of 1524), Luther did not proceed to establish an authority structure in the church, as Jean Calvin later did. This was partly a matter of default, because for decades Luther hoped and expected that a general council of the church would be called to decide about the theological issues he had raised and their consequences for church order. The default mode, in which the secular princes became the de facto bishops, became a permanent feature of the Lutheran church in Germany for many years to come. Thus, while Luther had freed secular government from the embrace of the church, he allowed the church to be embraced by secular government.

But Sturm had a different vision—more like that of the Swiss cities—which was to coordinate the roles of church and government, but not to put one above the other. Sturm's assumption of responsibility for the church in Strasbourg, strengthened by his alliance with the Lutherans, was a subsection of his overall concern for Strasbourg's security and therefore also subject to Machiavellian rules.

Marpeck in Strasbourg saw the events of the early Christian centuries repeated when in 1531 he wrote that "the pope as a servant of the church was married to Leviathan, that is, temporal power."[3] Thomas Hobbes in 1651 argued in his famous work, *Leviathan*, that government

---

2. See Martin Luther, *An Appeal to the Ruling Class of the German Nation*, 1520.
3. Rempel, *Later Writings by Pilgram Marpeck*, 38-39.

should have complete control over all aspects of national life, including the church. More than a century earlier, the astute Marpeck declared that in Strasbourg it already did.

All these developments Marpeck observed with his keen eye, and all of them were intimately linked with his forced departure from Strasbourg. The situation was scarcely better elsewhere, since everywhere the marriage between the church and Leviathan was in place among Catholics and evangelicals alike. Still, during 1531-32, a breathing space developed in the religious struggle in the empire. The Ottoman Turks under Suleiman were on the move again. The Muslim empire invaded Habsburg Hungary, Carinthia, and Croatia on a broad front. This threat of invading armies required Ferdinand to conclude the Peace of Nuremberg with the Protestants, providing for the free exercise of religion until a general council of Christendom could be called within a year. Only with this promise could he get military support from the Protestant princes. The Turkish attack was repelled but the threat remained.

A Clear Destination

For at least a month before January 1532, Pilgram and Anna knew that they could not stay much longer in Strasbourg and had carefully considered where they should next live. It may be that they had been in touch with the Anabaptist noble woman Helena von Freyberg, who had settled in Constance after her flight from Kitzbühel in the Tirol. They may have spent some time with her there. Martin Bucer had written to Ambrosius Blaurer, the Reformer in Constance, warning him about Marpeck. It may be that Bucer knew of Marpeck's intention to go there.[4]

Pilgram and Anna may have gone briefly to Constance, but most students of Marpeck's movements assume that, once they left Strasbourg, he and his wife travelled to the vicinity of St. Gallen, in the northeast of Switzerland, where Marpeck put his engineering skills to work once again. Almost certainly their destination was somewhere in the Canton Appenzell, south of the city of St. Gall.

In 1532, St. Gall itself was not a safe place for an Anabaptist leader. Although the Reformation had been successfully introduced in the city by 1527, in that same year St. Gall joined Zürich and Bern in a decree to suppress Anabaptism, providing for severe penalties.[5] This decree was repeated in 1530 and 1532. Switzerland at this time was a loose confederacy, a collection of Catholic and Protestant cantons. The defeat of the

4. Boyd, *Pilgram Marpeck*, 98, n5.
5. *Ostschweiz*, Heinold Fast, ed., *QGT* 2. (Zurich: Theologischer Verlag, 1973), 5-6.

Protestant armies (including a force from St. Gall) by the Catholic cantons at the Battle of Kappel in 1531 sharpened the religious conflict everywhere, including St. Gall. Turmoil arose when, in the settlement after the defeat, St. Gall's ancient monastery again passed into the hands of the Catholic abbot. As part of the settlement, the city had to pay the monastery an indemnity of ten thousand guilders plus six hundred guilders to the victorious Catholic cantons as reparation. The abbot rode into the Protestant city on March 1, 1532, accompanied by a delegation from the Catholic cantons.[6] Soon after, a wall ten metres high was built around the monastery to separate and protect it from the Protestant city.

The city government of St. Gall had enough to do to reach a peaceful accommodation with the abbot and therefore had little patience with Anabaptists in the city. In July 1532, when the Anabaptist Hans Marquart sharply criticized the evangelical preachers in a sermon, he was put in prison. After participating in a public disputation, he was expelled.[7] For Marpeck as an Anabaptist, life in St. Gall would have been a repetition of what had happened to him in Strasbourg. The Reformer and chief politique of St. Gall, Joachim von Watt (known as Vadian), no doubt understood both Martin Bucer and Jakob Sturm very well, for his religious policy closely followed theirs. As a result, Pilgram and Anna probably chose to avoid the city and moved instead to the adjacent rural canton.

The northern border of the Canton Appenzell stretched a stone's throw to the south of the city of St. Gall, with the intervening rural area around St. Gall belonging to the city. Marpeck and Anna were attracted to Appenzell for reasons that were similar to what initially had drawn them to Strasbourg four years earlier. First, Appenzell had a reputation for tolerance of dissenters. It was not party to the decrees issued by the major Swiss cities against Anabaptists in 1527.[8] The whole Swiss Confederacy except Appenzell issued a second decree in 1530.[9] Appenzell's policy of toleration was a matter of concern to the other members of the Swiss Confederacy, and on January 10, 1530, its government was admonished to cooperate.[10] In June 1531 the Swiss cities sent a second strong admonition to Appenzell, warning the canton to get serious about the suppression of Anabaptists. The cities complained that Appenzell had given

6. Johannes Kessler, "Sabbata," in *St. Galler Reformationschronik 1523-1539*, ed. Traugott Schiess (Leipzig, 1911), 97.
7. Ibid., 98; Fast, *TA: Ostschweiz*, 461-68.
8. Ibid., 5-6.
9. Ibid., 8.
10. Ibid., 208.

Anabaptists shelter, to the harm of the other cantons. They pledged their help to Appenzell in an upcoming public disputation with Anabaptists.[11] In August 1531, the Protestant pastor in Teuffen, the main urban centre in Appenzell not far from St. Gall, wrote to the Swiss Protestant leader Ulrich Zwingli complaining that the Anabaptists were taking over as a result of government neglect.

A third decree against Anabaptists was issued in May 1532 by all the cantons, this time including Appenzell. It included the instruction that those who would not recant should be drowned without mercy.[12] Fortunately, even though Appenzell had been signatory to the decree, its officials were not at all diligent at carrying out its provisions. Apart from a few temporary imprisonments in 1530,[13] the most the authorities were prepared to do was to forcibly baptize the children of Anabaptists.[14] Apparently the prospects for Anabaptists in Appenzell in 1532 were no worse and probably better than they had been in Strasbourg in 1528.

The second reason for Appenzell's attraction to the Marpecks was the continued existence of Anabaptism there. The movement had begun with great enthusiasm in 1525 with a large number of believer baptisms by the eloquent peasant preacher Bolt Eberli. In Teuffen the local priest was replaced by the Anabaptist Johannes Krüsi. Anabaptist congregations were formed in several towns, but lack of strong leadership soon allowed the growth of foolish and dangerous behaviour that required public intervention. In one instance, a woman named Frena Bauman persuaded many to stop working and throw away clothing and food in the expectation that God would supply their need.[15] Nevertheless, a public disputation called for by the evangelical clergy in 1527 brought out four hundred Anabaptists, according to a contemporary report. But after that, the movement shrank.

Threats of suppression contained in the edicts of the Swiss cities, including St. Gall, persuaded some Anabaptists in 1530 to try to get to Moravia. This group of ten men and a number of women, led by the former monk Wolfgang Ulimann, were arrested and executed at Waldsee in Swabia. The few who recanted were allowed to return. But an Anabaptist presence remained in Appenzell, no doubt due to the more lenient policy of the cantonal government.

There may well have been a third reason for the Marpecks initially

11. Ibid., 220.
12. Ibid., 9.
13. Ibid., 214.
14. Ibid., 208-10, 216ff.
15. Ibid., 621-22.

avoiding St. Gall and going instead to rural Appenzell. It is based on an interpretation of what Marpeck saw as his vocation at the beginning of this new stage in his life as an Anabaptist leader. Marpeck never repeated the lively, articulate confrontation with government officials and clergy that he experienced in Strasbourg, even though the twelve years that he later spent in Augsburg could have presented another such opportunity, protected as he was there by his role as city employee. It is possible that the 1527 public disputation in Appenzell offered Marpeck a glimmer of hope for public dialogue, although it would have been obvious to him that forces increasingly were working against such open discourse.

Marpeck may have concluded that the growing determination of both Catholic and Protestant governments to suppress Anabaptism made a repetition of the lively debates of Strasbourg impossible. Perhaps he also recognized that the religious confessional positions by the Lutheran, semi-Lutheran (Strasbourg) and Reformed (Swiss) cities had been staked out and hardened by political realities. Continued controversy with leaders like Bucer was no longer likely to be productive. As a result of all this, he seems to have concluded that he would concentrate on quietly building up and strengthening the scattered groups of Anabaptists, thereby seeking to unify them as a truly reformed church alongside others whom he recognized as Christians but who had stopped short of a full reformation of the church. There seem to be good reasons for supporting these suppositions because they appear to be confirmed by Marpeck's life and activity from 1532 onward.

Strangely, there is no evidence in the public records of Appenzell or St. Gall that Marpeck lived in Appenzell. But live there he did, although not visible as an Anabaptist elder or as a public employee. He must have been privately employed to make a living for Anna and himself. Meanwhile, the storms of persecution were devastating Anabaptist communities elsewhere.

The Impact of Münster

The year 1535 was a landmark one for Anabaptists. Anabaptism in the Netherlands and Westphalia had developed into a militant movement centred in Münster, an episcopal city (i.e., seat of the bishop) of seven thousand to eight thousand inhabitants in northern Germany. Anabaptists now constituted a considerable portion of the population. They had gained control of the city in the civic elections of 1534 and proclaimed "the New Jerusalem." Three days later, all non-Anabaptist inhabitants were told they either must leave Münster or be rebaptized. That same day the Catholic bishop, who had set up military headquarters nearby, began a sixteen-month successful siege of the city with the help of Protestants (in this case, primarily Lutherans). Thus ensued months of increased radicalization among the Anabaptist leadership—including polygamy and forced community sharing of goods—and growing misery among Münster's beleaguered citizens, many of whom resorted to eating grass in a desperate attempt to ward off starvation. In the three months prior to the taking of Münster, several hundred men lost their lives attempting to flee. The final capture of the city by Catholic and Protestant forces resulted in a two-day bloodbath in which about seven hundred people were killed.[16]

Münster's conquest and the suppression of its Anabaptist regime came on June 25, 1535. The bloody radicalism of the Anabaptists of Münster sent a chill of fear and loathing into western Europe. The city's Anabaptist leaders believed and publicly announced that God had put the sword of divine vengeance into their hands to execute his fierce judgment on all their persecutors, particularly the Catholic clergy. They clearly meant to carry out this divine mandate. This turn toward apocalyptic violence had fatal consequences for Anabaptists everywhere.

Even before the fall of Münster, Archduke Ferdinand of Austria had intensified measures against Anabaptists in his part of the empire. Many were killed by beheading and burning at the stake. By 1528, this fierce persecution had also caused a refugee movement out of Tirol—including, of course, Marpeck. Marpeck and many hundreds of others fled to the relative safety of Moravia and settled in large communities, many under the leadership of Jakob Hutter, himself a Tirolean. Pushed by the events in faraway Münster, Ferdinand now began to see Münsters everywhere, but especially in Moravia, where Anabaptists had gathered in large numbers. Early in the summer of 1535, he compelled the Moravian nobles to expel the Anabaptists from their estates. Some Anabaptists who had fled to Moravia now returned to Tirol. The distress among those in Tirol and elsewhere now exceeded anything they had experienced in earlier years.

In the midst of this tribulation and at the height of Anabaptist persecution, there is some evidence that Marpeck may have returned to Kitzbühel, a small city in Tirol not far from his home community of Rattenberg. This possibility arises from a letter of Anna Scharnschlager, wife of Marpeck's close associate, Leupold. Anna wrote to her brother-in-law Hans Steger, who was a lawyer in Kitzbühel, about a property matter. She asked him to send his reply to her via Marpeck.[17] Anna's letter is not

---

16. Hubertus Lutterbach, *Der Weg in das Täuferreich von Münster. Ein Ringen um die heilige Stadt* (Münster: Dialogverlag, 2006), 147-48; and Ralf Klötzer, "The Melchiorites and Münster," in *A Companion to Anabaptism and Spiritualism, 1521-1700*, eds. John D. Roth and James M. Stayer (Leiden: Brill, 2007), 217-56.

17. Fast, *TA: Ostschweiz*, 511-13.

dated precisely, so we don't know when during 1535 Marpeck might have been in Kitzbühel. If his journey was occasioned by Ferdinand's persecution of Anabaptists in Moravia, it may have been in July or August, soon after their dispersion.

If Marpeck did indeed travel to Kitzbühel, whatever could have persuaded him to leave a safe haven in Switzerland for the bloody storms of Tirol, where he was a hunted man? Was he exercising his office of elder to give pastoral care to the persecuted, some of whom he may have known personally? Did some of the refugees who returned to Tirol flee from one or more of the fellowships with whom Marpeck was associated in Znaim and Austerlitz and other places? In 1533 an official report claimed that Anabaptism had been totally exterminated in Kitzbühel. The report was mistaken, but did Marpeck go there to determine the facts for himself? Whatever the reason for possibly going there, it would have been important because it was a long and hazardous journey, most of it through hostile territory, whichever route he might have chosen to take. All we know is that he was soon safely back in Appenzell.

At Work Once Again

Perhaps a year or two after his arrival, Marpeck was again offered work as an engineer; this time, to build a fulling mill for the finishing of linen cloth. He likely did this work before his journey to Kitzbühel so that the mill could be used during the summer months when the bleaching of linen took place. This new professional challenge could well have been a fourth reason for the Marpecks' move to Appenzell.

The production of linen in and around St. Gall is confirmed as early as the year 1260. Hemp for the manufacture of linen was grown nearby in the area between Constance and St. Gall. The spinning and weaving of the hemp fibres was a cottage industry involving thousands of peasants and artisans in city and country. Once woven, the raw linen was sold on the market, bought by merchants who fulled (cleansed and thickened) the material, bleached it, and then sold the finished product all over Europe and North Africa. The craft guilds exercised strict control of quality and measurement so that St. Gall linen bore a special mark guaranteeing its high quality. At the bleaching ground, likewise, everything was controlled and regulated in detail. The bleach masters were required to post a bond to ensure quality. Only water and sun worked the bleaching process. The result was that some of the linen was so fine that a square metre of linen could be pulled through a finger ring.[18]

18. Paul Stein, *Die Industrie des Kantons St. Gallen. Chronik des Kantons St. Gallen* (Zürich: Verlag Franz Brun, 1945), 160-65.

There is no certainty about who engaged Marpeck to build the fulling mill or where it was built. Jörg Probst Rothenfelder, usually known as Jörg Maler, stated in an interrogation in Augsburg in 1550 that he had first heard about Marpeck in St. Gall, where, he said, Marpeck had built a magnificent fulling mill. His reference sounds somewhat distant, as though they were not personally acquainted at that time. As already suggested, Marpeck was not based in St. Gall. Indeed, his name never shows up in the St. Gall civic or church records. Maler, however, lived near St. Gall and in Appenzell, arriving from Baden, Switzerland, in the fall of 1534. Perhaps he was attracted by the weaving industry, inasmuch as he was a weaver. He left again for Augsburg in March 1535. Whether the two met during these months is not established.[19] We will learn much more about Maler and his ensuing relationship with Marpeck in chapter 15.

The building of the mill in 1535 is supported by circumstantial evidence. The St. Gall chronicler Johannes Kessler reported that a new bleaching business was established in 1535. Scholars quite properly linked the two events, since bleaching and fulling were both essential for the production of linen cloth.[20] Although the location of the mill is not known, Kessler's report leads to the assumption that it was in St. Gall territory because he says that the new bleaching ground was established on the *Kugelmos* meadow. It was known as the *Schytlin bleiche* (Schytlin's bleaching ground) because a widow named Scheitlin had bought it.[21] Kessler also reports that water was supplied, perhaps by a tributary of the Sitter River, which flowed on the west side of the hill.[22] There would have to have been enough water, perhaps dammed up, to drive the water wheel that powered the mill. The mill, if indeed it was built at the same time, must have been near there. Kessler also reported that the new bleaching ground was established as a protective measure against competition from Constance. There is reason to suppose that Marpeck could have been hired to build a fulling mill on that location.

On the other hand, it is tantalizing to speculate that the mill Marpeck built was not connected at all with the establishment of the bleaching ground in St. Gall. The production of fine linen in the St. Gall area was on

19. Heinold Fast, "Pilgram Marbeck und das oberdeutsche Täufertum. Ein neuer Handschiftenfund," *Archiv für Reformationsgeschichte* 47 (1956), 198.

20. Klassen, *Covenant and Community*, 33.

21. There is still today a hill named *Scheitlinbüchel* about 1.2 kilometres southeast from the centre of St. Gall. This could therefore be the location mentioned by Kessler.

22. Kessler, "Sabbata," 102.

the way to its greatest expansion, peaking in 1550. We already mentioned the competition from Constance. Competition also came from Appenzell, when in 1535 the canton made an attempt to draw the entire industry away from St. Gall and establish its own mark of quality.[23] It is possible that, because Marpeck lived in Appenzell, his work was part of the industry takeover attempt, even though it failed due to the intervention of other cantons of the Swiss Confederacy.

The Appenzell centre immediately southeast of St. Gall was Teuffen, which five years earlier had included a large Anabaptist congregation. To the west and a few kilometres from St. Gall lay the village of Niederteuffen, which is served by the Sitter, the main river in the area. It is possible that Marpeck built a fulling mill near there to take advantage of a plentiful flow of water and of a new professional opportunity in an area of religious tolerance. His hydrological skills had been important for mining in Tirol and bringing timber into Strasbourg. It is likely therefore that he also built the water system required for bleaching and fulling in Appenzell.

The mill built by Marpeck would have had basically four parts. The first was a trough into which bunches of wet cloth were laid. Above it were two heavy oaken hammers on a shaft at the two-thirds point of the handle from the head. Behind the hammers, the main shaft was driven by a waterwheel. On the wheel shaft were cams, four hard wooden projections each ninety degrees apart, which, as the shaft turned, raised the hammers and dropped them heavily onto the cloth in the trough. The oaken hammerheads were shaped so that each time they dropped on the cloth they rotated it a little, thus assuring uniform processing. Part of this system of processing cloth was the drying frame, a simple structure of two horizontal wooden rails supported by vertical posts. After fulling, the wet cloth was stretched on this frame to dry. Once that was done, the cloth was spread on drying fields where the bleaching took place over eight to sixteen weeks, regularly sprinkled with clean water.[24]

Apart from being a power source, a considerable supply of clean water was essential to the industry. Fulling mills were used to clean woven cloth, to further separate bunches of fibres and then soften them—all of which was done prior to bleaching.[25] Special pools had to be created for separating hemp fibres before they could be spun and woven. This process

23. Stein, *Industrie*, 164.

24. See *A History of Technology* 3, ed. C. Singer, et al. (New York: Oxford University Press, 1957), 169-70.

25. See also *History of Technology* 2, Singer, et al., 218.

would pollute any waterway and had therefore to be isolated from the source of water used for bleaching.[26]

We may imagine Marpeck's excitement at the opportunity to put his technical skills to use again. It would have been a task taking some time. The proper wood, at least some of which was oak, would have to be procured and dried. Contemporary illustrations of a fulling mill suggest a machine that stood taller than a man, with a wooden frame built of timbers 25 by 15 centimetres (10 by 6 inches), at least 2 to 3 metres (6.5 to 10 feet) in length. The main shaft was 25 centimetres (10 inches) thick, the length depending on the distance to the water wheel, again perhaps 2 or 3 metres. The weight of the impact of the hammers would depend on the length of the handle as well as of the cam, and all that would in turn depend upon the cloth that was to be processed.

Although the location of the mill built by Marpeck cannot be determined with certainty, we may conjecture that it was built in the winter of 1534-1535 and completed in the spring to take advantage of the boom in the industry and to meet the competition. So once more Marpeck, owing to his engineering competence, was at the centre of local enterprise. We may be sure that his machine continued to serve the linen industry in the area for many years to come. But unlike his engineering efforts in Strasbourg, except for the brief mention by Maler, we never hear of his fulling project again.

For the next seven years, until 1542, Marpeck remained invisible most of the time. Occasionally we get a glimpse of him, particularly in Moravia and Augsburg. The visible traces of his life "are like footprints in the sand of the seashore. Where once there was a complete set of footprints coming onto the beach and leaving it again elsewhere, the waves have now erased so many that one cannot be at all certain how all the remaining prints relate to each other."[27] Switzerland appears to have been his base of operations as an Anabaptist elder until 1542.

Two Men of One Mind

Two associates and friends of Marpeck make their appearance soon after his arrival in Switzerland. We have already mentioned Jörg Maler, the weaver. The other was Leupold Scharnschlager, who had become a close associate of Marpeck's while they both lived in Strasbourg. Anna Scharnschlager's letter to Hans Steger, referred to earlier in this chapter, places her in Appenzell near Marpeck in 1535. She and her husband

26. *A History of Technology and Invention*, ed. Maurice Daumas (New York: Crown Publishers, 1969), 513.
27. Walter Klaassen, "Schwenckfeld and the Anabaptists," 389.

Leupold likely joined Pilgram and Anna in Appenzell after their expulsion from Strasbourg in 1534.

It is entirely possible that Scharnschlager and Marpeck had known each other earlier in Tirol, where Scharnschlager had an estate at Hopfgarten near Kitzbühel.[28] Leupold and his wife were forced to flee in 1530 after their conversion to Anabaptism became known. They had made their way to Strasbourg, likely following the Marpecks there. Scharnschlager worked in Strasbourg with Marpeck and in the region beyond—especially in Speyer, some 100 kilometres (60 miles) north of Strasbourg along the Rhine. This working relationship is revealed in a letter of comfort and encouragement that Scharnschlager wrote to Michel Leubel, a recent convert to Anabaptism, as well as in a lengthy record of the interrogation of Leubel and Thomas Adolf by the authorities of Speyer.[29]

Scharnschlager and Marpeck were contemporaries, although Scharnschlager was probably five or six years older than Marpeck. He was married about 1509. If one assumes him to have been about twenty at the time, that would put his birth at around 1489. The two men came from the same social stratum and were both educated and economically well off. Scharnschlager was an independent landowner; there is no indication of any special professional skill. He is referred to in the Strasbourg records as *Seifensieder*,[30] which means soap maker. He uses this designation of himself in his petition to the Strasbourg city council.[31] It may therefore be assumed that he made soap to support his wife and himself, although there is no direct evidence of this. In his later years, he became a school teacher in Ilanz.

Life for the Scharnschlagers in Strasbourg after Marpeck's expulsion was apparently quiet. This may be in part because the Anabaptist church in

---

28. For a biography of Leupold Scharnschlager, see the article on him by Gerhard Hein and William Klassen in *ME* 4, 443-46, and Walter Klaassen, "Anna Scharnschlager," in *Profiles of Anabaptist Women*, 58-63.

29. These documents reveal that Scharnschlager had baptized Adolf, who had reported to Scharnschlager about Leubel. Adolf had gone to Strasbourg to be baptized, but because baptism had been suspended for a period, it was not done. He carried Scharnschlager's letter of late December 1532 back to Speyer for Leubel and another convert, Caspar Schuhmacher, whom Scharnschlager had baptized. Schuhmacher had recanted and this led Scharnschlager to include in his letter his view of baptism, which conformed in every respect to Marpeck's. Early in January 1533, Leubel and Adolf were questioned and both recanted. However, the official record states that Leubel was executed by drowning at midnight on January 30, remaining faithful to his Anabaptist convictions. See *TA: Baden und Pfalz* 4 (Gütersloh: Bertelsmann Verlag, 1951), 419-21, 421-25.

30. Krebs and Rott, *TA: Elsass* 2, 311, 343. Sebastian Franck also practised that trade until he was hired by a printery.

31. Ibid., 353.

Austerlitz, Moravia, had ordered a temporary suspension of baptism caused by the strife over this issue among Anabaptists in Strasbourg,[32] although we don't know how long the suspension lasted. The Anabaptists' public challenging of Strasbourg's Reform clergy and city council that occurred during Marpeck's last months there was not repeated. Scharnschlager gave quiet and moderate leadership to the group that previously had gathered around Marpeck. He must have continued contact with other Anabaptists in the city, including Melchior Hoffman, who regarded Scharnschlager as an opponent because he rejected Hoffman's docetic christology, which downplayed the fully human Christ in favour of the heavenly Christ.[33] Scharnschlager also parted company with Hoffman because Hoffman had assigned Strasbourg a role in the events of the end time.[34] Hoffman never agreed with Marpeck and Scharnschlager that the functions of government and church should be radically separated.[35]

Even so, in May 1534, Scharnschlager was apprehended and interrogated by members of the Strasbourg council—perhaps a function of the alarm caused by the events taking place in Münster. Strasbourg councillors knew that Hoffman had been an inspiration to the Münster Anabaptists. Bernhard Rothmann, who had become the theologian of Münster and articulator of the conviction that the Münster Anabaptists were God's avengers, had spent time in Strasbourg in 1531.[36] The siege of Münster by the joint Catholic-Protestant force had begun on February 27, 1534, and the events in and around Münster were big news throughout the empire. Evidently the Strasbourg authorities had voiced the opinion that if Anabaptists gathered in as large numbers in Strasbourg as they had in Münster, they would take over the city and coerce everyone else to their point of view, just as the Anabaptists in Münster had done.

In his plea for tolerance, Scharnschlager responded to these fears. He was interrogated again on May 27 when his questioners tried unsuccessfully to get information from him about other Anabaptists and Anabaptist meetings. Scharnschlager declared that the betrayal asked of him was the work of Judas Iscariot and he would not do it.[37] It was at this interrogation that Scharnschlager talked to his accusers about their denial of reli-

32. Klassen, *Covenant and Community*, 32.

33. Krebs and Rott, *TA: Elsass* 2, 19.

34. Hoffman predicted that 144,000 witnesses (Rev. 14:1-5) would go out from Strasbourg into the whole world.

35. This was apparently also true of Menno Simons, according to Helmut Isaak, *Menno Simons and the New Jerusalem* (Kitchener, Ont.: Pandora Press, 2006), 104-7.

36. William Klassen, "Bernd Rothmann," in *ME* 4, 368-70.

37. Ibid., 343. For English translation, see William Klassen, "Scharnschlager's Farewell to the Strasbourg Council," *MQR* 42 (1968), 211-18.

gious liberty to him and his fellow believers. This led to his lengthy plea for toleration, which he submitted to the Strasbourg council and which they read on June 16, 1534.

Scharnschlager's highly articulate petition[38] is the first exhibit of many that demonstrate how interwoven the life and thought of Marpeck and Scharnschlager had become. Like Marpeck, Scharnschlager admitted that he had been attracted to Luther's early teachings when Luther had questioned infant baptism and rejected coercion in matters of faith. But both Luther and Zwingli had departed from their early vision when they agreed to use the sword to defend the gospel against pope and emperor. The gist of the argument in Scharnschlager's petition was that even as the evangelicals expected to be granted freedom of faith, they ought to extend the same freedom to Anabaptists. We left the coercion of the papacy to come to you for safety, he wrote, and now it is being denied us.

Agreeing with the Reformers, Scharnschlager suggested there are two legitimate swords. One is secular, wielded by the government for the punishment of evil and protection of the good. The other is the sword of the Spirit, which is wielded by the Christian community for internal correction but which kills no one. The killing sword of the magistrates is legitimate but has no place or function in the community of faith. It was a breathtaking position to adopt and defend in 1534 although, as Scharnschlager notes, it was saying in another way what Martin Luther had said at the beginning of the Reform movement: "The Word will do it!" No other power was necessary for the triumph of the gospel.

One can imagine the Reform clergy and councillors squirming in their chairs at the force of the argument, especially Scharnschlager asking of them only what they demanded from the emperor and pope for themselves, for they were not insensitive people. But they were being tarred with their own brush, a rebuttal that is never received kindly by those who hold power, no matter how logically persuasive the argument is. Perhaps it is not surprising that no written response or justification from either clergy or council is extant. Both Scharnschlager and Marpeck accurately judged that Strasbourg's security in the empire was the primary consideration of the clergy and council, swallowing all inconsistencies.

Scharnschlager and his wife were banished from the city in 1534, just as Pilgram and Anna had been two years earlier. His farewell letter to the council illustrates that Leupold left uncowed: "If this is the way one is to proceed in Christ, with force and scandal and offensive cases," he wrote, "who would win the neighbour for the Kingdom of Christ? This would

38. Ibid., 346-53.

not be winning but driving them away." And then, to drive the point home, "If . . . you, my lords, call yourselves Christians and scandalize us innocent ones, how will you answer for this before God?" Nevertheless, he softened somewhat in his closing comments, noting that it was his duty to offer this testimony to the best of his understanding and conscience. "If it is not being done as cordially as I should, I beg you my beloved Lords, not to hold it against me. If I could be of further service to you, I would be inclined to do so. If you no longer desire me to sojourn here, I will commit you to Christ, my Lord, and by God's grace pray for you that God may, if possible, give you insight."[39]

Marpeck and Scharnschlager are clear evidence that it was not only the dispossessed who looked to Anabaptism and were prepared to take high risks for it. For the poor, the Anabaptist message of God's love and the equality of believers was a way out of social inferiority and impotence. For these two relatively wealthy men, the Anabaptist way represented a thought-out, consistent, internally coherent view of Christian faith and of the Christian's relation to God and Christ, the world, and especially government. It was a set of convictions worked out in the crucible of the religious controversy of the time. In terms of social status and reputation, they put at risk as much as anyone and ultimately surrendered all "creaturely" things in submission to Christ. Both men signed letters with the words "a partner in the tribulation which is in Christ." They understood themselves to be part of the reform of the church that went all the way. They were "full gospel" reformers, which for them that was not a slogan but a reality in which they lived.

Tensions Without and Within

On October 28, 1538, Hans Felix Uhrmacher, son-in-law of Leupold and Anna, wrote them a letter from Austerlitz. We learn that it was Scharnschlager who had been instrumental in Uhrmacher's conversion to Anabaptism. For a long time, wrote Uhrmacher, he had desired to see his father-in-law again but so far had been prevented from doing so. Now, however, such a visit might happen, for he had heard that Leupold and Anna might not be able to stay *oben*, meaning "above," a reference to mountain territory, which could therefore be a reference to Appenzell. He anticipated that they would come down to Moravia.[40] The question is, what had Hans Felix heard that would make the continued residence of the Scharnschlagers in Appenzell impossible?

39. Klassen, "Scharnschlager's Farewell," 218.
40. Fast, *TA: Ostschweiz*, 513.

By 1538 everyone knew that sooner or later, when peace was forged between Emperor Charles V and King Francis I of France, the emperor would yet again have a free hand to attempt by force of arms a solution to the religious controversy brought on by the Reformation. A ten-year peace treaty between the two monarchs was signed on July 14, 1538. Although Switzerland was not formally part of the Holy Roman Empire, the waves created within the Habsburg lands often washed over the Swiss Confederacy, so that even there religious dissenters were fearful.

But there were also more immediate threats. On August 28, 1538, the Swiss mandate of 1526 against Anabaptists was renewed and brought up to date in St. Gall. The official complaints were familiar. Some Anabaptists were charging the evangelical clergy with preaching false doctrine; others refused to attend evangelical church services and forbade their households to do so. They refused the civic oath, and those who had the franchise would not vote in council elections. These last refusals, especially, constituted a danger to the public order. The decree announced that all who were convicted of these charges would be exiled from the city,[41] affecting those Anabaptists who lived in the city of St. Gall and the adjacent countryside.

There was no new decree in Appenzell, where the Marpecks and Scharnschlagers were living. But the Anabaptist community to which they belonged spanned the border between St. Gall and Appenzell, so that the new threat in St. Gall would have affected the whole Anabaptist community.

When Hans Felix, the Scharnschlagers' son-in-law, warned Leupold and Anna that they might be forced to leave Appenzell, the reason for the rumour he cited may also have been an internal one. A former Anabaptist named Johannes Spichermann reported that between 1535 and 1537 there had been a suspension of the Lord's Supper in the Anabaptist community in St. Gall. This was done, as the report said, to allay public fears of insurrection. The Anabaptist practice of daring to take communion outside the established church was viewed by many people as a serious threat to public order. This increased public anxiety was part of the big wave that washed over Europe after the debacle at Münster—much like public anxiety in the wake of the September 11, 2001, terrorist attacks in the United States—and Anabaptists everywhere were tossed about by it.

The Swiss Anabaptists may have thought that suspending the Lord's Supper, which was so central to the life of the community, would help to allay the fears of the government. But the suspension could also have been

41. Ibid., 477-78.

a reflection of internal strife. "Occasionally the devil lights a fire because he always resists those who desire to live out the Word of God in purity," Spichermann was reported to have said. That may be an indication of the problem of legalism that plagued the fellowship. A central part of the dispute was the meaning of the Lord's Supper. Was it a joyful celebration of divine forgiveness or was it the occasion for separating the genuine Christians from the false?[42] The letters of the early 1540s by both Marpeck and Scharnschlager to the Anabaptists of Appenzell address this issue repeatedly, as we will see later. It is not hard to imagine that this dispute could be the cause of the suspension.

Spichermann also reported that on Easter Day, April 1, 1537, the Appenzell fellowship had again elected elders, one of whom was Jörg Maler.[43] Marpeck and Scharnschlager must both have been involved in these events even though the report makes no reference to them. It may be that because of the external and internal threats to the continued existence of the community, once again they had discussed moving to the Anabaptist community in Austerlitz, where public pressure and internal tensions were less intense.

It is possible that Scharnschlager's important work, *The Common Order for Members of Christ*, may be part of these events.[44] Scholar Heinold Fast had tentatively dated this work at 1540, but there seems no good reason for not moving the date back a few years to 1537.

An important feature of *The Common Order* is found in articles 5 and 6, which deal with church discipline. Scharnschlager approached the potentially difficult matter of discipline within the church in a manner that was not legalistic. From his perspective, discipline should be exercised not so much to keep the fellowship pure, but always to keep it intact and to foster an environment in which Christians can grow.[45] He called the form of discipline known as the ban a "ban of forgiveness" or a "ban of love." Always it was an action—whether merely a rebuke or, in more serious situations, excommunication from the group—carried out by the Holy Spirit through members of the community, so it was also called the "ban of the Holy Spirit." In this and many other examples, it

---

42. Heinold Fast, "Vom Amt des 'Lesers' zum Kompilator des sogenannten Kunstbuches. Auf den Spuren Jörg Malers," in *Aussenseiter zwischen Mittelalter und Neuzeit*, eds. N. Fischer and M. Kobelt-Groch (Leiden: Brill, 1997), 199-200. Reprinted in Fast and Rothkegel, *Kunstbuch*, 42-70.

43. Ibid., 200.

44. See Packull, *Hutterite Beginnings*, 33-53, and especially pp. 49-52, for a detailed discussion of this *Order* and its relationship to the Swiss and Hutterite orders.

45. If the above reconstruction approaches accuracy, it is easy to see where Maler obtained the *Order* to include it in the *Kunstbuch* many years later.

is clear that Scharnschlager's work reflects Marpeck's views in sentence after sentence. A close parallel to article 5 is found in the *Admonition*, a treatise on baptism and the Lord's Supper on which Marpeck and Scharnschlager were working during these years.[46]

There is no overt evidence that the Marpeck community in Appenzell moved at this time to Moravia. Presumably the crisis passed and the Anabaptists in Appenzell and St. Gall struggled on, dealing with their internal problems. Once more, these events suggest a close relationship between the group of churches with which Marpeck was affiliated and the Swiss Brethren. In Appenzell, it appears, the two groups were not separated. They were kept together in dialogic tension by the devotion of Scharnschlager and Marpeck to the oneness of the church. They continued to affirm that oneness even when Marpeck moved to Augsburg in 1542 and Scharnschlager to Ilanz, where he carried on as an Anabaptist leader until his death in 1563.[47]

Anabaptist scholar Arnold Snyder has argued in several articles that the Marpeck legacy in the Swiss Brethren community continued into the seventeenth century.[48] In the Swiss region of the Grisons, the same can be said of the Scharnschlager legacy. In Appenzell, this legacy became much richer as Marpeck and Scharnschlager began collaborating on one of their most influential works.

---

46. Klassen and Klaassen, *WPM*, 279.

47. See J. Ten Doornkaat Koolman, "Grisons," in *ME* 2, 584-86, which notes that Ilanz was an Anabaptist centre for many years (585).

48. Arnold C. Snyder, "The (Not-So) Simple Confession of the Later Swiss Brethren, part 1, Manuscripts and Marpeckites in an Age of Print," *MQR* 73 (1999), 677-722. Snyder also argues that the Schleitheim Articles were appealed to by the Marpeck group, as for example in Scharnschlager's discussion about whether a Christian can be a magistrate, where he quotes Schleitheim; see Fast and Rothkegel, *Kunstbuch*, 518-20.

-11-

Focus on the Sacraments

Sometime probably in the late 1530s, a manual on the sacraments came into the hands of Pilgram Marpeck and Leupold Scharnschlager. It laid the foundation for one of their most important works. The manual's authors included several men who had gained notoriety as the theologians of the Münster uprising and the conceptualizers of Anabaptists as God's avengers. They seemed most unlikely figures to have had such influence upon Pilgram and Leupold.[1]

Bernhard Rothmann, who came first in the list of authors and whose name is most associated with this work, had helped introduce the Reformation to Münster in 1533. Shortly after that, he became an opponent of infant baptism, and on November 8 of that year he published a work entitled *Confession Concerning the Two Sacraments*. In it, he described baptism as dipping into water, which for the one baptized signified dying to sin, burial with Christ, and resurrection to a new life of doing God's will. The Lord's Supper was described as a loving gathering of Christian believers in remembrance of Christ.

Reading this work several years later in north-German Flemish dialect, Marpeck and Scharnschlager recognized its potential value for their own communities and the larger Anabaptist fellowship. They knew perfectly well that it had come out of the notorious and bellicose Anabaptist kingdom of Münster and that it had been written at least a year before the

1. The authors are listed in the preface as Bernhard Rothmann, Johann Klopriß, Hermann Staprade, Henrick Rol, Dionysius Vinne, and Gotfrid Stralen. The preface several times claims the manual is a statement of the "Predikanten," preachers of Münster. Rol, a former Carmelite priest, was a gifted writer and Anabaptist leader who may have left Münster in protest of what was happening there (see van der Zijpp, "Henric[k] Rol, in *ME* 3, 704-5). He was burned at the stake at Maastricht in September 1534. His writings deserve to be compared with the *Confession* (*Bekentnisse*) to ascertain his role in that document.

201

adventurer and street actor Jan van Leyden had proclaimed himself king of Münster in September 1534.

In the introduction to their version of this work, which they named the *Admonition* (*Vermanung*), Marpeck and Scharnschlager avoided naming the authors of the original work, stating that it had been "published by others and . . . tested by us and purged of all the errors which we have found. . . . These other witnesses we have cleansed and corrected, omitting the mistakes and errors in them."[2] They also referred to "destructive sects," possibly a reference to the events in Münster that occurred after the publication of the original manual. Indeed, Marpeck and Scharnschlager explicitly condemned the claims made by the Münsterites that they were the kingdom of Christ on earth.[3]

We can be sure that Marpeck and Scharnschlager gave their reworking of the manual very careful thought and took a calculated risk. They were convinced that the work was well thought out and could be cleansed of all error and dross. It was a dangerous game they were playing, but it was not exposed until 1956 when Franklin J. Wray detected a link between the two works.[4] Had their borrowing been exposed in the 1530s, the consequences would have been grave.

One scholar has accused Marpeck and Scharnschlager of plagiarizing Rothmann's work.[5] However, while much of the *Admonition* was a direct appropriation from Rothmann (a borrowing that is openly acknowledged), Marpeck and Scharnschlager made the text their own from the opening sentences to the concluding lines.

Offering Instruction

The authors clearly stated the purpose of the *Admonition* at the beginning of the work. It sought to unify the scattered Anabaptists, many of whom were discouraged and ready to give up, so that in the mercy of God "all wounded and tired consciences may be restored, healed, and gathered together and united into one." The work reveals that there was a serious, ongoing struggle of many Anabaptists to find the true path and avoid the alluring side roads offered by the spiritualizers and evangelicals,

2. Klassen and Klaassen, *WPM*, 166.

3. Ibid., 209.

4. Frank J. Wray, "The 'Vermanung' of 1542 and Rothmanns 'Bekenntnisse,'" in *Archiv für Reformationsgeschichte* (*ARG*) 47 (1956), 243-51.

5. Rempel, *Later Writings by Pilgram Marpeck*, 68. In a similar criticism, Robert Stupperich claimed that the *Admonition* writers used the Rothmann work "without correction in individual details." See Stupperich, *Die Schriften Bernhard Rothmanns* (Münster: Aschendorff, 1970), 139.

and perhaps even the militancy that had characterized the Anabaptists in Münster five years earlier.

The *Admonition* was not intended to be a polemical attack on opponents, as Marpeck had done in his Strasbourg writings. Rather, it offered instruction on the use of the term "sacrament," the nature of baptism and the Lord's Supper, and the understanding of the nature of the church. It also clearly identified the errors of the papists, evangelicals and what it termed "false Anabaptists" and their teaching on baptism and the Lord's Supper. The false Anabaptists were, in a manner of speaking, insiders and therefore much more dangerous than the Catholics and Reformers. These "messengers of Satan mixed with members of the covenant of truth" and "joined themselves with the members of the church in order to spoil, blind, and embitter." This appears to be an allusion to Bünderlin, Entfelder, Schwenckfeld, and perhaps also Melchior Hoffman. Nor should we rule out the Münsterites themselves, for later on they are explicitly mentioned and chided.

The work was intended for the Anabaptists in St. Gall and Appenzell, in Strasbourg and surroundings, and likely also in Moravia. Although the book was unsigned, for reasons already cited we know the authors were Pilgram Marpeck and Leupold Scharnschlager, and perhaps even others, because the writers identify themselves as "members of the covenant community." In the concluding sentence, the authors refer to themselves as "participants in the tribulation which is in Christ." This line was the trademark signature of Marpeck and Scharnschlager. Virtually all of the themes appearing in Marpeck's Strasbourg publications—in his *Confession* of 1532, and in Scharnschlager's *Plea for Tolerance* of 1534—appear again in the *Admonition* and confirm the identity of the two revisers.

Two Covenants

Marpeck and Scharnschlager set out to correct for their readers an important error with respect to the concept of covenant. Their comments provided an addition to the original text arising from their concern about the growing popularity of the notion of one testament. They rejected the teaching of the Swiss and South German Reformers that Scripture offered only one covenant from Abraham to their own time. This was a major issue in Switzerland, where they now lived, and the primary focus of a book by Heinrich Bullinger, an articulate successor to Zwingli, which was widely circulated in 1534 in both German and Latin.[6]

6. Translated, the title is *Concerning the One, Eternal Testament or Covenant of God.* The Bullinger book is listed in the original German in the bibliography as *Von dem einigen vnnd ewigen Testament oder Pundt Gottes* etc.

This one-covenant view held together in continuity both the secular (as embodied by the king) and the sacred (the priest and prophet). Together they formed an indivisible unity, a God-ordained unity visible in the Old Testament and also in the history of the church. It was a unity that was staunchly defended, especially in the evangelical city states of Switzerland and south Germany.[7] The signs of the one covenant were circumcision and baptism, Passover and the Lord's Supper.

But the authors of the *Admonition* rejected the one-covenant view and identified two covenants: an external one found in the Old Testament and an internal covenant in the New. The distinguishing difference was that in the external covenant (manifested in part in circumcision and the promise of the land) every physical descendant of Abraham was included, while the internal covenant required an individual response that was sealed by baptism. It followed, therefore, that circumcision and baptism were not equivalent. The advent of Christ had also separated government from church in a way that allowed government no role at all in the church.

The system of the one covenant was very alluring in 1540 because it relieved people from having to make a personal decision. For most of society, baptism occurred soon after birth, and conformism to the laws of government and the church was the norm. To establish a community of the new covenant, as the Anabaptists did, required a nonconformity to the existing European practices that immediately put life and liberty at risk. The gravity of this issue helped to explain the efforts of Marpeck and Scharnschlager to clarify in detail what the differences were between Old and New Testaments—in other words, between Israel and the church of Christ:

> In summary, the ancients had a sketchy, figurative, yet symbolic faith which focussed on hope. Such a faith was reckoned as a figurative righteousness which all the ancient believers as followers of Abraham and his righteousness had. Just as the shadow points forward to the light and the figure to the essence, the faith of the ancients pointed forward to Christ and His true believers, and pointed to the regenerate righteousness; it became really essential only in the righteousness of Christ, when He had become justified, and when, in His true glorified humanity, he took His seat at the right hand of the Father.[8]

The authors refer to themselves as partners in covenant (*Bundsgenossen*). "We have dedicated ourselves," they wrote, "as those committed

7. For Calvin's impact in Geneva, for example, see H. H. Wolf, *Die Einheit des Bundes. Das Verhältnis des alten und neuen bundes bei Calvin* (Neukirchen Kreis Moers: Verlag der Buchhandlung des Erziehungsvereins 1958).
8. Klassen and Klaassen, *WPM*, 233; an addition to Rothmann text.

to the covenant of the banner of divine righteousness and truth." Under this banner they had pledged themselves to follow "Jesus Christ our Lord and General" and fight "with the weapons and sword of the Holy Spirit"—not for an earthly kingdom but for a heavenly one.[9] The dominance of military metaphors in this "call to arms" is a direct appeal to cast off the literal warfare used in Münster and take on the true spiritual struggle to which the writers invited the children of peace. Everywhere people cry "covenant, covenant!" but deny the truth of it, they observed. The true covenant, instituted by Christ, is "his binding covenant of the good conscience with God" (1 Pet. 3:21), which was Anabaptist language for baptism.

True Baptism

The discussion of baptism occupies fully two-thirds of the *Admontion*, and one-third of that was added to Rothmann's original work by Marpeck and Scharnschlager.[10] When we recall Marpeck's disappointment at not being able to find people in Strasbourg brave enough to publicly explore the meaning of baptism, it is no surprise to see the emphasis that he and Scharnschlager placed on this topic in the *Admonition*. During his final days in Strasbourg, Marpeck was finally able to have a dialogue with Martin Bucer, who also believed that the two testaments "were essentially one thing" (*so gar ein Ding*). However, this discussion took place in court as Marpeck defended himself from charges of heresy. It wasn't quite the open discussion he had envisaged.[11]

According to Marpeck and Scharnschlager, the apostolic Scriptures described true baptism as follows:

> Those baptized shall thereby confess their faith and commit themselves, by the power of their faith in Christ, to lay aside their old being entirely and, henceforth, be inclined to live a new life. . . . Accordingly, baptism is a burying of the old being and a resurrection of the new.[12]

Further, the good conscience

> can be created and achieved only by the Spirit of God, who cleanses the heart and unites us through faith. Insofar as this covenant of con-

9. Cf. 2 Cor. 10:4-6 and Eph. 6. See also appendix B.

10. Additions to the Rothmann text by Marpeck and Scharnschlager are marked in italics in the English translation by Klassen and Klaassen, *WPM*, 159-302.

11. In the early years of Anabaptism, major discussions on baptism were led by Balthasar Hubmaier and others. Christoph Freisleben in 1528 wrote a brilliant tract that was widely distributed. See Seiling, "Christoph Freisleben's On the Genuine Baptism of John, Christ and the Apostles," *MQR* 81 (2007), 623-54.

12. Klassen and Klaassen, 186.

science is sincere, when they in baptism totally commit themselves to God and to the obedience of the truth, the believers thereby purify their souls and are washed from all sins. Otherwise, baptism is of no use and is only a mockery in the presence of God.[13]

Infant baptism, they taught, could not fulfil the scriptural teaching about baptism. Faith has to be personal; it cannot be the faith of the sponsors or godparents, who can make no promises for the child before God because they do not know what the child will do when it becomes an adult. Marpeck and Scharnschlager considered the general lack of faith and Christian obedience among those baptized in infancy a consequence of this practice of sponsorship.

As for the argument of the infant baptizers that God, being omnipotent, can give faith even to a newborn, they responded by reminding them of the distinction between God's absolute power and his ordained power (*potentia absoluta, potentia ordinata*).[14] "For God has sealed His might in the order of the word; he who attributes other powers to God blasphemes His order and power, and suggests that God has not adequately demonstrated His power and glory in and through the order of His word." Baptism therefore requires a personal, not alien, faith. It is the order of God's word.

To Marpeck and Scharnschlager, baptism is not only a sign; it also agrees with the promise and co-witnesses to it. The outer action and the inner commitment are one thing. In fact, it is not a sign at all but rather one essential union with the inner. Baptism "is the external work and the essence (*Wesen*) of the Son." Baptism "is a portal of entrance into the holy communion or church of Christ." Only by it are believers "joined together and accepted into a holy church." Careful instruction in Christian faith has to precede baptism to ensure that the one baptized has full awareness of the gravity of the step being taken.

The two writers also laid to rest the ancient concern about original sin in the child: i.e., if the child was not baptized, original sin remained and the child therefore was condemned. "Original sin," they wrote, "is inherited only when there is knowledge of good and evil." Small children have no such knowledge and therefore "they remain in the promise of Christ until they can be instructed, and until they can believe, confess, and desire baptism." Further, "the proclamation of faith in Christ capture[s] the

---

13. Ibid., 187.

14. See H. Oberman, *The Harvest of Medieval Theology* (Grand Rapids, Mich.: Eerdmans, 1967), 41-43. Unbelievers live under the absolute power but believers under the ordained power of God.

knowledge of good and evil . . . under the obedience of faith, to leave the bad and to choose the good."[15]

It has sometimes been argued that, in contrast to the Reformers, Anabaptists adopted an optimistic view of human nature because of the emphasis on choice. But Marpeck and Scharnschlager, like Martin Luther, argued that only when faith arrives is it possible to choose.

They inserted a seventeen-page excursus on infant baptism and the arguments advanced by its defenders.[16] The issue for them was no twenty-first-century denominational difference, generously accepted by everyone. They understood biblical baptism to be a foundation stone of the church and infant baptism as the cause of much of the church's corruption.

> Infant baptism is the true beginning, ground, and root of the total antichristian regiment and realm, and an abrogation of the true covenant of Christ, and of His cross and tribulation, under which the treasure of Christ is hidden. . . . Infant baptism is an introduction to the realm of the Antichrist, a true and real entrance, beginning, door, and reason for its being, and an instigation to all evil and idolatry, which is maintained through his deceptive guise of Christ, a secure anchor to deceive the people. As soon as infant baptism were to be abolished, the disruption of the realm of the Antichrist would immediately follow.[17]

Without a personal, conscious commitment in baptism to live according to the example of Christ and exemplify the fruits of the Spirit, bonding Christians into the church, the church remained unprotected against the wiles of the antichrist.

The Lord's Supper

Marpeck and Scharnschlager then offered a relatively short treatment of their views of the Lord's Supper. The communion of the Lord's Supper, they wrote, "is a physical gathering of those who believe in Christ" and only for those who have been baptized and become part of the new covenant community. Believers eat and drink the bread and wine as a remembrance of the Lord.

Remembrance has two parts. First, "we believe and proclaim that the Son of God became man, conceived by the Holy Ghost in the Virgin Mary, conceived and born by the seed of the woman as a true, natural, earthly man of the lineage and seed of David. In death He has given His earthly,

15. Klassen and Klaassen, *WPM*, 206-7.
16. Ibid., 223-40.
17. Ibid., 219, 259.

natural life and body, and shed His blood for the forgiveness of our sins." The second part is the acknowledgment of the debt of gratitude and its direct consequence of love for one another. Not only that, but "through patience, we should show our love to all our enemies and also pray for them, even unto death."[18]

Discipline

If that love is not present and a participant shows a contrary disposition (i.e., not being in mutual peace), such a person should be regarded as an outsider until he or she repents and shows improvement. The authors were anxious to clarify that "we are not to be like those who maintain the ban, banning people from the face of the earth, seizing life and land, forbidding place and people. Such a ban does not belong in the Christian church." This passage describes the church discipline in the medieval church and among the evangelicals. Understandably, Anabaptists were always regarded by their secular and religious authorities as church members in error. What Anabaptists experienced as persecution was regarded by the authorities as church discipline.

The Meaning of Sacrament

In the opening section of the *Admonition*, there is a brief discussion of the word "sacrament." Marpeck and Scharnschlager defined the word in its basic meaning as an obligation sealed with an oath. It is an act that is carried out voluntarily. Baptism and the Lord's Supper are properly called sacraments because they involve an obligation, freely undertaken, to be of one mind and conduct with Christ. "The spirit of the action is more important than the elements which are used." More important for their view of sacrament was their understanding of the bread and wine and the water, the external elements, as participating in the spiritual action so that they became absolutely indispensable.

Community of Goods

In the discussion of the Lord's Supper, there is a brief reference to the community of goods in the early church. To this Marpeck and Scharnschlager added some reflections of their own, perhaps because they knew that the *Admonition* would be circulated beyond Appenzell to the Austerlitz Brethren in Moravia. The community of goods had become a mandatory feature of the Hutterite Anabaptists in Moravia, zealously enforced among Hutterites even to this day.

18. Ibid., 274-75.

Marpeck was familiar with and used the mystical concept of *Gelassenheit* (yieldedness). He wrote a tract on it which is lost.[19] The main feature of this concept was that the true believer surrenders all attachment to created things, especially to property. In *Exposé of the Babylonian Whore*, Marpeck states that adherence to property is self-centredness, which has no place in the church of Christ. Despite this severe judgment on property, Marpeck himself does not appear to have argued for community of goods while he was in Strasbourg. However, the Austerlitz Brethren, with whom Marpeck was closely associated, appear to have practised some form of the community of goods before 1535.[20]

There is no trace in the *Admonition* of Marpeck's earlier negative comments on property. Rather, Marpeck and Scharnschlager argue that the sharing of all things in common should be done voluntarily out of love and should not be required as a necessary part of church life. Moreover, they note that it was not practised by all the churches in New Testament times. "Among true Christians who display the freedom of love," they wrote, "all things are communal and are as if they had been offered, since they have been offered by the heart."[21] Neither Marpeck nor Scharnschlager lived communally, but they were strongly committed to sharing with those in need.

Nonviolence and Noncoercion

Finally, Marpeck and Scharnschlager introduce an important theme that runs through the whole treatise, identifying it as their work: that is, the nonviolent, noncoercive nature of the kingdom of Christ. Jesus Christ is the Lord and General and his host are heavenly, not earthly knights. The kingdom of Christ is timeless—unlike earthly kingdoms—and the weapons are not material but spiritual. "We fight as in the light and not with physical power, as do the rulers and lords of the darkness of this world." Throughout Christian history, the authors observed, there were those who

> wanted to fight with the physical sword, as if they were fighting, like the Jews, for an earthly kingdom or land. The Peasants' War and, after that, Zwingli's[22] and, now in the appearance of the true baptism of Christ, the Münsterites in Westphalia have done the same. . . . The kingdom of Christ is not of this world. Thus no true

19. Ibid., 554.
20. Packull, *Hutterite Beginnings*, 61.
21. Klassen and Klaassen, *WPM*, 279.
22. The Kappel Wars, into which Zwingli went as a combatant chaplain, and lost his life.

Christian needs to occupy or defend either city, land, or people, as earthly lords do, nor to carry on with violence, for such belongs to the earthly and temporal rulers and not at all to the true Christians. Those Christians who take up the sword will perish by the sword.[23]

Written for Lay People

Both Rothmann and the reviser-authors emphasized their desire to write as simply as possible because they were writing not for other theologians but for lay people. "We hope our effort will help the poorly educated find the truth."

The *Admonition* was published during the first half of 1542. The place of printing is unknown, as is the number of copies printed. As late as 1553, Marpeck was sending twenty copies of the book to congregations with which he was affiliated in Moravia. Two printed copies are known to have survived, as well as a handwritten copy in a Hutterite codex. Additional evidence of the widespread circulation of the *Admonition* comes from Heinrich Bullinger, a successor to the Swiss Reformer, Ulrich Zwingli, who noted that the Anabaptists carry it everywhere and almost "make an idol of this work."[24]

The book became an important basis for discussion among Moravian Utraquists, the mainstream of the Hussite movement in Bohemia, which had its roots in a rebellion against Rome after Jan Hus was burned at the stake in 1415 for advocating church reform.[25] The Utraquists had no direct ties with the Anabaptists but were led to review their understanding of the gospel and Christ's mission by reading the *Admonition*.[26] An Utraquist priest, Beneš Optàt, had some fundamental objections to Marpeck's theology, but he followed a tolerant path and made some compromises that led Utraquists and Anabaptists to work together toward a common goal: the renewal and union of Christendom. An official analysis of the *Admonition* by the Utraquists was carried out between 1556 and 1559 and is just now being studied and made available to scholars.

A Very Personal Feud

There is one historic irony concerning publication of the *Admonition*. Caspar Schwenckfeld, Marpeck's main theological opponent (see chapter

23. Klassen and Klaassen, *WPM*, 209.
24. Neal Blough, *Christ in Our Midst* (Kitchener, Ont.: Pandora Press, 2007), 106. See also Heinold Fast, *Heinrich Bullinger und die Täufer* (Weierhof: Mennonitscher Geschichtsverein, 1959), 140.
25. MacCulloch, *The Reformation*, 37.
26. Rothkegel, "Beneš Optàt, On Baptism and the Lord's Supper," *MQR* 79 (2005), 359-82.

6) and prominent spiritualist, became convinced that the *Admonition* was a direct attack against him. It wasn't, but Schwenckfeld took its criticisms personally and wrote a hefty attack against the book, skewing the theological agenda of the Marpeck group for the next two decades.

In 1540, Marpeck travelled to Ulm in south Germany not only to visit with Schwenckfeld but also to give pastoral care to his people there. His destination was Austerlitz to meet with the congregation there in his role as elder. But first he travelled north and stopped to visit Schwenckfeld, who had been forced by the Lutheran clergy to leave the city of Ulm and had found shelter in the castle of Baron von Freyberg at Justingen, perhaps 10 kilometres (6 miles) southwest of Ulm.

We are not given any reason for Marpeck's visit with Schwenckfeld. Perhaps he was trying to reestablish face-to-face contact with this fellow religious dissenter in the wake of their disagreements over the content of Marpeck's various publications. Marpeck demonstrated many times in his life that he relished vigorous discussion with those with whom he differed in their understanding of aspects of Christian faith.

During the 1540 visit, Marpeck and Schwenckfeld evidently talked about mutual acquaintances, one of whom was Wolfgang Sailer. A former roommate (*Stallbruder*) of Schwenckfeld's from his Strasbourg days, when they may have both roomed in Capito's house, Sailer had been a follower of Schwenckfeld but had then turned to Anabaptism, likely under Marpeck's influence. He later became a Hutterite and songwriter. Schwenckfeld complained to Marpeck that Sailer had neglected him.[27] Later in his travels, Marpeck met with Sailer in Austerlitz, and told him about Schwenckfeld's complaint. He also told him that the Lutheran theologians at Schmalcald had condemned Schwenckfeld's doctrine. Sailer then wrote to Schwenckfeld on June 4, 1540, about Marpeck's visit and reported what he had said about Schwenckfeld.[28] Sailer indicated that the theologians' condemnation of Schwenckfeld came as no surprise; in fact, Sailer had expected it to happen long ago. He suggested it might be time for Schwenckfeld to learn humility and to assess what the Lord was saying to him through these developments. Sailer's comments did not sit well with Schwenckfeld and may have helped set the stage for his increasingly acrimonious exchanges with Marpeck.

27. CS 7, Elmer Ellsworth Schultz Johnson, ed. (Leipzig: Breitkopf & Härtel, 1926), 163. See also Christian Neff and William Klassen, in *ME* 4, 400. Sailer's letter is translated by Victor Thiessen.

28. The text of Sailer's letter is not published in the *Corpus Schwenckfeldianorum*, although Schwenckfeld's reply is (see above CS 7, 163-67). However, a copy of Sailer's letter was obtained from the Woelfenbüttel Library by Joe Springer of the Mennonite Historical Library. Victor Thiessen translated the handwritten script cited here.

⤚

If Marpeck's journey was undertaken for pastoral reasons, it makes sense to imagine that after meeting with Schwenckfeld in Justingen, he had travelled to Strasbourg to meet with Anabaptists there. There may be evidence of a trip to Strasbourg in a letter written by Scharnschlager to those at Strasbourg indicating they had been given pastoral oversight by Marpeck. After Strasbourg he had made his way to Austerlitz, where he met with Sailer and other Anabaptists. His route likely took him from Ulm on a safe riverboat down the Danube to Moravia.

One of the people with whom Marpeck visited during his travels in 1540 was Magdalena von Pappenheim, a former Benedictine nun who led a circle of friends who had at first been drawn to Schwenckfeld but then became followers of Marpeck. Marpeck was also on friendly terms with Helene Streicher, the widow of an Ulm shopkeeper. Streicher had begun a correspondence with Marpeck, hoping to persuade him to Schwenckfeld's position. Several exchanges of letters between them followed Marpeck's visit to Ulm, with Magdalena providing postal services.

Marpeck's second letter to Streicher[29] was written early in 1542.[30] It sought to refute four arguments she had made that revealed her as a committed follower of Schwenckfeld: first, that Christ's humanity had been swallowed up by his divinity; second, the claim that the material and spiritual should be radically separated; third, the belief that Paul had not been sent to baptize; and finally, Streicher's rejection of a gathered church (meaning, no organized, permanent church community). The tone of the dialogue between Marpeck and Streicher is remarkable in the honesty that both display to the other. When Streicher says she does not belong to the Anabaptists, Marpeck replies with "Nor did Christ command you to do so. He commanded you to belong to Him alone" (in other words, simply to be a Christian). But Marpeck was blunt in his criticism of her perception of Christ (and that of other followers of Schwenckfeld).

> According to your boast, you know a proud, lofty, arrogant Christ, for whom poor folk are far too unimportant. Neither you nor your kind could learn humility or gentleness from them, but prefer to invent your own artistry. We have no other consolation but to put forward our poverty with all lowliness. . . . Alas, what a difficult thing, what a poor work, it is for you and your kind to recognize that Christ opened the eyes of the man who was born blind. . . . May God preserve his own from blindness.[31]

29. Klassen and Klaassen, *WPM*, 376-89.
30. Boyd, *Pilgram Marpeck*, 104, n49.
31. Klassen and Klaassen, *WPM*, 384-85.

Marpeck tried to explain Anabaptist simplicity to her, saying it is a biblical attribute available to all who open themselves to it. He invited Streicher to do Bible study as the Anabaptists did, thus highlighting a fundamental difference between the Schwenckfeld followers and the Anabaptists. In the Marpeck group, all people read the text and shared their understanding of it. In Schwenckfeld's, he told his followers what the text meant and how they should respond. Marpeck urged Streicher not to force the text, saying that the true meaning can emerge only when it is openly, freely sought. In order for Christ to be present when this stretching of the mind occurs, he said, you do not need many people. "Two or three" meeting in the name of Christ are enough to seek and find his will.

If the 1542 date for the letter to Streicher is accurate, we may conclude the controversy over these disputed points predates Schwenckfeld's reply to Marpeck's *Admonition* in mid-1542. The conflict seems to have begun in earnest with Schwenckfeld's arrival at the von Freyberg castle at Justingen, and prior to that, of course, in Strasbourg in 1530 and 1531.

After Helena von Freyberg received a copy of the *Admonition*, she also sent a copy on to Schwenckfeld, requesting his opinion on it. Schwenckfeld immediately assumed, even though the *Admonition* had been published anonymously, that it was the work of Marpeck and at least one other person.[32] Because of the similarity of its arguments to those in Marpeck's letter to Streicher, Schwenckfeld also immediately assumed that it was written against him, even though there was no indication in the book that it was.[33]

By August 21, 1542, Schwenckfeld noted in a letter to Magdalena that he had written a lengthy appraisal of the *Admonition* titled the *Judicium* (*Judgement*) at the behest of several brothers.[34] This work was never published because Schwenckfeld desired that it be used only in the circles of Schwenckfeld and the Anabaptists. A copy of *Judgement* was sent to Marpeck by a friend. An exchange of letters between Schwenckfeld and Marpeck then ensued, with Marpeck responding to Schwenckfeld immediately upon receiving the *Judgement*.[35] He complained that the treatise was unjust and that Schwenckfeld had perverted his views and interpreted them in the most negative way possible. Furthermore, he reprimanded Schwenckfeld for writing in a manner that benefited no one but created only vexation.

32. *CS* 8, eds. C. D. Hartranft and Elmer Ellsworth Schultz Johnson (Leipzig: Breitkopf & Härtel, 1927), 162.

33. Schwenckfeld's suspicion was also expressed in his letter to Helena von Freyberg on May 27, 1543, *CS* 8, 618.

34. *CS* 8, 161.

35. This letter is not extant, but its contents can be deduced from Schwenckfeld's reply.

Schwenckfeld's sharp response was dated September 25, 1542.[36] Anyone who had a healthy Christian understanding, he wrote, would see that while there was a lot of good in Marpeck's *Admonition*, it was confused and superficial. He advised Marpeck to abandon his practice of speaking about divine matters in terms of human wisdom, which, he said, Marpeck had wrongly called simplicity. This pretension, he charged, conflicted with Marpeck's aspiration to be one of the foremost Anabaptist leaders. Schwenckfeld offered to speak face to face with Marpeck, provided a place and enough time were available. Finally, he admonished Marpeck to reconsider and to think more carefully about the issues under discussion. Specifically, he asked Marpeck to read *Judgement* carefully alongside of his own *Admonition*, to respond point by point in writing to *Judgement* and send his response to him at the Justingen castle.

This exchange of writings and letters in August and September 1542 gives us a clue as to Marpeck's whereabouts during this period, indicating that Marpeck was present in both Ulm and Augsburg. Schwenckfeld's invitation to Marpeck on September 25, 1542, to meet personally for discussion,[37] and a repeat of that invitation four days later to come to Justingen, can make sense only if Marpeck were nearby. Another letter of Schwenckfeld's from September 27 reported that Marpeck had discussed the faith of the patriarchs with Wolfgang Musculus in Augsburg.[38] In May 1543 Schwenckfeld wrote to Helena von Freyberg, asking her to pass his letter as well as a summary of his *Judgement* on to Marpeck.[39] Since Helena was in Augsburg, this request could locate Marpeck there by that date.

Marpeck's initial reply to Schwenckfeld's request for a point-by-point response to *Judgement* came in 1544 in the first instalment of a herculean effort that occupied Marpeck virtually until his death. Known as the *Verantwortung (Response)*, the work attempted over and over again to stake out Marpeck's own understanding of the issues as over against the views of Schwenckfeld. As we will see in chapter 13, by the time it was finished, Schwenckfeld had long since tuned out, paying no more attention to Marpeck.

36. *CS* 8, 269-79.
37. *CS* 8, 277.
38. *CS* 8, 289. See also T. Bergsten, *Pilgram Marpeck und seine Auseinandersetzung mit Caspar Schwenckfeld* (Uppsala, 1958), 54-58.
39. *CS* 8, 681.

-12-

Seeking to Reunite Anabaptists

The unity of the church was very much on Marpeck's mind when he visited Austerlitz in 1540. In addition to visiting his people in the area, he also began to lay the groundwork for his efforts a year later to unite the Anabaptists in Moravia. Church unity was the theme of the first of his letters preserved in the collection of Anabaptist writings known as the *Kunstbuch*.[1]

Writing to Marpeck on September 27, 1542, Caspar Schwenckfeld noted that he had received a letter from Marpeck dated September 25, 1540,[2] with an address in the *Grauen Bund* (the Grisons), which was the largest of the Swiss cantons bordering on Tirol in the east and on the Republic of Venice in the south. The Reformation had been introduced there in 1526 as a result of a public debate between Catholics and evangelicals in Ilanz. Schwenckfeld's letter suggests that Marpeck had left his residence in Appenzell. All of that is confirmed by a letter written by Marpeck on December 21, 1540, from Probin, a small hamlet near Ilanz in the westernmost part of the Grisons. Ilanz lay on the Rhine River, some 175 kilometres (105 miles) south of St. Gall.

We are in the dark about the reason for this move from Appenzell to Ilanz or somewhere near there. Perhaps Marpeck had been sent there by the church in Austerlitz to give oversight to Anabaptists living in the area. He may also have gone to Ilanz to work with Leupold Scharnschlager on the

---

1. Klassen and Klaassen, *WPM*, 521-27. The authors were unable to refer to the critical English edition of the *Kunstbuch* because it was not yet in print at the time of writing.

2. Marpeck's letter was an epistle sent to Valentin Ickelsamer, one of Schwenckfeld's close co-workers. According to Ickelsamer, Marpeck argued that Christ, being human, could be tempted. Ickelsamer forwarded the letter to Schwenckfeld, which is why it took two years to reach him. See *CS* 8, 290, and appendix B, "The *Kunstbuch*."

Admonition, which was published in 1542. We know that Scharnschlager moved to Ilanz sometime in the 1540s and made it a base from where he taught and gave leadership to Anabaptists.[3] But there could have been yet another reason for Marpeck's journey to Ilanz. To judge from letters he wrote later, he had found his association with Anabaptists in Appenzell increasingly difficult because of their growing legalism, and he perhaps concluded that a separation would reduce the tension. There is no hint that he went to Ilanz for professional reasons.

The Treasure of Unity

Marpeck's December 1540 letter from Probin was written to his followers in Strasbourg, Alsace, and the Kinzig and Leber Valleys in response to a letter he had received from them.[4] It is also possible that he wrote with the memory of a visit to them earlier in the year.[5] The theme of the letter is the unity of the church, the treasure without which there is no Christian love. To make his point about love, he directed their attention to the Canticle, the Song of Solomon, and in particular the figure of the bride whose love unfolds in the beauty of the returning spring. The spring, Marpeck explained, represents the New Testament—the totally new season begun by the coming of Christ—in contrast to the winter of the Old Testament, the time before Christ.

"Unity," he wrote, "is the highest adornment of love. This treasure, unity, brings with it all other virtues and treasures, namely peace, joy, comfort in the Holy Spirit, as well as humility, meekness, temperance, modesty, knowledge, friendliness, endurance, patience, wisdom, perseverance, courage, and much else." He warned them not to be careless with this treasure of unity. "I do not write this to accuse you but to entice you to emulate the true and proper humility of Christ, that the innocent may not rise up against the guilty to insist on their rights, but rather to act like the Lord who in his innocence gave Himself for us."

The unity for which he was striving was based on love and all the wholesome virtues that are part of it, he said. It could not flourish in the winter of the time before Christ. The temptation to live in the old legal order, of which coercion was a part, was as real for Anabaptists as for other Christians. It was a theme to which he often returned in the years that followed.

3. J. Ten Doornkaat Koolman, "Grisons," in *ME* 2, 584-86.
4. Klassen and Klaassen, *WPM*, 521-27.
5. Boyd, *Pilgram Marpeck*, 102, n31.

~⌐

Early in 1541 Marpeck again travelled to Moravia, this time with the purpose of reuniting the Anabaptists there.[6] But before recounting what followed, we need to describe Anabaptism in Moravia. In the early sixteenth century Moravia was part of the kingdom of Bohemia. It lay in what is now the most easterly part of the Czech Republic, directly north of the Austrian capital of Vienna. In 1526 Archduke Ferdinand became king of Bohemia. He immediately launched an effort to force the pre-Reformation dissenting church of the Czech Brethren, which had widespread support in Moravia, back into the Catholic fold. But the Moravian nobility were very jealous of their autonomy and resented the king's interference in the status quo. However, recognizing that Ferdinand was king, they elected a governor (*Landeshauptmann*) as their representative and spokesman at the royal court. Some of the nobles had become Protestant, among them Leonhard von Liechtenstein, the lord of Nikolsburg in southern Moravia, just north of the Austrian border.

A Magnet for Anabaptists

This is where the Anabaptist presence began in Moravia. With the support of humanist Reformers in the Nikolsburg clergy, von Liechtenstein had invited Balthasar Hubmaier (who had been expelled from Zürich in March or April 1526) to come to Nikolsburg and lead the Reformation there.[7] Nikolsburg quickly became a magnet for other Anabaptists including Hans Hut and Lienhart Schiemer, who had been baptized by Hut.

The first split in Moravian Anabaptism took place there in 1527. A group under the leadership of Jakob Wiedemann separated from Hubmaier's Anabaptism, which was officially supported by the secular authority of von Liechtenstein. Wiedemann's followers refused to bear arms and were opposed to the use of government coercion in matters of faith. During the winter of 1528, Wiedemann and his followers moved north to Austerlitz, a distance of about 50 kilometres (30 miles). As discussed previously, Hubmaier was arrested at Nikolsburg in July 1527 by Ferdinand's police on a charge of sedition. He was burned at the stake on March 10, 1528, a scant two months after the departure of Pilgram Marpeck from Rattenberg.

The growing persecution in the Holy Roman Empire produced

6. Boyd, *Pilgram Marpeck*, 102.

7. Martin Rothkegel, "Anabaptism in Moravia and Silesia," in *A Companion to Anabaptism and Spiritualism, 1521-1700*, eds. John D. Roth and James M. Stayer (Leiden: Brill, 2007), 165-72.

waves of refugees heading for the relative safety of Moravia. Anabaptist communities formed in a number of places under the protection of the Moravian nobility. Between 1528 and 1533 there was a constant struggle over leadership in these communities, especially over the issue of property, according to reports in the *Hutterite Chronicle*.[8] The original community of goods under Wiedemann was an accommodation to immediate critical needs in the winter of 1528. It eventually became the distinguishing mark of a number of Anabaptist communities in Moravia under the leadership of Jakob Hutter, beginning in 1533.

By the mid-1530s there were a number of separate groups of Anabaptists, among whom were the congregations with which Pilgram Marpeck was affiliated at Austerlitz:[9] Eibenschitz, Nikolsburg, Poppitz (Popovice), Znajim (Znojmo), and Jamnitz (Jemnice). According to Jarold Zeman's research, there were seven of these communities, two of which Zeman was unable to identify with a name. Martin Rothkegel has noted the existence of these "Austerlitz Brethren," who called themselves "the fellowship of those who have entered into a covenant with God."[10] There were also "Swiss Brethren" in a number of places who were not always distinguished from the groups with whom Marpeck was affiliated. By the time Marpeck travelled to Moravia for his reunification attempts in 1540 and 1541, the Hutterites constituted the largest and most stable group of Anabaptists. Zeman identified Anabaptists in 185 Moravian communities.

The *Hutterite Chronicle* described in detail the schisms that plagued the Anabaptist communities in Moravia in 1530 and 1531. One of Marpeck's co-workers, Wilhelm Reublin, in 1531 wrote Marpeck a letter concerning these schisms, including details about the events in Austerlitz and the role of Wiedemann.[11] Those Anabaptists with whom Marpeck was associated were in small and scattered groups.[12] That being so, the settlement of differences was urgent if they were to survive at all. The growing strength of the Hutterite communities represented a temptation to the struggling fellowships of Austerlitz Brethren, with whom Marpeck was connected.

---

8. *Die Älteste Chronik der Hutterischen Brüder*, ed. A. J. F. Zieglschmid (Ithaca, Cayuga Press, 1943), hereafter referred to as *Hutterite Chronicle*, 79-131.

9. J. K. Zeman, "Historical Topography of Moravian Anabaptism," *MQR* 41 (1967), 40-52. The following numbers refer to pages in the article: Austerlitz (45-46), Eibenschitz (58), Nikolsburg (118), Poppitz (126), Znaim and Jamnitz (126).

10. Rothkegel, "Anabaptism in Moravia and Silesia," 186-89.

11. The letter was first translated into English by J. C. Wenger, published in "A Letter from Wilhelm Reublin to Pilgram Marpeck," *MQR* 23 (1949), 67-75.

12. Packull, *Hutterite Beginnings*, 137-38.

By 1541, six years had gone by since the Hutterite communities had begun to flourish under Jakob Hutter's leadership. It had not been easy. In 1531 Sigmund Schützinger and Jakob Hutter separated from the first such community of shared goods in Austerlitz, which was led by Jakob Wiedemann. As mentioned earlier in this chapter, Wiedemann's group itself had splintered from the followers of Balthasar Hubmaier. Hutter and Schützinger's group began again at Auspitz (Hustopeče), a short distance to the south. Among those who came with them were eighty to ninety Tiroleans who had come to Austerlitz from Krumau in 1528[13] (see chapter 5). The rest stayed at Austerlitz.

Marpeck's earlier visit to Moravia in 1532 was likely undertaken to mediate the schism about which Reublin had written. Marpeck had heard conflicting accounts of it from his compatriots who were now divided between Austerlitz and Auspitz. During 1533 a leadership struggle took place in the Auspitz community and Jakob Hutter emerged as the most prominent leader. Then, in 1535, Hutter and his supporters left the politically untenable site at Auspitz and moved to Schakwitz (Šakvice).[14] The community had a strong sense of identity partly associated with the practice of the community of goods. A number of the North Tiroleans who had come from Krumau had remained at Austerlitz, where Cornelius Veh was now a leader and Marpeck's contact man.

The *Hutterite Chronicle* of the day recorded a rather volatile episode of Marpeck's attempt at unification of the different Anabaptist groups. As the first stage of the attempt to reunite Anabaptists in 1541, Veh and several others travelled from Austerlitz to Schakwitz, a distance of about 60 kilometres (40 miles). Schakwitz at that time was a main centre of the followers of Hutter. It is important to note here that the account of what follows was written by Kaspar Braitmichl perhaps twenty-five years after the event. Braitmichl was a devoted follower of Hutter and a leader in the Hutterite community in later years. The incident is therefore seen belatedly and entirely through Hutterite eyes. We don't have a parallel account from Marpeck or someone sympathetic to him.

Veh and those with him were given a hearing before the whole community, but, as Braitmichl reports, "they did all they could to weaken some of the believers [i.e., Hutterites] and make them fall away."[15] This judgment conceals the potentially persuasive attempt of the visitors to propose a compromise on issues that divided Moravian Anabaptism, particularly on the central Hutterite conviction concerning the community of goods and likely

13. Ibid., 135.
14. Ibid., 224-25, 237.
15. *Hutterite Chronicle*, 210.

also on issues of church discipline. Both of these were issues of concern in Veh's letter to the Anabaptists in Appenzell and Zürich in March 1543.[16] Veh and his companions returned without having achieved their goal.

Arriving 'Full of Guile'

The Hutterite report on the visit of Marpeck is more extensive. He arrived at Schakwitz "soon afterward," which probably means after Veh's return and report of his reception. The *Chronicle* reports that Marpeck arrived "full of guile and intrigue" and that his stated purpose was "to gather and unite all groups that had split up over matters of faith."

The leaders at Schakwitz regarded his presence as very disturbing and disrupting. Why then did they even allow the people to assemble in order to hear Marpeck? Only a year before there had been a rebellion against the leadership, and perhaps refusing to hear Marpeck would have created only more dissatisfaction and insubordination.[17] What the leaders referred to as Marpeck's "slanderous talk" was likely his criticism of the lack of Christian freedom among them because of the coercion they applied to enforce the community of goods. Marpeck must have been very persuasive, because the meeting soon turned chaotic.

While Marpeck kept talking about why he had come and what could be done to bridge their differences, the gathering knelt down to pray. Marpeck wanted to join them but the leaders would not permit it because "he had poured contempt on them." He likely tried to explain that the New Testament evidence for community of goods as a mark of the true church was at best ambivalent. In 1531 Marpeck seems to have had some appreciation for community of goods, but by the early 1540s he had changed his mind. He believed that only the Jerusalem church had practised it.[18]

The local leaders orchestrated the meeting in such a way that Marpeck would be prevented from getting a genuine hearing, likely because they were afraid that some of the assembly would be influenced by him. There had been sufficient disagreement with the leaders in the last year or two to justify their fear.

Finally, unable to achieve his purpose, the *Chronicle* says Marpeck "became incensed and said openly that he would rather unite with the Turks or the pope than with this church, and he left in a rage." Marpeck obviously lost his temper. He had been able to keep control of himself in other settings when his views were challenged, but to be ignored by means

16. Fast and Rothkegel, *Kunstbuch*, 476-89.
17. *Hutterite Chronicle*, 198-99.
18. Klassen and Klaassen, *WPM*, 278-79.

of loud prayers meant to drown him out was too much for him. The *Chronicle* says that he stormed out, flinging at them the testy judgment that they were worse than infidels and papists. Fast was somewhat sceptical of this graphic account.[19] It's possible that descriptions of the event may have been embellished in the twenty-five years between the actual visit of Marpeck and the writing of this version of it.

Whatever actually happened, Marpeck seems to have made no further attempts at unity with the followers of Hutter.

His unsuccessful encounter with the Hutterites wasn't the first time that his anger got the better of him. As readers may recall, he snapped at Martin Bucer during the public debate in Strasbourg, saying "whoever calls on government is cursed" (chapter 9). And he lashed out at the Swiss Brethren, as we will see later in this chapter. Marpeck's temper was also referred to by one of his primary opponents, Caspar Schwenckfeld, who called him an intemperate and wrathful man.[20] Given the animosity between the two men, one might question the accuracy of this characterization of Marpeck. As for Pilgram's angry outbursts, we should note that there is recorded evidence of only three or four such incidents over the course of a lifetime. Marpeck was certainly known for his zeal. But given the stress that he lived under weighed against his success at building a community of believers and the fond devotion of his followers, he does not appear to be a "wrathful" individual.

Still Seeking Unity

Despite the failure of his attempted rapprochement with the Hutterites, there is no reason to doubt Marpeck's honest determination to seek a way of unifying the various Anabaptist groups. He understood that a first step would have to be to win the Hutterites over to his plan. Perhaps this is a question from hindsight, but was Marpeck not fully aware of the strength and numbers of the Hutterite communities by 1541? Did his own allies in Moravia, especially Cornelius Veh, not properly brief him for his venture into Schakwitz? Or did he simply attempt to do what he believed to be God's will, knowing full well what he was up against? We don't know, since he himself never referred to the event, and there was no post mortem report of it in the Marpeck community.

When it became clear that unity could not be achieved by negotiating with the Hutterites, Marpeck continued his work with the Moravian

19. Fast, "Pilgram Marpeck and South German Anabaptism," *ARG*, 233; also Fast and Rothkegel, *Kunstbuch*, 33, n86.

20. CS 8, 167. The same page lists many other insults and invectives that Schwenckfeld hurls at Marpeck and other Anabaptists.

Anabaptists, and together with his colleague Leupold Scharnschlager, completed work on the *Admonition* to try to foster the unity of Anabaptists.

In addition, sometime during 1542 Marpeck wrote a long letter addressed to "the Swiss Brothers." A companion letter is more precise and identifies these Swiss Brothers with the Anabaptists of Appenzell.[21] Heinold Fast wrote that these Anabaptists, among whom Marpeck had lived and worked for about eight years, occupied a special niche within the Anabaptist movement that had originated in Zürich and spread throughout Switzerland, south Germany, and Moravia.

According to Marpeck, the Appenzell Anabaptists distinguished themselves by their lack of capable leadership as well as their practice of harsh church discipline involving frequent excommunication. In other words, not all of the Swiss Anabaptists were censured by Marpeck in these letters but only those in St. Gall and Appenzell. As Arnold Snyder has shown, the Marpeck group and the Swiss Anabaptists were of the same mind on most issues. The division that had developed over leadership and excommunication was the occasion for the letter, and Marpeck expressed the hope that they would all soon be united again.

According to Heinold Fast's analysis, the letter appears to be composed of some previously written parts and some new pieces.[22] There is first the letter proper at the beginning and the end, and between the two parts of the letter there are twelve clear, distinct sections, each of which could exist separately. This could account for the considerable repetition in the letter, since the separate pieces are not identified as such, except two of them. Indeed, Marpeck refers near the beginning to "these my writings." On the other hand, all of them relate directly in some way to the central theme of the letter, namely the making of hasty, unconsidered judgments about the behaviour of members of the church.

The first section of the letter[23] is a ringing manifesto of Christian freedom from legalism and from what he calls *Eigentum*, that is, everything that is outside of Christ. The meaning of this term included actual things owned, but also social status, profession, reputation, and the fearful clinging to them. This freedom could be won for Christ's own by obedience to Christ, who established love as the fulfilment of all divine requirements. Here and many times throughout the letter Marpeck defended himself

21. These two letters are in Klassen and Klaassen, *WPM*, 309-61 and 362-68. Fast and Rothkegel, *Kunstbuch*, 200-36, 237-41.

22. The actual letter regarding the issues between him and the people he wrote to is at the beginning, 311-13, and at the end, 360 line 27, to 361 line 25, of Klassen and Klaassen, *WPM*.

23. Klassen and Klaassen, *WPM*, 313 line 29 to 323 line 3.

against a charge made against him by those to whom he was writing. His accusers, people who favoured harsh church discipline, felt that he had staked out this liberty of Christ too widely so that it became a cover-up for wickedness.

Christians are obligated to make judgments concerning unchristian behaviour, he wrote. But in doing so, they need to be considerate and to make careful distinctions. To make himself clear, Marpeck used the analogy of a plant with leaves that blossoms and eventually bears fruit. Summary judgments, including excommunication, should be made only when the fruit of evil is clearly evident and when that fruit is manifest unbelief. Until then, at the leaf and blossom stage, admonition and warning are the rule. Judging someone summarily for an instance of unchristian behaviour pre-empts the role of the Holy Spirit, who determines when that is necessary. Provision has to be made for growth and development. Marpeck viewed hasty judgments and interference in the work of the Holy Spirit as so serious that he called them the "abomination" spoken of by Daniel and Jesus; that is, putting oneself in the place of God. At the end of the letter, writing with considerable gentleness considering the gravity of the issue, he said that he was not certain in his conscience that he could be part of the practice of church discipline as exercised by the letter recipients.

While Marpeck was a champion of Christian unity, he was very emphatic about what, for him, prevented it. A section of this letter clearly staked out the parameters within which Christian unity was possible. These are the issues where Marpeck drew the line on church unity, determining the foundation on which it rests. These are his personal statements, what he and the church should tolerate and not tolerate. The letter is written at the same time that he and Scharnschlager were completing work on the *Admonition*.

The controversy with the Appenzell Anabaptists—and especially their charge that he was too easy-going in matters of discipline—forced him to declare very specifically where the limits of Christian faith were to be placed. It is worth quoting the whole section. The points are enumerated in the margin by Marpeck (or more likely by the copyist, probably Jörg Maler, who later copied the letter into the collection of writings known as the *Kunstbuch*):

> 1. I will especially avoid those who use the bodily sword, contrary to the patience of Christ, who did not resist any evil and who likewise commands his own not to resist tribulation or evil, in order to rule in the kingdom of Christ.
> 2. I avoid those who institute, command, and forbid, therewith to rule in the kingdom of Christ.

3. I also avoid those who deny the true divinity, Spirit, Word, and power in Jesus Christ.

4. I avoid those who destroy and deny His natural, earthly humanity which was received from man, of the seed of David, born without man's seed and sin, born of Mary the pure virgin; he was crucified and died a natural earthly death, from which he arose again, and has now seated Himself at the right hand of God.

5. I also avoid those who, living in open sin and gross evil, want to have fellowship in the kingdom of Christ but without true repentance.

6. I avoid all those who tolerate such a thing.

7. I avoid all who oppose and fight against the words and the truth of Christ. With all such, regardless of what they are called in the world, I will have no part or fellowship in the kingdom of Christ unless they repent. . . .

8. I also reject all ignorant baptism which happens without true, revealed, personal faith whether in children or adults.[24]

A Hostile Response

This letter and the following one may be an explanation for Marpeck's departure from Appenzell in 1540. The letter evidently produced a spirited and hostile response in which the writers complained that Marpeck no longer regarded them as a church of Christ. Apparently they also returned the charge, saying that they, likewise, did not regard him and his community as a church of Christ because his view of the liberty of Christ opened the door to no discipline at all. Yet in his letter of 1542, Marpeck nowhere specifically says that the Swiss of Appenzell are not a church of Christ. So either they read it between the lines, or they learned of his views in another way, perhaps by a letter not preserved. In any event, in the letter of 1543 Marpeck says so very clearly.

The 1543 letter is addressed to the brothers in Appenzell and specifically to Uli Scherer and Jörg Maler, both elders of the church. "We write you again," Marpeck began, "hoping that God in his mercy would grant us to achieve unity and communion in Christ."

His repeated use of the first person plural suggests that the letter was likely from him and Scharnschlager,[25] who, although we don't hear about him as living in Ilanz until 1546, could well have been there in 1543. The recipients were addressed as being zealous for God, which Marpeck regarded as a basis for hope that unity with them might yet be

24. Ibid., 332-33.
25. The letter may also possibly be from a Marpeck congregation (or Austerlitz Brethren congregation) that was distinct from the Swiss Brethren congregation in Appenzell.

achieved. He plunged right into the water of controversy and told them bluntly that by their slander and anger they had so grievously harmed themselves that they were close to destruction. But it got even more serious. Schism, he wrote, has three causes: false prophecy, lack of watchfulness, and lack of understanding—and the last one was the reason for this trouble. It was, he said,

> lack of understanding: ignorant, angry, hasty zeal for old customs, for blood relatives, for fellowship based on natural love, for one's own teaching, knowledge and understanding, which loves to puff itself up, and which causes communal strife before it has come to self-knowledge. Still, the law and fear of God is by nature written on their unclean hearts. Because of this, but still not washed from sin, they accept faith in Christ in baptism, discipline and the Supper without the accompanying work of the Holy Spirit, presuming in ignorant zeal to be teachers before they have become disciples of Christ. Such persons bring schism into the church of Christ. Nor may they be called a church of God in Christ. But one may be zealous and work for them with hope until they are brought to true understanding.[26]

Marpeck wrote in the third person perhaps to mitigate the sharpness of his judgment, but there can be no doubt that he was here describing what he saw in this Swiss Brethren congregation or in the Swiss Brethren generally, given that they were poorer and less sophisticated and lacked the educated leadership of the Austerlitz Brethren. We get a picture of a church community that was ingrown, self-sufficient, and having all the marks of a faithful Anabaptist community but presumptuous and unfree. Toward the end of the letter, Marpeck said that he and those with him justifiably excommunicated them because of their unjustified censoriousness and use of the ban. He had given them a clear reason for no longer regarding them as a church of Christ. They, on the other hand, had not given him a single reason for not regarding him and his as a church of Christ.

What, one may ask, gave Marpeck the right to issue such a scathing judgment on the Appenzell church, a judgment that apparently infuriated them? There are several good reasons for Marpeck's anger. First, he was speaking by virtue of his authority as an elder. In the letter of 1542, he wrote that once one is chosen as elder and having received the Holy Spirit, a status has been conferred that cannot be revoked.[27] He was thus speaking by

---

26. Klassen and Klaassen, *WPM*, 364.
27. Ibid., 361.

divine authority. But he also said that one must learn to understand how to use Scripture. According to prophets, apostles, and Christ, Scripture is used in three ways that should not be confused. It is used, he said, for teaching to instruct the ignorant, for admonition and warning, and finally, for bringing commandments and prohibitions. If these distinctions are carefully applied, he said, it will help avoid hasty and wrongful judgments.

Nevertheless, one could argue that the Swiss were justified in their anger against Marpeck. When Marpeck refused to acknowledge the Anabaptist communities in St. Gall and Appenzell as true congregations of Christ, he was abandoning his own primary rule about making hasty judgments. He repeated this rule in these letters over and over again, namely that one should wait for the evil fruit—outright unbelief—clearly to reveal itself and not judge according to leaves and blossoms. It appears that his extreme antipathy to legalism led him to adopt the course of action he so bitterly criticized in the Swiss. Or perhaps he was persuaded that he had already seen the evil fruit in the form of hasty and unconsidered judgments. If so, then he should have excommunicated those congregations, since he did allow for exclusion from the church in extreme cases.

Jörg Maler, who was to become an associate of Marpeck's in Augsburg and whom we shall meet again in chapter 15 in much greater detail, was part of the Swiss group of believers to whom the letters of 1542 and 1543 were addressed. Marpeck's comments evidently rankled him for years. In 1561, when he copied these letters in what became the *Kunstbuch*, he added glosses (comments) in the margin at a number of points.[28]

He actually put his finger on the problem in a comment to the 1543 letter. Marpeck had written: "Where judgement is perverted, all of God's action, bodily and spiritually, is suspended."[29] To this Maler responded: "It follows that it was suspended for the Romans, too. But Paul does not do that." Maler had in mind Romans 14:3ff., 10 and 13, which Marpeck himself had cited at this point. Indeed, if Marpeck had read, for example, the first epistle of Paul to the Corinthians more carefully in the heat of his censoring of the Swiss, he would have seen that in spite of all the troubles in that church, Paul never refused to recognize it as a church of Christ. The Corinthians were immature, quarrelsome, and wayward, but Paul never cut them off from the grace of God. Marpeck had ignored his own advice.

But it should also be said that Marpeck was better than his hasty judgments indicated since, like Paul, he never gave up on the Swiss. In his

28. Klassen and Klaassen, *WPM*, 333-34, 346, 357, 360-61, 366.
29. Ibid., 366.

letter to them in August 1551, he had left behind any bitterness about the Anabaptists of Appenzell and St. Gall. There was no word of them not being a true church. In fact, they were included with all others as subjects for his mature teaching.

When Marpeck called for Christian liberty without coercion he was concerned not only with repressive governments and their coercion of believers but also specifically with the actions of Anabaptist churches. He believed that among Anabaptists, above all, liberty should be preserved without the coercion of legalistic church discipline. He regarded such coercion, whether used by Catholic and Protestant governments or by Anabaptists in their own communities, as denying the Christ who had coerced no one, not even his persecutors, even though he had the power to do so.

Christ's refusal to use his power to dominate and coerce was a theme to which Marpeck returned frequently in his writings. Marpeck insisted that all who claim to be followers of Jesus should follow Christ's example in their relationships within and without their communities.

Differences over the Oath

Marpeck's letter of 1543 to the Appenzellers comes to an abrupt end without his usual signature. The pagination of the *Kunstbuch* shows that one page is missing at that point. The last sentence on the previous page reveals the subject of the missing page to have been a discussion of the oath. The last sentence before the missing page reveals that Marpeck held a position on the oath different from that of the Swiss Brethren.

As a public servant and civic leader in Catholic-dominated Rattenberg, Marpeck grew up with the practice of the oath as a standard part of sealing an agreement or affirming a relationship. The fundamental meaning of the oath is to call on God as a witness to what one is doing and in a sense to draw God into the transaction as a guarantor. Oaths made perfect sense in a society that believed that God alone could protect a person from false testimony.

When Marpeck became an Anabaptist, he joined a community in which the prohibition of oaths was taken very seriously. The Anabaptist argument rested on several passages of the Bible. James 5:12 declares, "Above all, my beloved, do not swear, either by heaven or by earth or by any other oath, but let your 'Yes' be yes and your 'No' be no, so that you may not fall under condemnation." And Matthew 5:33-37 states:

> "You have heard that it was said to those of ancient times, 'You shall not swear falsely, but carry out the vows you have made to the Lord.' But I say to you, Do not swear at all, either by heaven,

for it is the throne of God, or by the earth, for it is his footstool, or by Jerusalem, for it is the city of the great King. And do not swear by your head, for you cannot make one hair white or black. Let your word be 'Yes, Yes' or 'No, No'; anything more than this comes from the evil one."

The same year that Pilgram became an Anabaptist, those Anabaptists under the leadership of Michael Sattler met at Schleitheim and tried to come to a common mind about a number issues, including refusal of the oath. They agreed to take the words of Jesus literally, believing that people who are serious about following Jesus would have the kind of integrity that does not require an oath to reinforce a promise or a relationship.

Not all Anabaptist leaders agreed with the Schleitheim declaration. Among them were Hans Hut and Hans Denck, whose views were published soon after Denck's death in November 1528. Denck drew in part from Paul, from 2 Corinthians 1:23, "I call on God as witness against me: it was to spare you." Denck argued that Paul was swearing an oath in this instance. He also noted that to make a solemn promise—as one does in marriage or baptismal vows—has the same effect as an oath.[30] This text was published a month after Marpeck arrived in Strasbourg and almost certainly came to the attention of the Reformer Wolfgang Musculus when he carried on discussions with Marpeck and other Anabaptists.[31] Denck had been in Strasbourg and had debated in public with the evangelical preachers there about Anabaptist issues.

By the time Marpeck entered the debates in Strasbourg he appears to have decided he would employ a selective refusal of oaths, depending on their different categories—a position that would guide him for the rest of his life. As a result, he told the Swiss some years later that he would not be bound by their restrictions on the oath; rather, he would be guided by his own conscience.

We know that Marpeck had sworn the oath of citizenship required for his employment in Strasbourg.[32] He could not have gained employment without it. It appears that he did not, however, swear an oath to protect Strasbourg with force. He also apparently encouraged others in his community to decline such an oath, because both Martin Bucer and Jakob

---

30. Clarence Bauman, *The Spiritual Legacy of Hans Denck* (Leiden: Brill, 1991), 259.

31. Musculus, one of the finest biblical scholars of the Reformation, devoted a major treatise to the subject of the oath, published in 1533, two years after he had left Strasbourg and moved to Augsburg. It was soon translated into Dutch and became part of the Anabaptist and Reformed discussions in Holland and in Augsburg.

32. Boyd, *Pilgram Marpeck*, 58.

Sturm stated that Marpeck taught his people not to swear.[33] The same pattern was true in Augsburg, where he must have sworn an oath to become a civic employee,[34] making him an exception among Anabaptists.

We don't know what Marpeck wrote about the oath to the Anabaptists in St. Gall and Appenzell, because, as noted above, the page containing his statement was for some unknown reason cut out of the *Kunstbuch*. However, the one remaining sentence by Marpeck pertaining to the oath on the previous page reads: "Concerning your understanding of the oath on which we have adequate clarity from you, we cannot bind anyone's conscience nor put a rope around anyone's neck, nor are we able to submit our consciences to your understanding." He clearly disagreed with what he regarded as a position that was coercive.[35]

Marpeck distinguished the civic oath from the oath concerning religious faith. The rejection of oaths that Marpeck taught (and that the Strasbourg authorities concluded was sufficient to have him expelled from the city) concerned oaths confirming recantation and the *Urfehde*, the oath promising never to return.[36]

Debate over the nature of oaths continued throughout Marpeck's lifetime. Scholar Craig Farmer has shown that from 1527 to 1602, nineteen treatises on the oath were published by Reformation-era theologians representing all major groups and supported by all major confessional statements of faith, each of them seeking in one way or another to prove that the Anabaptist position (whether Schleitheim's or Denck's) was wrong.[37] Many of the treatises recognized that the issue of the oath helped create a major rift among various Anabaptist groups.

Once More on the Road

The early 1540s were a time of intense (and often futile) efforts by Marpeck to unite the fragmented Anabaptist community. Despite all the correspondence we have, it is difficult to establish Marpeck's movements

33. *TA: Elsass* 1, 521, 350, 360.

34. Ibid., 164.

35. Fast and Rothkegel, *Kunstbuch*, 237-31. Also, Edmund Pries, "Anabaptist Oath Refusal: Basel, Bern and Strasbourg, 1525-1538," University of Waterloo PhD dissertation, 1995, dealing with the various types of oath among Swiss Anabaptists in Appenzell and St. Gall. See also William Klassen, "Oath," in *ME* 4, 4-8.

36. In March 1529, the Strasbourg Anabaptist Lux Zymerman stated to the authorities that he was prepared to swear what was not contrary to God. Perhaps he was expressing Marpeck's position on the issue.

37. Craig S. Farmer, "Reformation-Era Polemics against Anabaptist Oath Refusal," *MQR* 81 (2007), 207-26. The article specifically looks at Wolfgang Musculus, Urbanus Rhegius, and Johann Faber, all from Augsburg.

during this period with any certainty. As we indicated earlier, it seems likely that he spent time in the fall of 1542 in Ulm and Augsburg. Based on the flurry of letters between Marpeck and Schwenckfeld in 1542 and 1543, it seems probable that Marpeck and Anna once again moved on, leaving Switzerland and Moravia behind. They packed up their belongings and headed for Augsburg in south-central Germany sometime in late 1542.[38]

38. The effect of Marpeck's controversy with Schwenckfeld was not limited to the immediate participants and the several women involved (see chapter 9). A letter by Schwenckfeld to Michel Sporer in Stetten, north of Constance, on February 21, 1544, reveals knowledge of the *Admonition* and Schwenckfeld's replies to it by Anabaptists in Stetten and in Esslingen near Stuttgart. Even then there were relations between the Swiss Brethren and the Marpeck circle beyond the links with the Swiss in Appenzell and St. Gall. These links became more extensive as time went on. Jörg Scherer, alias Jörg Wernlin, a physician, was a leader of the Swiss Brethren in the Esslingen area and a personal acquaintance of Pilgram Marpeck (see *ME* 4, 918).

-13-

Arrival in Augsburg

When Pilgram and Anna Marpeck arrived in Augsburg toward the end of 1542, they were entering one of Europe's oldest and richest cities. Augsburg had begun as a Roman settlement in the year 15 BCE. A century later it had a population of ten thousand, strategically situated where the rivers Lech and Wertach met. Named after the emperor Augustus, the city was the capital of the ancient Roman province of Rhaetia, which included Regensburg in the north and Chur in the south, roughly bordered by the Rhine River in the west, the Danube in the north, and the Inn to the east.

Augsburg became a bishopric in the eighth century. Two centuries later the present cathedral was built at the north end of the main street of the city. To this day it offers the oldest stained-glass windows in Europe, dating from about 1050. Like tourists today, Pilgram and Anna undoubtedly would have gone to see the cathedral and its historic windows. We need not suppose that just because it was a Catholic Church, they would have avoided it. Nowhere in his writings does Marpeck ever denigrate church buildings in the cities where he lived. It is important to mention this because many Anabaptists did precisely that, referring dismissively to the luxurious churches with their grand images and paintings as places of idolatry.

In 1316 Augsburg became an imperial city—meaning that, like Strasbourg, it became a self-governing political and social unit within the Holy Roman Empire. It sent its own representatives to the diets, the annual meetings of the representatives from all the political units of the empire. Most of those units—regions like Bavaria, Hesse, Saxony, and Württemberg—were ruled by princes who were situated in the imperial hierarchy directly below their common overlord, the emperor. There were also the ecclesiastical domains, such as the lands ruled by the archbishops of Augsburg, Cologne, and Salzburg. As bishops they were responsible to the pope; as rulers they were answerable to the emperor.

By the late fifteenth century, long-standing tensions between the Augsburg city government and the church led the bishop to relocate his official residence to Dillingen, about 65 kilometres (39 miles) north of Augsburg. This effectively left the city government in control of religious affairs within the city. Augsburg was governed by a "small council," headed by a mayor, and a "large council" composed of the small council and twelve representatives from each of the various worker guilds.

When Marpeck arrived in Augsburg, it was a Protestant island in a Catholic sea. Immediately to the east of the city lay the duchy of Bavaria, which through all the years had remained loyally Catholic. On the west side was the small county of Burgau, held by the Habsburgs. To the south, and north on the west side of the Lech River were the lands of the bishopric of Augsburg. Travelling to Augsburg from any direction therefore required crossing Catholic territories. Any one of the Catholic rulers of these territories could endanger the city's welfare by refusing passage of food and water. Although Augsburg was Protestant, a strong Catholic minority remained, composed mostly of old patrician families like the Fuggers, Welsers, and Baumgartners—all bankers—as well as some merchants loyal to the emperor and a few clergy.[1] Estimates of the city's population in 1544 vary between 35,000 and 50,000. Given its vulnerable location and its encirclement by potential enemies, Augsburg was a heavily fortified city surrounded by a continuous wall with seven ramparts and at least thirty-five defence towers, most of them on the east wall facing Bavaria.

Marpeck's previous moves to Strasbourg and Appenzell had been motivated partly by the presence there of Anabaptists. But that was not the case with Augsburg, whose early important Anabaptist community had been virtually extinguished in 1528. The Anabaptist movement had numbered in many hundreds, but the followers were regarded as politically unreliable and suppressed by arrest, imprisonment, and expulsion by the evangelical leaders of the city. The Anabaptist community reemerged a few years later but never again achieved its original numbers. There appears not to have been a functioning congregation in Augsburg in 1542.

In 1539 Helena von Freyberg had been allowed to settle in the city, and it may be that she was instrumental in bringing the Marpecks to Augsburg. It may also be that Marpeck had been looking for work there.

---

1. H. Immenkötter, "Augsburg," in *Oxford Encyclopedia of the Reformation* 1, ed. H. J. Hillerbrand (Oxford: Oxford University Press, 1996), 89; Immenkötter, "Kirche zwischen Reformation und Parität," in *Geschichte der Stadt Augsburg*, ed. Gunther Gottlieb, et al. (Stuttgart: Konrad Theiss Verlag, 1985), 401.

A position in Augsburg must have been waiting for him, because he seems to have begun work soon after he and Anna arrived. However, it appears that soon thereafter, he also began a period of intensive writing.

A Massive Work

Upon receiving a copy of Caspar Schwenckfeld's *Judgement*, Marpeck began to work immediately on a reply to it as requested by Schwenckfeld. Entitled the *Response*, Marpeck's work was laid out in a hundred statements and answers, with the statements in the form of direct quotations from the *Judgement* and the answers written by Marpeck.[2] As Pilgram passionately compiled his detailed treatise, the *Response* evolved into a massive work, totalling 518 modern printed pages! The ninety-sixth statement and answer regarding the Lord's Supper alone runs to eighty-eight pages. As a help to the reader, Marpeck thoughtfully divided it into five chapters. (A detailed summary of the *Response* appears in appendix A.)

The first part of the *Response*, sections 1-54, was completed by the end of 1543. Marpeck's accompanying letter is dated New Year's Eve, 1544, which is generally taken to mean December 31, 1543.[3] When we consider this date, it makes sense to conclude that Marpeck was already in Augsburg, perhaps as early as late 1542, and devoted a major part of 1543 to the *Response*.[4] He would have needed major stretches of time for the sustained work required of him.

A letter to Schwenckfeld[5] accompanied the first part of the work. Its themes are an echo of earlier exchanges between the two men. In the letter, Marpeck expressed his hurt and anger because of Schwenckfeld's put-down of his *Admonition* as confused and superficial. He was deeply offended by Schwenckfeld's aristocratic contempt and intellectual arrogance when he accused Marpeck and his people of being unlearned and ignorant.

Marpeck hit back in kind. He wrote sarcastically that Jesus himself was judged by his opponents to be an uneducated carpenter's son. He charged Schwenckfeld with "fabricated, carnal wisdom, reason, and self-selected spirituality." Schwenckfeld regarded Marpeck's concern for the importance of materiality as intellectually inferior, whereas Marpeck regarded it as foundational to his theology. Schwenckfeld assumed that

2. Rempel, *Later Writings by Pilgram Marpeck*, 68. Rempel calls the work a "first draft of a systematic theology."

3. Klassen, *Covenant and Community*, 48-49.

4. "Pilgram Marbecks Antwort auf Kaspar Schwenckfelds Beurteilung des Buches der Bundesbezeugung von 1542," in Loserth, *Quellen und Forschungen*.

5. Klassen and Klaassen, *WPM*, 369-75.

his doctrine of Christ's celestial glory was fundamental to true Christian faith, whereas for Marpeck it was unrooted and abstract when not combined with the physical man Jesus.

Marpeck insisted, as he did in the *Admonition*, that for ordinary, uneducated people there was need to write simply and concretely, and to avoid abstraction, which he referred to as artfulness, affectation, and sophistry.

Marpeck was genuinely dismayed by Schwenckfeld's attack on him in the *Judgement*. "I should never have thought it possible," he wrote, "that you would first write behind my back, and then accuse me to such an extent without having asked to investigate anything. You have previously discussed so many matters of faith with me, and yet you attribute such things to me." The offence was heightened when Schwenckfeld had sent his *Judgement* to Magdalena von Pappenheim.

Marpeck uttered the classic cry of the person who feels defamed. "Because you continuously add more untruthful accusations against me, and because you have composed and widely distributed an entire book of accusations against me . . . which supposedly indicate my beliefs about Christ my Lord, I am attacked by many. Therefore, I am forced to defend myself."

If it be God's will, he said, Schwenckfeld could confess his treachery and it might be forgiven. He then extends an olive branch. "I, too, heartily desire forgiveness for those times when, for His sake, I did too much against you or others. . . . If you can show me that I falsely accuse you of something, either in this matter or some other, you and others shall find my heart and mouth . . . open to confess and apologize, because we are all fallible and deficient persons."

Then, once again protesting his innocence, Marpeck said he would send a reply to Schwenckfeld to half of his *Judgement*. "Then you might see," he said, "that we are not as fearful of your writing as you believe when you suggest that we do not allow it to appear before our congregation and thus bar the good-hearted from knowing the truth."

Debate over Authorship

There is a debate among scholars as to whether the writings attributed to Marpeck were actually products of Marpeck and his co-workers or just Marpeck alone. We have already concluded that Scharnschlager assisted Marpeck in the translation and rewriting of the *Admonition*. The claim of multiple authorship of the *Response* is based mainly on the use of the plural pronoun throughout the work. This could simply mean that what Marpeck wrote represented the conviction of his whole group. But there is another argument for multiple authorship. The Zürich manuscript of the *Response* once belonged to Walpurga von Pappenheim, a niece of Magdalena. The manuscript was copied and "corrected from the original given by Marpeck to Magdalena." Notes added to the manuscript tell us that Marpeck had sent a copy of the first part to Caspar Schwenckfeld.[6]

A further note (presumably written after the death of Marpeck and many of his associates) tells us that the *Response* was offered to Schwenckfeld by "the late brothers." Their names are appended to the preface: Pilgram Marpeck, Leupold Scharnschlager, Sigmund Bosch, Martin Blaichner [Plaichner], Valtin Werner, Annthoni Müller, Hans Jakob, and other deceased brothers. The note does not claim that all these participated in actually writing the *Response*. They were the ones who offered the work as a response to the errors of Schwenckfeld, and one or several of them personally delivered it to Schwenckfeld. Finally, following the list of names, we are told that all these, representing the Marpeck communities everywhere, had given their approval to what was written.[7]

John Rempel has argued for the single authorship of this work by Marpeck,[8] although recently he has acknowledged that he is "less convinced" of his position than he once was.[9] Whatever the authorship, there is no question that the personal tone of the *Response* indicates that at the heart of this work it was a person-to-person polemic.

The first part of the *Response* was sent out quickly, with a sense of urgency. The reason for the haste, the text explained, was so that "our fellow believers and other true-hearted people would not be overtaken by these false, mistaken spirits, prophets and calumnists," and that those who had already been seduced by the arguments of the *Judgement* might be restored. As we have seen, Schwenckfeld received this work but never responded to it. Although part 2 of the *Response* was announced and produced, Schwenckfeld failed to respond to it as well.[10]

No firm date can be assigned for the second part of the *Response*. Work on it must have begun immediately. Because Marpeck was its author (or primary author), it must have been completed before 1556, the year of his death. Since Schwenckfeld never received the second part, it could be concluded that it added nothing new to their debate. But it also should be remembered that the whole work was written not for

6. Loserth, "Pilgram Marbecks Antwort," 174.

7. Ibid., 49-50.

8. John D. Rempel, *The Lord's Supper in Anabaptism* (Scottdale, Pa.: Herald Press, 1993), 103-4.

9. Rempel, *Later Writings by Pilgram Marpeck*, 19, n8, 1999.

10. Loserth, "Pilgram Marbecks Antwort," 174.

Schwenckfeld himself, but rather to help the Marpeck churches resist Schwenckfeld's teachings.

Schwenckfeld had a significant following in Augsburg, including members of the city's distinguished families. Thus, refuting Schwenckfeld with part 2 was very important. The authors had to make this refutation, they stated, even though they found the whole matter distasteful and would rather not have done it.[11] Schwenckfeld's view of the church continued to be attractive to Anabaptists because it made the church invisible: no baptism, no Lord's Supper, and no visible church structure to catch the eyes of the ever vigilant authorities everywhere. At the end of the *Response*, Marpeck put his finger on what he thought was the issue:

> [Schwenckfeld] wanted to be spared the true offence of Christ's cross and remain in peoples' good graces. He sees how they abuse, dishonour, mock and crucify those whom they call "Anabaptists" while he and his adherents are not greatly reviled or hated.

This was a serious charge and not altogether fair, but it illustrates the threat that, despite Marpeck's comments to the contrary, Schwenckfeld and his views represented for Anabaptists.

It is impossible to give a detailed description of the argument in the *Response* because of its length. The endless argumentative hair-splitting and the constant repetitions may be explained by Marpeck's compulsive attempt to clarify his position. He feared the persuasiveness of Schwenckfeld's reasoning. The unwieldiness of the work was also due to the unfamiliar intellectual territory into which Marpeck was venturing. The words of the Lord's Supper, especially, invited controversy over the ancient philosophical question of the visible and material as related to the invisible and non-material in human experience—questions as old as the philosophical enterprise itself.

Although he had written about these matters in his first published works, Marpeck continued to struggle with the vocabulary at the heart of his discussion; words such as *essence*, *sign*, *symbol*, *ubiquity*, *local*, *figurative*, and *sacrament*. The reader is left with a feeling that Marpeck continued to be uncertain about how to use these terms. Prodded by Schwenckfeld, who was more familiar with this territory, he tried again and again to clarify them and capture just the right nuance—but never quite succeeded.

Despite many years of tension between Marpeck and Schwenckfeld, a meeting between the two does appear to have taken place, perhaps after Schwenckfeld had received the first part of the *Response*. In a letter dated

11. Ibid., 429.

February 21, 1544, Schwenckfeld wrote about a face-to-face dialogue with Marpeck regarding the *Admonition*. In a second letter written years later (April 30, 1560, four years after Marpeck's death), Schwenckfeld said he recorded the dialogue because Marpeck had always accused him of inaccuracy. "I recorded all his words more or less."[12]

In the 1560 letter to Daniel Graff, Schwenckfeld summarized all that he saw was wrong with Anabaptism, focusing primarily on Leupold Scharnschlager and his associates, Marpeck included.[13] He noted that he had been dealing with the errors of the Anabaptists for thirty-two years,[14] which would date back to 1528 and the meetings he, Capito, and Bucer had with Marpeck and Kautz in Strasbourg. In the 1560 letter, he warned that the terrible state of the church could be a divine punishment for those who were "usurping the Holy Spirit" through their baptizing and trying to build a community of Christ. He singled out the many errors of doctrine and what he termed heretical views, which he said disqualified Anabaptists from being the church.

Marpeck never made any reference to the 1544 dialogue with Schwenckfeld, which was probably the last time the two ever met. Interestingly, the *Response* existed only in handwritten copies in the sixteenth century. It survived in three such copies, which may now be found in Zürich, Olmütz (Olomuc in the Czech Republic), and Munich. It was transcribed, edited, and finally published in 1929 by Johann Loserth.

Professional and Domestic Life

Despite all the time and energy Marpeck obviously devoted to the *Response*, much of his time in Augsburg was spent working as an engineer, first involved with timber cutting and transport, and later waterworks. Although Pilgram and Anna apparently arrived in Augsburg in 1542, the first official record of his name in the city books appears for work done on February 16, 1544. There he is referred to as "Baumgartner's servant," with payment for work "in my lord's forests." Baumgartner was the feudal lord of Hohenschwangau in the Alpine reaches of the Lech River south of Augsburg.[15] Thus, no sooner was he formally employed than Marpeck was off to supervise timber-cutting in the Alpine woods, and Anna Marpeck once more was on her own, having to organize a household in a strange city during the extended absence of her husband. She and Pilgram lived in a house just north of the church of St. Moritz, not far from the

12. *CS* 8, 862.
13. *CS* 17, 213-32.
14. Ibid., 217:6ff.
15. Boyd, *Pilgram Marpeck*, 134.

Interior of a sixteenth-century house similar to the Marpeck home in Augsburg.

modern Bürgermeister-Fischer Street. Nearby were the guildhalls of the weavers, the merchants, and the patricians.[16] It was a prestigious part of the city. The house, presumably rented from the city's paymaster (*Baumeister*), again suggests that Marpeck came with some financial means, or perhaps such a residence came as part of his employment.

In 1544 an influx of families had created a severe housing shortage, followed by rising rents. To meet the emergency the council decreed that from that date onward, only those who had acquired citizenship by marriage or by action of the council would be allowed to live in Augsburg, unless they had been working in the city for at least ten years.[17] The Marpecks must therefore have been granted residence rights along with Pilgram's professional appointment. They were registered residents (*Einwohner*) but not citizens. As such they paid no taxes, and Marpeck was not liable for military service.[18]

What might the Marpeck dwelling have been like? Pilgram and Anna occupied rooms in a bourgeois house, not a tenement. They likely had a bedroom or two, a living room, and a kitchen. Given that Marpeck spent a lot of time writing, he probably had a room with a desk and some shelves for books. We can presume they had a large, wood-panelled living room

16. Ibid, 136.

17. *Augsburger Stadtlexikon*, ed. Günther Grünsteudel (Augsburg: Perlachverlag, 1998), n378.

18. Boyd, *Pilgram Marpeck*, 136.

probably furnished with a solid oak table, a large cupboard for storage, and shelves on the wall for dishes and cooking utensils. According to the styles of the day, there would have been chairs and benches along the wall. The walls of such houses were up to 60 centimetres (2 feet) thick. The bedroom would have had a four-poster bed with heavy curtains for warmth, and a bedside table with some shelves above. Walls normally were papered in bright colours, and floors were wooden or tiled. The ceiling formed the floor of the upper storey, resting on exposed beams.

Entry doors of the time were narrow and opened inward. They were often decorated with intricate wrought-iron hinges and locks. There would have been several windows, likely quite large and deeply recessed because of the thickness of the walls. They would have been glazed with glass roundels set in lead, with a single opening leaf to admit fresh air in the summer. There were wooden shutters on the outside of the house.

The fireplace would have been situated in the living room with the chimney above. The base would have been brick, with andirons to hold the wood logs. In the chimney of such homes was an iron pot hanger which could be raised or lowered to adjust the heat for cooking, as well as an iron cooking-pot holder on a hinge that could be swung over the fire. On the wall near the fireplace were hung cooking pans with long handles. The mantle and the wall above it were normally decorated, perhaps even with a painting.

The Marpecks may even have had a calendar on the wall, since calendars had been in use for about a century. Such a calendar would have seasonal pictures above the name of the month. The days were lettered from "A" to "G" to determine Sunday, and saints and feast days were identified. The revolutions of the moon could be calculated and the signs of the zodiac appeared at the appropriate places.[19]

There would have been a bench in front of the fireplace where the Marpecks warmed themselves in the winter. A table would likely have been nearby so that when they ate, they sat with their backs to the fire. There were no toilets, but bedrooms of the time had chamber pots under the bed. Baths were taken in a wooden tub and soap was available. The house was probably serviced with cold running water. All lighting was with candles. Their diet probably consisted of meat and fish, eggs, dairy products, and bread. Salt and spices were important for flavour and for preserving food.[20] All of this was possible because of the professional salary Pilgram received from the city.[21]

19. Eugen Diederichs, *Deutsches Leben der Vergangenheit in Bildern* I (Jena: Eugen Diederichs, 1908), 43, n126.

20. Based on Fernand Braudel, *The Structures of Everyday Life: Civilization and Capitalism 15th–18th Century* 1 (New York: Harper & Row, 1981), 266-310.

21. Ibid., 187-226.

Ordinary wage-earners lived in much more crowded quarters, with fewer amenities and with much less comfort. In the summer they suffered from heat and in the winter from cold. Smoke from wood fires was a constant health hazard. The Marpecks had no personal acquaintance with poverty and the suffering it caused, except through Pilgram's work with miners and gardeners—an exposure that underscored his commitment to sharing a substantial amount of his own wealth with others less fortunate. The Marpeck home must have been a quiet refuge from Pilgram's public professional activity, as well as from the political storms that were brewing in the empire.

A Woman of Her Time

We hear nothing about Anna Marpeck apart from three references to her in Marpeck's letters and a mention of her attending a birth. Nothing ever "went wrong" in Anna's life; that is, she was never arrested. The arrest of Anabaptist women usually involved interrogation, which often produced information about personal convictions and activities. For every known story of an Anabaptist woman, "there are thousands of stories that cannot be told at all."[22] Anna Marpeck's life story is one of those. In the words of Robert Cleaver, a Puritan writer of the late sixteenth century, "The duty of the man is to be skilled in talk; and of the wife, to boast of silence."[23] His words describe Pilgram and Anna, who in this respect were very much people of their time.

Even though we have very little knowledge about Anna's daily life, we do know the normal responsibilities of women in her position. The wife's duty was to oversee the domestic household and order everything that related to its furnishings and conveniences. As the person responsible for procuring food, she likely would have made purchases of vegetables, fruit, meat, and spices at the market on the Perlachplatz, which was near their first residence. Anna also would have looked after the preserving and storing of food that was dried and salted. Perhaps she and Pilgram also had a garden plot to grow cabbages and herbs. She would have been responsible for preparing and serving meals. The purchase and sewing of clothing and bed linens would have occupied her time, as well, perhaps, as embroidery and other needle crafts. She would also have had the care of the household finances.

22. Snyder and Hecht, *Profiles of Anabaptist Women*, 8.
23. Robert Cleaver, 1598, in Joyce L. Irwin, *Womanhood in Radical Protestantism 1525-1675* (New York: Edwin Mellon Press, 1979), 79.

Interior of a sixteenth-century house similar to the Marpeck home in Augsburg.

Anna had a servant named Barbara Nagensenfftig, who would have been responsible for cleaning the dwelling, washing floors, removing ashes, cleaning the fireplace, and bringing in firewood. She would have assisted in other household tasks such as removing human waste and rubbish, which accumulated even in frugal households. Being people of means, the Marpecks would have been able to acquire manuals for managing a household as well as cookbooks and books on herbal lore that were published in Augsburg at the time by the printer Heinrich Steiner.[24]

A Conventional Marriage

What can we say about the marriage of Pilgram and Anna in the light of the almost total silence of our sources? As suggested earlier, Anna may have been one of a group of Anabaptist refugees who had fled from the lower Inn Valley to Krumau before Pilgram arrived there in February 1528.[25] The refugees came from the same area of Tirol and may even have known each other before their flight. They shared a common ethnic heritage and language. We have no reason to think that the Marpeck marriage was anything but conventional for its time. The husband was the head of the household and the wife obeyed the husband.

24. Josef Bellot, "Humanismus-Bildungswesen-Buchdruck und Verlagsgeschichte," in *Geschichte der Stadt Augsburg*, ed. G. Gottlieb, et al. (Stuttgart: Konrad Theiss Verlag, 2nd ed., 1985), 346.
25. Packull, *Hutterite Beginnings*, 135.

But we do need to place the marriage of Anabaptists within the context of an enormous change in the view of marriage brought on by the Reformation. Protestants had all rejected the Catholic teaching of marriage as a sacrament, a rejection with which Anabaptists certainly agreed. Protestants viewed marriage as a holy estate and eventually agreed that its legitimacy was based in civil law. They therefore created marriage courts to regulate it.

Anabaptists, however, developed the view of marriage as "a covenantal relationship between a man and a woman as freely consenting and fully responsible members of the conventicle of the faithful." It was more than the Protestant view of marriage as a hedge against sexual chaos, because it was regarded as "a direct expression and result of redemption and salvation."[26] This view made Anabaptists as concerned as Protestants with the quality of marital relations. Protestant writing on marriage and what it should ideally be, based as it was on the admonitions in the New Testament, would therefore also be descriptive of Anabaptist marriages of the time.

There were manuals on Christian marriage available during the sixteenth century, such as ones written by the Zürich reformer Heinrich Bullinger in the 1540s and, as mentioned, the English Puritan Robert Cleaver in 1598. Although Cleaver wrote long after the death of the Marpecks, his concise words may serve to describe some features of a Christian marriage in the 1550s. The husband, he wrote, should guard and govern his wife, admonish and instruct her, but should never "lay violent hands on her."[27] A woman could legitimately leave her house for four reasons:

> First, to come to holy meetings, according to the duty of godliness. The second, to visit such as stand in need as the duty of love and charity do require. The third, for employment and provision in household affairs committed to her charge. And lastly, with her husband, when he shall require her.[28]

None of these rules would conflict in any way with the Anabaptist view of the covenanted marriage relationship. The few hints we have of the Marpecks' marriage—again, Marpeck refers to Anna in his letters three times—point to a stable, loving relationship between the two. As we saw earlier, Pilgram once refers to Anna as "my Andle," a loving diminutive; once as his matrimonial sister Anna, an expression of the covenantal rela-

---

26. Thomas M. Safley, "Marriage," in *Oxford Encyclopedia of the Reformation* 3 (New York: Oxford University Press, 1996), 20.
27. Irwin, *Womanhood*, 78.
28. Ibid., 82.

tionship referred to above; and once as "my Anna," which suggests intimacy.[29] The information is meagre, but what there is reflects Marpeck's affection for and commitment to Anna.

Was Anna literate? Perhaps so, seeing that many Anabaptist women learned to read so that they could have access to the Scriptures themselves. Her own Anabaptist convictions were never challenged. Even if she had not shared Pilgram's faith, the authorities most likely would have interrogated her about him, as they normally did. There is no indication that she did not participate in Anabaptist meetings, especially since the Marpeck home was one of the meeting places for Anabaptists in Augsburg.

Anabaptist Midwives

The most interesting snippet of information we have about Anna is that she might possibly have been a midwife in Augsburg. According to testimony given in 1562 by a woman named Kunigunda, wife of Hans Jakob Schneider, a leader in the Marpeck community in Augsburg, Anna was present at the delivery of Kunigunda's babies.[30] It's not clear whether she was the attending midwife or there as a friend. (It was common for women friends and relatives to gather for the birthing process.) Whatever Anna's situation, it's worth noting that there appear to have been a large number of midwives among the Anabaptists in both Augsburg and Strasbourg.[31]

Anabaptist women needed to be able to trust a midwife to be sure that she would not baptize an infant if the child appeared to be near death. For Catholics and Protestants, it was essential for a child to be baptized to be certain that he or she would get to heaven. In the fifth century, Augustine had declared that infants who die without baptism were consigned to hell. By the thirteenth century, church theologians began to suggest that such children would instead go to "limbo," a place where unbaptized babies were deprived of the vision of God but did not suffer because they did not know what they were deprived of. Whether they were fearful of limbo or hell, the vast majority of Christians during Marpeck's time believed it was essential for a sickly infant to be baptized if it looked as if the baby might die.

Thus, a midwife or any other layperson had the power to baptize a baby immediately if the child was at risk. In fact, a pamphlet entitled *An*

29. Klassen and Klaassen, *WPM*, 416, 426, 483.

30. Friederich Roth, *ARG* 4, 1547-1555 (Munich: Theodor Ackermann, 1911).

31. William Klassen, "Midwives," in *ME* 5 (Scottdale, Pa.: Herald Press, 1990), 584-85. For further information on midwives, see also Merry E. Wiesner, *Working Women in Renaissance Germany* (New Brunswick, N.J.: Rutgers State University Press, 1986), especially 55-62 and 188-89.

Instruction for Midwives, How they are to baptize in an emergency, was circulated during the latter part of the sixteenth century, partly as an attempt to counter the ridicule of Anabaptists who made fun of emergency baptism.[32]

Anabaptists believed all children would go to heaven even though they weren't baptized. To prevent emergency baptisms, they began to encourage Anabaptist women to become midwives. They wanted to do everything possible to ensure that baptism occurred only when persons reached the age of informed consent, in their teens or adulthood. Anabaptist midwives were even encouraged to lie: to say that they had indeed baptized a deathly ill baby when in fact they hadn't, in order to protect the parents and themselves from retribution by authorities.[33]

On September 25, 1554, midwives were ordered by the Augsburg city council to report every neglect of baptism and bring it to the attention of the council.[34] If Anna was practising midwifery at the time, she and other Anabaptist midwives would have felt intense pressure to change their ways. It is a testimony to the courage of these women that, even under threat of prison or exile, most appear to have held true to their beliefs and steadfastly refused to baptize the infants they delivered.

Interestingly, the question of what happens to infants and children who die continues to be debated to this day. In April 2007, the Vatican's International Theological Commission issued a document declaring that, after several years of study, it had concluded that the concept of limbo reflects an "unduly restrictive" view of salvation.[35] Reflecting a significant shift from Marpeck's time, the commission said "there were serious theological and liturgical grounds for hope that unbaptized infants who die will be saved and enjoy the beatific vision." But speaking cautiously, it added, "We emphasize that these are reasons for prayerful hope, rather than grounds for sure knowledge."

32. Klassen, Ibid.
33. Klassen, Ibid.
34. Council decree in Roth, *ARG* 4, 618, n17.
35. John Thavis, "Limbo teaching a 'restrictive view of salvation,'" *The Catholic Register*, Toronto, May 6, 2007, and at www.catholicregister.org/content/view/670/849/.

-14-

Daughters Shall Prophesy

The quiet but stubborn defiance of authority by Anabaptist midwives is but one indication that we should not assume all Reformation-era women were quiet homemakers. Nor should we assume that Marpeck's relationship to women typified that of other men of his time. During Marpeck's life, for example, there was disdain, especially among intellectuals, for "old women." Johan Fabri, whom we encountered in chapter 3 as an advisor to Ferdinand and Cardinal Lang, criticized Martin Luther in 1520 because he "pays little heed when he scatters his teaching, so that every old woman on the street knows what Luther proclaims."[1]

Arnold Snyder has written that the degree of equality between men and women in Anabaptism hovered between complete inequality and total equality. "While Anabaptist women usually were not 'equal' to men in terms of 'official leadership roles' within the movement," he says, "they did experience far more freedom of choice than was the social norm, especially in the earlier more pneumatic stages of Anabaptist development."[2] Women were actively involved in virtually all aspects of the life of the movement. Even in the small Anabaptist community of Augsburg, there were ten women who were considered by their group to be heads of households. Perhaps their husbands had died or been killed, or perhaps the women had been forced to flee to a safer town, as happened to Marpeck's

---

1. The quote is taken from a letter by Johan Fabri (then called Faber) to his friend Joachim Vadian, a leading Reformer in St. Gall. (See Herbert Immenkötter, "Johann [sic] Fabri," in *Theologische Realencyclopedie* 10: 784-88.) Fabri is also the Catholic theologian who took the notorious 1487 proclamation against witches, the *Malleus maleficarum*, and in 1520 transformed it into the *Malleus in haeresim Luth-eranam*, to use against Lutherans (see chapter 3).

2. Snyder and Hecht, *Profiles of Anabaptist Women*, 9.

close associate Helena von Freyberg, whom we shall meet in more detail later in this chapter.

Marpeck in his earliest writings noted that women were among the earliest disciples commissioned by Jesus. He and other Anabaptists also drew inspiration from the biblical passage "your sons and daughters shall prophesy" (Joel 2:28 and Acts 2:17) and from Acts 21:9, which gives stirring examples of prophesying by the four daughters of Philip.

Anabaptists were also influenced by a number of outspoken women whose names and publications became known throughout much of German-speaking Europe. They were part of what some might call a sixteenth-century liberation movement that began when women started reading the Bible and classical texts for themselves, often in small groups in each other's homes.[3] Encountering the Bible in their own language, some of them for the first time, they came to the conclusion that the Holy Spirit could touch women as well as men and could give them the courage and freedom to speak.

Argula von Grumbach was one such person whose story could well have made an impact on Pilgram and Anna and their associates. Born to a prominent family in the Bavarian nobility, Argula was given a copy of the Coburg Bible in German at age ten. She first came into public view in 1523 when she took on the establishment of the University of Ingolstadt for what she considered gross mistreatment of a young scholar accused of Lutheran ideas.[4]

The confrontation began when eighteen-year-old Arsacius Seehofer was arrested in a series of clumsy efforts by the Bavarian authorities to stamp out Lutheranism. On September 20, 1523, von Grumbach wrote a letter of protest to the university, asking that a debate be held in German. "You lofty experts," she fumed, "nowhere in the Bible do I find that Christ, or his prophets, put people in prison, burned or murdered them, or sent them into exile."[5] She warned university officials that if they tried to silence her, other women would take up the pen and the university would become a laughing stock. Her call for a debate was either ignored or rejected. A furious Argula then gathered townsfolk together and read

3. Silke Halbach, "Argula von Grumbach als Verfasserin reformatorischer Flugschriften," in *European Highschool Writings, Series 23, Theology 468* (Frankfurt, 1992).

4. See *Argula von Grumbach, A Woman's Voice in the Reformation*, ed. Peter Matheson (Edinburgh: T & T Clark, 1995). Also, Susan Karant-Nunn, "Grumbach, Argula von," in *Oxford Encyclopedia of the Reformation* 2 (New York: Oxford University Press, 1996), 199.

5. Matheson, *Argula von Grumbach*, 102.

her letter in the public square—an action that historian Peter Matheson describes as one of the first "modern media events."[6]

According to Matheson, the Ingolstadt theologians responded by attempting to tame the "silly bag." Their efforts proved fruitless. Von Grumbach's letter began circulating as a pamphlet that eventually went through fourteen editions! Matheson notes that the last ten editions became "information packs" containing the pamphlet and Seehofer's propositions, which had been condemned by the university, as well as an introduction by the well-known preacher Balthasar Hubmaier. Argula then began a letter-writing campaign to some of the leading princes of the empire, calling for reform and an end to censorship and coercion. Her first pamphlet was followed by seven other writings.

As her fame grew, so did the epithets against her. Soon she was labelled a "female desperado," a "shameless whore," a "heretical bitch," and a "wretched and pathetic daughter of Eve." Thus, what began as a private criticism soon became a cause célèbre. Matheson estimates that thirty thousand copies of her eight writings circulated throughout the Holy Roman Empire in just two years. There is little doubt that the people of Tirol, located next to Bavaria, would have been among the first to become acquainted with her challenge to authority. Among them would have been Marpeck and his family friend, Helena von Freyberg.

Another influential woman of the time was Ursula von Weydin, who in 1524 published *Against the Unchristian Writings and Accusations of an Abbot Simon*. In the book, von Weydin describes herself as a "well-grounded Christian writing about the Divine Word and married life."

Citing Matthew 10, von Weydin declared that a woman has a duty to speak out. The specific text to which she was referring was probably Matthew 10:19, "When they hand you over, do not worry about how you are to speak or what you are to say; for what you are to say will be given to you at that time." It's a verse that both von Weydin and von Grumbach said applied to women as well as men. (Argula admitted that for a time she had tried "to be silent" as Paul had urged the women of Corinth, but she had found it unbearable.)

With biting irony, Ursula von Weydin suggested that if the clergy didn't wish to get educated, they might consider turning the task of preaching over to milk maids, many of whom knew the Bible better than they did.[7] She knew she was thwacking a hornets' nest. "I know very well that for a

6. Ibid.
7. The similarities between this comment by von Weydin and the writings of Erasmus suggest that one probably had read the other; see Erika Rummel, ed., *Erasmus on Women* (Toronto: University of Toronto Press, 1996).

woman to reprove such bigwigs will be seen as ludicrous and a waste of time. Yet I know that Christ has addressed Matthew 10 to me as much as to any bishop," she asserted. "To remain silent would be to make one-self accountable before God for their follies."

A Tirolean Noblewoman

Such outspoken writing doubtless had a strong influence upon the Tirolean noblewoman Helena von Freyberg, who was in her late thirties when von Weydin and von Grumbach began speaking out. Several years later von Freyberg would become a leader in the Anabaptist movement and a lifelong associate of Pilgram Marpeck. In fact, Helena could well have been responsible for encouraging Pilgram and Anna to move from Appenzell to Augsburg.

The ties between Marpeck and von Freyberg go back to their shared roots in the Tirol. Helena von Münichau was born about 1491, about four years earlier than Pilgram, in her family's feudal castle near Kitzbühel, not far from Marpeck's home community of Rattenberg. In 1491 Helena's father, Gilg, bought mining and grazing rights from Pilgram's father, Heinrich. Thus, as Linda Huebert Hecht observes, the family connection between the Marpecks and the lords of Münichau had been well established one genera-tion before Pilgram and Helena became members of the same Anabaptist congregation.[8]

By 1506 Helena had married Onophrius von Freyberg, a Bavarian nobleman. Beginning in 1508, she gave birth to four sons. Nothing is known about her until 1523, when she took up residence in her family's Münichau Castle in the spectacular Inn Valley foothills of the Alps. As we saw in chapter 2, there were many reform-minded clergy (including Jakob Strauss and Stefan Castenbaur) preaching in the valley by 1526. By the end of 1527 Helena was welcoming Anabaptists to her castle and soon became converted to the gospel they preached. She and all her domestic help were rebaptized, although her husband and sons were not. He became a Lutheran and continued to dwell in his own family castle in Bavaria.[9]

Early in 1528 the goings-on at Münichau Castle became known to the authorities in Innsbruck, who said she was "the primary cause of so many people joining this movement."[10] In spite of the mortal danger to those involved, the castle had become a refuge for persecuted Anabaptists.

8. Hecht, "Helena von Freyberg of Münichau," *Profiles of Anabaptist Women*, 125.

9. Ibid.

10. Ibid., 138, n19.

The family castle of Helena von Freyberg in Kitzbühel, Austria.

Helena apparently became head of the local Anabaptist congregation, and as such fearlessly visited thirty-six Anabaptists who had recanted in prison in July 1528. She supported the growing movement by assisting its leaders and providing financial help to the persecuted.

In 1529 an order was issued for her arrest. By this time, sixty-six Anabaptists had been executed in the area of Kitzbühel alone.[11] Helena's position in society could no longer save her. Soldiers came to arrest her at her family castle in Münichau. When it was clear that she had already fled, they tried unsuccessfully to find her at her husband's castle at Hohenaschau. She had escaped first to Bavaria (possibly her husband's castle), then returned to Tirol, and finally to a house she owned in Constance early in 1530.

In Constance she encountered Ambrosius Blaurer, a Zwinglian reformer and strong opponent of Anabaptism. It was probably through Helena that Ambrosius's sister, Margaret Blaurer, became acquainted with the writings of Pilgram Marpeck, much to the alarm of her brother. As we saw in chapter 8, Margaret discussed these writings at length in her correspondence with Martin Bucer, the leading evangelical clergyman of Strasbourg. Margaret and Helena may also have had contact with Marpeck himself after his expulsion from Strasbourg in 1532. It is quite possible that Ambrosius, a city patrician of considerable influence in Constance, helped

11. Ibid., 127.

turn leading Protestants of the town against Helena because of her association with Marpeck and her continuing advocacy of Anabaptism. She was expelled in 1532 and her house confiscated.

Meanwhile, friends and family of Helena interceded with Ferdinand, and she was offered a rare pardon on the condition that she would renounce her Anabaptist views. Ferdinand also assured her that she could return to her castle near Kitzbühel if she acceded to his demands. By the end of 1533, after a long struggle and many efforts to avert the archduke's demands, she decided to recant. She may have agreed to do so thinking that she could utter the words, get the recantation over with, and then resume her Anabaptist life. Such an approach was not unheard of among those who suffered religious persecution, although it was rejected by many Anabaptists.

The process of recantation was meant to involve as much public humiliation as possible in an effort to discredit the confessors and their illegal faith. Since she was such a notable social figure and had been so influential in the Anabaptist movement in the area, Helena was ordered to make a public recantation in the Kitzbühel parish church. The authorities hoped her public confession would weaken the resolve of other Anabaptists and lead to more recantations. She appealed against a public recantation, knowing how badly it would reflect on the movement and her family's reputation. With the help of the local Innsbruck government representative, Helena finally was given the right to a private recantation before a lower government official in Innsbruck.[12]

Late in 1534 she recanted "with loud clear words" that she was departing from her state of error, and swore the required oath. She left Tirol immediately, never to return. Why she left remains a mystery. It's possible she didn't feel safe, despite Ferdinand's assurances. The experience of others had taught her to be careful. Whatever the cause, it must have been a heart-rending departure for her, leaving not only her traditional family home but also, as far as we know, any chance to be with her husband and sons. In 1535 she moved to Augsburg, where she immediately turned her back on her recantation and once again became an active member of an Anabaptist fellowship.

Although Helena lived in Augsburg for most of the time between 1535 and 1545, initially she had little peace there. Anabaptism in Augsburg had been successfully suppressed for the most part by 1532. It survived only among a small group of believers who occasionally gathered in the homes of members or in the woods outside the city.

12. Hecht, *Profiles of Anabaptist Women*, 128.

Soon after her arrival, Helena was arrested for reportedly hosting Anabaptist meetings in her house and was interrogated on April 11, 1535. In her testimony she reported that she had visited and eaten with the evangelical clergymen Bonifacius Wolfart and Michel Keller, as well as with the mayor (a Dr. Wolf), and Georg Regel, all of whom were leading citizens of Augsburg and each of whom had come to her residence. Wolfgang Musculus, whom we first met in Strasbourg where he had come to know Marpeck and Schwenckfeld, also took time to meet with Helena after his move to Augsburg.

The clergy came calling with more than just friendly discussions in mind. Wolfart and Keller had both been given the paid assignment by city council to seek recantations from Anabaptists. Their visits were closely related to the interrogation of Jörg Maler in April 1535. Maler, who later became a major figure in Anabaptism as the compiler of the *Kunstbuch*, was interrogated just four days before Helena herself was arrested. It may well have been Maler's reference to her while he was being tortured that caused authorities to bring her in for questioning.[13]

Imprisoned and Exiled

Helena said in her testimony that she was not aware she had done anything wrong. However, if she could be shown that she was in error, she was ready to be instructed. She did admit that she had been rebaptized in Bavaria. However, she said, no one had been baptized in her house in Augsburg, carefully adding that she knew of no brothers and sisters (i.e., Anabaptists) except those in prison who had been arrested with her. (It was illegal to perform adult baptism in Augsburg, but not illegal to have been rebaptized elsewhere.) There were indeed meetings in her house, she admitted, but they involved only a few brothers at a time talking about the Word of God.

On April 13, 1535, she was imprisoned overnight in irons and expelled from the city the next day.[14] There is no hint of where she went, since the records about her are silent until January 1539, when two of her sons, both knights, wrote a letter to the Augsburg city council pleading the case of their "beloved mother."[15] Citing "her miserable plight" and the persecution she had endured, they observed that Helena had experienced difficulty in returning to her husband, "an old man who has almost come to the end of

13. Fast and Rothkegel, *Kunstbuch*, 698.
14. Roth, *ARG* 2, 422, 427.
15. Letter written by Panngratz and Christoff Georg von Freyberg, signed and dated at Aschau January 3, 1539. Taken from Roth, *ARG* 3, appendix ii, 427-28, trans. January 7, 2005.

Kitzbühel, home of Helena von Freyberg and where Marpeck delivered silver ore.

his life." She had been unable to return to their home, even though she desired to do so, "to spend the few remaining days of her life with him."

Appealing to the city council's "generosity and wisdom as a renowned lover of the word of God," her sons asked the council to persevere in its generosity with their mother and to let her live in Augsburg once again. "We are fully convinced that . . . she has lived in a Christian manner and carried herself well and will also do so in the future, which we assume she will do to the end."

Their heartfelt plea, reinforced by a reminder that they were people of means, was successful. Helena was permitted to return to Augsburg, apparently without conditions. She remained in the city until her death in 1545.

Immediately after her return to Augsburg, Helena began to involve herself with the local Anabaptists. As indicated earlier, she was probably instrumental in helping Pilgram and Anna Marpeck settle in the city in 1542. The resumption of their acquaintance in 1542 came as a result of Caspar Schwenckfeld's response to Marpeck's *Admonition* (see chapter 11). Helena was involved as a courier in an exchange of letters between Marpeck and Schwenckfeld because she was one of the few people who knew where they both were.[16] Over the years Helena had obviously acquired strong theological views of her own; otherwise Schwenckfeld would not have given her any attention. She was well acquainted with Schwenckfeld's views, which he tried to persuade her to share, but she never wavered in her adherence to Marpeck's vision.

Along with Magdalena von Pappenheim, Helena represented a strong woman's voice in the Anabaptist community of Augsburg. There is no hint in Augsburg that women were not equal with men in the Anabap-tist church in status, rights, and obligations. In sixteenth-century Protestant writings there was frequent reference to Paul's directive that women should be silent in the church (1 Cor. 14:34 and 1 Tim. 2:12). To our knowledge, however, Marpeck never cited these passages to fix the place of women. This is significant because it supports the claim that in the Augsburg Anabaptist community, there was "neither male nor female" (Gal. 3:28 RSV).

We should note that Helena also never assumed superiority because she was a noblewoman. It is likely that she was familiar with Marpeck's views on the link traditionally made between nobility and virtue, about which he wrote to Magdalena von Pappenheim in 1547.[17] Marpeck rejected that traditional view, which combined the two and asserted that the only virtue that mattered was instilled in Christians as the vassals of Christ by their true Lord, Jesus Christ. In terms of leadership, although the Augsburg group was often known as the Marpeck community, it's also worth noting that Helena herself was a strong leader in the community. In fact, she appears to have recruited a number of people to Anabaptism.

A Heartfelt Confession

We are fortunate to have Helena's confession of guilt,[18] written in her own hand sometime between 1539 and her death in 1545. Her confession is considered a positive response to "communal admonition" and a recommitment to serve God and the Augsburg congregation.[19] It was considered important enough to include in the collection of Anabaptist materials known as the *Kunstbuch*.

Her confession follows a general pattern that was well-established in the broader Christian community. Helena lived at a time when a literary

16. For the larger topic of Schwenckfeld and the von Freybergs, see Franz Michael Weber, *Kaspar Schwenckfeld und seine Anhänger in den freybergishcen Herrschaften Justingen und Oepfingen* (Stuttgart: W. Kohlhammer Verlag, 1962).

17. Klassen and Klaassen, *WPM*, 464-83. Also, Fast and Rothkegel, *Kunstbuch*, 595-609.

18. Translated by Linda Huebert Hecht in *Profiles of Anabaptist Women*, 132-35.

19. Hecht, *Profiles of Anabaptist Women*, 130-31.

form known as the "penitential psalm" was very popular, in part because of Luther.[20] This popularity was fed by some of the psalms from the Bible and especially by the Prayer of Manasseh from the Apocrypha, which Luther had translated and sent forth in many editions. Luther had opened up the issue of the relation between penance and penitence—in other words, the relationship between one's own guilt and what one does to repent of one's sins. The Catholic theologian Johan Fabri considered that women were not qualified to sort out the complex relationship between guilt and penance. It was a difficult issue even for classical theologians, he argued. How could women possibly understand? Fabri might have learned a thing or two from Helena, whose confession and acceptance by her Anabaptist church may be considered a model for the practice of a listening and forgiving community.

Helena's confession is a rare example of Anabaptist penitential literature. Furthermore, according to Hecht, it is unusual to have anything written by an Anabaptist woman, since most of them (and the majority of men of the sixteenth century) could neither read nor write. While repentance was considered essential to the advent of faith in Christ, confessions like Helena's are few, perhaps because of the emphasis within much of Anabaptism on living an upright, moral life in the strength of the resurrection of Christ. A confession of guilt, therefore, would be considered a clear admission of failure.[21]

Yet it was also at the heart of the gospel. Confession of sin and the acceptance of forgiveness by the community of the faithful lie at the foundation of the church's existence. In the sixteenth century, Catholics used indulgences and the private confessional to deal with sin. Luther became increasingly convinced that the public confession of sins was of value. It appears that the Marpeck group, like other Anabaptists, also practised public confession. Helena's example suggests that the process was not a quick one but was drawn out over time. The "sinner" was approached by a member or members of the group to recognize the wrong that was done and to repent. In Helena's case, it appears that she rejected the initial advances, believing she'd done no wrong. Only after repeated approaches did she begin to recognize her "sin" and then reached the point of wanting to do a heartfelt confession.

20. William Klassen, *The Forgiving Community* (Philadelphia: Westminster Press, 1966), 231, n6.

21. Two other well-known pieces that qualify as penitential prayers are Menno Simons's *Meditation on the Twenty-fifth Psalm*, in *The Complete Writings of Menno Simons*, ed. John C. Wenger (Scottdale, Pa.: Herald Press, 1956), 63-86, and the prayer of Hans Schlaffer composed on the night before his martyrdom, in *Spiritual Life in Anabaptism*, ed. C. J. Dyck, 195-209.

Helena's confession is transparent in its expression of her sense of unworthiness and of being overwhelmed with guilt and in need of cleansing and acceptance. It is possible that Helena experienced guilt because of her departure from her family. We don't know why she had been separated from her husband, whom she had hardly seen in a dozen or more years. Perhaps she stayed away from her family to protect them from the wrath of Ferdinand and others who would not take kindly to any family members attempting to protect her. She also may have felt badly because her sons and husband had helped negotiate a private recantation for her in 1534. Her confession makes reference to two oaths, probably referring to those she swore in her 1534 recantation: an oath to leave Anabaptism and an oath once again to embrace the Catholic mass and rites of penance. She kept neither oath but apparently could not dismiss them from her conscience.

It is our conclusion that her recantation came after nearly two years of negotiation with Ferdinand in which her sons and husband were intensely involved.[22] She recanted with considerable verve but immediately left for Augsburg instead of returning to her family in Tirol. On the basis of her family's negotiations with the authorities, this was an outcome that her loved ones did not expect. We can assume that Ferdinand also would have felt betrayed, having agreed (probably grudgingly) that Helena could stay in Kitzbühel, only to have her leave.

It would appear that as time went on these matters weighed heavily on Helena's conscience, eventually leading her to seek restoration with a public confession.[23]

Helena presented her confession to the Augsburg Anabaptist community led by Marpeck and Valtin Werner, both of whom she names in the confession. She decided to write her confession and then either have someone else read it or read it herself. However it was presented, the document offers us a special window into the life of von Freyberg and the community of which she and Pilgram were a part.

22. The evidence for the intervention of others on her behalf is now abundantly provided by Linda Huebert Hecht's discovery of a considerable cache of letters between Christoff Fuchs, a relative of Helena who was Ferdinand's representative in Kitzbühel, and members of the family, including Helena herself. Fuchs apparently visited Helena on his trips to Augsburg and worked energetically on her behalf.

23. The private recantation is part of Ferdinand's record. See Johann Loserth, "Der Anabaptismus in Tirol von seinen Anfängen bis zum Tode Jakob Hutters (1526-1536), Aus den Hinterlassenen Papieren Des Hofrathes Dr. Josef R. Von Beck," in *Archiv für Österreichische Geschichte* 78 (1892), 490; Causa Domini III. 10, 16 nos. 141, 143, in the Stadthalter Archiv. Fast and Rothkegel still refer merely to Helena's "willingness to recant" (see Fast and Rothkegel, *Kunstbuch*, 512) but the record has been clear for many years: She *did* recant and that recantation was a burden impeding her spiritual growth for at least a decade.

The bulk of her confession of guilt deals with a very specific burden. The members of the community to whom this confession was addressed were clearly familiar with the ongoing struggle described by Helena. Reading it four and a half centuries later, we have to fill in the gaps. What exactly was the sin Helena was confessing that caused her to be "red with shame," resulting in prolonged spiritual conflict and destroying her inner peace?

> Beloved in God, I ask you through God's will that you hear my accusation of myself, and the recognition of my guilt, in writing, since I truly cannot speak of it with my mouth, without turning red with shame, for flesh and blood have refused to confront it, sought escape where possible and remained silent when I have tried for a long time in the past (to deal with it).[24]

What could have produced such vexation in the church, and what could gradually impair her spiritual life, reducing it (according to her own words) to a veneer of devotion? What indeed was Helena's sin? She refers to it indirectly. She sinned, she wrote, *fürnemlich mit den hunden* (literally, "particularly concerning the dogs"). The identification of the sin hinges on the meaning of these words, especially "the dogs." The words must have been intelligible to the readers of the confession, but today we are forced to conjecture.

It has been suggested that her reference was literally about dogs, that Helena, being a noblewoman, had kept kennels of dogs, and that she had lavished too much attention on them and neglected the poor.[25] That may be possible, but two factors speak against this interpretation. First, the tone of the whole confession suggests a much more serious sin than preoccupation with dogs. Were it only about actual dogs, one would have to conclude that Helena was spiritually infantile to make such a fuss about spoiling her hounds. Second, the Marpeck community rejected legalism, that is, making a moral issue out of the socially trivial.[26] If Helena was spiritually mature, which we have every reason to assume, it is not likely that she would have become a spiritual cripple over an obsession with dogs during her privileged life of many years ago.

A more illuminating conjecture about the meaning of *Hünde* (dogs) is offered by Helena's biographer, Linda Huebert Hecht,[27] who translates this portion of the confession as follows:

> Especially I have sinned and become guilty concerning those in civil authority [*Hündt*] about which I was spoken to in the begin-

24. Hecht, *Profiles of Anabaptist Women*, 132.
25. "Briefe und Schriften oberdeutscher Täufer 1527-1555," in Fast and Rothkegel, *Kunstbuch*, 512-17.
26. See Klassen and Klaassen, WPM, 364.
27. Hecht, *Profiles of Anabaptist Women*, 124-39.

ning; according to my understanding and intention it was not sinful according to the evangelical order. I have resisted at this point with impatience and tactlessness in word and deed. I forcefully wanted to retain the freedom which I thought I had, not wanting to be restricted or compelled, seeking my own good to the detriment of my neighbour.[28]

As Hecht indicates, one of the metaphorical uses of *Hünd* was to designate a lower public official but without any derogatory intent. If that meaning is used, it could refer to the public officials[29] before whom Helena had to make her recantation in 1534. This explanation is not without problems, but it fits with the two objections made against a literal reading.[30] In fact, when we assume that she was confessing the sin of her recantation, the rest of the confession makes perfectly good sense.

She had, she wrote, "carelessly sworn by the name of God." She had been afraid of injustice if she did not swear to recant, and had not been mindful of Jesus, who had not objected when injustice was done to him. She stated that "according to my understanding and intention [my action] was not sinful according to the evangelical order." It's important to place her comment in historical context. In the sixteenth century, some Christians "considered an oath extracted under duress to be at least morally invalid."[31] She apparently had held to this view for a long time and tried to ignore the painful fact that members of her community did not share that view, but considered any recantation a betrayal of Christ.

There had been a long, drawn-out controversy over her action in the fellowship, for there were those who resisted her in her refusal to acknowledge wrongdoing. They had uttered angry, hasty words, and she had threatened to leave the community. She had, she confessed, fallen prey to self-deception, self-justification, and impatience with others. Her pride had rebelled against submitting to the community.

Was this perhaps a welling up of resentment that she, a noblewoman, was being called to account by commoners? She confessed that she had failed against love as described in 1 Corinthians 13. In her pride she had pre-

28. Ibid., 134.
29. These officials are called *Stadthalter* in the official government texts.
30. Hecht referred the question of the meaning of "dogs" to scholar Matthias Schmeltzer, who in turn consulted with Dr. Rudolf Tasser, a linguistic expert in sixteenth-century Tirolese dialect. In a February 4, 2004, letter to Hecht, Schmeltzer said that Tasser confirmed Hecht's interpretation of *hund* or *hunde*, saying that such usage was found in many areas of Austria and continues to be common among older people when referring to civil servants and other people offering service to the community.
31. J. S. Oyer, '*They Harry the Good People out of the Land*,' ed. John D. Roth (Goshen, Ind.: Mennonite Historical Society, 2000), 43.

sumed to teach others when she herself was not teachable. The result of all this self-justification was that her spiritual life was at a low ebb. "I barely grow or increase in the body of Christ, as an old woman in the faith [should], so that I feel worthless and shameful before God and His own."[32] Until now she had not been able to understand, "but God has revealed it to me, through His Holy, generous Spirit." This revelation led her to "yield myself to the discipline and punishment of my heavenly Father, his holy congregation and Christian church." Specifically, "I also ask his holy congregation, especially here at Augsburg, whom I have offended greatly, in particular Pilgram and Valtin, to forgive and pardon."

Discipline Tempered by Love

This confession tells us a great deal about Helena, but it tells us at least as much about the Augsburg Anabaptist community in the early 1540s. The Anabaptists of Augsburg held the view that recantation was a betrayal of Christ and his work of redemption. They believed that such a lapse of loyalty had to be dealt with in the community by a process of church discipline.

Helena's confession reveals that even in her small fellowship, likely in part because it was small and always under pressure, there were dangerous tensions, anger, procrastinations, and threats of leaving. It also shows clearly that the church discipline in this fellowship was marked by firmness tempered by love and patience. Helena was not excommunicated, even though recantation was regarded as very serious and even though for years she had declined to acknowledge what she had done.[33] She drew her strength, she said in her confession, from her identification with the prodigal son, who had come to his senses and returned to his father's embrace in Luke 15, and from the penitent tax collector in Luke 18, who pleaded in the temple, "God be merciful to me, a sinner."

The Augsburg fellowship headed by Marpeck was enough of a community of love and concern that Helena was able to acknowledge her error, safely confess, and then receive forgiveness. It was a community in which a woman in her own confession of wrongdoing could also expect those who had sinned against her in the heat of disagreement to acknowledge their own sin and receive her forgiveness in turn.

There is no sequel to the confession except its inclusion in the *Kunst-buch*.

---

32. Hecht, *Profiles of Anabaptist Women*, 133. Since von Freyberg was in her mid-fifties and had lost her husband and three of her four sons (who by this time had been killed in war), she likely was feeling the effects of old age.

33. For a discussion of Marpeck's vision of church discipline, see Walter Klaassen, "Church Discipline and the Spirit in Pilgram Marpeck," in *De Geest in het geding* (Alphen aan den Rijn: Tjeenk Willink, 1978), 169-80.

Helena was the only female contributor to that collection. Her inclusion reflects the leadership role she played in the Anabaptist community in both Tirol and Augsburg at enormous sacrifice to her own family life.

Some may wonder why there is no mention of Helena in Marpeck's own writings despite the decades of contact they must have had. Marpeck probably didn't name her (or others in his group) because he didn't want to put their lives at risk. It was one thing to write a letter of friendship to a named individual; it was something else to name someone in a pamphlet or book concerning Anabaptism. Authorities might have wondered if a given individual was an Anabaptist, but they needed some form of proof before arresting and charging anyone. As we saw from Maler's disclosure of Helena's identity and activities, to identify an Anabaptist, especially in writing, could be just the evidence the authorities needed to arrest, imprison, expel, or execute a follower of the faith.

After Helena's death, her tailor Hans Jakob Schneider spoke freely of the fact that she had brought him to the Anabaptist faith and taught him what it meant. Hans Jakob and Jörg Maler, who we will meet shortly, both held steadfast to their faith in Augsburg despite continuing adversity. They may have drawn strength from their associate, Helena von Freyberg, who forsook family and wealth to remain a dedicated Anabaptist to the end.

15

From Rogue to Faithful Follower

One of the most intriguing members of the Marpeck group in Augsburg was Jörg Maler, also known as Jörg Probst Rothenfelder. His story offers a vivid portrait of an unlikely figure to play such an important role in fostering Anabaptism and preserving the legacy of the Marpeck community.

Born about 1500, Maler was an Augsburg native whose life changed forever one November evening in 1526. Maler and several male companions were headed home from a tavern when they encountered a young woman who had been sent by her master to obtain a container of wine. According to court records,[1] the extremely inebriated Maler began to badger and harass the maiden. As his companions egged him on, his comments became more and more threatening. Terrified, the young woman fled to a nearby garden and then into what she hoped would be the safety of a house. Witnesses reported hearing loud cursing and verbal abuse as Maler lurched after the young woman. Pushing his way into the house, Maler menacingly used his beret to put out the light. He then threatened the maiden with a "weapon" (the court record did not specify if it was a stick, sword, or knife). Her cries of distress brought help, and the young woman was soon rescued. The drunken Maler, still surly and abusive, was then hustled outside. Only after the intervention of a city watchman did he allow himself to be pacified. He staggered home and shortly afterward was arrested and imprisoned.

At his trial on November 16, 1526, Maler admitted that he had drawn his weapon but couldn't recall if he'd actually hit the woman. He blamed alcohol for his memory lapse. "I had a good drink," he explained.

1. Fast and Rothkegel, *Kunstbuch*, 682-83.

He expressed regret, begged for mercy and grace, and promised never to do such a thing again. On November 22, the judges rendered their verdict. Maler was guilty of entering "into the house of (Haffner) Egelhoffer by force and had in this house hit a woman." He was convicted, imprisoned, and then exiled from Augsburg. He was not allowed to return until he paid a fine for the purchase of a Dutch enamelled oven tile (a *Kachel*) for a city project.

Up to this point, Maler had been a painter. He must have had some talent because in 1513, in his early teens, he was taken on as an apprentice by the royal artist in charge of portraits for Emperor Maximilian I. In 1525, he joined the painters' guild by paying half the required fee and thereby became what today we might call an associate member. It was a year and a half later that he was convicted of assault and expelled from Augsburg for the first time. The last we hear of Maler as a professional artist is in 1530 when he reportedly was the official painter for a tournament that took place in Augsburg during the 1530 diet in the presence of Charles V. No example of his artistry has survived.

At some point, we don't know when, religion became a major force in Maler's life. Early in 1532, after developing quite a reputation as a speaker, he was considered for a position as an evangelical (i.e., Protestant) pastor in Augsburg. However, he also had become exposed to Anabaptist theology and became increasingly drawn to it. In March 1532, he was rebaptized in the home of George Nessler in Augsburg and committed the rest of his life to Anabaptism.

It's not clear how and when Maler returned to Augsburg. Anabaptism in the city had been successfully suppressed for the most part by 1532 (a decade before the Marpecks were to arrive) and survived only as a small group gathering occasionally in the homes of members or in the woods outside the city. In late February 1533, a group of about a dozen people, including Maler, was arrested. Authorities interrogated them and demanded they recant. The Anabaptists insisted that they had gathered only in small groups where they had read the Bible and discussed the truth.

It was here that Bonifacius Wolfart and Wolfgang Musculus, Protestant ministers in Augsburg, enter the picture, seeking a recantation from Maler just as Wolfart was to do two years later with Helena von Freyberg. As one of the evangelical clergy, Wolfart apparently spoke kindly to Maler. When Maler expressed doubt that if he recanted, he would be able to keep what he was asked to promise, Wolfart assured him that the Augsburg Council was divided and would not act even if Maler failed to uphold his promise and returned to Anabaptism. That assurance led Maler to recant on April

29, 1533[2]—and then to meet with his Anabaptist group immediately thereafter. But he soon discovered that he had been misled by Wolfart. On September 18, 1533, he was expelled from Augsburg as an Anabaptist and threatened with more severe punishment if he returned.

Maler travelled to Baden in Switzerland where he learned the weaving trade. Then, during the summer of 1534, he journeyed to Moravia, apparently to acquaint himself with the Anabaptists there. It was likely on his way from Baden to Moravia that he visited Anabaptists in St. Gall and Appenzell, and there heard about or met Pilgram Marpeck. The renewal of Anabaptist persecution in Moravia brought him back to Augsburg in March 1535.

Once More in Trouble

Returning to Augsburg in 1535 was extremely risky. The Anabaptists of Münster in Westphalia were causing consternation everywhere with their bellicose threats against church and governments. Along with all others in the empire, the citizens of Augsburg had been compelled to pay a special tax to combat the Münster Anabaptists and their supporters, and were therefore in no mood to tolerate Anabaptists in their own midst.

Maler had planned to stay in Augsburg only long enough for him to reunite with his wife, Anna, and for them to dissolve their household and leave. To earn some money he worked for a local weaver. He also met with an Anabaptist group in a ravine outside the city. On April 4, 1535, authorities swooped down on one of the meetings, catching participants by surprise. The Anabaptists were arrested, imprisoned, and interrogated. Maler was in serious trouble. Having returned to Augsburg as an Anabaptist against the express wishes of the city council, he faced severe punishment.

His interrogation took place on April 5 and 7 as authorities questioned him about an alleged plot. With the recent events in Münster fresh in their mind, the interrogators probed for answers about Anabaptist leaders and gathering places, and the names of others whom they feared were part of a similar plot. There was no plot, Maler replied. He did not know any leaders. Rather, members of the group gathered by twos and threes in the homes of the masters for whom they worked and admonished each other

---

2. This recantation was a most unusual procedure in that he signed a letter (document) that borrowed heavily from the so-called Recantation of Hans Denck, first published by *Oecolampadius* after Denck's death in 1528 and in modern edition in *TA: Denck 2, Hans Denck: Religiöse Schriften*, ed. Walter Fellmann (Gütersloh: Bertelsmann, 1956), 104-10. For details, see Klassen, "Rothenfelder," in *ME* 4, 364. Fast has also collected documents from the Augsburg Archives pertaining to Maler in Fast and Rothkegel, *Kunstbuch*, 681-729. This reference, 716.

Torture of an Anabaptist.

to be faithful to the gospel. Maler refused to provide the names of other Anabaptists, saying that Scripture forbade him to do it.

Maler declared the interrogators could tear him limb from limb before he would betray anyone. They took him at his word. In the torture chamber they tied his hands behind his back, fastened a rope between his hands and strung it over a pulley. Twice they hoisted him off his feet, dislocating his shoulders. The pain in hands and shoulders was excruciating. When they finally let him down, he talked.

According to the written record of the interrogation, he named Helena von Freyberg as an Anabaptist. Yet on the title page of this record, "Freyberg" was crossed out and the name "Rechberg" inserted. (We have no record of who this person was or why the change was made.) In the testimony itself, Maler named von Freyberg and five other people, stating that they met in Helena's house by night and talked about the gospel. He did not know, he said, if Helena was baptized or not, or if she had given them money. Despite providing this information to authorities, Maler said he would not recant.[3]

At this point the council record makes note of testimony by Maler's

3. The account of the hearing is found in Fast and Rothkegel, *Kunstbuch*, 699. It is interesting to note that even under torture, Maler never again recanted.

wife, Anna, who explains with the help of a lawyer that Maler had come to Augsburg only to gather up their belongings and leave again, with her joining him. Her efforts to help her husband were in vain.

Maler and another Anabaptist spent a week in the pillory as perjurers and then were whipped out of the city. Later Maler did go back into Augsburg, having apparently been given permission to bring out Anna and their possessions.

The Swiss Years

Jörg and Anna Maler made their way to St. Gall and Appenzell, where he was employed as a weaver and where he became an important member of a Swiss Brethren congregation that had seen better days. When Maler arrived, the congregation had no leaders and the Lord's Supper was not being observed. This crisis was relieved in part on April 1, 1537, when Maler and one other person were elected elders. Although we have local records that refer to Maler as "a good looking man with curly hair,"[4] no direct information is available about his leadership or the spiritual condition of the church there at that time. The letters of Pilgram Marpeck to members of Maler's church in 1542 and 1543, however, shed some harsh light on the church's difficulties (see chapter 12).

The ultimate cause of their trouble, Marpeck wrote, was their understanding of Christian life and the life of the church as being governed not by the freedom of Christ's Spirit but by rules and laws. It seems that Marpeck may have regarded Maler as partly responsible, because the letter of 1543 was addressed specifically to him and Uli Scherer. We don't know Maler's response to Marpeck's accusations, but the marginal glosses that Maler added to the two Marpeck letters (perhaps when Maler prepared the *Kunstbuch* two decades later), may represent his recollection of how he responded to the letters in the 1540s.[5] Despite the angry notations, it's worth observing that the letters are included in the *Kunstbuch* at Maler's choice.

Maler reported later that he spent six years in St. Gall and eight in Appenzell, making his living in the textile industry. It is possibly during this period that, despite early disagreements, he began to develop a positive working relationship with Pilgram Marpeck. Maler's role as an elected elder of the local Swiss Brethren congregation is vague. He was a reader of Scripture and participated in discussion of what was read.[6] When arrested

4. Fast, *TA: Ostschweiz* 2, 581. For English translation of the marginal comments, see Klassen and Klaassen, *WPM*, 362-68.

5. Klassen and Klaassen, *WPM*, 334, 346, 354, 357, 360-61, 364, 366.

6. C. Arnold Snyder, "The Birth and Evolution of Swiss Brethren Anabaptism (1520-

in Augsburg in 1550, he reported that he had baptized just two women in St. Gall and Appenzell, but only because a designated baptizer was not available and he had been ordered to do it.[7] He consistently denied that he was a preacher.

Sometime in 1547 Maler wrote *An Account of the Faith*.[8] The *Account* is a series of Scripture passages strung together but arranged according to the different parts of his confession. Maler prepared it, he said, to help comfort the faithful to remain steadfast in tribulation and to offer edification for those who desired the truth. Heinold Fast has called it a mature expression of theology, without the polemical edges against Marpeck or various other Anabaptist and non-Anabaptist groups that had been characteristic of some of his other work.[9]

The work gives us no internal clue as to its setting or what specifically caused him to write it. The only point of reference may be the letter Pilgram Marpeck wrote to the Swiss on February 1, 1547.[10] Although there are no obvious links between Marpeck's letter and Maler's *Account*, it is possible that Maler wrote it as a way of clarifying his own thinking. If Maler earlier shared the legalism of the St. Gall-Appenzell church, he appears in his *Account* to be closer to Marpeck—especially when he writes about the virtue of patience, the Christian life as discipleship, and the meaning of suffering for Christ.

On the Move Again

The end of the Schmalcald War in 1547 created a dangerous situation in Switzerland and, indeed, throughout Europe. Threats uttered by the emperor against Protestant Switzerland caused consternation in Appenzell. Every available able-bodied man was called to arms. Maler was called but asked to be excused because he had "no desire to harm anyone nor to go to war against any."[11] He was promptly expelled from Appenzell. Where to go? Because virtually anywhere was dangerous for an Anabaptist, he was left calculating where he might encounter the least difficulty. Thirteen years had passed since he had been expelled from Augsburg. After all that time, he thought the authorities there might finally allow him to return.

Maler and his wife decided that she would be the best person to apply

---

1530)," *MQR* 80, 2006, describes the difference between reader and preacher, which Maler invoked also later in Augsburg.

7. Fast and Rothkegel, *Kunstbuch*, 716.
8. Ibid., 490-96.
9. Ibid., 59 n69.
10. Klassen and Klaassen, *WPM*, 427-63.
11. Fast and Rothkegel, *Kunstbuch*, 713.

to civic officials in Augsburg for approval for their return. Anna was a confident woman who knew her way in official circles and could intercede effectively on his behalf. She apparently travelled to Augsburg to ask the city council to allow her husband to come home.

She returned to wherever they were staying temporarily and reported that the mayor had said that even the council did not know what the emperor would decide about the religious situation in Augsburg. It would be best for them to wait where they were until the Diet of Augsburg had ended and the emperor had left the city. After another inquiry in February 1548,[12] Maler was encouraged that perhaps old scores were now forgotten. When a new council was installed on August 3, Maler and his wife felt confident they could safely return.

After some months delay, they set out for Augsburg only to have an accident in which Maler seriously injured his foot. He recuperated in Augsburg at the home of his brother-in-law Peter Herbe, and then went to work at his profession as a weaver,[13] quietly living for about eighteen months outside the city gate in rented quarters. He worked and paid taxes but did not attend any Anabaptist meetings. He did meet with various individuals, however, including his landlord and brother-in-law, to talk about the gospel.

Since the Marpecks and Malers were both living in Augsburg during this time, we know from city records of interrogations that he was invited to the Marpeck home on several occasions to discuss current affairs and what the Bible had to say about them.[14] It must have seemed to Maler and his wife that they could now expect to spend the rest of their days in their home city.

The peaceful times were not to last. On March 17, 1550, the authorities announced that a new imperial diet would commence in Augsburg on June 25. Since the emperor was going to be in the city again, the authorities probably felt it was time to offer proof to the imperial officials that they were serious about suppressing Anabaptism, as the city had earlier pledged to do. Jörg Maler and Jörg Seifrid were arrested on April 23 and the interrogations began once more. Seifrid recanted on April 29. Maler was interrogated on April 23, 28, and May 5.

The interrogators asked the usual questions: how and when had Maler returned, with whom was he staying, what was he doing, and where had

12. Heinold Fast, "Vom Amt des 'Lesers' zum Kompilator des sogenannten Kunstbuches. Auf den Spuren Jörg Malers," in *Aussenseiter zwischen Mittelalter und Neuzeit*, eds. N. Fischer and M. Kobelt-Groch (Leiden: Brill, 1997), 207.

13. Fast and Rothkegel, *Kunstbuch*, 714.

14. Ibid, 713.

he been before he returned? Again and again they asked him whether he was preaching. The term "preaching" as most people of Marpeck's day defined it involved speaking to large gatherings, like Protestant preaching services. The supposition was that if Anabaptists had preaching meetings, they were setting up an alternative church. Maler fervently denied this and explained that they met occasionally in small numbers to discuss Scripture. He was asked about the basis of his faith. He replied that he accepted the teaching of Christ and the apostles and the Twelve Articles (the Apostles' Creed). He said he always carried two books with him: the Bible and *The Imitation of Christ*, the classic devotional manual from the fifteenth century by Thomas à Kempis.[15]

He also tried to persuade his interrogators that he was not a sectarian like the Swiss Anabaptists and that he disagreed with them on seven points.

First, unlike the Swiss, he held that a Christian may swear an oath for the preservation of justice and truth.[16] Second, the Swiss would not agree to even carry a sword. He did not, he said, regard carrying a sword as a sin as long as it was not misused. Third, he did not agree with their insistence never to marry anyone who was not Anabaptist. Fourth, he rejected their rule never to wear brightly coloured clothing. Fifth, he did not agree with the Swiss that a man should not physically punish his wife. Apparently Maler believed that a wife should be punished just like a child if she did not behave.[17] Not only was Maler at odds with the Swiss Brethren on this matter, but he certainly would have been out of step with the Marpeck Anabaptist communities, which strongly emphasized equality of women. (One could well imagine what Helena von Freyberg and Anna Marpeck would have to say about Maler's views!)

Finally, Maler did not accept the Swiss Brethren rejection of civil marriage, making marriages "known among themselves."[18] Maler believed the authorities should be involved with marriage since part of their God-

---

15. Fast and Rothkegel, *Kunstbuch*, 61, n82.

16. See "Why I changed my Mind about the Oath," in Fast and Rothkegel, *Kunstbuch*, 407. Fast and Rothkegel date this statement around 1548, when Maler joined the *Marpeck-Kreis* or Marpeck circle in Augsburg. The issue of his changing his mind on the oath is likely slightly more complicated than they indicate. See our treatment of "Oath Refusal" in chapter 12.

17. Klassen, *Covenant and Community*, 90, n68.

18. Snyder, *Anabaptist History and Theology*, 288. These differences between Maler and the Swiss deserve more detailed treatment than we can give them here. The differences Maler describes were first noticed by modern scholarship in a transcribed document in the Pennsburg Schwenkfelder Library and were cited in Klassen, *Covenant and Community*, 90, and also in the Maler biography by Klassen in "Rothenfelder," in *ME 4*, 365-67.

ordained governing function was the punishment of marital misdeeds.[19] Clearly he expected that the Augsburg authorities would be more lenient if they knew his views on the oath, the sword, and civil marriage.[20]

The interrogation revealed the continuing legacy of fear among the authorities from the debacle in Münster fifteen years earlier. If there were many Anabaptists in the city, they might be plotting a takeover of Augsburg just as they had done in Münster. Maler rejected the supposition and caustically observed that the Münster Anabaptists were not Christians. The authorities asked only one specific question related to belief: whether Maler held the views of Arius, a heretic of the fourth century who provided an alternative to the orthodox doctrine of the Trinity, arguing that Jesus was neither divine nor human. It was a test about theological orthodoxy to determine if he believed that Jesus was divine. Maler responded that he accepted the Apostles' Creed as his statement of faith.

When the interrogators threatened to torture him, Maler replied that he would suffer whatever they did to him. Surprisingly, this time they refrained, explaining that he had a foot injury and that his health was not good. They decided instead to keep him in prison to continue to interrogate him further in an effort to get him to recant.

A short piece in the *Kunstbuch*[21] by Maler himself records that three Protestant clergy and one Dominican friar came to him and questioned him chiefly about baptism.[22] He replied that he held to the words of Christ and the apostles. But Maler was courageous and asked them a few questions of his own. Did Christians persecute or were they persecuted? And what did they mean by "world"? On the one hand they regarded the world as Christendom and on the other they preached against it as the realm of the devil. The result of this theological debate was that neither side changed the other's minds. The conversation ended and Maler remained in prison.

On April 23, 1552, after two years of confinement, it was decided to interrogate Maler again to persuade him to recant. If he refused, he was to be expelled from the city permanently. Two days later the authorities relented and said he could stay if he kept to himself and spoke to no one about his views. Maler replied that he would be an obedient citizen but that he could not "be bound concerning the word of God." He could promise

19. Snyder, *Anabaptist History and Theology*, 288 and 298, n78.
20. Klassen, "Rothenfelder," and Klassen, *Covenant and Community*, op. cit.
21. Fast and Rothkegel, *Kunstbuch*, 416-17.
22. Ibid. The identity of the friar could easily be Johann Faber, who wrote a book on the Anabaptists in 1550.

nothing and would suffer whatever punishment they laid on him. On April 26, 1552, he was banished from Augsburg yet again.

A Letter Carrier for Marpeck

After he was released from prison, Maler went back to St. Gall, leaving Anna back in Augsburg working as a seamstress to support them both. Over the years, in addition to gathering material for the *Kunstbuch*, he also devoted himself to the welfare of the scattered congregations of Marpeck followers, who called themselves "*Marpeck volk*" (Marpeck people) after Pilgram died. Maler became a letter carrier for Marpeck to Moravia. Several other members of the group were also letter carriers, most notably an old man named Thoma Schumacher, who travelled the long distances from Augsburg to Moravia and Appenzell. In 1553, Maler indicated that he wanted to "ride the circuit" of the Anabaptist congregations associated with Marpeck, presumably to offer pastoral care and to attempt to maintain the unity of the widely scattered congregations.

Only a few specifics are known about the aging Maler during his seven-year exile. He evidently travelled back to his friends near St. Gall and spent some time with them. On October 15, 1552, he wrote a letter from St. Gall to Ulrich Ageman in Constance, attempting to win Ageman to Anabaptism. Constance had been thoroughly re-Catholicized following the Schmalcald War and was therefore a dangerous place for an Anabaptist. Maler invited Ageman to take upon himself the cross of persecution, daring to speak with the integrity of Maler's own experience and his own physical pain.[23]

In December 1552 he returned to the vicinity of Augsburg, likely to visit Anna. He must also have reported to Marpeck about his visit to St. Gall. Early in 1553, travelling with Jacob Schumann, he carried a letter from Marpeck to the churches in Moravia[24] and brought back their answering letter of March 19, 1553.[25]

We have from his hand a confession of faith dated 1554, which he also included in the *Kunstbuch*.[26] A personal commentary on the Twelve Articles of the Apostolic Creed, the confession sought to demonstrate (we don't know to whom) that Maler shared with Catholics and Protestants

---

23. Fast and Rothkegel, *Kunstbuch*, 65. This letter is included in the *Kunstbuch*, 389-405. It is possible its inclusion is meant to serve as a model for recruitment and bears witness to Maler's own enthusiasm for Anabaptism.

24. Klassen and Klaassen, *WPM*, 549-54. Also, Fast and Rothkegel, *Kunstbuch*, 418-22.

25. Fast and Rothkegel, *Kunstbuch*, 423-27.

26. Ibid., 637-42.

the basics of Christian faith. Indeed, his commentary is entirely orthodox. Even the statement on baptism, part of his commentary on one of the Twelve Articles, "I believe in the holy, Christian church, the communion of saints," would have been acceptable to other Christians if he had not slipped in the words that one was planted into the church "through personal faith." In the article on the Holy Spirit, he confessed his trinitarian faith, saying he believed "that God desires to be my father, to forgive my sins through Christ, and through his Holy Spirit to give me eternal life."

The commentary also hinted that his exile, which would last for the next five or six years, was a difficult time for him. He referred to "all my anguish and distress, and that which opposes me for His name's sake." He affirmed his belief that "almighty God would shelter him from everything that assailed him and tried to turn him away from God." His words suggest he may have been experiencing more persecution. However, his anguish may also have been caused by the death of Anna, because we hear no more about her.

In April 1559, Maler once more begged to be allowed to come home to Augsburg. His request was denied, and he was forced to remain outside the city. But on June 1, 1559, the Augsburg council decided that the clergy, at Maler's request, should present him with theological theses to which he should respond. Maler addressed five topics: the external (oral) word, infant baptism, the substance and essence of the Lord's Supper, secular government, and swearing the oath.[27] These topics, similar to those raised during Maler's various incarcerations over the years, are a template of the times. Evidently Maler's responses satisfied the authorities, for the council decided to pardon him and open the city to him. Maler for his part agreed to appear before the council and make his confession.[28] This has all the marks of a final accommodation, short of calling it a recantation.[29] It would appear that Maler could no longer accommodate the exclusive bitterness of the religious controversy of his time and decided to withdraw from it. The eclectic nature of the *Kunstbuch* collection may be testimony to a similar shift in Maler's position from engagement to withdrawal. Or perhaps the old man, now nearing age sixty and in poor health, was simply tired and desired a few more quiet years in his beloved Augsburg.

This permission to live in Augsburg provided him with the opportunity

27. All five are also contained in Hans Denck's "recantation" of 1528 and in Maler's recantation of 1533.

28. Stadtsarchiv Augsburg, Ratsbücher nn30, 31.

29. Hans Denck's so-called recantation of 1527 has been compared to this statement by Maler. See Klassen, "Rothenfelder," in *ME* 4, 364. Denck also did not recant. See *TA: Denck* 2, 104-10.

to collect all the remaining available writings of the Marpeck community that he wanted to include in the *Kunstbuch*. It is ironic that none of Maler's early work as an artist survives, but his production of the *Kunstbuch* offers us one of the greatest treasures of Anabaptist culture.

Channelling a Mighty Stream

Before the discovery of the *Kunstbuch*, the modern world had only a few letters of Marpeck, who through these few writings seemed to project an image of a dogmatist seeking to build a correctly fashioned tower of faith. Thanks to the material that Maler collected, we now see Marpeck as a pastor, theologian, and passionate advocate of change. Throughout the writings of Marpeck and his associates there is a passion for *Gottseligkeit*: a sense of being filled with the blessedness of the presence of God's love and mercy, with full and free forgiveness.

Maler worked on the *Kunstbuch* as if he was following Marpeck as they attempted to channel a mighty stream. Occasionally on the margins he pushed some impurities to the side or reminded the reader to see a different point of view. Throughout, members of the church were encouraged to speak freely and clearly what their hearts and minds urged them to say.

Jörg Maler died in 1562. Despite his many faults and transgressions, over the course of his turbulent life he nevertheless allowed himself to be used as an instrument to assist in building the community of those who called themselves fellow sufferers with Christ.

-16-

Works Amid War and Intrigue

There are differing views about the nature of the Anabaptist community in Augsburg from the time Pilgram Marpeck entered the imperial city in 1542 until his death in 1556. According to Stephen Boyd, Marpeck was the leader of a persistently strong Anabaptist group.[1] Boyd's observation gives the impression that Marpeck took over the leadership of an already existing Anabaptist community. However, according to Hans Guderian, when Marpeck arrived in Augsburg there were only a few Anabaptists in the city. Guderian maintains it was under his leadership that the Anabaptist community developed there.[2]

To understand Marpeck's accomplishment, it's important to review the struggles of Anabaptists in Augsburg for twenty years prior to his arrival. Like Strasbourg, Augsburg was an open city in 1525 and 1526, and therefore it was the major centre of Anabaptism in south Germany. A number of major figures of early Anabaptism spent time there: Hans Denck, Hans Hut, Balthasar Hubmaier, Lienhart Schiemer, Hans Schlaffer, and many more. They were initially tolerated by the city authorities when they appeared to be committed to the teaching of the evangelical party in the city.[3] But when believer baptisms increased early in 1527—including the baptism of several prominent citizens—the city council began to worry that the common people would all become Anabaptists.[4]

From August 20 to 24, 1527, Augsburg was the site of a major gathering of about sixty Anabaptists that has become known as the Martyrs' Synod. Its purpose was to develop a missionary strategy and to resolve

---

1. Boyd, *Pilgram Marpeck*, 138.
2. Hans Guderian, *Die Täufer in Augsburg: Ihre Geschichte und Ihr Erbe* (Pfaffenhofen: W. Ludwig Verlag, 1984), 98-99.
3. H. Immenkötter, "Kirche zwischen Reformation und Parität," 396.
4. Guderian, *Die Täufer in Augsburg*, 37.

some differences over the interpretation of the events of the end times. Hans Hut, one of the leaders attending the meeting, had predicted that these events as found in Matthew 24 and the book of Revelation would happen by Pentecost 1528. Others disputed his interpretations.

When city authorities learned of the meeting, they decided to take swift action against the Anabaptists. All Anabaptist leaders in the city were arrested and imprisoned. Attempts were made by the evangelical clergy to persuade them to recant. Torture was used to produce confessions, as in the case of Hans Hut.[5] Many of those not arrested fled the city. Yet despite this harsh treatment, the movement continued to grow.

If life was difficult for Anabaptists in Augsburg at that time, it was even worse in nearby Swabia, where the persecution was much more intense. Swabian Anabaptists fled to Augsburg in fear for their lives. Because of the hostility of the Augsburg authorities, they gathered mostly in rural places outside the city. Through stealth and courageous persistence, local Anabaptist leaders managed to keep the little groups in touch with each other. What's more, there is clear evidence that the number of Anabaptists in Augsburg grew not just from people moving into the city. From October 1527 to April 1528, 203 believers baptisms are documented![6]

Meanwhile, civic officials became increasingly agitated. A letter written by Joachim Helm, an Augsburg citizen, reveals a high level of alarm about the heretics flourishing in Augsburg, among whom were adherents to several varieties of Anabaptism. These people, Helm wrote, are so foolish that even young girls welcome death for their cause. When one of the Anabaptists preaches, he wrote, thousands flock to hear him. But when the educated Catholic clergy preach, he lamented, there are scarcely six or seven.[7] No wonder the authorities were concerned.

In September 1527, Hans Hut, one of the Martyrs' Synod participants, was arrested and interrogated. Under torture, he admitted his link to Thomas Müntzer, the mystical theologian and revolutionary peasant leader in 1525 and to his teachings about the end times. To his alarmed interrogators, Hut's predictions could mean only one thing: a bloody insurrection by thousands of Anabaptists that could be a repeat of the 1524-26

5. Christian Meyer, "Zur Geschichte der Wiedertäufer in Oberschwaben," part 1 ("Die Anfänge des Wiedertäufertums in Augsburg") in *Zeitschrift des historischen Vereins für Schwaben und Neuburg* 1 (1874). See also Gottfried Seebaß, *Müntzers Erbe: Werk, Leben und Theologie des Hans Hut* (Göttingen: Gütersloher Verlagshaus, 2002).

6. Guderian, *Die Täufer in Augsburg*, 34-39.

7. G. Kawerau, "Zur Reformationsgeschichte Augsburgs," in *Beiträge zur bayerischen Kirchengeschichte* 2 (1896), 131-32.

peasant uprising led in part by Müntzer, during which thousands were wounded or killed[8] (not to be confused with the upheaval in Münster in 1534-35, in which a great many also died; see chapter 10).

In the Name of Peace and Order

On October 11, 1527, a mandate against Anabaptists in Augsburg was made public. It listed as offences the rejection of infant baptism, rebaptism, sectarian gatherings, and secret and seductive teaching "against God, Christian order, good morals . . . leading to schism, contrariness, rebellion and revolt against the government."[9] From that point onward the Augsburg council was not interested in differences with the Anabaptists in theological matters but only in the preservation of peace and order and the elimination of any tendencies to insurrection.[10] If arrest, torture, expulsion, and/or death were needed to preserve this order, so be it. The order and safety of Augsburg needed to be protected from this dangerous group.

The council appointed Conrad Peutinger, a noted humanist, to the task of keeping the city safe from Anabaptists. He saw in them only subversion. The nighttime meetings, their own care for the poor, and the sending out of Anabaptists by the Martyrs' Synod to proselytize elsewhere were regarded by Peutinger as evidence of a sinister plot. He was convinced that a new uprising was at hand, especially because of Hut's participation in the peasant uprising three years earlier. Peutinger decreed that Anabaptists should be denied employment and thus encouraged to leave the city.

In the first half of 1528, no fewer than one hundred Anabaptists in the Augsburg area were punished by branding, cutting out the tongue, imprisonment, expulsion, and even the rare execution. Nevertheless, in the years that followed, city officials did not carry out the draconian decree of the Diet of Speyer of 1529 or of the Swabian League, of which Augsburg was a member. As we saw in chapter 8, the infamous decree, agreed to by all members of the diet, was a reactivation of provisions against rebaptism first enacted in the sixth century.[11] The decree provided the death penalty for Anabaptists with no need for a church court, which had traditionally

8. For a record of the interrogation see Christian Meyer, "Zur Geschichte der Wiedertäufer in Oberschwaben." See also Johann Loserth and Robert Friedmann, "Hans Hut," in *ME* 2, 846-60.

9. Guderian, *Die Täufer in Augsburg*, 84.

10. Ibid., 82.

11. H. J. Goertz, "Ketzer, Aufrührer und Märtyrer. Der Zweite Speyerer Reichstag und die Täufer," in *MGBl* 36, N.F. 31 (1979), 8.

decided cases of heresy. The "rebellious agitators of this vice of Anabaptism" were not to be pardoned under any circumstances. Only those who confessed their error and were willing to accept the penalty could appeal for clemency. Exile was forbidden so that the authorities could keep an eye on any who might revert to Anabaptism. Whoever gave shelter or kindness to Anabaptists would likewise be subject to the penalties of the decree.[12]

Interestingly, Protestants (i.e., Lutherans and other Reformers) criticized the city's undifferentiated condemnation of Anabaptists. Aware of their own vulnerability to charges of heresy, they argued that not faith but rebellion and insurrection against constituted government should be punished.[13] Hence the officials of Augsburg were especially careful not to prosecute for theological or church reasons.[14] But the policy was firm: Anabaptists were not to be tolerated in their city. A 1536 letter revealed that indeed they were not expelled for theological reasons but because of their disobedience and contrariness. By withdrawing from full participation in civic life—such as refusing to bear arms to protect the city—they were perceived as thereby destroying civic order.[15]

This policy continued into the 1540s and '50s, when Marpeck lived in Augsburg.[16] He and others survived by treading a narrow path and trying as much as possible to avoid confrontation with civic officials. Since the government did not regard Anabaptism as a religious movement, there was no possibility for Marpeck to engage in public theological debate as he had done in Strasbourg, even if he had desired it. Since Anabaptists were regarded as insurrectionists, their safest response was to submit to government authority so as not to be condemned. In fact, one reason for the republication of the *Exposé of the Babylonian Whore* in 1544 was to clarify for the authorities in Augsburg that Marpeck and his group had no thoughts of political disloyalty.

At the Centre of Action

The turbulent events leading up to the Schmalcald War between Emperor Charles V and the Protestants had begun to unfold early in 1544 after the Marpecks had already been in Augsburg for several years.

12. Johann Loserth, "Reichsgesetze gegen die 'Wiedertäufer,'" in *MGBl* 1 (1936), 27-28.
13. Goertz, op. cit., 17.
14. Guderian, *Täufer in Augsburg*, 86-95.
15. Boyd, *Pilgram Marpeck*, 133.
16. From an interrogation of Jörg Maler on April 7, 1535, we learn that the first question he was asked was about the conspiracy of Anabaptists against the city. See Fast and Rothkegel, *Kunstbuch*, 696-97.

The city was a member of the Lutheran Schmalcald League, the Lutheran military league founded in 1531 at Schmalcald to prevent the suppression of Protestantism. Consequently, Augsburg was repeatedly at the centre of conflict. Thus, whatever Marpeck's motivation for relocating to Augsburg, he likely would not have gone had he known that it would become a seething cauldron of war and all its attendant miseries until his death fourteen years later.

In his 1531 booklet, the *Exposé of the Babylonian Whore*, Marpeck had warned members of the newly formed Schmalcald League that their proposed armed resistance to the emperor's threats of military action could never be justified on the basis of the gospel.

Throughout the 1530s there followed a bewildering succession of alliances, wars, treaties, and betrayals involving all parties: the emperor, the pope, France, the Ottoman Turks, and the Protestant principalities and cities. Charles V had one aim throughout: to restore religious unity under the banner of the papal church. He was prevented again and again from doing so by having to repel the French on the West and the Turks to the East, campaigns for which he needed the military support of the German princes of his empire. They included those who had become Protestant but whom, at the same time, he was planning to force back into the papal church.

The Imperial Diet met at Speyer, on the Rhine, in February 1544. There the emperor promised the Lutheran members of the Schmalcald League that their ongoing dispute over religious issues could be solved by a church council in which they could take part. He had one proviso, however. They would need to assist him in his war against France and the Turks. They agreed. Given their fractious history, it was a strange alliance that prompted an even stranger union on the opposing side.

Many must have shared the astonishment of Martin Luther when he wrote on March 8, 1544, of the latest news announcing an alliance of France, the Turks, and the pope against the emperor. The lineup was breathtaking: His Holiness Pope Paul III ("the Successor of Peter") and Francis I (known as the "Most Christian King of France"), as well as the Muslim Turks headed by Suleiman the Magnificent, the great enemy of Europe—all were allied against His Apostolic Majesty, the Catholic Emperor Charles V!

To understand this bizarre partnership, it must be remembered that the pope was also the secular ruler of the papal states. These states stretched across the Italian peninsula and shared a border with the Holy Roman Empire, which for centuries the popes had considered a military threat to their papal states. Even in the 1540s, the emperor and pope were regarded as the two equal heads or shepherds of Christian Europe. The jockeying for power and position with each other had been a feature of European politics for five hundred years. Francis I had been a rival of Charles V ever since 1519, when Charles triumphed over Francis in being selected emperor by the electors of the Holy Roman Empire. The Ottoman Turks had attempted to expand into Europe for the better part of two centuries and were the main external threat to the empire. The fact that the pope, Francis, and Charles were all Catholic Christians did not prevent them from using whatever means were available to extend and consolidate their own power.

After eight months of fighting, in September 1544 Charles won the war against this formidable alliance on both fronts, and peace treaties were signed. His hands were now free to turn to his main task, bringing renegade sectors of his empire back to the Catholic fold. While Charles still hoped for a church council to settle the religious differences, he also decided on a military solution to deal with the religiously disobedient who had only recently been his allies. Now, in an about-face, the pope once again became the emperor's ally and supplied him with money and the promise of troops to use against the Protestants and other heretics within his realm.

Renewed Call for Nonviolence

These were the events that prompted Marpeck to issue a second edition of the *Exposé of the Babylonian Whore* in Augsburg sometime in 1544.[17] Part of Marpeck's title, which was typically long in the style of the sixteenth century, stated his purpose clearly: "... *concerning the victory, peace and rule of the true Christians, and published to show in what manner they obey the authorities, and bear the cross of Christ without rebellion and resistance, with patience and love.*"[18] Because of Charles's renewed desire to restore the Catholic Church's dominance throughout his empire, the threat of war was much more immediate now than in 1531, the date of the first edition. Augsburg was a member of the Lutheran Schmalcald League and in 1536 had signed the Lutheran Wittenberg Accord, a Protestant agreement written mostly by Martin Bucer about the articles of belief, especially pertaining to the Lord's Supper.

Marpeck's argument against the Lutherans' willingness to take up arms to advance their beliefs was therefore more timely than ever. The reissued publication was also designed to help strengthen a commitment

17. The reissue was printed by Philip Ulhart. Werner O. Packull, "Preliminary Report on Pilgram Marpeck's Sponsorship of Anabaptist *Flugschriften*," MQR 75 (2001), 87. English text translated by Walter Klaassen, "Exposé of the Babylonian Whore," in *Later Writings by Pilgram Marpeck and His Circle* 1, 24-28.
18. Klaassen, *Later Writings by Pilgram Marpeck and His Circle* 1, 24.

to nonviolence by members of the Marpeck churches, since they feared—with good cause—that some of them could well be required to render military service. That's exactly what happened in Augsburg in July 1545, when several men were called to render sentry duty on the city walls.[19] They refused and were expelled from the city.

Difficult Times for Anabaptists

All in all, 1544 was a taxing year for Marpeck. Soon after he and Anna had established a new household in Augsburg, he began his work as a professional engineer, with assignments that sometimes took him many miles from home. In addition to working on the second edition of the *Exposé*, he and others were completing the first part of a magisterial document, *Response to Caspar Schwenckfeld (Verantwortung)*, exploring the relationship between outer and inner (the material and the spiritual) Christian experience of the Divine.

How Marpeck had the time to combine his leadership in Anabaptist writings with his professional work is not clear. It is possible that the terms of his employment included some flexibility, being task or project-oriented rather than requiring set hours from him day by day, morning to night.

Sometime in July of that year, a cry for help came to Marpeck from Chur in the Swiss Grisons, where he had so recently lived and where Anabaptists were now being persecuted. The *Kunstbuch* preserved a letter by Marpeck written in August 1544 from the city of Chur. It appears that he had travelled to Chur briefly,[20] likely going there in his role as elder to help and encourage local Anabaptists in distress. The visit also gave him an opportunity to make contact again with his long-time co-worker, Leupold Scharnschlager, who at that time was already living in Ilanz, not far from Chur.

Two letters of Scharnschlager,[21] one written on May 24, 1544, and the other soon after, shed light on the purpose of Marpeck's visit. The first was addressed to Martin Plaichner, an Anabaptist leader at Chur, offering comfort to Plaichner and several other Anabaptists who had been served with a notice of expulsion from Chur. The letter spoke of the love of God

---

19. Boyd, *Pilgram Marpeck*, 141.

20. There is evidence that by October 4, 1544, he was again back in Augsburg. See Fast and Rothkegel, *Kunstbuch*, 541, in the introduction written by Fast in his transcription of the *Kunstbuch* letters. The letter is in English translation in *WPM*, 390-401. Marpeck's letter in Fast and Rothkegel, *Kunstbuch*, 541-49.

21. Fast and Rothkegel, *Kunstbuch*, 526-29; Gerhard Hein, "Two Letters by Leupold Scharnschlager," *MQR* 17 (1943), 165-68.

in Christ that is sufficient for whatever trials afflict God's children. These are the days, Scharnschlager wrote, when we need to be ready for the rough road of pilgrimage. Please read this letter to the discouraged and fearful, he continued, especially the sisters. For their benefit, he called attention to the heroic figure of Judith in the Old Testament Apocrypha as an example of steadfastness in the faith.

The second letter, written soon after the first, began with the knowledge of the expulsion of several Anabaptists from Chur, with the expectation that others would soon join them. Scharnschlager addressed especially the temptation that comes from those who call themselves Christians, by which he undoubtedly meant the Protestant authorities in Chur.

To quote Scharnschlager, the authorities say to the Anabaptists: "Where will you go? You won't be welcome anywhere. Give in a little! After all, you are fussing only about details which do not affect your salvation. Just give up on your insistence [on baptism] and the persecution will stop!"[22] Scharnschlager warned that down that road lies total surrender. Instead, he counselled, "He who is faithful in what is least, will also be faithful in what is great." He comforted the faithful with Jesus' words that those who are persecuted for righteousness sake are blessed. Besides, he said, others of us (he was likely thinking of the Anabaptists in Tirol) have experienced much more severe suffering and have been faithful even to death. Cast aside all "creatures," everything earthly, so as not to be delayed in your pilgrimage, he continued. Let us not by any surrender of conviction strengthen our persecutors in their injustice. Scharnschlager included himself among the persecuted, so we may conclude that he was living in Ilanz, not far from Chur, at least by 1544 and possibly earlier.

During his stay in Chur, Marpeck wrote a letter addressed to "the elect true believers in Württemberg." Dated August 15, 1544, it is quite different from the letters he wrote to the Appenzellers. The believers in Württemberg were members of fellowships Marpeck had begun when he worked in the Black Forest for the city of Strasbourg from 1530 to 1532. They were located in the Kinzig Valley and at Langnau, and most likely other places as well. It was a letter of teaching and edification with no reference at all to persecution or to trouble in the churches. In fact, the government policy concerning Anabaptists in Württemberg was lenient. Duke Ulrich, who had regained his principality from King Ferdinand in 1534, was advised by Johannes Brenz, a Reformer in Nuremberg and a champion of religious tolerance. Brenz insisted that Anabaptists should be won over only by persuasion. The alternative he

22. Fast and Rothkegel, *Kunstbuch*, 523.

favoured was recantation. According to Brenz, putting them to death forever prevented a change of heart, while exerting pressure on them to leave only meant that Anabaptism would spread elsewhere.

In Praise of the Love of Christ

Marpeck's letter to Anabaptists in Württemberg is a fine example of his use of allegory in his interpretation of the Bible. It also reveals clearly the mystical strain that characterized the South German and Austrian Anabaptism that had Hans Hut as its progenitor. Marpeck addressed his people as scattered in Württemberg and elsewhere but united in faith and spirit. This letter offers a stark contrast to his letters to the Swiss in Appenzell, which were dominated by his concern about disunity among the faithful. The unity of spirit he detected in Württemberg gave him the freedom to share with the believers there some theological reflections for those already mature in faith.

Marpeck began his Württemberg letter with a paean of praise on the love of Christ, which flows from the one trinitarian God and is the unity of all faithful hearts. Describing this as female personification of love, Marpeck said it is the eternal beginning "stretching from the highest height. She takes to herself the influx of whatever is loved and may in truth be loved. In particular love, which is God in all, is the observer of that which she herself has created and formed in the likeness of her image."

What she has created is supremely the human being in whom she is reflected in her essence and by whom, in turn, she is eternally loved. There she beholds her likeness fully when she lives "in the new heaven and the new earth as a holy city, the New Jerusalem." She descends from heaven as a bride prepared for her husband. This love is the banner, seal, and promise imprinted on the hearts of all the faithful for their eternal security and victory over all hate and enmity.

The figure of the bride was the transition to an interpretation of parts of the Song of Songs (1:2-4 and 2:10-14). Marpeck here was participating in a long tradition of interpretation that began in the second century and was most developed by Origen in the third century and Bernard of Clairvaux in the twelfth century. The Song of Songs—called the Song of Solomon in many modern Protestant Bibles—was the biblical book most read and commented on in the monasteries of the Middle Ages.[23] The celebration of the love that united the believer to God and to the church was a standard feature of mystical writing. Marpeck must have had access to

23. J. Pelikan, *The Growth of Medieval Theology* (Chicago: University of Chicago Press, 1978), 122-23; Klassen, *Covenant and Community*, 120-23.

interpretations of the Song of Songs because his interpretation carefully tracks the traditional allegorical approach to the book.

The apparel of the bride represents the virtues of the Holy Spirit in their perfection. The person who has not known this bride does not know divine love and has no self-knowledge. Marpeck said that he had had a brief glimpse of her, as had many others.

> I, along with many others who testify to it through faith, have had only a glimpse of her form. This glimpse has created great longing in our hearts to see her again, fully and as she really is. Perhaps we, with all who desire it, may get another glimpse of her, and see her form, so that our hearts may be more eager with desire to seek her and see her form.

He expressed an intense desire to be clothed with garments like hers; that is, the adornment of divine love that unites eternally. These lines testify to the intensity of Marpeck's inner life as well as to his acknowledgment of the unity of his faith with that of others in earlier centuries.

Marpeck wrote that the Canticle, as he called it, employs the image of natural love to direct believers to supernatural love through which they are led into God: they in God and God in them. This is what sixteenth-century mystics called "the gospel of the creatures"—created, material things pointing to divine spiritual realities.

> Partly drawn as it is from nature, these brief words show the nature of love. Nearly the whole of the Canticle presents and illustrates the real, supernatural love by means of the natural parable of love. By this means, all faithful hearts are led into the real, supernatural love, into God Himself; yes, into God Himself and God into them.

One of the sections of the 1542 letter to the Swiss summarized Marpeck's understanding of this concept derived from Hans Hut.[24] This bride is the mother of all believers. She bears them to Christ and nourishes them. These are the legitimate children of God, born figuratively of Sarah from her husband, Abraham. But many who claim to be Abraham's children are in truth the children of Hagar, said Marpeck, and therefore not heirs with the true heir, Isaac. Their father is indeed God as creator, but they are not children through the spirit of the figurative Sarah, the church. They are not nourished by the true Sarah, and mother and child perish in the gruesome desert of this world. Marpeck saw the figurative Hagar as the mother of all the sects, meaning primarily Catholics and Protestants.

24. Klassen and Klaassen, *WPM*, 352-59.

Care for the Churches

Sometime before the end of 1544, Marpeck wrote an anxious letter to Cornelius Veh and a man named Paul, two of his fellow leaders in Austerlitz, Moravia.[25] Something about the way these men exercised their leadership must have come to Marpeck's attention. The theme of the letter is what scholars term antinomianism, a word that describes a lifestyle that assumes there are no laws to govern Christian behaviour. Marpeck's phrase "the freedom of Christ" could have been interpreted in those terms. It was the diametrical opposite of the legalism that had exercised him in earlier letters to the Anabaptists of Appenzell. Legalism was the view that the Christian life was the inflexible observance of rules regarding all aspects of living, including the kind of clothing Christians were allowed to wear and especially that every infraction of the rules was a betrayal of Christ.

Did Veh and Paul conclude that because such legalism was contrary to the Spirit of Christ, Christians therefore were free from every restraint? Marpeck did not mention any specific actions, but the expression of fear in the second-to-last paragraph of his letter suggests that he was concerned about more than a general admonition related to a long-standing Christian dilemma, the tension between law and liberty.

He became personal in the last paragraph, as though he had heard something specific concerning Veh, either with respect to his own actions or his leadership. He was concerned, Marpeck wrote, with those who do not want to be responsible to or for anyone and claim that this is the liberty of Christ.

> They boast about their freedom, yet remain servants of destruction. In their invented liberty which, according to the lust of the flesh, they imagine they possess, they live in open offence and scandal to those who have tender consciences. . . . Of this kind of liberty we know of no instance in Christ's teaching.[26]

This liberty is as destructive as legalism, he warned. Outside of love of God and the neighbour there is no liberty. Here as in other issues, Marpeck— like an ancient mariner trying to avoid disaster—tried to steer between Scylla, the mythological monster on one side of the Strait of Messina, and Charybdis, the whirlpool on the other side.

A letter by Leupold Scharnschlager during this time apparently was closely linked to this issue of freedom and legalism. Entitled "General admonition and reminder," Scharnschlager's letter appears to have been a

---

25. Ibid, 402-6. Fast and Rothkegel, *Kunstbuch*, 148-53.
26. Ibid., 151.

circular message sent to scattered groups of Anabaptists in the mountain country around Ilanz, written "to all [who are] spiritually asleep and luke-warm in the Lord in these last times, in all four corners of the earth."[27]

Scharnschlager began with an expression of dismay that people have neglected the assembly, the discipline, and the admonition that are proper to the church. Next comes a "call to arms" to those who are still awake to deal with the emergency. The third section specifically mentions the care-less attitude of some to brotherly correction. If one person tries to admon-ish another, the response is: "My friend, who are you? Don't you also do this or that?"

What we may be seeing here is the gradual erosion of church disci-pline, induced in part by the campaign of Scharnschlager and Marpeck against legalism among the Swiss Anabaptists. But Scharnschlager's letter also clearly illustrates how the external circumstances of physical distance as well as social and economic pressure on the Anabaptists around Ilanz gave support to the reluctance to exercise "brotherly correction." He refers to single Anabaptist women, for example, who wanted to marry for economic security but could find partners only outside Anabaptist circles. Others wanted to pursue better secular employment to provide for their families.

Could these actions of the Anabaptist women near Ilanz be a form of complaint against Scharnschlager and Marpeck, who were among the priv-ileged members of society? With Scharnschlager hired as a schoolmaster and Marpeck as an engineer, their economic circumstances were a notch above those of most other people. These Anabaptists at Ilanz also observed the lives of their Protestant neighbours, who were not burdened with "brotherly correction" and with social and economic disabilities. This may have been a quite deliberate relaxation by these Anabaptists of the tension between legalism and liberty in order to survive.

More Wars and Invasions

Wars and rumours of wars were the order of the day in the 1540s. The Holy Roman Empire and France were at war, and the Turks once more invaded Hungary and Austria. The Treaty of Crespy on September 18, 1544, brought all these conflicts to a temporary halt. But the end of war was to be a beginning of other things, and the city council of Augsburg knew it. Council members were being lobbied by the bishop and a high imperial official to abandon the Schmalcald League and support the emperor. The effect was to strengthen the Protestant resistance in the city.[28]

27. Fast and Rothkegel, *Kunstbuch*, 446-50, translation by Victor Thiessen.
28. Heinrich Lutz, "Augsburg und seine politische Umwelt 1490-1555," in

Augsburg had joined the Schmalcald League in 1536. The resulting sense of security prompted the Protestant city council to take action to complete religious reform in the city. The mass was abolished on January 17, 1537. These developments in Augsburg and similar ones elsewhere led to the formation in 1538 of the Catholic League of Nuremberg, uniting the Catholic principalities of the Holy Roman Empire to oppose the Lutheran Schmalcald League.

A general church council, which was to restore peace to Christendom and unite everyone for the war against the Turks, failed to take place and was postponed for a year. Gains for the Protestant reform in 1542-43 further alarmed the Catholics. By 1545, both Catholics and Protestants were raising armies.

The Augsburg bankers made a loan of 110,000 guilders to Charles V with no awareness that the money was to be used to wage war against the people of Augsburg. When council members learned about the deception, they forced the bankers to give them an equal amount for their own war effort. The Protestant mayor Jakob Herbrot doubled property taxes for three years and prepared for a defensive war against the emperor.[29]

These alarming public events unfolded amid the efforts of both Catholics and Protestants to dominate the other and force them to their will—especially in personal confession of faith and the ordering of the life of the church. The uncertainty of the times and the ruthless confrontations of Christian versus Christian are reflected in a letter Marpeck wrote toward the end of 1545 to Scharnschlager in Ilanz.[30]

He began by saying that he had recently written to Leupold and brother Martin, and hoped they had received the letter. "Brother Martin" is likely Martin Plaichner, to whom Scharnschlager wrote in May 1544. The crisis of persecution, which was the subject of that letter, had evidently passed and Plaichner was again at home. Marpeck was at pains once again to underscore the role of Christians in a disordered world, especially the world of Protestant and Catholic Christians who by their actions denied Christ.

There is violence, coercion, and domination everywhere, Marpeck wrote, and everywhere people claim that it expresses the mind and will of Christ. He undoubtedly had in mind Catholics and Protestants alike.

Geschichte der Stadt Augsburg. 2000 Jahre von der Römerzeit bis zur Gegenwart, ed. G. Gottlieb (Stuttgart: Konrad Theiss Verlag, 2nd ed., 1985), 426-27.

29. Boyd, *Pilgram Marpeck*, 128; Hermann Kellenbenz, "Wirtschaftsleben der Blütezeit," in *Geschichte der Stadt Augsburg*, ed. G. Gottlieb, et al. 289.

30. Klassen and Klaassen, *WPM*, 412-17; Fast and Rothkegel, *Kunstbuch*, 500-5.

> There are many rulers, many temporal and spiritual tyrants who, while appearing to be Christian, violate, judge and condemn. They run ahead of Christ, and seize His power like thieves and murderers; they rob Him of His honour and glory. They become powerful before they have humbled themselves, they rule and govern before they serve, they condemn and judge before they have judged themselves.

True Christians have been placed by Christ in the world not to rule, judge, condemn, destroy, and inflict suffering and evil on others but to serve them and offer them God's grace and salvation. Human beings have few such servants, he observed, but those few must offer themselves under the banner of the truth in tribulation with Christ.

In May 1546 the emperor rode alongside the Rhine and Danube Rivers from Maestricht in the Netherlands to the Diet at Regensburg. He journeyed with a very small military guard through enemy territory to prove that he had no hostile intentions. By deliberately exposing himself to danger, he used a calculated piece of deception to hide his hectic but successful round-the-clock negotiations for military support wherever he could get it. No one knew what his intentions were, causing fear and suspicion all around. When the Protestant convert Juan Diaz was horribly murdered at Neuburg sometime in May by his own brother—a member of the emperor's entourage—there was high alarm.[31]

The emperor's seemingly peaceful journey in May turned out to be the lull before the storm.

31. Karl Brandi, *Deutsche Geschichte im Zeitalter der Reformation und Gegenreformation* (Munich: Bruckmann 1969), 238.

-17-

Anabaptist Vulnerability Increases

Sometime around the middle of 1546, concerned members of the Schmalcald League were sent to ask Charles V why he was preparing for war. "The emperor desires to restore unity, peace, and justice in the empire," he replied. He would deal with "the disobedient" according to the law and his authority.[1] The emperor's message was unmistakable. War against the Protestants was imminent. Alarmed by the prospect, a large group of empire-friendly merchants—the Fuggers, Welsers, and Baumgartners, among others—left the Protestant-dominated city of Augsburg.[2] Weeks later, the Schmalcald War broke out, pitting Charles V against the Lutheran princes.

The first action of the war occurred on July 23, 1546, when Protestants captured the town of Dillingen, where the bishop of Augsburg lived. Before long, their armies threatened the imperial centre of Innsbruck. In spite of these gains, however, the Schmalcald League frittered away its initial military superiority through poor leadership, and by year-end its army had disintegrated and the forces of Charles V were winning. In the end, Augsburg was conquered and was required to pay 150,000 guilders to Charles for the cost of the war, an amount equal in 2008 to 75 million dollars. By April 1547, eight months after it began, the war was over, and for the first time in his reign, Charles seemed to be unquestioned military master of the Holy Roman Empire.

---

1. Joseph Lortz, *Die Reformation in Deutschland* 2, 5th ed. (Freiburg: Herder, 1962), 262.
2. Heinrich Lutz, "Augsburg und seine politische Umwelt 1490-1555," in *Geschichte der Stadt Augsburg. 2000 Jahre von der Römerzeit bis zur Gegenwart*, 2nd ed. G. Gottlieb (Stuttgart: Konrad Theiss Verlag, 1985), 427.

These stormy events directly affected Marpeck's work for the city of Augsburg, particularly his efforts to bring wood into the city, which were interrupted for several years. It could have been Marpeck's work for the wealthy banker, Baumgartner, that led to his later employment delivering wood to the city of Augsburg.[3] He came there at a time of economic crisis. In November 1543, when Marpeck was already in the city, the Augsburg council authorized the distribution of 150 cords of firewood to the poor to alleviate the suffering caused by a severe wood shortage in the cold of early winter.[4] Marpeck may have talked to city officials about his work supplying Strasbourg with firewood and building timber, using the rivers to float logs into the city. Augsburg, like Strasbourg, was strategically situated beside a major river. The Lech was an important waterway linking the Alps to the Danube.

Between October 18, 1544, and February 28, 1545, Marpeck was occupied with drawing plans for a new civic water system for Augsburg. We may confidently conclude that he had a work room provided by the city that would have included drafting tables and the necessary tools. He must have prepared what today would be called blueprints for the system. In May 1545, a cabinet maker was commissioned to construct a model of Marpeck's plans. That summer he supervised the construction of the new waterworks. Historian Stephen Boyd conjectures that what was referred to in the city records as "Pilgram's waterwork" (*Pilgrims pronnenwerckh*) corresponded to a new waterwork "at the bleacher outside Jacob's gate."

It appears that Marpeck was drawing on his experience in St. Gall by providing water service to a bleaching operation to strengthen the city's weaving industry.[5] The weavers were the largest trade guild in town. From the beginning they had been solid in their support for the Reformation. The industry had been in constant crisis since the start of the century because of outside competition and had received steady support from successive city councils. Moreover, the weavers represented a political block that could threaten the stability of the government. Marpeck's work was therefore important for the economic and political health of Augsburg.[6]

The Jacob Gate was on the east side of the city at the end of the present street of Pilgerhausstrasse; the waterwork and the bleaching ground were on the left side, between the city wall and the Lech River. Marpeck

3. Boyd, *Pilgram Marpeck*, 134.
4. Paul von Stetten, *Augsburger Stadtlexikon*, ed. Günther Grünsteudel, (Augsburg: Perlachverlag, 1998), 370.
5. Boyd, *Pilgram Marpeck*, 136.
6. Lyndal Roper, *The Holy Household, Women and Morals in Reformation Augsburg* (Oxford: Clarendon Press, 1989), 11, 30.

also had the larger task of providing a better water supply system for the whole city, as well as providing wood for heating and construction.

In April 1545 the council appointed a commission of four men to develop a plan to relieve the wood shortage. The forests around Augsburg had long ago disappeared as firewood for the city's houses, so the commission had to look farther afield. Marpeck saw his opportunity and suggested that the city purchase forest lots on the northern slopes of the Alps near the Lech River. Seeing the economic advantage of Marpeck's advice, the council on May 12 hired Marpeck as supervisor of the work (*oberster Werkmann*).[7] The councillors acted promptly on Marpeck's suggestion and on June 27 signed a twenty-eight-year lease on a forest belonging to a convent not far from the border city of Fuessen for the price of 2,400 guilders,[8] an amount about seventy-five times the annual salary of a carpenter. Councillors fretted that the value of the wood—calculated as one guilder per cord—seemed too high. They charged the members of the commission to bargain for a lower price but to pay the full guilder if the vendor could not be persuaded.[9] Whatever they worked out, the official work for the transport of wood into the city was complete.

By June 1545 Marpeck was not only supervising work in the city's forests and transporting timber into the city, he also held the position of top technical employee of the city, responsible for the wood supply and in some measure for water too.[10] He continued to be responsible for work in the forests, for in 1549 he was provided with a horse and an expense account for his work there.[11] By 1546 he received an annual salary of 150 guilders, five times the salary of a carpenter.

Continued Vulnerability

At the end of the Schmalcald War in 1547, the Anabaptists in Augsburg comprised a small group of fewer than one hundred members, including city employees like Marpeck, a number of craftsmen, labourers, and women in charge of households.[12] They met in the homes of the Marpecks, Jörg Maler, and others.[13] They had a simple order of service that focused on what God had done and what God promised would still

7. *Die Chroniken der deutschen Städte vom 14. bis ins 16. Jahrhundert 32. Augsburg 7* (Göttingen: Vandenhoeck & Ruprecht, 1917/1966), 70.

8. Boyd, *Pilgram Marpeck*, 135.

9. *Die Chroniken der deutschen Städte, Augsburg 7*, 70.

10. Boyd, *Pilgram Marpeck*, 135.

11. Ibid., 136.

12. Helena von Freyberg is believed to have died in 1545, leaving a significant vacancy in the Augsburg Anabaptist community.

13. Boyd, *Pilgram Marpeck*, 138-39.

be done through a community that allowed itself to be led along the path of peace. They often ate together, with each person paying for his or her own food. Those who did not have the money to cover this cost were provided for by others.

The emperor's victory resulted in a drastic change in daily life for Protestant Augsburg. For the Anabaptists, it merely intensified their vulnerability. Theirs was a precarious existence: uneasy, uncertain, and illegitimate. Yet the letters that emerge from the group during this time bespeak a firm conviction that behind the ever-present threats was a sense of victory, wherein this community of faith could lean on the arms of the God of peace, knowing that their life would continue to flow as part of the tribulation and suffering of Christ.

In the summer of 1545, when preparations for war were already being made and Protestants were still fully in control, Augsburg's city council had passed ordinances to control Anabaptist activity that it felt could harm the city. Midwives were placed under restrictive control to ensure that no infant remained unbaptized.[14] Printers were served notice that they were allowed to publish only what had the permission of city council.[15] This was new. Printers had faced virtually no interference in Augsburg, which maintained a civic policy of openness[16] that had been in place for twenty years. The control of printing, no doubt directed at Anabaptists, was also imposed to prevent Catholic materials from being circulated.

In August, the police were ordered to keep an eye on gatherings of Anabaptists. With growing concern for the security of the city, civic officials were taking no chances. Although there had not been a hint of trouble for two decades, Anabaptists were still regarded as politically unreliable.

On July 8, 1546, the day before the Schmalcald War broke out, five Anabaptist men refused to do watch duty on the city walls. Most of them had a connection with Marpeck and were treated by authorities as belonging to his fellowship. Yet the council seems not to have pressed the question of their affiliation with Marpeck. His Anabaptist ties were surely an open secret in Augsburg. Possibly the authorities didn't want to jeopardize the important civic work that Marpeck was doing. Perhaps he also gained some protection from his close association with several influential clergy, including Wolfgang Musculus, whom he probably came to know from

14. William Klassen, "Midwives," in *ME* 5, 584-85. Also, Wiesner, *Working Women in Renaissance Germany.*

15. *Augsburger Stadlexikon,* 386.

16. Rolf Kiessling, "Augsburg in der Reformationszeit," in *Augsburger Stadtlexikon,* 67.

their encounters during the Bucer debates in Strasbourg.[17] It could also be that Marpeck developed a different operating style in Augsburg, one that was more low-key than his more up-front, confrontational approach in Strasbourg. He probably took care, for example, to observe Augsburg's rules that no assemblies should exceed ten or twelve people.

~

Among the Anabaptists on trial for refusing guard duty was Hans Jakob Schneider, a member of the Marpeck group who had received his instruction on Anabaptism from Helena von Freyberg and who emerged as a spokesperson for the five men. Schneider's statement stands as a simple testimony to civil disobedience: refusing to obey authorities on the grounds of conscience.

"Did you take the annual oath of citizenship?" Schneider was asked.
"Yes," he replied.
"Why, then, do you now refuse to serve as a guard?"
"I want to carry out all my civic responsibilities," Schneider answered, "as far as that is possible. However, I cannot find it in my conscience to keep the watch and especially to assail the enemy. I would rather die than do so."[18]

It was not timidity that compelled Schneider to refuse guard duty. Rather, it was a higher loyalty arising from Anabaptist interpretation of Scripture, which incorporated the love of enemies into its quest for justice and peace. His teachers were Helena and Pilgram, who themselves had endured life-altering consequences for refusing to submit to the dictates of the ruling powers.

At trial's end, all five of the men who refused guard duty were expelled from the city.[19] Marpeck himself was warned about his Anabaptist activity on July 16, but no action was taken against him.

Takeover of Augsburg

A year later, on July 23, 1547, a triumphant Charles V rode into town precisely at noon. He came with a large retinue of soldiers, princes, and nobles, including Spanish grandees dressed in black velvet. The emperor,

---

17. Musculus was Martin Bucer's secretary in Strasbourg before moving to Augsburg in 1531 and in 1549 to Bern. He appears to have had an impact on both Marpeck's and Maler's understanding of the nature of swearing an oath. See the discussion on the oath in chapter 12 and "Oath," by William Klassen in *ME* 4, 6-8.
18. Boyd, *Pilgram Marpeck*, 141.
19. Ibid.

also garbed in a black velvet coat and hat, rode by himself, preceded by his imperial marshal, the Marschalck von Pappenheim,[20] who carried the regal sword. Then came the cardinal of Augsburg and after him, the three mayors of the city along with the city's mercenaries, all dressed in black. The mayors and members of council had ridden out of the city to meet the emperor. They dismounted and fell on their knees. Charles graciously ordered them to rise and accompany him into the city. They, in turn, were followed by Neapolitan, Italian, Spanish, Burgundian, and German cavalry units fully armed in colourful ceremonial uniforms, followed by ten companies of infantry.

Marpeck and his group could well have been among the citizens who witnessed the entry of the emperor to Augsburg. One can imagine the populace lining the parade route in stunned silence at the overwhelming demonstration of this military victory and dreading its consequences. The question "where will all these foreign soldiers be billetted?" was no doubt murmured through the crowd. But the soldiers were not the only ones who marched into town. Preceding the emperor, the whole supply train of Charles's army had swept into the city at eight o'clock that morning: countless wagons, donkeys, and horses plus teamsters and supply personnel.

Once he had demonstrated his military strength, Charles was anxious to scatter his soldiers into the populace at large. When the emperor arrived at his quarters at the Fugger house (to the left of today's Maximilianstrasse), he dismissed most of the military—including the supply train—and sent them to be billetted outside the city in nearby villages. He ordered the expulsion within twenty-four hours of all soldiers who were not on his payroll, regardless of nationality, as well as now-unemployed mercenaries. They were ordered to go home or to a chosen place of residence and not to linger. One by one, the cavalry units and infantry marched out of town, leaving via the Jacob Gate and thereby passing the waterworks that Marpeck had designed and built just two years earlier. As the troops descended on the villages, their residents fled into Augsburg in fear, for no one was safe from the rampaging soldiers.[21]

Demobilized soldiers and mercenaries were a plague caused by the many and continuing wars. Given to robbery and violence, they were a threat to the order of Augsburg, which was already imperilled by the legitimate mili-

---

20. The Marschalck von Pappenheim was a member of an ancient Augsburg family who for many years had been the imperial marshals. This line of the family had become Protestant and was known to Pilgram Marpeck. See *Die Chroniken der deutschen Städte, Augsburg* 8, 326-27.
    21. Roth, *ARG* 4, 154-55.

tary.[22] Within months, the violence caused by increasingly unhappy soldiers was to come to full boil.

On September 30, 1547, four companies of soldiers and one of musketeers marched noisily and threateningly through the city to the emperor's lodging at the Fugger house, demanding to be paid their back wages. There had been previous episodes of vandalism and riotous behaviour by soldiers to the point that citizens shut themselves up in their houses. The emperor was so alarmed by the angry soldiers that he promised immediate payment. But he was also determined to set a public example that would discourage any repetition of threats toward him. The ringleaders of the rebellious soldiers were caught and executed. On November 3, the master gunner of the Lutheran elector of Saxony was taken to the weavers' guild house for punishment after he reportedly threatened to assassinate the emperor. A pillar was erected on the street in front of the guild house, a place very near Marpeck's house, and the man's right hand tied to it. With one swing of the axe, the executioner lopped off his hand. Sadly for the master gunner, this was only the beginning of his travails. The unfortunate man was then taken to the Perlachplatz at the city centre and laid across the wheel, drawn, and quartered. No wonder Charles was surrounded by armed guards, even when he went to church.[23]

The occupation of Augsburg by the emperor's own troops placed extra burdens on the townspeople, including probably the Marpecks. It may have been to help with these burdens that Magdalena von Pappenheim, a member of the family of the imperial marshal of the emperor, at this time sent a support gift to Anna Marpeck.[24] Both Magdalena and her niece, Walpurga von Pappenheim, had become Anabaptists. It was Pilgram who mentioned the gift in a letter to Magdalena. He wrote: "My sister Anna [his wife] thanks you kindly, and I too, for your gift and donation."

A New Reality Takes Hold

An imperial diet was called for September 1, 1547, to deal with the new reality in the empire following Charles's victory. Charles now seemed to be undisputed master in the Holy Roman Empire. The days of negotiation with the evangelical princes were over; he could now order that his wishes be carried out. The diet of 1547 is sometimes referred to as *der geharnischte Reichstag*, meaning the armed or military diet, alluding to Charles's military supremacy and his intention to force his will on the van-

22. *Die Chroniken der deutschen Städte, Augsburg* 8, 326-27.
23. Ibid., 330-32.
24. Klassen and Klaassen, *WPM*, 483; Fast and Rothkegel, *Kunstbuch*, 609.

quished. But the sense of power was short-lived. The deliberations dragged on for a year for reasons with which Charles was all too familiar. Even before Charles's military victory was complete, the pope had recalled the troops he had sent to assist Charles, fearing an emperor too powerful for Rome to deal with. This raised again the threat of schism and conflict between the two heads of Christendom, the pope and emperor.

Perhaps this renewed uncertainty contributed to the deliberate tactical obscuring of Charles's theological position and to his hesitation to make political commitments to the princes attending the diet.[25] He knew that he might have to compromise yet again, as he had so often been forced to do in the past. Over the long winter, the sordid behaviour of the defeated princes brought the diet into further disrepute, scandalizing the inhabitants of Augsburg with their drunkenness and lewd conduct.

The result of the diet of 1547-48 was the so-called "Interim," an imposed preliminary settlement of the religious discord between Catholics and Protestants that became the law of the empire in May 1548. It was designed to last only until a general council of the whole church—including Catholics and Protestants—would produce a final settlement. Under the Interim, Protestants were allowed to have married clergy (i.e., priestly marriage) and Protestant laity could partake of communion with both bread and wine. The basic Catholic doctrines were to remain in place. Several days after May 15, 1548, Granvella, Charles's chief minister, summoned the Augsburg council and demanded that it declare whether it would accept the Interim. After some diplomatic back and forth, it was accepted under threat of unilateral action by the imperial government.[26]

The Interim eventually failed because of the resistance of the people, who simply rejected the presence of priests in Protestant churches and refused to listen to them.[27] The Protestant residents of Augsburg knew that the Catholic clergy (who, along with its prominent citizens, left the city before the war) had lobbied the emperor for the diet to be held in Augsburg as a punishment for their religious defiance of pope and emperor between 1530 and 1547.[28]

Emperor Charles and his entourage remained in Augsburg for a full year. Interestingly, his brother Ferdinand also visited Augsburg to attend the diet during this time. He arrived on October 20, 1547, three months after Charles marched into the city. In contrast to Charles's grand entrance,

25. Lortz, *Die Reformation in Deutschland*, 266, 269.
26. *Chroniken der deutschen Städte, Augsburg* 7, 27-31.
27. Karl Brandi, *Deutsche Geschichte im Zeitalter der Reformation und Gegenreformation* (Munich: Bruckmann, 1969), 248.
28. *ARG*, 4, 43.

Ferdinand quietly rode into town at eight o'clock in the morning with only eight companions by his side. To underscore the low-key, friendly nature of his visit, he left his army in Bavaria. Moreover, he even declined civic plans for a ceremonial reception.[29]

Thus Ferdinand and Marpeck were once more in the same city, but neither Marpeck nor official records make any mention of this coincidence. Both must have known about the other's presence. Why Ferdinand did not demand Marpeck's extradition is a mystery. Perhaps the volatile situation in the city or Ferdinand's preoccupation with larger issues precluded him from taking action against Marpeck. But perhaps there was another reason for it as well. No other person of Marpeck's stature and function in the city was in any way interfered with, and that could mean that Marpeck and others like him had immunity because of their importance as indispensable employees of the city.

On August 3, 1548, Charles suspended Augsburg's ancient constitution and dissolved the city's craft guilds and their control of the city council. He also gave Augsburg a new constitution stipulating that both Catholics and Protestants should have an equal number of members on the city council, even though Catholics now accounted for only 10 percent of the population. Charles had no intention of abrogating Augsburg's independence as an imperial city, but rather sought to ensure that in the future it would have a government more faithful to him. Members of council were now to be chosen from the patrician families.[30] The council was forced to surrender the ancient rights of the city, in particular its 1383 constitution. In the religious settlement, Protestants—as indicated, comprising 90 percent of the population—were given just three churches and two preaching localities. The occupying forces stayed on, despite all pleas from citizens, because the emperor and the clergy were determined to punish Augsburg for its refusal to conform. But even with the emperor present, no one—whether Protestant or Catholic—was willing to serve on the council or as mayor.[31]

The many inequities and resulting civic surliness were, in Marpeck's view, the consequence of trying to resolve religious differences by force. We may be sure that those Protestant theologians who had heard Marpeck on this issue in similar crises (and who earlier had disagreed with him) must now have had some second thoughts. It was at this time that Martin Bucer, the Reformer from Strasbourg, chose exile in England over accepting the

29. *Die Chroniken der deutschen Städte, Augsburg* 8, 330-31.
30. H. Immenkötter, "Augsburg," in *Oxford Encyclopedia of the Reformation* 1, 90; Lutz, "*Augsburg und seine politische Umwelt*," 428.
31. *ARG* 4, 312, 65-66.

emperor's terms because, he said, his conscience would allow him no choice. The Augsburg settlement did not interfere with the church life of the Anabaptists because they had no legal standing to begin with. There is little doubt, however, that the general disorder during the year of the diet must have disrupted their gatherings from time to time.

'The Deep Humility of Christ'

On February 1, 1547, Marpeck wrote a long letter that the copyist, entitled "The Deep Humility of Christ" to those who were part of the Marpeck fellowships scattered in small clusters in the Grisons, Appenzell, St. Gall, and Alsace.[32] The Schmalcald War was not yet over, but its eventual outcome was already predictable by any careful observer. Certainly Marpeck was familiar with the incoming bulletins about the military triumph of Charles's forces, which would bring disaster to Augsburg. Just two days before he wrote this letter, a delegation of officials from the city had travelled to Ulm and submitted to the emperor on their knees. Soon after Marpeck wrote the letter, the first occupation force entered Augsburg.[33] It was, he wrote, a demanding and dangerous time. Referring to armed soldiers who were ostensibly in the service of Christ, he bluntly called them "ignorant and unbridled animals."

Marpeck felt compelled to write to members of his fellowship, many of whom were also affected by the war, to help them understand why Catholics and Protestants—all of whom claimed the name of Christ— acted as they did. He began where he always began, with the humiliation of Christ in the incarnation. But he raised the theological stakes by writing about the "deep humiliation" of Christ in the *descensus ad inferos*, the decent into hell, based on 1 Peter 3:18-20.[34]

Some say that the descent into hell was a descent of triumph, he wrote. Indeed, the triumphant harrowing of hell was a favourite subject of medieval painting and sculpture. But for Marpeck, the descent was the nadir of Christ's humiliation. Only after total humiliation, only after going down to the ultimate depth, could he ascend and be exalted in glory. "The true warrantor went Himself into the depths of hell with our sins, and yet without any sins of His own, through His torment on earth in order to make payment."

---

32. Klassen and Klaassen, *WPM*, 427-63; Fast and Rothkegel, *Kunstbuch*, 558-85.
33. Lutz, "Augsburg und seine politische Umwelt," 428.
34. In the sixteenth century this theme was very popular, nurtured in part by mystical piety and also by the Gospel of Nicodemus, a widely read apocryphal book. See Klassen, *Covenant and Community*, 183-86, and literature there cited.

Every believer must make the same journey of descent and ascent with Christ, and there can be no glory for the believer unless the deep humiliation come first, Marpeck said. This is a very difficult lesson for Christians to learn. The descent with Christ is the "severe water of baptism" through which the believer goes into the depths of death with Christ and only then can be raised up with Christ. This can be learned only through understanding the depth and humiliation of Christ in the incarnation revealed through his holy humanity. But none of those who imagine themselves to be Christians want to have any part of this humiliation, he caustically observed. As proof, look at their attempts not to submit but rather to dominate.

To pursue his line of argument with greater clarity, Marpeck used the image of the ark of the covenant from 1 Samuel 4:10-7:1, in which the ark was temporarily captured by the Philistines. The ark typified for him the container of all the divine treasures available to God's people through the offices of Christ. According to Marpeck, the Philistines—that is, the world, including those who believe themselves to be Christians—accept the ark. But when they perceive that it brings only trials and testing (the natural lot of true Christians) they send it away by means of their military, employing armour, weapons, and guns. It can be clearly seen in today's events, said Marpeck, that they have no use for the patience of Christ, who never used weapons to subdue others.

> If one wishes to, one can see that such is the case these days. There are those who have adopted the gospel, but they only appear to adopt the patience of Christ; the Philistines now send the ark back home again. Are these not truly the unspiritual Philistines who, together with their Goliath, trust only in human power?[35]

A patient, peaceful approach is one of the chief treasures in the ark, Marpeck declared. The earnest copyist of the letter added his own note in the margin here, citing as examples the Swiss wars of Kappel, in which Zwingli perished, and the Schmalcald War. As a final caution, Marpeck warned that all the faithful who are on pilgrimage through the desert of this world must take care that the treasures of this ark are not lost.

Marpeck's ministrations to the ordinary faithful were tame compared to his verbal upbraiding of the wealthy. Within walking distance of Marpeck's home was the palatial residence of the financier Anton Fugger. Marpeck had worked in the Tirolean mines owned by the Fugger family twenty years earlier and therefore had personal acquaintance with their worldwide financial empire and their methods of doing business—both of

---

35. Klassen and Klaassen, *WPM*, 448.

which reminded him, he said, of Peter's denial and Judas's betrayal of Jesus. The financiers of today, wrote Marpeck, have sold the Lord through envy and hate. "Whole lands, armies, and peoples[36] . . . are betrayed, sold, and bought by their loans, finance, and usury," he declared.[37]

What really galled Marpeck was that all this greed and ruination happened under the name of Christ among both "the old and new enforcers of faith." It was common knowledge that the Fuggers had advanced the money for the enormous bribe that resulted in Charles being made emperor in 1519 and that they had financed Charles's wars throughout his reign. Only two years earlier, as previously mentioned, they had loaned Charles a vast sum that was then used to subjugate Augsburg.

See what has happened to those who supposed themselves to be Christians, Marpeck pointedly observed. It is God's righteous judgment upon their unbelief. Perhaps the news from Ulm about the humiliation of the Augsburg officials there prompted Marpeck to write this letter.

Repetition with a Purpose

It is easy to dismiss with impatience the long, often tedious discourse of sixteenth-century writers on theological topics. Marpeck's letters are a case in point. He was repetitive and did not always follow through on what he announced he would do. He also sometimes painted himself into a logical impasse.

That said, Marpeck's writing technique may be more insightful than it might first appear. Marpeck was writing to lay people, not to rhetoric-trained theologians. He was not arguing the rightness of his views but writing for the spiritual edification of his readers, to help them strengthen their faith. One common method to help believers internalize Scripture was repetition, even for those who were literate. For those in Marpeck's community who could not read, repetition was even more important. Going over the same ground again and again may not have been accidental or indicative of lack of skill or imagination. Rather, it may have been a useful teaching tool.

Marpeck's letters demonstrate a total immersion in the mental and spiritual world of the Bible. This biblical world was Canaan and the language was the language of Zion. The most important reason for repetition was to fix in the minds of the readers that this was the *truly* real: the unshakable, permanent reality compared to the world of nations, govern-

---

36. An example of this was the extensive control of mining in South America by the Fuggers and Welsers. See H. G. Koenigsberger, "The Empire of Charles V in Europe," in *The New Cambridge Modern History* 2, *The Reformation*, ed. G. R. Elton (Cambridge: Cambridge University Press, 1958), 312-13.

37. Klassen and Klaassen, *WPM*, 449; Fast and Rothkegel, *Kunstbuch*, 575.

ments, and wars, which was a world that was capricious, unreliable, imper-manent, and ruinous.[38] For example, 1547 was a disastrous year for Augs-burg and its people. More important to Marpeck, however, was "this new and acceptable" year of the Lord (Isa. 61:2; Luke 4:19).[39]

Nor was this spiritual world an abstract world. Marpeck wrote about the mystical body[40] of the church that is beyond human sight, but he anchored this body firmly on his favourite theological rock—the human-ity of Christ—and with it the church, which is visible in history in a given place on the map at a given time in the years of our Lord. It is this living, visible community that lives its true life already in the Promised Land, liv-ing both there and in exile here on earth at the same time.

The letter Marpeck wrote to Magdalena von Pappenheim in December 1547 can be read similarly. It is about sinners, repentance, and forgiveness.[41] Those who sin, wrote Marpeck, are invited to repent so that they may receive grace. Whoever receives grace is free from the tyranny of sin. Thus they are able to live out the virtues of Christ in the commun-ion of saints. Even those who have made their natural virtues and customs into idols, he says, may through faith in Christ be granted the nobility of true godliness. Those who are weak and fearful and believe in God but don't do his will and sink into sin can also be led to repentance and the state of nobility and virtue.

Few True Nobles

To illuminate this point further, Marpeck reached for a metaphor, "peasant nobility," which he probably chose because Magdalena was a member of a noble family. But his discussion of the term is general, which suggests perhaps that this letter was addressed to others of his group as well.

"Peasant nobility," as Marpeck used the term, was an oxymoron, thereby immediately alerting his readers to the fact that it had nothing to do with the actual peasantry or nobility of his time. The medieval ideal of chivalry[42] (at the centre of which was the virtuous knight) had by Marpeck's time become a generalized ideal especially common in the bourgeois circles

38. The letter of February 1, 1547, is a particularly good example of this contrast. Everything is understood in terms of the divine economy of salvation. Every facet of the relationship of Christ and the believer, as well as the believer and the world, is given attention.
39. Klassen and Klaassen, *WPM*, 441; Fast and Rothkegel, *Kunstbuch*, 568.
40. See his letter "On the Inner Church," *WPM*, 418-26; Fast and Rothkegel, *Kunstbuch*, 588-94.
41. Klassen and Klaassen, *WPM*, 464-84; Fast and Rothkegel, *Kunstbuch*, 595-609.
42. Diaz de Gamez, "The Chivalric Ideal," in *The Portable Medieval Reader* (New York: Viking Press, 1949), 91-92.

to which Marpeck belonged. In the original ideal the knight was both noble and virtuous, without reproach in reputation. He upheld the virtues of courage, honour, piety, fidelity, and service. Noble lineage was very important, as was the coat of arms, which was a kind of guarantee of the virtue of the bearer. Because of the close link between chivalry and the Crusades, the knight was understood to be a knight of Christ, the *miles christianus*.

The peasant, on the other hand, had no noble pedigree and was popularly considered to be ignorant, crude, and brutish—a person without moral restraint. The sixteenth-century paintings of Pieter Brueghel as well as contemporary woodcuts clearly illustrate this judgment. Marpeck's use of the metaphor should therefore not be interpreted to be either approval of the actual nobility of his time or disapproval of the actual peasantry. He used "noble" to mean Christian and "peasant" to mean sinner.

Marpeck's use of the metaphor begins with the biblical concept of the kingdom of God, of which Christ is the king. He is head of "the high nobility of Christ." The actual material jewels of the earthly nobility do not, of course, guarantee virtue, but they are images of the virtues of Christ. In the earthly nobility it is a scandal to possess gold, ceremonial chains, jewels, and the appropriate apparel and at the same time lack all honour and natural virtue. Indeed, he writes, there are few true nobles today.

At the beginning, God endowed Adam and Eve with nobility, complete with all the noble virtues. But they rejected this nobility with its virtues when they disobeyed God and were expelled from "the garden of delights." They were turned into labouring peasants in the "great village of this bleak world's wilderness." Marpeck then contrasts the manicured pleasure gardens of the nobility, with their aroma of roses and herbs, with the rudeness of the village with its rubbish and foul smells. Thus this divine nobility in the persona of Adam and Eve became "wretched, coarse peasants . . . working the earth in falsehood and deceit, in all wickedness, shame, and licentiousness . . . and made into coarse, undisciplined slaves of sin."

Marpeck ends the letter with a prayer that God would preserve his readers and himself from error in a world where people run hither and thither looking for the peace of Christ and not finding it. He was concerned especially that his people not be seduced by the sects, a reference no doubt here to Schwenckfeld but also to the Protestants, who were mostly Lutheran.

At the end of the letter to Magdalena, he conveys thanks for the gift to Anna and sends greetings from her and the community in Augsburg. Behind the expression of appreciation for the gift to Anna lies gratitude for the gift that words alone cannot begin to express: God's grace as seen in the Son.

We are not aware if a response to the letter was given.

-18-

Engineer by Day, Theologian by Night

While theological issues were a matter of intense interest for Marpeck, more down-to-earth concerns also consumed considerable amounts of his time and energy. For a while, he had as many challenges on the engineering front as he did evangelizing the faith.

As part of the constitutional change of the Interim settlement, the city's paymaster (*Baumeister*), in whose house the Marpecks were living, was replaced by three members of the patriciate. Now that the political situation had stabilized, these men turned their attention to the interrupted project of getting wood into the city. Marpeck's position as an employee of the city seems not to have changed, even though the whole senior administration had.

He immediately had the ear of the new officials. It may be that because he was neither Catholic nor Protestant, he was viewed as neutral and therefore didn't constitute a threat. Marpeck had spoken to the new council members and had rashly persuaded them that he would bring the wood into the city at the low cost of a few *batzen*, a small local coin similar to today's penny, for one cord. To assess this offer, one of the three new members of the paymaster's office and a second official rode out to the forests with Marpeck. Once in the woods, they conferred and agreed that the wood could be cut into suitable lengths, thrown into the Lech River, and allowed to float freely into Augsburg. Near the city, wooden barriers would need to be built at great cost across the river to stop the logs and enable them to be hauled onto the land. Expert woodsmen were hired to determine whether or not the wood could be floated downriver by the devised system.

They judged that the Lech often ran very high and overflowed, creating many tributary channels. They warned against Marpeck's plan, saying that the flow would be strong enough to destroy the barrier, resulting in loss of the wood. But Marpeck and Melchior Ilsing, the patrician in charge, persuaded the council that there was no insuperable problem, and the project continued late in 1548. Whether Marpeck was relying on his experience successfully transferring wood from the Black Forest to Strasbourg or some other plan, his engineering judgment related to this particular project failed him quite spectacularly.

As the experts had predicted, logs from the raging waters smashed into the barrier near Augsburg and destroyed it. Needing to capitalize on the high-water flows, the city immediately rebuilt it. Some men worked from boats while others toiled in the cold mountain water. Another shipment of logs was then hauled from the forest and dumped into the fast-flowing Lech. Once again, the high waters caused the heavy logs to pound against the barrier and break it. Finally, for the third time the logs came hurtling down the river and smashed the barrier yet again. This time, the river swept away the entire barrier and all the wood, some of it floating into the Danube as far away as Linz, more than 300 kilometres (180 miles) away.

In the end, only a fraction of the wood from the forest was saved for Augsburg. Worse, the logs ended up costing the city not a few batzen as Marpeck had boasted, but four or five guilders per cord.[1] All this must have been very embarrassing for Marpeck, whose technical work normally was accomplished (as best we know) with considerable success.

Surprisingly, this signal disaster did not cost him his position. Even though this method of transporting large quantities of logs was not tried again for another fifteen years,[2] Marpeck seems to have continued floating wood into Augsburg on a smaller, more manageable scale.[3]

It was Marpeck's work with the civic water supply that probably helped him keep his job with the city despite his log-transport fiascos. Since the fifteenth century, there had been ongoing work to regularize Augsburg's supply and use of water. A burgeoning production-oriented business climate in the city sparked new industries such as paper mills, fulling for the weaving sector, and oil production for domestic use. Increasingly these industries were built along waterways diverted from the Lech River. Thus the city was compelled to steadily improve the technology of supplying water for its industrial and domestic use.[4]

1. *Die Chroniken der deutschen Städte vom 14. Bis ins 16. Jahrhundert 32. Augsburg* 7 (Göttingen: Vandenhoeck & Ruprecht, 1917/1966), 70-73.

2. Ibid., 73, n2.

3. Boyd, *Pilgram Marpeck*, 136.

4. Anton Werner, *Die Wasserkräfte der Stadt Augsburg im Dienste von Industrie und Gewerbe* (Augsburg: Verlag der Math. Rieger'schen Buchhandlung, 1905), 10.

When Marpeck came to Augsburg, two water towers stood to the right of the Red Gate, which had just been completed in 1544 at the main southern entrance to the city. The water supply for the towers was the Brunnenbach, a strong-flowing brook into which flowed a number of smaller brooks arising from a large aquifer to the south of the city, the main water source for Augsburg even today. The southernmost and oldest of these towers had been built in 1416 to provide water for the fountains in the southern part of the city through a system of wooden pipes. There is evidence that Marpeck renovated this old tower and lived with Anna in a residence atop it after 1548. It can still be identified by the decorative balustrade around the top.

The other tower near it had been built in 1470 as the city's demand for water rose. Marpeck added two more storeys to the existing two. Wooden pumps were used to raise the water from the Brunnenbach into the towers, from where it flowed by gravity to the users. The addition of storeys to the newer tower enabled the water to be raised higher, which in turn enabled gravity to take the water further into the city. Marpeck also helped expand the existing network of wooden pipes to distribute the water. Due to his work, the citizens of Augsburg had running water in their homes after 1558 at ten guilders per annum.[5] However, since that amount constituted the equivalent of a third of an artisan's annual salary, only the wealthy could afford it.

A part of the water system was the so-called lower tower at the northern end of the city at the Mauersberg, a short distance southeast of the cathedral. In 1538, the former defence tower was rebuilt as a water tower, and the famous *machina augustana* was installed.

The machina was a system of seven screw propellers or augers enclosed in pipes, one above the other, driven by a water wheel that in turn drove a mechanism of wooden cogwheels. The bottom of each auger sat in a trough, the lowest one at stream level. It raised the water from one trough into the one above it until it finally flowed into a tank at the top from which it fed by gravity into the service pipes. The tower with its machine was one of the mechanical marvels of the time and was described complete with drawings in 1554 by Jerome Cardanus, a scientist from Milan.[6] This tower was supervised by Georg Loscher, Augsburg's director of waterworks

---

5. Wilhelm Ruckdeschel, "Die Brunnenwerke am Roten Tor zu Augsburg zur Zeit des Brunnenmeisters Casper Walter," in *Zeitschrift des historischen Vereins für Schwaben* 69 (1975), 63-64; W. Ruckdeschel, "Das untere Brunnenwerk zu Augsburg durch vier Jahrhunderte," in *Zeitschrift des historischen Vereins für Schwaben* 75 (1981), 86-87; Boyd, *Pilgram Marpeck*, 137-38.

6. Ruckdeschel, "Das untere Brunnenwerk zu Augsburg," 90-91.

(*Brunnenmeister*). There is no indication that Marpeck had anything to do with it. However, Marpeck received a much higher salary than Loscher, a fact that suggests he may have been Loscher's superior. Whatever the case, Marpeck seems to have had the more senior administrative responsibility for the water system.

By 1550, Marpeck was listed first among the technicians, indicating he likely was public works director. Certainly he employed a number of workmen and commissioned others to provide parts and materials. Marpeck's projects represented a separate file in the city administration, a file accorded its own funding.[7] We also know that in 1550 Marpeck supervised the early stages of constructing a dyke on the Reichstrasse,[8] an imperial road that ran between Augsburg and Innsbruck along the Lech River. The dyke may have been built to prevent the road from flooding during times of high water. Despite his logging mishaps and his quiet but influential existence as an Anabaptist leader, Marpeck continued his employment in Augsburg until his death.

A Rare Stability

It should be noted that no other Anabaptist—let alone Anabaptist leader—at that time ever enjoyed the kind of stability and lifestyle that Marpeck appears to have had while in Augsburg. His wages were far above those of the average worker. Marpeck's hydrological skills provided him with a financial security that was a source of much envy for his main theological opponent, Caspar Schwenckfeld. In a letter to a follower, Schwenckfeld expressed his surprise that Marpeck was allowed to remain in Augsburg while he was not. "I did not think he was still there," he wrote. "That is the way it goes when you consider your own advantage. . . . But of course error has a place to live in this world where as justice and truth have no place in this world but must wait till the new world."[9]

Yet it's clear that Pilgram and Anna lived very modestly at an economic level far below what they could afford. Marpeck's writings repeatedly stressed the need for Christians to share whatever blessings they had with each other, particularly with the poor. There is every indication that in this and many other respects, Marpeck strived to live what he preached.

Lutheran church historian Friedrich Roth describes Marpeck in Augsburg as *der alte Schwaermer*—a pejorative term that at best meant "the old enthusiast" and more typically, someone with bees in his bonnet—who, he says, would have been recognized as such by many city dwellers and cer-

7. Boyd, *Pilgram Marpeck*, 136-38.
8. Ibid., 137 n63.
9. Letter to Sibilla Eiseler, CS 7, 657.

tainly by the members of the city council and clergy.[10] However Marpeck was regarded, it is important to note that while other Anabaptists in the city were harassed, imprisoned, and expelled, he was warned but not touched.[11] There is no indication that he was in any danger even when his former nemesis Ferdinand was in the city from 1547 to 1548 and again for some months from 1550 to 1551.

Ferdinand and Marpeck must have known about the other's presence in the city. Given the close working relationship they once had, each one doubtless harboured a sense of betrayal against the other. Ferdinand must have been tempted to swoop down on Marpeck and make him pay for duping his royal master and fleeing Rattenberg to pursue a life of illegal activity as an Anabaptist. The fact that Marpeck wasn't touched suggests that local authorities either hid Marpeck's identity from the king or warned Ferdinand not to proceed against him. As mentioned earlier, the city could ill afford to lose his engineering skills.

Yet Marpeck's life was not trouble-free. Augsburg city council warned him about his Anabaptist activities in 1545, 1550, 1553, and 1554.[12] On the first date council officials warned him not to have anything to do with his sect. The second warning had to do with the appearance of the work *The Explanation of the Testaments* (*Testamenterleutterung*). Apparently they suspected that he was the author. On the third occasion they warned him that if he was holding meetings, he would be punished; and on the fourth, if it could be shown that he was spreading his "error," he would be ordered to leave town. Despite the intensifying rhetoric against him, it is possible the warnings were pro forma to satisfy the imperial watchdogs overseeing the implementation of royal edicts against Anabaptists. Whatever the cause, no action was ever taken against him.

A Tempered Approach to Government

Marpeck's own views of government and a Christian's relationship to it may have had something to do with his political security. As we saw earlier, he did not object to swearing the civic oath in Strasbourg wherever it did not conflict with his primary loyalty to Christ.[13] He evidently swore the oath again when he was hired in Augsburg. We do not know what passed between Marpeck and the Augsburg city council in terms of a ver-

10. See Roth, *ARG* 3, 249. It should be noted that the term *Schwaermer* generally implied uncontrolled religious mania.
11. In contrast, see the story of Jörg Maler in chapter 15.
12. For a summary of these warnings, see Klassen, *Covenant and Community*, 35-36.
13. But see the unpublished dissertation of Edmund Pries, *Anabaptist Oath Refusal*.

bal agreement regarding his employment. But he apparently demonstrated in word and deed what he counselled his followers to do, namely not to provoke government. Governments do not carelessly persecute people, he stated, but are concerned with order and security. Clearly Marpeck had in mind the lower orders of governments (especially Protestant ones) like city councils, and not the policies of Charles V and Ferdinand I. He counselled quiet submission so that the few remaining places of refuge for Anabaptists might not be lost.[14]

There seems to have been a gentlemen's agreement between the Augsburg council and Marpeck that, in the interests of the welfare of the city, they would not provoke each other. Marpeck's attitude has sometimes been characterized as a kind of pietist quietism, implying he was guilty of un-Anabaptist compromise.[15] Looking at the available evidence, we see no basis for Marpeck being called a quietist or a secret conformist. He participated in Christian communion with other Anabaptists in and around Augsburg and continued active service as an Anabaptist elder counselling, writing, publishing, and visiting Anabaptists in communities near and far.

Time and Money into Publications

While Marpeck did not engage in any public debates with the evangelical clergy in Augsburg as he had done in Strasbourg, he energetically continued with the publishing activity he had begun there, making available to his churches pamphlets and books across a fair spectrum of theological views.

Historian Werner Packull concurred with Adolf Laube and Helmut Claus[16] in concluding that the first publisher Marpeck engaged in Strasbourg was Jacob Cammerlander, who published *A Clear Refutation* and *A Clear and Useful Instruction* in 1531 and the *Exposé of the Babylonian Whore* in 1531. Marpeck may also be credited with seeing to the publication of *The Schleitheim Articles* (1533) and the *Micah Commentary* attributed to Hans Denck (1534). He continued his publishing activity in Augsburg with second editions of the *Exposé of the Babylonian Whore* and of the *New Dialogue*. Packull further claims that the little tract *How*

14. Klassen and Klaassen, *WPM*, 514.

15. Robert Friedmann, *Mennonite Piety through the Centuries* (Goshen, Ind.: Mennonite Historical Society, 1949), 10, 22. Actually Friedmann's judgment is odd, given that he identified Marpeck as the great opponent of the proto-pietism of Caspar Schwenckfeld. (See Friedmann, 29, 84, 86, 193.)

16. See Werner O. Packull's article "Preliminary Report on Pilgram Marpeck's Sponsorship of Anabaptist *Flugschriften*," *MQR* 75 (2001), 75-88. See also Adolf Laube with Helmut Claus, *Flugschriften vom Bauernkrieg zum Täuferreich (1526-1535)* 1 (Berlin: Akademie Verlag, 1992), 708-27.

the Scriptures Are to be Understood, attributed earlier to Michael Sattler and published in *The Legacy of Michael Sattler*,[17] could be written by either Michael Schneider, an associate of Jörg Maler, or more likely, represents the co-authorship of Marpeck and Scharnschlager because it reflects their approach to Scripture.[18] These were printed by Philip Ulhart in 1544.

In 1546 in Augsburg, Heinrich Steiner published the Hubmaier works, *Old and New Teachers on Believers' Baptism and Dialogue with Zwingli's Baptism Book*, and *A Christian Order* by Jörg Haugk von Juchsen.

After that, publishing became dangerous in Augsburg because of the political situation, and the publication activity shifted back to Strasbourg and the printer Sigmund Bund. Packull suggests that it was perhaps Bund who printed the *Admonition* in 1542 and then the *Explanation of the Testaments* by 1547. Finally, he believes that Marpeck was responsible for the 1550 publication of Christoph Freisleben's *On the Genuine Baptism of John and the Apostles* on the Bund press.

Marpeck's publishing efforts represented an enormous amount of work as well as expense. In Augsburg, he had the financial resources to commission what might have been print runs of three hundred to five hundred copies, which would have been adequate for his churches. Perhaps they were also distributed to the Swiss Anabaptists. It is known that the Hutterites in Moravia used the 1547 work, *Explanation of the Testaments*.

Writing and publication were Marpeck's method of evangelism to and edification for his people. If Packull's reconstruction is accurate, it must have involved travel to Strasbourg for Marpeck or other members of his church to commission the printing. They would then have had to transport the books back to Augsburg for distribution. Even though the Augsburg censors were lenient, all this work had to be done clandestinely. The printed Anabaptist material was invariably transported through hostile territory, exposing those members of the church who did it to serious danger.

In addition to the demands on Marpeck's time and resources, he also had to contend with the anxiety and stress of the enterprise. Ironically, several decades ago at least one scholar referred to the "quiet and seclusion" of Marpeck's life in Augsburg.[19] In fact, his life was anything but

---

17. John H. Yoder, trans. and ed., *The Legacy of Michael Sattler*, CRR 1.

18. The authors concur that Marpeck and Scharnschlager are most likely the co-authors of *How the Scriptures Are to be Understood*, written to deal with their concerns about divisions within the church arising from what they argue is faulty reading and interpretation of the Scriptures. Marpeck had written on this topic to Helen Streicher in the 1540s (*WPM*, 180-83), and Scharnschlager spelled out similar views in the preface to the *Explanation of the Testaments*.

19. See n13 above.

quiet and secluded. Marpeck lived on the edge, carefully navigating his fervent commitment to witnessing to an Anabaptist vision of the gospel alongside his more public persona as a highly skilled professional living in relative political and financial security.

We may assume that Marpeck's professional work and his Christian leadership were guided by the same basic theological axiom—the humanity of Christ—with the resulting hallowing of material things as bridges to the divine. Thus we can suggest that he had a sacramental view of his professional work as well. His work was a direct expression of his faith. It was not simply a means to make a living and support his vocation as a Christian leader but an integrated part of his life.

A Concordance in German

On May 5, 1550, the Augsburg Anabaptist Jörg Seifrid was interrogated by city officials trying to get information on the publication of books and tracts by Anabaptists. Seifrid was entirely open with his information. He knew very well, he said, that Pilgram Marpeck and his brotherhood had a printing press, but he did not know where it was housed. He had asked to buy a book from them with the title "The Explanation of the Old and New Testaments."[20] This testimony is a clear reference to the book known as the *Explanation of the Testaments*, another major work of the Marpeck-Scharnschlager partnership, which became known again in the twentieth century with the discovery of two copies, one at Zürich and the other at the erstwhile Prussian State Library in Berlin. Today nine copies are known to exist: two in Slovakia, two in Munich, and one each in Bratislava, Berlin, Wolfenbüttel, Vienna, and Zürich.[21]

The *Explanation of the Testaments* was apparently published early in 1547. This date is supported by a letter of Caspar Schwenckfeld to Leonhart Hieber on May 1, 1547, in which he wrote: "Pilgram and the Anabaptists have produced a big book I have read. [In it] they concern themselves with the salvation of the [Old Testament] patriarchs."[22] The book was not new by 1550 but only then came to official attention.

During the second day of his interrogation, Seifrid is specifically reported to have said that Marpeck "had a book on Anabaptist teaching printed." The exact meaning and intent of this section of the council's recorded minutes are not clear. The minutes seem to suggest that coun-

20. Fast and Rothkegel, *Kunstbuch*, 717-18.

21. We gratefully acknowledge the help of Joe Springer of the Mennonite Historical Library, Goshen, Ind., in assembling this information.

22. CS 11, 21.

cillors intended to confront Marpeck when he returned to Augsburg and demand that he submit a copy of the book to them for examination.[23] It seems safe to assume that this too was a reference to the *Explanation of the Testaments*.

The Augsburg authorities first learned of this book from Seifrid and then called Marpeck to explain its publication, since it would have been illegal. No record of the meeting with Marpeck has been preserved. Caspar Schwenckfeld in 1551 reported that Marpeck was required to submit a book to the Augsburg censors.[24] Although Marpeck may have been responsible for the book, Helmut Claus has shown that the work actually was printed by the Strasbourg printer Sigmund Bund between 1547 and 1550.[25] Interestingly, the censors subsequently approved the book, evidently because it was not a theological treatise but a kind of concordance, and because it was not published in Augsburg.

Although we have no supporting evidence, Seifrid's report that the Marpeck group had a printing press may well be accurate. Certainly Marpeck had the means to purchase and operate one. But so far no publication from such a press has been established. Whoever owned and/or operated the publishing house, it seems to have functioned primarily as a distribution centre for Anabaptist materials.

⸔

The *Explanation of the Testaments*, as a German-language concordance, reflected a relatively new development of the sixteenth century. Concordances to the Bible were first prepared for biblical scholars, not lay people. The earliest known was a Latin concordance to the Vulgate, the official version of the Bible before the Reformation. Even in the sixteenth century, Latin concordances were the norm. The earliest concordance in German was published in Strasbourg in 1524, and another specifically for lay people in 1525. The Zürich publisher Froschauer added a concordance used by the Swiss Brethren to his German New Testament in 1525.

In 1540 the Swiss Brethren brought out their own concordance. Its arrangement was topical, not alphabetical. Arnold Snyder describes it as "a condensed Swiss Brethren Bible, distilled to what was considered to be its essentials" and especially designed for people with little or no education.[26]

23. Fast and Rothkegel, *Kunstbuch*, 720.
24. *CS* 7, 657.
25. Packull, "Preliminary Report," 76-77.
26. C. Arnold Snyder, ed. *Biblical Concordance of the Swiss Brethren*, 1540, trans. Gilbert Fast and Galen Peters (Kitchener, Ont.: Pandora Press, 2001). In the book *Gesprächbüchlein* by Jobst Kinthis, published in Worms, 1553, on the Swiss and South

Snyder judged that the *Explanation of the Testaments* (*Testamenterleutterung*) was not dependent on the Swiss Brethren concordance. Although the arrangement of both is topical, the Swiss Brethren Concordance mixed Old and New Testament passages, whereas the *Explanation of the Testaments* dealt specifically with the relationship of the two. Further, it proclaimed that the Old Testament was not equivalent to the New but that they stood in a historical relationship to each other, the New being the fulfilment and completion of the Old.[27]

A Response to Zwinglian Theologians

The introduction to the *Explanation of the Testaments* is ambivalent about the book's authorship. Six instances suggest a single author[28] and two, multiple authorship. One clearly states that there was "another faithful worker,"[29] and the other that "he did not prepare the book by himself."[30] The main author, who is now generally thought to have been Leupold Scharnschlager, was at the time living in Ilanz in the Grisons. The disciplined style of the introduction suggests that he was the author and that he was assisted by Pilgram Marpeck. It is certain that he and Marpeck were in touch with each other as the work progressed.

A discussion of this work by Scharnschlager is necessary because it so clearly expresses the mind of Marpeck, especially his view of the relationship of the Testaments to each other. It was written to clarify the view the Marpeck-related churches took of the relationship of the Testaments in contrast to that of their opponents, the evangelical clergy in Switzerland, Württemberg, Alsace, and the imperial cities, especially Strasbourg and Augsburg. In each of these locations, Anabaptists had to answer to the Zwinglian theologians who periodically interrogated them. The debate over this issue had begun between the Zürich Anabaptists and Zwingli in 1524.

The Zwinglians held to a theology of a single covenant between God and the people; it continued without interruption from Old to New Testament, from Abraham to the present. The life of the community of Israel in the Old Testament in fact provided a model for the little Protestant Christendoms in Switzerland and South Germany. The pastor was seen as the successor of the prophets and the government as the successor of the kings. Normally the elected council, as the representative of Christian com-

---

German Anabaptists, he referred to one of the Swiss groups as those with "the small concordance." Since the Marpeck-Scharnschlager concordance was some eight hundred pages, it probably is not the one used by the Swiss group to which Kinthis referred.

27. Snyder, *Biblical Concordance of the Swiss Brethren*, ix-xiii.
28. Klassen and Klaassen, *WPM*, 558, 560, 562, 563, 564, 565.
29. Ibid., 560.
30. Ibid., 564.

munity, had the decisive voice in establishing the form of faith and church discipline.[31] Within this theology the parallel significance of circumcision and infant baptism and the use of the sword to discipline in the divine community made perfect sense. To the Zwinglians, the difference between the Old and New Testaments was that in the New, things were somewhat brighter than in the Old. They held that the New Testament was simply an interpretation of the Old and especially that Jesus confirmed the validity of the one covenant. The baptism of infants, the use of the sword, and the Swiss-South German Reformed assumption that the church and civic community were one were all justified by appeal to this covenant theology.

In the introduction to the *Explanation of the Testaments*, Scharnschlager lists the dangerous consequences of the Zwinglian view. First, it was a denial of the creedal statement which says "he descended into hell." If all were Christians under the one covenant, he asked, why would Christ have gone down to preach the gospel to the spirits in prison? It was generally assumed in church doctrine that these "spirits" were all those who had died before Christ. How, he wondered, can they so disregard the faith of the teachers of the early church who all accepted this doctrine? According to the Zwinglians, he said, either the *descensus* did not happen or it was meaningless. If all were Christians in the one covenant and still are, what is the point of the suffering, death, resurrection, and ascension of Jesus? What do they make of all the passages in the New Testament in which it is clearly stated that what Christ brought by his work was totally new and not present before? He also suggested that the roles of church and government are confused in their theology. Government should be allowed to remain in the place where God has put it, and not in the holy place, the church. To confuse government and church is to create the abomination of which Daniel and Matthew spoke.

At this point Scharnschlager declared that the violation of God's order has led to God's punishment for many people, a clear reference to the troubles of the Schmalcald war and its aftermath. There are no grounds for saying that "no one can exercise worldly government better than a Christian." In fact, God gives to secular rulers his special wisdom for the task by which they can rule justly. Because they have God's special wisdom, they do not need the specific wisdom of Christ, which never coerces or kills as rulers are sometimes obligated to do.

"These are the arguments," he continued, "which have moved the workers to produce such a book."[32]

31. J. Wayne Baker, "Bullinger, Heinrich," *Oxford Encyclopedia of the Reformation* 1 (New York: Oxford University Press, 1996), 228-29.

32. For a translation of the Introduction see Klassen and Klaassen, *WPM*, 555-59.

Scharnschlager had done his homework well. There can be no doubt that he had at his disposal the writings of Zwinglian clergy, for his criticisms of their position are cogent and direct. He chided them by implying they had not read the church fathers carefully enough or had ignored them outright, a criticism that would strike home with scholars who often appealed to the fathers as authorities. It also means that Scharnschlager had read the fathers on the *descensus* in some form.

A Massive Work

The book itself is a massive concordance of 836 pages divided topically into 125 chapters. Some random topics from the index indicate what the author was doing:

> Salvation, saviour, yesterday and today, chapter 8, 15-16.
> Understanding yesterday and today, chapter 35, 100-1.
> Revelation yesterday and today, chapter 37, 104-5.

Under each topic follow the related Scripture passages, those for "yesterday" drawn mostly from the Old Testament and for "today" from the New. Included also are a number of explanatory notes by the author. Only the chapter references are given, since Bible text had not yet been divided into verses. (The practice of dividing chapters of the Bible into verses had not yet begun. The English Geneva Bible, published in 1557, was perhaps the first Bible with this feature.) "Thus," Scharnschlager wrote with evident pleasure, "everyone who has a taste for it may take wholehearted delight, joy and pleasure as in a rose garden or a meadow with a variety of colourful flowers."

The Bible used was the Zürich Bible, first published by Froschauer in 1531.[33] Scharnschlager hastened to assure the reader that he would not be responsible for errors in translation. Occasionally he used the Worms edition of the prophets and so noted.[34] He did not deem it necessary to describe the arguments he was seeking to refute since, he wrote, they "are known to everyone since they have been frequently printed." This comment supports the view that the book was directed chiefly against the Zwinglian theologians. He admitted that there may be mistakes in so large a work but trusted that the mature judgment of the reader would not for that reason dismiss the whole work.

It is evident that the *Explanation of the Testaments* also functioned

33. Ulrich Gäbler, *Huldrych Zwingli Eine Einführung in sein Leben und sein Werk* (Munich: Beck, 1983), 94-95.
34. Ludwig Haetzer and Hans Denck translated the twelve prophets into German at Worms in 1527.

as a reference work in the second part of the *Response* and thereby also had its place in the ongoing debate of the Marpeck group with Caspar Schwenckfeld. Scharnschlager specifically stated that the book's argument was with opponents who held views "much like Schwenckfeld." This is especially true when they argued that the suffering of Christ was retroactive to the Old Testament.

Finally Scharnschlager added a paragraph that is as accurate for the twenty-first century as it was for the sixteenth. Many who want to buy or read a book are more concerned about the author than about the truth, he observed. Is the author socially prominent and what religious party does he belong to? Some are offended by a book "because it is too academic or too popular, too erudite or too ignorant." He admitted there was some justification for this attitude because

> these last and dangerous times are full of error, sects, schisms, and opinions concerning faith. . . . In order to prevent this and to point the reader solely to the truth of God's Word the name of the author of this book is omitted. It is omitted also because he did not prepare this book by himself.[35]

It is not known how many copies of the *Explanation of the Testaments* were printed. Subsequent references and allusions to it are scarce. It figured in a 1571 debate at Frankental in which Hans Buechel, a close co-worker of Marpeck, was a participant.[36] One of his letters is preserved in the *Kunstbuch*.[37] The fact that two copies are found in Bratislava in Slovakia suggests that the Hutterites used it, perhaps unaware that the book came out of the Marpeck circle. The copy in Zürich points to its use among the Swiss Brethren. A Lutheran minister, Jacob Andreae, mentioned the book in a sermon at Esslingen in 1568, and there is another reference to it from a Lutheran as late as 1598.[38]

Rescuing Church from Government

One other reason for Scharnschlager writing the book related to the place and function of government. His argument that the role of government should be disentangled from that of the church echoed Luther's boast in his early writings that he had done precisely that. Whereas Luther claimed that he had rescued the government from the church,[39] Scharnschlager said that by disentangling the two he was rescuing the church

35. Klassen and Klaassen, *WPM*, 563-64.
36. Klassen, *Covenant and Community*, 53.
37. Fast and Rothkegel, *Kunstbuch*, 586-87.
38. Op. cit.
39. See especially Luther's 1523 work, *Secular Authority: To What Extent it*

from the government. He also implied that a secular government, which is equipped by God with special wisdom for the task, is more likely to deal justly because it has unqualified clarity about its mandate. Evangelical governments are confused about their mandate, he explained, and consequently act unjustly—especially toward people who don't share their religious views.

We have here, therefore, not merely fulminations against other Christians but careful and informed arguments characterized by internal consistency. Unfortunately, the evangelical clergy for the most part were not free to engage this work or Anabaptists in general in terms of biblical interpretation because they were allied with—and sometimes subject to—governments of evangelical Christians who were concerned, above all, with the security of their city or territory in an empire headed by a deeply committed Catholic emperor. This is stated by the "Preacher" in the *New Dialogue*, published under Marpeck's auspices in Strasbourg in 1531, when he admits that the governmental authorities won't permit the baptism of adults.[40]

⤙

It was within this polarized context that the Augsburg Interim was issued. Instead of serving as a breathing space for the resolution of religious differences, the Interim simply strengthened Protestant resistance throughout the empire to any imposed religious peace. Protestants expressed this resistance in a flood of satirical pamphlets. The emperor was now the "antichrist" and his Spanish officials and soldiers "the true Turks." Pope Paul III was called the "pope-devil" who had pulled the wool over people's eyes to accept his godless Interim and to deny and blaspheme Christ and his living word. A thunderhead of vexation and hate was building up, threatening the emperor's hopes for religious peace.

Historian Karl Brandi wrote that in Germany, this period was the last time until the eighteenth century that the voice of ordinary people was heard.[41] During the next two centuries autocratic governments all over continental Europe (in contrast to the revolutionary upheavals in the British Isles) expected their citizens to be seen but silent.

Should be Obeyed, John Dillenberger, *Martin Luther: Selections from His Writings* (New York: Doubleday, 1961), 363-402.

40. Rempel, *Later Writings by Pilgram Marpeck*, 58.

41. Karl Brandi, *Deutsche Geschichte im Zeitalter der Reformation und Gegenreformation* (Munich: Bruckmann, 1969), 248.

19

Unsettled, Discouraging Times

The Imperial Diet met again in Augsburg in 1550, two years after the previous one concluded. The arrival of Ferdinand was in marked contrast to his previous low-key entrance to the city. Accompanied by about 1,500 soldiers and court officials as well as his ten-year-old son Charles, Ferdinand I—still king of Bohemia and Moravia, and archduke of Austria—rode into the city in majestic style through the Red Gate at the south end of town. The date was July 4, 1550, five years before Marpeck's death.

Once more, trouble loomed with the presence of so many armed men from different parts of the empire. As the soldiers came to the plaza St. Ulrich in the centre of the city, several of the gunners fired their weapons either as a prank or a threat. A stray ball hit the eye of a servant girl and killed her. Public anger intensified when Ferdinand's soldiers were then billetted in the houses of weavers in the suburbs of Holy Cross, a new part of the city. The billetting was a great hardship for the townsfolk because the city had not yet recovered from the previous diet when restless soldiers had destroyed so much property. Complaints about the large numbers to be housed (including many prostitutes, who were a regular addition to every European army) were of no avail. People had to provide hay, straw, and bedding for ten to twenty soldiers in each house. In addition, the city was forced to build 1,400 stalls for the many war horses.

Even though the events surrounding this diet were more peaceful than those of the previous one of 1547-48, the presence of so many idle soldiers caused a rash of crime and continual unrest. Chronicler Paul Mair wrote that military police were kept busy arresting and executing troublemakers. Even the threat of capital punishment didn't halt the rampaging.

The diet began its sessions on July 26. On August 14, a group of Spanish troops fell upon the Church of St. Ulrich, where Protestant vespers were being sung, and destroyed the place. Complaints to the city authorities were fruitless because local officials were reluctant to tangle with armed soldiers. Only the intervention of the emperor's own men finally stopped the Spaniards.[1]

Pilgram and Anna lived in the middle of all this turmoil and confusion. There is no reason to think that they escaped the demand to billet soldiers, although we hear nothing of it. The Church of St. Ulrich was very near the water tower where they lived. The commotion there could not have escaped their notice, but there is no word of it from sources relating to them.

⤙

In August 1550 the emperor summoned all ten of the evangelical clergy to appear before his councillor, the bishop of Arras, to be questioned. The clergy had no end of troubles. Harassed by imperial soldiers and officials, the Protestant clergymen were charged with fostering rebellion. They vigorously denied the charge but to no avail. They were ordered to leave the city within three days, after which all evangelical preaching and ministering in the city ceased.[2] The Anabaptists, who were not considered evangelical but heretics, continued as before: holding clandestine meetings and worship services and publishing illegal tracts.

Within fourteen days of the clergy being forced out of town, the Augsburg chronicler Mair triumphantly wrote that the emperor had received word that the Turks had taken Tripoli and that Spain was now vulnerable to attack. He believed the emperor would need to leave Germany and look after the defence of Spain, thus giving the citizens of Augsburg some breathing space. In Hungary there was renewed fighting between the Turks and Ferdinand's forces, while to the west the French were on the move again with an invasion of the Holy Roman Empire in Lorraine.[3]

Meanwhile, the emperor's Spanish troops continued to cause havoc in Augsburg. There were only a few of them, Mair noted, but "they do as they please and no one dares to call them to account." There is no order; no one is in charge, he lamented. Women and children are victimized, and no property is safe.[4]

1. *Die Chroniken der deutschen Städte vom 14. bis ins 16. Jahrhundert*, Augsburg 7, 202-7, 217-20; 8, 375.
2. Ibid., 245-48.
3. Ibid, 245 n2; Karl Brandi, *Deutsche Geschichte im Zeitalter der Reformation und Gegenreformation* (Munich: Bruckmann, 1969), 254-55.

The troubles in the city seemed never to end. Although the conditions of the Interim had restored Catholic government and worship, by early 1551 Protestant resistance had become public, even during the sitting of the diet. On Thursday, March 13, 1551, the Augsburg city council publicly announced after trumpet calls in all the city squares that there was to be no interference with the priests who took consecrated oil to the sick. There had been an incident in the street of the blacksmiths when the smiths had mocked and yelled loudly at the priests.[5]

The continuing civic unrest seemed to underscore a frequent theme in Marpeck's writing: resorting to the sword to defend the gospel only produces more strife.

The 'Evil Monk' Attacks

Two years before the Augsburg Diet, as part of the rejuvenation of Catholicism, a Dominican friar named Johann Faber, who also signed his work Fabri, was installed as preacher in the cathedral of Augsburg. (This is a different Faber/Fabri from the senior church official whom we met in chapter 2, who died in 1541.) The Faber of Augsburg was referred to by Protestants as the "evil black monk" because of his intemperate zeal in restoring Catholic faith and practice in Augsburg. In July 1550, he published a book against Anabaptists in which he addressed three issues: the oath, the community of goods, and the joy and steadfastness of Anabaptists under sentence of death.[6] The three parts were originally preached as sermons, one of them in Schlettstadt in Alsace, where he had worked some years earlier.

At the beginning of his appointment to the Augsburg cathedral, Faber made the charges against Anabaptism that were current among both Catholic and Protestant polemicists. Anabaptist teaching, he wrote, destroys Christian and civic unity, polity, and peace. The proof of this was their rebellious, proud, truculent war against the Holy Empire at Münster. Christian governments, he said, were obligated to resist this damaging rebellion, to root it out, and get rid of it.

The gist of the work, however, involved Faber's discussion of the oath and community of goods. This discussion is scriptural throughout. Faber obviously attempted to speak to the Anabaptist appeal to Scripture on both subjects. "The obscure dark Scriptures must be sprinkled with the salt of divine wisdom and Christian understanding," he wrote, "so that

---

5. Ibid., 189.

6. Johann Faber, *Von dem Eyd Schwören. Auch von der Widertauffer Marter. Vnd woher entspring das sie also frölich vnnd getröst die pein des tods leyden. Vnd von der gemainschafft der Widertauffer*, 1550.

the word of life and truth does not become to the proud the occasion for death and error in the fire of hell."[7]

Why would this book have been published at this precise time? Anabaptists in the city were not numerous and generally avoided publicity. Along with Marpeck, they may have been ready to swear any oath that did not require the bearing of weapons or that would bind them in their confession of faith. There is no evidence of the practice among them of the Hutterite style of community of goods in which no private property was allowed. As we noted earlier, Marpeck himself opposed the Hutterite approach, advocating only the voluntary sharing of goods among members of his community.

Still, 1550 was the year when two leading Anabaptists, Jörg Maler and Jörg Seifrid, were arrested and interrogated under Faber's supervision. At no time during their interrogations during April and May were they questioned about the oath or the community of goods. There was only one oblique, possible allusion to the community of goods when Maler was asked whether Anabaptists planned a takeover in Augsburg like the one in Münster in 1534-35, where a form of compulsory sharing of goods was practised. Thus, local Anabaptists hardly posed a threat concerning these two issues, the practice of which could be seen as dangerous to the city.

We therefore need to look elsewhere for the reasons for Faber's book. It could be that events in Moravia beginning in April and May of 1550 were relevant to the publication of this work. Early in 1550 at the meeting of the Moravian Diet at Brünn (Brno), King Ferdinand took steps to arrest the progress of the Reformation by ordering the expulsion of Anabaptists living in Moravia. They were ordered to leave by St. John the Baptist Day (June 24). The *Chronicle of the Hutterian Brethren* describes vividly what happened, especially the brutal treatment of defenceless people, causing the loss of many lives, especially the young and the sick.

> A group made camp by the waterside and put up tents, but the marshal's men drove them away and set fire to the camp so that the faithful would have nowhere to go. The men even destroyed their oven to deprive them of bread as well. There was no end to fear and need for the poor little flock. Like owls, they could not go anywhere in the daytime. People shook their heads when they saw them. They were a laughingstock. Everybody shouted at them, mocked them, and chased them off.[8]

7. Ibid., D iv.
8. *The Chronicle of the Hutterian Brethren* (New York: Plough Publishing House, 1987), 307.

Sometime that summer Peter Bakich de Làk, a landowner and one of the most violent opponents of Moravian Anabaptists, travelled to Augsburg. On his return he attacked Anabaptists in Gätte, Hungary, with the utmost cruelty in the early winter of 1550. "They came at night," the *Chronicle* records, "surrounded the house, and drove old and young out into the cold. Their cruelty, violence, and malice knew no bounds."[9]

It is possible that the publication of Faber's book in Augsburg was part of the campaign to destroy Moravian Anabaptism, especially as community of goods was a highly visible feature of Anabaptist life there. Was Faber trying to justify Ferdinand's actions against the Anabaptists when he discussed their readiness to suffer with patience, attributing it to the work of Satan? Did Bakich de Làk, a violent opponent of Anabaptists, meet with Ferdinand in Augsburg in July 1550? If Faber met with Ferdinand and de Làk, perhaps the book and the actions of de Làk were part of Ferdinand's program of extermination.

Four and a half centuries later, there is no way of knowing how all these separate pieces fitted into a complete whole. There is no allusion to Faber's book or attending events in Marpeck's writings. However, the fate of the communities in Moravia with which Marpeck was affiliated must have been of great concern to him.

The 'Holy Household'

In the midst of (and perhaps because of) the turmoil of the military occupation and religious repression, the Anabaptist group in Augsburg appears to have been small.[10] According to the testimony of Jörg Seifrid, they met four times a year or whenever the need for a meeting arose.[11] When Maler and Seifrid were interrogated during 1550, they both denied that there were Anabaptist gatherings as such. Rather, they said, they talked to individuals about the Christian gospel and faith when they were asked. The overall impression is that there was a group of perhaps twenty to thirty persons, although during the twenty years between 1542 and 1562, some forty-five people appear to have been part of the group. According to one account, the members were all converts of Pilgram

9. *Chronicle*, 305-9.
10. The letters of the *Kunstbuch* and the public records of Augsburg offer us bits of information with a few names. Boyd lists fourteen names: Anthony Hildebrand (Marpeck's assistant and successor as hydrologist), Jörg Maler, Helena von Freyberg, Hans Jakob Schneider, his wife, Kunigunda, Hans Schmidt and his wife, Anna, Jörg Weckerlin, Jörg Seifrid, Hans Schleiffer, Georg Kraft, Hans Eberlin, Ulrich Knoll, and Hans Jakob. See Boyd, *Pilgram Marpeck*, 139, 141.
11. Fast and Rothkegel, *Kunstbuch*, 707.

Marpeck. Apart from Marpeck and another person, who were both city employees, the group comprised primarily craftsmen and labourers, a few domestic servants and, as previously mentioned, ten women who were heads of families.[12]

The reference to women in charge of households may be a clue to the Anabaptist strategy of accommodation in Augsburg, designed to set off in some measure their political vulnerability. From the beginning, the vision for accomplishing the Protestant reform in Augsburg had been that it would be done through the "holy household." This term described the method of production by the guilds in households composed of a family of parents and children as well as apprentices and even journeymen. The household was under the leadership of the husband, whom everyone obeyed, and it was hoped that the reform of Christian faith would take place in the intimacy of the family.[13]

Social historian Lyndal Roper, who described this way of accomplishing reform, pointed out that, like Protestantism, Anabaptism as well was "based on household forms of association." But in the case of Anabaptists, women exercised considerable authority. This was a notably different practice from other Christians that probably arose from Anabaptist theology, which placed a strong emphasis on the equality of all people. It is perhaps for this reason that Roper refers to ten women as important members of these groups,[14] perhaps the ten heads of households referred to above.

It may be, therefore, that meeting in houses instead of larger assemblies was deliberately used by Anabaptists as a way of appearing to accept the public model of reform. Although there is no supporting evidence, it is possible that Anabaptists actually participated with others in the production model of the "holy household." It may also be possible to see the hand of Marpeck here, helping his people to survive in Augsburg through appropriation of acceptable social forms of living and working.

The other members of the fellowship were not treated as generously by civic authorities as Marpeck was; they had to have strong spiritual constitutions to surmount the persistent threats and sufferings they repeatedly endured. Nevertheless, with the exception of Jörg Maler (see chapter 15), others in the Marpeck group seem to have been left alone by the authorities after 1547, probably because they did not have Maler's chequered history. Evidently they were successful at remaining mostly invisible. When they met, it was in small numbers in the houses of members, including

12. Boyd, *Pilgram Marpeck*, 138-39.
13. Roper, "The Holy Household, Women and Morals," 15, 28, 252-53.
14. Ibid.

Marpeck's and several others. Yet the civil and religious turmoil that unsettled the empire—particularly Augsburg—during the mid-years of the sixteenth century was a constant source of anxiety in their lives.

Hidden Fire of the Enemy

Despite the difficulties created by the events around him, Marpeck assiduously tended the care of his scattered churches. For some time, he had been especially troubled yet again by the churches in St. Gall and Appenzell. During August 1551 in the midst of Augsburg's tribulations, Marpeck wrote a letter to these Swiss churches warning them about the hidden fire of the enemy in human hearts.[15]

In 1542 and 1543, the issue had been legalism; now it was self-will. Some months earlier he had written a letter to the faithful in St. Gall and Appenzell that has not survived. In a letter written to him, they did not acknowledge this letter. Instead, they made some demands of Marpeck that totally perplexed him.

We know about Marpeck's first letter because of his response on August 9, 1551, to their demands. He was deeply discouraged and expressed it. The enemy of our souls, he wrote, goes about the world inciting strife and conflict but claiming everywhere that it is all for the cause of God. He creates distrust, flattery, self-seeking, slander, envy, and arrogant pride, such that no one will yield to anyone else. All the while people have no idea what is happening but are being fatally wounded and brought to destruction.

Marpeck was merely describing what he was observing every day in the political manoeuvring at the diet and the chaos in the city. But his deep discouragement flowed from the fact that even in the little Anabaptist churches, these same powers of destruction were at work, with the believers likewise claiming to be motivated by godly zeal. From Marpeck's point of view, there seemed to be no self-surrender—only self-assertion. He did not mince his words:

> There is among you a hidden fire which has an evil, stinking smoke
> and taste of fire, which the enemy of truth is seeking to conceal in
> order that he may ignite, destroy, and burn to ashes many hearts
> before it is discovered. . . . Thus he also kindles his strife with deceit,
> lies . . . faultfinding, mistrust . . . greed for personal honor . . . boast-
> fulness, and pride. From this it follows that no one will yield to any-
> one else.[16]

15. Klassen and Klaassen, *WPM*, 498-506. Fast and Rothkegel, *Kunstbuch*, 550-57.

16. Klassen and Klaassen, *WPM*, 501.

There is no listening to the Spirit of God, he said, but only to human voices.

> I do not write this to point at someone specifically but only for our mutual warning so that we put out the fire and save, [that we] apply the greatest earnestness, care, and diligence to get each other out of the fire before we perish, and learn to fight with the sword of the Spirit before we are attacked, wounded, and killed by the enemy.[17]

God had called and driven him, he wrote, and that was why he was compelled to speak like Jonah after the fish released him. He confessed that, like Jonah on the ship, he was ready to take on himself the cause of the trouble so that, even if it gave him great displeasure, he could serve them to help them cope with what concerned them. Almost throughout he uses the first person plural pronoun. In a short prayer of confession Marpeck admits that the fault was not solely on one side of the estrangement.

> Thus, my God, you have ample right to tell us that we ought to be ashamed of our request because we have regarded as trifling your gift and grace. Nevertheless, we will continue shamelessly and importunately to beg with hope that you will listen to us for the sake of our own peace.[18]

Perhaps it was this letter acknowledging his own fallibility that turned things for the better between him and the Swiss. He ended on a conciliatory note, greeting them in Jesus Christ and with the prayer that they would all be saved from the time of trial. His signature was his trademark, "a servant and comrade in the tribulation of Christ."

Ruling Flip-flops

The French invasion of the empire in September 1551 was successful in good measure because the French had the help of the German Protestant princes. On April 4, 1552, coalition troops of the French and German princes entered Augsburg, immediately reestablishing the pre-1548 order in the city. On June 11 Augsburg's city council called all the evangelical clergy back to the city. They were reinstated in their places on Sunday, August 12.

Meanwhile, the main coalition army pursued the emperor, who had already fled south to the city of Innsbruck, the capital of the Habsburg-ruled

17. Ibid., 502.
18. Ibid., 503-4.

Tirol. As the army approached the mountain passes above Innsbruck, Charles fled over the Brenner Pass to Bruneck, nestled in the Alps of what is today northern Italy. The Council of Trent, which was meeting nearby, scattered as the hostile army approached Innsbruck. Under intense pressure to avoid a bloody confrontation, Ferdinand hastened to meet with the Protestant prince elector, Maurice of Saxony. They managed to cobble together a truce at Passau, where the Danube and Inn Rivers meet. The cessation of hostilities freed the emperor to gather an army against France and reassert his authority in his own imperial cities, including Augsburg.

Thus, just one week after a modicum of religious freedom had been restored in Augsburg, the city once again was forced to open its gates to repressive rulers. First, the feared Duke of Alba entered the city. A day later, Charles V and his entourage marched into town. The constitution of 1548 was again imposed, although according to the agreement at Passau, the religious situation was not altered. Protestants retained the privileges granted them under the Interim.[19] The status quo for the churches would remain in force until the next diet, scheduled to meet in Augsburg in 1555. These flip-flops apparently made little difference to the Anabaptist congregation in Augsburg. The ruling councils were probably too preoccupied with their own troubles to bother with a few dissenters.

Leaders Must Be Servants

At the end of 1552, several months after the countervailing power struggles in Augsburg, Marpeck wrote a letter to the congregations in Moravia, expressing edification and encouragement.[20] Moravia was not in the eye of the storm, as Augsburg was. Indeed, the Anabaptist communities there were to have relative peace for the next decade. Nevertheless, Marpeck returned again to the familiar servanthood theme. Those in charge of the church must follow their Master and be servants rather than rulers.

> This intention was proclaimed in the midst of heaven by an angel and is eternally so proclaimed [Rev. 14:6ff.], that all creatures of God should, like the Son of the Father, submit freely and without compulsion to such service and lowliness. Any creature that has not thus voluntarily served man with and in Christ until the coming revelation of the mighty glory of the Son is cursed and eternally damned.[21]

19. Immenkötter, "Kirche zwischen Reformation und Parität," 402-3; Lutz, "Augsburg und seine politische Umwelt 1490-1555," 429.
20. Fast and Rothkegel, *Kunstbuch*, 418-22.
21. Klassen and Klaassen, *WPM*, 551, amended.

These words identify the "eternal gospel"[22] with the central Christian affirmation of the lowly incarnation of Christ.[23] Part of this gospel is the inclusion of the followers of Christ in the lowly incarnation of God to save the world. The denial of this central doctrine of servanthood puts a person forever outside God's grace. The fallen angel-serpent was thrown down on earth (Rev. 12:9) and now alienates those on earth from the "eternal gospel." Together with the enemy of all truth they now inherit the curse. For Marpeck, this was yet another reflection on the refusal of some—especially those referred to during this time as evangelicals—to embrace the renunciation of all coercion and dominance as the true Christian way. The curse of alienation from God and its effects can be seen everywhere, warned Marpeck. All the more reason, he wrote, not to abandon this servant discipleship no matter "the offence, frustration, and affliction of the enemy . . . we must endure." The outcome of faithfulness to the eternal gospel, he said, is the eternal blessing of God.

Marpeck's letter was carried to Moravia by Jörg Maler and Jakob Schumacher. They also took with them twenty copies of a work thought to have been Marpeck's *Admonition* of 1542[24] and two other letters, both of which have been lost, one dealing with the favourite Anabaptist topic of *Gelassenheit* (true surrender) and the other with the Lord's Supper. The *Gelassenheit* epistle had been carried to them earlier by the elderly letter carrier named Thoma. The churches had not confirmed its arrival and so it was sent again.[25] The carrying of Anabaptist materials was always dangerous and one can imagine Thoma, anticipating a search, depositing the epistle somewhere with the intention of recovering it later. Unable to do so, he returned to Silesia from where he had come.

The answering letter (written on March 19, 1553, at Eibenschitz),[26]

22. Rev. 14:6: "Then I saw another angel flying in midheaven, with an eternal gospel to proclaim to those who live on the earth—to every nation and tribe and language and people."

23. The special use of this formulation stems from Joachim of Fiore in the twelfth century. He identified the "eternal gospel" with the gospel of the Holy Spirit "which proceeds from Christ's gospel." It belonged to the third and final age, the Age of the Spirit, after which there would be no other gospel. The Spiritual Franciscans also adopted the term but used it for the writings of Joachim which, according to the teachings of Gerard of Borgo San Donnino about 1250, belong to the Third Age. The term probably made its way into the Reformation era and into Anabaptism by way of the Third Order of the Franciscans. For Joachim's teaching, see Bernard McGinn, *The Calabrian Abbott: Joachim of Fiore in the History of Western Thought* (New York: Macmillan, 1985), 99-204.

24. Klassen and Klaassen, *WPM*, 586, n6.

25. Ibid., 554.

26. Fast and Rothkegel, *Kunstbuch*, 423-27.

reveals a good deal about the churches in Moravia associated with Marpeck and their relationship to him. The writers said they knew that Marpeck would not be with them much longer. Was he sick or had he been ill? He was now at least fifty-eight years old. He had devoted much toil and labour to the churches over a long time, they wrote, and he and others continued to work untiringly. They addressed him several times as "our much beloved brother." They expressed their gratitude for all of God's grace "in this last and perilous time." It was a wonder to them that the churches still existed. The letters that Marpeck had sent them had been read in all the congregations associated with Marpeck, which were listed: Austerlitz, Poppitz (Popovice), Eibenschitz, Jamnitz (Jemnice), Znaim, and Vienna. The Moravian writers desired that greetings be given if possible to Leupold Scharnschlager and the aged Sigmund Bosch.

The letter was signed by the elders of the congregations. Because we have few names of the members of the Moravian Anabaptist churches associated with Marpeck, it is fitting to record the names of the elders as they appear in the letter: "Andre Schuster from Austerlitz, Peter Fruewirt from The Stone and Boppitz, Balthasar Grasbanntner, carpenter from Eibenschitz, Rup Dachennsteiner, smith from The Forest and from Jemnitz, and Bastel Schlosserr from Vienna and from the elders and churches in the land of Moravia, your brothers in the Lord Christ." It was a warm letter with no hint of disunity or strife. Marpeck's efforts had evidently borne fruit.

Balancing Work and Writing

Throughout Augsburg's troubles from 1546 to 1553, Marpeck worked as director of public works for the city. There is no indication that he was unable to do his work or that there was any interruption in his employment.

He was responsible for the maintenance of the water towers with their wooden pumps. They would have required constant attention and repair; wooden machinery had a short lifespan because of wear from the sand that invariably arrived with the water from the aquifer. Marpeck had to keep the water flowing into the city, as well as be constantly vigilant to prevent silting and keep the complex system of pipes in repair. He had to make sure that the weavers always had fresh water for the fulling process to cleanse and thicken cloth. He continued to be responsible for the supply of firewood to heat businesses and homes in the city, including the mansions where Charles and Ferdinand lived during their lengthy stays in Augsburg.

We have no idea of Marpeck's working hours. We do know that in addition to his professional duties, which must have claimed most of his work day, he was responsible for the care of his congregations in Augsburg and others scattered from Alsace to Moravia. Most of Marpeck's time spent on the churches was devoted to writing. One can imagine Marpeck reading and writing by the light of one candle after another, well into the night after his day's work was done.

Marpeck's later years were occupied with part 2 of the *Response*. It was never published but survived in three handwritten copies which are now available at Olomouc in the Czech Republic, and in Zürich and Munich.

His available letters addressed specific problems in the churches that formed his Anabaptist community. He set a high standard for them and attempted to raise them up to the level of his vision for them. Mostly, however, he was a teacher, helping them to interpret the Bible in a situation of constant pressure on them to surrender their convictions. Tirelessly throughout his writing, he called on his followers to identify courageously with their Lord in his humble renunciation of every use of power to dominate and control. Only thus could true freedom be achieved. It was a high order for ordinary mortals, but such a commitment was central to Marpeck's theology.

-20-

Marpeck's Final Years

Less than two years before Marpeck died, there was yet another occasion when he and Ferdinand found themselves in the same city and at opposite ends of the church-state spectrum. Once again Augsburg was selected as the site for the Imperial Diet, where the ruling monarch met with the clergy and secular leaders of all the constituent parts of the empire. The diet was called for 1555, but on June 10, 1554, Charles V announced he would not attend and turned its leadership over to his brother Ferdinand instead.

Ferdinand arrived in Augsburg on December 29, and the diet opened on February 5, 1555. It was not an auspicious beginning. Following the example of the emperor, six of the seven imperial electors (Ferdinand was himself an elector as king of Bohemia) chose not to appear, but sent representatives.[1] Then, on March 23, Pope Julius III died and all the papal representatives at the diet were recalled to Rome. No replacements were sent. The diet eventually made its decisions without either the emperor or the pope, finally drawing to a close on September 25.

Despite its problems with attendance, in historical hindsight it was the most important meeting of a diet since 1530. That diet had also met in Augsburg and became famous for the Lutheran "Augsburg Confession," the document that has been the creed of the Lutheran church to the present day. Yet to contemporaries, the diet of 1555 must have appeared to be anticlimactic. The absence of so many of the ruling authorities suggested that they simply did not care. For most people, the momentous news of the final day came not from the diet but from Charles V. The emperor knew that his dream of restoring the Holy Roman Empire to its former glory of political and religious unity was over. He'd had enough. On the last day of the diet,

1. *Die Chroniken der deutschen Städte vom 14*, 413.

an imperial official brought the message of the abdication of Charles to his brother, Ferdinand.[2] The subjects of the empire were stunned.

Nevertheless, the announcement of Charles's departure had far fewer long-term ramifications than the proclamation issued that final day, a document naively and in blind confidence entitled "the eternal religious peace." The proclamation, which has come to be known as the Peace of Augsburg, was neither visionary nor peaceful. Its terms were the result of a standoff: an impasse that lasted until the beginning of the next century and then fell apart amid repression and bloodshed that lasted for decades.

There were four main terms to the "eternal peace." First, the Lutheran princes and imperial cities were guaranteed security equal to the Catholics. Second, and more important, each unit of the empire was given the right to choose between Catholicism and Lutheranism according to the principle *cujus regio, ejus religio*, meaning that the faith of the ruler is the faith of the subjects. (The phrase's exact translation is "whose the reign, his the faith.") Lutherans in Catholic territories were to be tolerated, while Catholic faithful in Lutheran jurisdictions were to be similarly treated. According to the third term, all lands of the Catholic Church seized by Lutheran rulers before 1552 were to be left to them, and fourth, every archbishop or abbot who became Protestant would forfeit title, lands, and privileges.

The settlement acknowledged only two confessions, Catholic and Lutheran. Zwinglians, Calvinists, and Anabaptists were excluded. The immediate effect in Augsburg was that, in order to enjoy the privileges of the peace, all Protestants had to become Lutheran or face expulsion or worse.[3] Augsburg, along with the other imperial cities, was required to assure that each confession—Roman Catholic or Lutheran—acknowledge the right of the other to faith, church usages, order and ceremonies, and properties.

The settlement was a necessary compromise rooted in mutual exhaustion. The only religious tolerance agreed upon was the agreement to live and let live. Beyond that, the doctrine of *cujus regio, ejus religio* was in rigid force. People who could not accept the faith of the ruler of their particular territory would have no choice but to emigrate. Thus, the legitimacy of religious dissent—a necessary precursor to religious freedom and diversity—was delivered a severe albeit temporary blow. Tellingly, within less than twenty years, the Calvinist rulers of the Dutch Republic were tolerating Catholics, Lutherans, and Mennonite/Anabaptists.

Ferdinand has been praised by scholars such as Fichtner, Laubach,

2. Lortz, *Die Reformation in Deutschland* 2, 283.
3. Immenkötter, "Augsburg," *Oxford Encyclopedia of the Reformation* 1, 90.

and Kohler. They place less emphasis on the human rights impact of the agreement and hail it for achieving a number of years of peace. Alfred Kohler, Ferdinand's most recent biographer, gives him great credit for finding a way for Catholics and Protestants to live together and thereby lessen religious tensions in Germany. Ferdinand favoured the diet's compromise in the hope that Catholics would prevail in most jurisdictions. It did not happen. Although they did prevail (and still do) in Austria, Bavaria, and Bohemia, Lutherans dominated most of northern Germany. What followed was an uneasy peace. The compromise did not end the struggle between Catholic and Protestant, and in 1618 led to the ferocious Thirty Years War.[4]

For Augsburg, the principal effect of the proclamation was that the link between civic and church communities was severed. It was the death knell of the Christian commonwealth, which had given imperial cities like Augsburg and Strasbourg their vital character as well as political stability and economic success. With two confessions—Lutheran and Roman Catholic—in the same city, the traditional unity between church and state was no longer possible, and the secular state was the eventual result. Religious leaders would no longer participate in the government of the city. In fact, regardless of confession, the church in these cities thereafter would not be independent (as we perceive of church-state separation today) but rather would be under government control.

⌐

Pilgram Marpeck lived another year beyond the declaration of the Peace of Augsburg. We don't know his assessment of this historic development. We do already know, however, about his reflections on the evangelical resort to arms in defence of the gospel and the consequences it would bring. At the time of the formation of the Schmalcald League in 1530, Marpeck wrote that the end result would be "great bloodshed which God will bring upon all. . . . With much greater and more awful bloodshed than in the Peasant War, they will all perish in the rebellion of Korah [Num. 16:1-35], which is not the same as dying for Christ."[5]

Marpeck's grim warning proved prophetic. In 1531 he had written about the "marriage" of the whore of Babylon: in other words, ultimate political power joined with religious piety. What he saw around him now was a further escalation of this disastrous mix. The great seduction about which he wrote continued, and most of society seemed to worship the

4. Kohler, "Father of the Augsburg Religious Peace," *Ferdinand*, 316.
5. Klassen and Klaassen, *WPM*, 27-28.

beast. Few recognized the incarnation of this lie, which then as now thrives via its greatest blasphemy: using the word *peace* to produce a system that carries the virus of war. The seeds of chaos were sown during the Schmalcald War and its aftermath, then harvested again in the Thirty Years War, the final bloody military contest between Catholics and Protestants. The so-called Peace of Augsburg only postponed the conflict.

Returning to First Principles

The last of Marpeck's letters that has survived was written two weeks before the Diet of Augsburg opened in 1555. The letter was sent to his congregation at Langenau, not far from Ulm, with the request that it also be sent on to the congregation in the Lebertal in Alsace. The *Kunstbuch* copyist gave it the title "Concerning the Humanity of Christ," which was, as we have seen, the starting point of Marpeck's theology.[6] As in his earlier letters, he addressed practical issues that had arisen among his followers.

The first topic to which he turned was theological. Early in 1554, a large conference of perhaps six hundred Anabaptists representing all the major groups had assembled in Strasbourg to discuss the issues of theology and church order that had divided them.[7] One scholar has suggested that Marpeck himself was present as a major participant, still working for unity among Anabaptists, but there is no evidence for this. Nothing is known about the outcome of this conference.

The next year Anabaptist representatives from the Netherlands, North Germany, and Switzerland gathered again to discuss, in their own words, "what could be known about the origins of the flesh of Christ."[8] Perhaps, as historian Stephen Boyd conjectures, some of the members of the Marpeck-affiliated churches from the Lebertal near Strasbourg were planning to be at the Strasbourg follow-up conference in August 1555 and had asked him for guidance.[9] Marpeck's last letter of June 22, 1555, reveals his passionate involvement with a key theological issue debated at that conference: the humanity of Christ.

The summertime debate concerned this central pillar of Marpeck's the-

6. Klassen and Klaassen, *WPM*, 507-15; Fast and Rothkegel, *Kunstbuch*, 408-15; Blough, *Christ in Our Midst*, 33 passim.

7. Jan Kiwiet, *Pilgram Marpeck* (Kassel: Oncken, 1957), 66, n43. A Strasbourg council minute of March 19, 1554, states that a large group of about six hundred Anabaptists had gathered near the long bridge the previous Saturday. Abraham Hulshof, *Geschiedenis van de Doopgezinden te Straatsburg van 1525 to 1557* (Amsterdam: J. Clausen, 1905), 218, n1.

8. Hulshof, *Geschiedenis van de Doopsgezinden te Straatsburg*, 220.

9. Boyd, *Pilgram Marpeck*, 146.

ological edifice, so it is not surprising that there is a note of alarm in his letter of June 1555. The number of Anabaptists associated with Marpeck who attended was small by comparison with the numbers of the followers of Menno Simons and the Swiss.

A compromise statement was issued by the conference in August, stating that some held too low a view of the incarnation, while for others it was too high, and that neither position was properly understood. Lists of Scripture passages supporting both positions were added. One list supported the claim that Jesus' flesh came from heaven and the other that he received it from Mary. The conference statement declared that Anabaptists would stick to Scripture; incarnation was one of those questions to which they did not know the answer. It is more important, they said, to keep the commandments of Christ than to press for an understanding of the mysteries of how Christ became flesh.[10] It is hard to imagine that Marpeck would have disagreed with this statement. For reasons not known, the document was signed by elders from the Netherlands only, with no parallel signatures from the Swiss (*Hoogduitschers*). There were no representatives from the Hutterite communities in Moravia.[11]

Unique Among Anabaptists

Marpeck's christology emphasized the humanity of Christ as the theological axiom on which everything else in his theology depended. It is important to note that Marpeck's formulation of this belief was unique among Anabaptists, and he may have worried that it would not be given proper attention.

In fact, his distinctive views were often at odds with those of many Anabaptist leaders. Marpeck was particularly appalled by the position of the followers of Melchior Hoffman and Menno Simons (after whom today's Mennonites are named), who argued that although Jesus was fully human, he did not receive his human body from his mother Mary but rather received his heavenly flesh in his incarnation, flesh like that of Adam before the fall.[12]

The fact that the Melchiorite christology and his own could be regarded by other Anabaptists as similar must have alarmed him even more. One of the most important concepts of the renegade kingdom of Münster was "The Word has become flesh and lives in us," a passage so crucial to Münsterite theology and life that it was even engraved on their

10. Harold S. Bender, "Strasbourg Conferences," in *ME* 4, 642.

11. Hulshof, *Geschiedenis van de Doopsgezinden te Straatsburg*, 221-24.

12. T. Finger, *A Contemporary Anabaptist Theology* (Downer's Grove, Ill.: InterVarsity Press, 2004), 385.

currency.[13] The thought that Anabaptists would actually forge a state—even worse, would do so by violence—and then engrave what Marpeck would have considered a wrong-headed theology on the state currency would have outraged him.

Marpeck emphatically proclaimed that the Son of Man was indeed human. Jesus was born a pure, true, and unalterable man who took his nature and kind from the human race both in and from Mary, the pure Virgin. His genuine humanity, Marpeck wrote, has been taken up into God the Father, and God the Father in the Son, eternally God of one essence and spirit. Precisely because he is the Son of Man all judgment has been conferred on him; not because he is also God's Son and of one substance with the Father. Marpeck warned that it is easy to call Jesus the divine Son of God, since even unclean spirits do that (see Matt. 8:28; Luke 4:34). But to acknowledge this Son of Man as a true man and then to confess him to be Lord and God can be done only by inspiration of the Holy Spirit.

This led Marpeck then to the question of how Christians can know whether or not they are led by God's Spirit. This was a very important question at the time since all people—whether Catholic, Protestant, Schwenckfeldian, or Anabaptist—each in their own way appealed to the Holy Spirit's work as the guarantor of theological truth. Marpeck confessed that he too had often acted with excessive zeal and with little of God's Spirit.

This is a theme that occurs a number of times in his letters during the final years of his life, offering a glimpse of a more introspective and compassionate Marpeck than the firebrand of earlier years. He chided himself for being a servant on these occasions rather than a son (see Gal. 4:7). His own experience, he continued, had also made him more generous toward others who ran with zeal but did not follow the direction of the Spirit. As a man who steeped his life in the book of Isaiah, he knew that the coming of God's justice depended ultimately on the faith that "the zeal of the Lord of Hosts will do this" (Isa. 9:7)—but also that God's zeal was made manifest through people. Those who are zealous, he observed, can do good. Not only that, but in part they do God's will—although not as those driven by the Spirit as God's children and friends but as servants who don't know what the Father is doing.

> Many men act because of zeal concerning the good, who do not know or suppose otherwise than that they are driven by the Holy Spirit. In part, it is probably true, that it is often of God, but not under the office of the true Holy Spirit of Christ, but driven by a

13. Max Geisberg, *Die Münsterischen Wiedertäufer und Aldegrever. Eine Ikonographische und Numismatische Studie* (Baden-Baden: Verlag Valentin Koerner, 1977), 59, 64-72.

servile service. God also uses such servants now, often as a provisional forerunner and preparer of the way for those who are rightly driven of the Holy Spirit of Christ, that they may make the path and the road, clear it, and weed it. They are however only servants, and not friends or children, who do not know what their Master is doing, nor what He has in mind. Such a servile compassion has frequently taken place in our time for quite a while now and contributed to all divisions and sects.[14]

But they also do God's will, he said, for they prepare the way for those driven by the Spirit.

This was Marpeck's version of Luther's teaching that the law of the Old Testament was the preparation for the gospel. Luther, Zwingli, Hoffman, Schwenckfeld, and Franck are cited in a margin note in the *Kunstbuch* as examples of those who were only servants, unaware of what their Lord was doing. This zeal *without* the Holy Spirit, Marpeck said, is the source of all the sects.[15]

Reflections on Domination

It was the division among Anabaptists and the larger division of Christians into papal and evangelical sects that led Marpeck to attempt to identify the marks or signs by which believers could know that they were being led by the Spirit. The first mark, he wrote, is the love "for God, and granting my neighbour that which God has granted and given to me for His praise." No one may receive God's gifts and then deny them to others.

The second mark is the readiness to surrender patiently all one has, including life itself, for the sake of Christ and the gospel. Marpeck's readers would have recognized in this mark an underlying principle that he held dear: the gospel cannot be defended by violent resistance.

The third mark or sign that he defined is the ability to recognize when God opens a door to the gospel. "No one should open a door which God has not opened, in order that the office of the Holy Spirit remain His own and free," he warned. Doing so leads to throwing pearls before swine, which then turn and destroy (see Matt. 7:6). Here Marpeck probably implies that to break down the door and promote the gospel through forceful domination causes only destruction, as the evidence of recent years showed.

The fourth and last mark, he concluded, is that in teaching and making judgments, the believer must be free and sound in the truth. Then one will know if the hearers desire the gospel, he said, because of the great need of their spiritual weakness and illness. For only believers need the holy

14. Klassen and Klaassen, *WPM*, 511-12.
15. Here he is in full agreement with Entfelder.

food and drink and the physician with his ointment—the words of truth that can heal the nations. Those who consider themselves to be healthy, and those who scorn the sustaining food and healing medicine, are excluded from them by their own choice.

Marpeck seemed to be echoing the words of Jesus that pronounce divine blessings on those of a gentle spirit as well as those who know themselves poor in spirit and who hunger and thirst for righteousness. God cannot bless those who profess not to need God, thereby seeking to control and dominate everything for their own ends. To recognize the truth of this difference is to be led by the Spirit.

It is important to notice how Marpeck tried to avoid saying that those with whom he disagreed were not Christian. He grounded that reluctance in his own experience of having zeal without the modification of love and patience. It was an issue Marpeck had struggled with during a lifetime of controversy with fellow Anabaptists, with evangelicals like Martin Bucer and with spiritualists such as Caspar Schwenckfeld. Unlike Martin Luther or Menno Simons, Marpeck appears to have become less rigid and more accepting of those with whom he differed toward the end of his life.

Harsh judgments on others were the stock-in-trade of religious people in the sixteenth century, especially of those fiercely committed to their convictions. They were afraid that if one's opponents were granted some measure of truth, one would betray the truth as one understood it. These dynamics are especially obvious in the controversy between Marpeck and Schwenckfeld. Impatience and anger often betrayed both of these men, although both accepted as fellow Christians those who differed from them. Marpeck, especially, showed that he was able to apologize to Schwenckfeld when he had made accusations that were not accurate.

At the end of this last letter that we have from Marpeck, he addressed the "brothers from Langenau." Apparently they had been threatened with expulsion by their authorities and had come to Marpeck in Augsburg for advice. He had urged them to return to Langenau. Perhaps God would grant them leave to stay there again. In the letter, he said he doubted that the threats of the government would be carried out. Threats are often made by the authorities to keep people quiet so that they won't have to act against them, he said. Perhaps they had been meeting openly too often. He counselled them to observe moderation and discretion. The government often exerts pressure, he explained, because they themselves will be punished if they don't.[16] They do not wish to persecute us, he wrote, and therefore we should not provoke them so that they don't act unjustly against believers.

16. All principalities and cities of the empire were required to carry out the mandates against Anabaptists. Many were unwilling to do so.

These words may capture more of the dynamic of Marpeck's survival in Augsburg than any of his other writings that exist today.

In the letter, Marpeck addressed Abraham Brendlin and admonished him not to endanger by ill-considered provocation what security they had. We don't know what had occurred, but Marpeck evidently regarded the provocations as not necessary for conscience's sake, for he added that where God's truth is concerned, they should all be prepared to surrender everything, even life itself.[17] Finally, he urged that special provision be made for the needs of an old sister (in other words, an older woman in the community).

Positive Role of Government

Marpeck's advice on the relationship of the faithful with government is likely indicative of his positive assessment of government and its function, as well as his own experience as a magistrate in the imperial system in Tirol. Nevertheless, one should not rule out a deliberate adjustment on Marpeck's part to the political and social realities in the milieu in which he worked and the security he evidently enjoyed.

When he admonished his people at Langenau not to antagonize the government so that the few safe places they had would not be lost, he was likely reflecting his own accommodation to the authorities in Augsburg. In order to be tolerated, he and his group apparently met quietly only about four times a year. He may also have known and remembered Jakob Hutter's aggressiveness against the Moravian authorities when, in the summer of 1535, his group was evicted from Schakwitz. Hutter had called King Ferdinand a bloodhound. He was then told to write his grievance in a letter to the governor of Moravia, John Kuna, in which he moderated his invective but threatened him with the fate of Pilate.[18] By all this, Hutter's ability to lead had been crippled. In the fall of 1535 he was forced to flee and his community was scattered.

It is possible that this episode, with its bloody sequel of Hutter being burned to death at the stake in 1536, influenced Marpeck to counsel his people not to antagonize governments. When he did criticize government or the state, he resorted to images such as "Leviathan" and "the Authorities" rather than use the scathing language of Hutter or the ridicule of Balthasar

---

17. For a detailed analysis of Marpeck's position regarding the relationship of the Christian to the state see William Klassen, "The Limits of Political Authority in Pilgram Marpeck," *MQR* 56 (1982), 342-64.

18. Packull, *Hutterite Beginnings*, 237-39. The "fate of Pilate" is perhaps a reference to the legend that, in despair, Pilate committed suicide.

Hubmaier.[19] Moreover, while Marpeck repeatedly wrote that obedience to God may require the surrender of life itself, he seemed never to have faced that prospect. He certainly did not strive for martyrdom. Moreover, he could easily rationalize that by his writing and pastoral care, he was doing what God had given him to do.

We note that there is no evidence that Marpeck ever came to a verbal defence of his persecuted brothers and sisters in the Habsburg Netherlands, where the Inquisition raged, or in Tirol, where persecution did not stop until the movement died out as a result of violent persecution and emigration. His very silence bears a question mark. Was that possibility open to him? By his apparent silence, was Marpeck trying to avoid drawing the attention of governments to himself and his group of churches for their own safety, since there was nothing he could do about those persecutions?

～

The last paragraph of the final letter we have from Marpeck offers us a glimpse of a caring leader. He concludes his letter to the Langenau brethren by describing a herbal remedy for rheumatism to help the wife of a brother in Christ addressed as Lorrentz. He tells the woman that valerian root should be put in water for three or four days, adding more root until it is strong enough. The mixture should not be boiled. The woman should drink it regularly, but she should not eat any cabbage or pork or drink any wine with this medicine. She should not take a bath, Marpeck cautioned, because that only drives the rheumatism into the head.

Interestingly, in the National Library (*Nationalbibliothek*) in Vienna there is another medicinal recipe written by Marpeck in 1555. It is found in a volume of writings on medicine and has the title "Pilgrimus (a Latin version of his name[20]) Marpeck: How to make the green juice of the black-thorn (sloe) as a remedy for figwarts and hemorrhoids."[21]

Marpeck's recipe explained how to make sloe juice from green sloe (i.e., cherry) pips so that it would last for a year.[22] The mixture was to be

19. Mention of the ridicule is included in Johan Fabri's booklet on the trial and execution of Hubmaier.

20. There are differing forms of Pilgram in Latin: In the censor's report it appears as "Pilgerinum" (Klassen, *Covenant and Community*, 36), in a reference by Walch as "Pilgramus" (ibid., 25 n49), and by Bucer as "Peregrinum" (ibid. 29, 62).

21. (*Wie man den gruenen Schlehensaft machen sol wider die Feigwartzen und Ausgang des Afters.*)

22. First, he advised, crush the green pips of the sloe well in a mortar and strain the mixture with rosewater through a fine sieve or through a cloth so that a pure juice results. Let the juice stand to settle. When it is clear, strain it, and put it in a clean

used when hemorrhoids bled or when itchy warts developed on a woman's private parts. The concoction would shrink the hemorrhoids, he predicted, and the warts would disappear. He then testified that the recipe had often been effective.[23]

Because the recipe was found in archives in Vienna and because there was a Marpeck-affiliated fellowship there, it may be proper to conclude that Marpeck sent the recipe to someone who was part of that group in 1555. The source for these recipes was likely one of the many books on remedies for common ailments that were frequently found in the homes of the well-to-do all over Europe.[24] It is also intriguing to wonder if Marpeck might have acquired the recipe through an Anabaptist midwife or from the medical genius Paracelsus, with whom he probably had contact during his years as mining superintendent in Rattenberg (see chapter 2).

A Final Glimpse

The last sign of life from Marpeck is a signature for funds related to the waterworks, dated October 31, 1556. A week later, he was dead. An entry for November 7, 1556, in the city books reads: "Anthony pays 11 guilders 59 kreuzer for Pilgram deceased." He died suddenly some time during that week at about age sixty-one. The cause of death is unknown. Boyd says that Pilgram's wife, Anna, probably received his last salary payment on December 16 and moved out of the water tower soon thereafter. Anna appears to have survived him for a few years. She may have moved in with Hans Jakob and Kunigunda Schneider, because they testified in 1562 that she had been with Kunigunda during her childbirth (see chapter 13).[25]

Pilgram Marpeck would have been buried within a day or two of his death, wrapped in a white shroud and likely laid to rest beside a cemetery established outside the city in 1494. It was the practice throughout the sixteenth century and beyond to bury Anabaptists outside the designated cemeteries in unconsecrated ground. In Speyer in 1530 an order was given

---

glass. To a quarter of the juice add alum (a double sulphate of aluminum and potassium, probably used for astringent qualities) about the volume of a hazelnut. The alum preserves it so that it does not spoil or grow mouldy, Marpeck explained. The sediment that settles at the bottom should be siphoned off and saved with the juice. When the sediment is to be used, it should be added to some rosewater, made into a paste and applied to the affected part.

23. *Nationalbibliothek Wien, Sammelband medizinischer Schriften*, Codex Nr. 11, 182, fol. 294 a and b, Rezept Nr. 36.

24. The manuals found in German-speaking areas also often contained dietary prohibitions to ensure effectiveness.

25. Boyd, *Pilgram Marpeck*, 146.

that any Anabaptists buried in a garden or cemetery were to be exhumed and buried in a field.[26] In some communities, the local executioner buried Anabaptists under the scaffold.[27] It was thought that anyone who had refused the sacraments of the church—baptism, the eucharist, and extreme unction—would defile consecrated ground. Those buried outside consecrated church or cemetery grounds were believed to be outside God's care.

Yet isolated voices from earlier times disputed this theory of exclusion. Honorius of Autun, a twelfth-century theologian, wrote: "It is in no way harmful to the just not to be buried in the cemetery of the church, for the whole world is the temple of God, consecrated by the blood of Christ. Whatever may happen to their bodies, the just will always remain in the bosom of the church."[28] The Waldensians and the Hussites of the fifteenth century believed that the place of one's burial was immaterial to salvation.

But Catholics and Protestants in the sixteenth century were much more particular. Official instructions were issued in the Palatinate in the year of Marpeck's death: "Whoever dies as an Anabaptist or a Schwenckfeldian, having refused the sacraments, is to be buried without the tolling of bells or a funeral sermon."[29]

The few references to Anabaptist attitudes to burial of the dead suggest that they were not greatly concerned by this official exclusion. In 1530 Anabaptists in Esslingen did not bury their dead in a cemetery "but under a tree with no funeral ritual."[30] In 1626 an old Anabaptist who had been urged to conform to the official Lutheran faith so that he could have a Christian burial said that he was not concerned "that he would be buried in the local garbage ditch" (*wuhlskaute*).[31] For people who were persecuted everywhere and for whom faith in God was experiential and relational more than creedal, their place of burial was not a matter of great concern. When "the earth is the Lord's," as they often said, every place was godly, not just a consecrated cemetery.

From everything we know about Marpeck, he too would not have regarded the manner and place of his burial as a vital issue. He believed that he was united to Christ by the Holy Spirit and therefore could not be

26. Ibid., 478.
27. Ibid., 380, 383-84.
28. Philippe Aries, *The Hour of our Death* (New York: Knopf, 1981), 41.
29. *Quellen: Baden und Pfals (TA: Baden und Pfals)* 4, ed. Manfred Krebs (Gütersloh: Bertelsmann Verlag, 1951), 150.
30. Claus-Peter Clasen, *Die Wiedertäufer im Herzogtum Württemberg* (Stuttgart: W. Kohlhammer Verlag, 1965), 89.
31. G. Franz, *Urkundliche Quellen zur hessischen Reformationsgeschichte* 4, *Wiedertäuferakten* (Marburg: Elwertsche Verlagsbuchhandlung, 1951), 523.

separated from Christ by any human decree. His community would have regarded him as a faithful victor, now reigning with Christ. Unconsecrated burial had no bearing on that ultimate reality, for they knew that no human institution, including the church, could control and prescribe for others what were the prerogatives of God.

⌐⌐

The death of Pilgram Marpeck would have been a major blow for his Anabaptist community in Augsburg and for members of Marpeck-affiliated churches in Switzerland, Moravia, and elsewhere. Six years after his death Hans Jakob Schneider, a member of the Augsburg Marpeck fellowship who we have encountered several times, said in an interrogation: "Pilgram of blessed memory had been their leader and teacher. . . . Those of his faith were all such because of Pilgram of blessed memory."[32]

---

32. Stadtsarchiv Augsburg, *Urgichten*, July 22, 1562.

-21-

A Full and Meaningful Life

Pilgram Marpeck had the unusual distinction among Anabaptist leaders of being a lifelong successful professional who by virtue of his technical skill died a natural death rather than being burned at the stake or beheaded. As we have seen, Marpeck never experienced official interference in his work because of his continued religious dissent. When he was hired, the city of Augsburg merely requested that he refrain from promoting his "sect." Despite repeated accusations that he had published Anabaptist texts and engaged in illegal activities, no official charges were laid. Furthermore, not once in the approximately nineteen years of his employment as an engineer is there a record of criticism of or dissatisfaction with his work. From this we may presume that he was highly competent.

Marpeck appears to have regarded his professional work as a service to humanity and to God. It also gave him the means and the time to be a Christian leader and author.

The question has often been posed whether Marpeck sensed any tension between working for the state and serving Jesus as Lord of the church. The answer is that he did indeed address this question, which was central in his debates both with the Swiss Brethren and with Caspar Schwenckfeld. For the Swiss Brethren, serving as a government official was no longer permissible as a result of the Schleitheim Confession, the first published Anabaptist statement of faith. Drafted by the Swiss in the spring of 1527, the Schleitheim statement not only ruled out government work but also forbad Anabaptists to serve as government-related mediators. Ironically, Marpeck served precisely those two roles in the several years preceding the Schleitheim Confession and his own conversion to Anabaptism late in 1527. Even after his conversion, he remained in public service for the rest of his life.

During his discussions with the clergy in Strasbourg, Marpeck took the position that serving as an official of the state was allowed for Christians as long as one remained conscious of the possibility of being required to do things that would violate one's allegiance to Christ. For example, it was always wrong for a Christian to use the sword and to make decisions involving life and death.[1] In the *Babylonian Whore* booklet, he cited the situation of loving one's neighbour and then seeing the neighbour attacked. Should you not rush to defend that person and thus show love for him or her? Marpeck suggested that using arms to ward off an attack could be done only if one decides to leave the company of the Lamb and join those who fight with physical, not spiritual, weapons.

> I admit . . . earthly rulers as servants of God, in earthly matters, but not in the kingdom of Christ; according to the words of Paul, to them rightfully belongs all carnal honor, fear, obedience, tax, toll, and tribute. However, when such persons who uphold authority become Christians (which I heartily wish and pray for), they may not use the aforementioned carnal force, sovereignty, or ruling in the kingdom of Christ. It cannot be upheld by any Scripture. To allow the external authority to rule in the kingdom of Christ is blasphemy against the Holy Spirit.[2]

Marpeck took issue with Caspar Schwenckfeld and Martin Bucer, who saw no contradictions between being a Christian and serving the state, even to enforce Christianity (their interpretation thereof) with the sword. Both Bucer and Schwenckfeld pointed to Acts 10 and claimed that Cornelius, a centurion in the Roman army, remained a centurion after he was baptized by Peter. Marpeck rejected this argument, saying that the Bible doesn't indicate what Cornelius did after he was baptized.

The clearest statement on the issue of Anabaptists serving the state comes from Marpeck's close associate, Leupold Scharnschlager, in a short piece in the *Kunstbuch* entitled "Whether a Christian can Serve as an Official in the state."[3] His reply was that the Christian first must do God's will and then must obey the command of Christ to love your neighbour as well as your enemy. He then quoted the Schleitheim Confession in support of his position that it would be difficult to be a government official and to obey the spiritual laws of God and Christ.

Marpeck made no hard and fast ruling on this matter but invited peo-

---

1. See Krebs and Rott, *TA Elsass* 2, 346-53, and in Loserth, *Quellen und Forschungen*, 303-4.

2. Klassen and Klaassen, *WPM*, 150.

3. Fast and Rothkegel, *Kunstbuch*, no. 29 "Ob der Christ ein Amt in der Obrigkeit Wahrnehmen Kann," 518-20.

ple to consider whether they could do justice both to God and the state.[4] It appears that Marpeck was able to live with this dilemma, perhaps because he did not allow himself to be placed in a situation where he had to use a sword to protect people's lives. Early in his working life when he was mining superintendent working directly with Ferdinand, at the point that he decided to live as an Anabaptist, he quit his job and secretly made his way to Moravia (see chapter 4). In subsequent years, as long as he was hired by the state to provide wood and water or to build fulling mills for weavers, it appears that he saw no tension between his job as civil servant and his work as an Anabaptist leader. Perhaps he saw his work in part as an avenue to loving his enemies: such as providing firewood for Spanish soldiers as well as for citizens of the city. Unfortunately, no text has yet been discovered in which Marpeck speaks directly to his own situation as a senior civil servant and church leader. The best we can say is that he appears to have a clear conscience with respect to this issue.

Man of Action

Marpeck is remembered today for his articulation of the way of a Christian in this world. He worked in a society in which Protestants and Catholics threatened each other with war, while the threat of invasion by the Turkish troops of Suleiman could not be ignored. What were the essentials of the vision to which he called his followers?

Marpeck did not develop his theology as a scholar might. His parents were rooted in Catholic piety and parish life in Rattenberg. The Augustinian priest Stefan Castenbaur began preaching at the parish church soon after Martin Luther took Europe by storm and made an impact on Marpeck that stayed with him through life. Exuding a passionate commitment to the Bible, Castenbaur boldly called for renewal of the church, arguing that the source of renewal began in the Old Testament and then moved on to the New. He was adamant that the ceremonies of the church had the potential both to enrich and renew people's lives and the church itself. He laid a foundation for Marpeck that underpinned the spirit and practice of his faith throughout his life.

Marpeck was a man of action who lived very much in the everyday world of his home and work places, mixing with professionals and business people, with politicians and clergy, wealthy patricians and poor labourers, armies and their commanders. He knew the comforts provided

---

4. Neal Blough's conclusion that "regarding civil government, Schwenckfeld was more flexible than was Marpeck" would be difficult to support with evidence even though the topic has been much discussed. See Blough, *Christ in Our Midst*, 183.

by a professional income and satisfaction in his work as an engineer. He also knew the uncertainty and stress that his form of Christian faith brought, not so much perhaps for himself as for those whom he had drawn into that faith and who did not have the protection of the relative wealth and position that he enjoyed. Marpeck knew from experience the hazards and weariness of travel, for an Anabaptist leader—despite professional or personal prestige—was never safe anywhere. He knew the unremitting tension of the careful balance of accommodation between his expression of faith and the political realities of his time and place.

He struggled with his uneasy estimate of other Christians, especially those Christian leaders who held power. Their actions were so often out of harmony with what he "had learned of Christ," that he sometimes feared they were not Christians at all—presenting him with a conflicting choice between charity and judgment. He also knew the frustration and sometimes the anger of having to disagree with others whom he knew to be Christians.

He also struggled with attacks against his integrity and worthiness as a follower of Christ. He knew his limitations as a lay theologian; hence his repeated frustrating attempts to clarify what he said to his opponents often resulted in annoying repetition and wordiness. He knew about the high demands made on his self-confidence by having to be for the world and at the same time against the world (*pro mundum contra mundo*) in a way not required of his Catholic and Protestant opponents. He was no dilettante playing at theology, any more than his churchly adversaries were. His theology, like theirs, was hammered out amid the human realities just described. What person in his or her right mind would set out into the world under those conditions with such steely determination unless he was certain that what he had found was important for the life of the world?

Traditional but Visionary

Marpeck's views were shared by only a handful of Europe's people, a small despised minority. In the estimation of a modern Reformation historian, their way "lay along the clouds"—that is, they nowhere touched the realities of life on the ground. But numbers are no guarantee of truth or falsehood, and humanity's visionary few deserve as respectful a hearing as the conforming multitude.

It is important to establish that in his *credo*, Marpeck was entirely orthodox.[5] Unlike other figures of the Reformation,[6] he had no quarrel

5. Despite accusations by Bucer and Schwenckfeld to the contrary.
6. To mention only three: Servetus, who questioned the church's teaching on the Trinity; Menno Simons, who denied that Jesus derived his flesh from Mary, his mother

on the central affirmations of Christian faith with Catholics and Protestants. His differences with his Christian contemporaries came in the consequences for faith, especially of the items of the creed dealing with Jesus. He accepted the church's teaching of the complete humanity and complete divinity of Jesus, but he struggled with the implications of that teaching. If we allow Marpeck to be judged by the teaching tradition of the church and not by the near inerrancy of interpretation often attributed to the Protestant Reformers, we can see that his interpretations run along traditional lines found elsewhere among Christian interpreters before the sixteenth century. As an example, one may point to the monastic life as a following of Jesus, emphasizing the need to adopt Jesus' humility, poverty, and nonviolence.

At the centre of Marpeck's theological construct stands the figure of the human Jesus, the man of flesh and blood who was the very revelation of God, the Creator of all things. God's self-revelation in a human being also revealed the manner of his working by the Holy Spirit to make himself known. This took place, wrote Marpeck, only and always through objective visible things: a man, his human voice and action, water, bread and wine, Scripture, and preaching. The Holy Spirit leads humans to invisible spiritual reality by means of these visible "creatures." These creatures, he insisted, are indispensable to human salvation, with water, wine, and bread actually participating in the process of cleansing from sin, and in making the believer a participant in the suffering and sacrifice of Christ.

None of this is to say that this emphasis on the visible as the gateway to the invisible was Marpeck's invention. It was a basic philosophical assumption of ancient sacramental doctrine. Among the Reformers, Martin Luther held this view, and it is entirely likely that Marpeck learned it from him as well as from other proponents of change, such as Lienhart Schiemer and Hans Schlaffer. This emphasis on the creaturely probably protected Marpeck from ever becoming part of the Spiritualist movement.

The following statement by Anglican John Donne, dean of London's St. Paul's Cathedral, from a 1621 sermon, reflects the depth and nuance of the conviction that was prevalent among Reformers and Anabaptists in the sixteenth and seventeenth centuries:

> He that undervalues outward things, in the religious service of God, though he begin at ceremoniall and rituall things, will come quickly to call sacraments but outward things, and Sermons and publique prayers, but outward things, in contempt. As some Platonique Philosophers, did so over-refine Religion, and devotion,

---

(a belief also shared by Schwenckfeld); and perhaps also Zwingli, who denied that baptism and the Lord's Supper were important for human salvation.

as to say, that nothing but the first thoughts and ebullitions of a devout heart, were fit to serve God in. If it came to any outward action of the body, kneeling, or lifting up of hands, if it came to be invested in our words, and so made a Prayer, nay if it passed but a revolving, a turning in our inward thoughts, and thereby were mingled with our affections, though pious affections, yet, say they, it is not pure enough for a service to God; nothing but the first motions of the heart if for him. Beloved, outward things apparel God; and since God was content to take a body, let us not leave him naked.[7]

For Marpeck and his colleagues, no issue was as central as what he calls the "enfleshment" of the Word. Their insight was drawn not just from Castenbaur, Luther, and other challengers of tradition, but also the fourth-century church father Augustine,[8] who set the agenda for theological debate with his focus on 2 Corinthians 3:6, "the letter kills, but the Spirit brings life." One of the most popular books of the sixteenth century was Augustine's *Spirit and Letter*, which was reprinted in German and published in many editions.[9] Augustine's writings were also prominent in one other aspect of sixteenth-century public debate, and that is in treating the Bible as a revelation of God intended for ordinary people in the belief that their lives could be transformed by understanding it.

Baptism for Marpeck was at the heart of "enfleshment." It is, he said, the means the Spirit uses to incorporate the new believer into the church: "the blessed company of all faithful people," to use the simple words of the *Book of Common Prayer*. The bread and wine of sacrifice define what the individual believer and the church now are; that is, one in mind, intention, will, and behaviour with Christ. The whole process was initiated and carried forward by God in grace and mercy and was not dependent on any human action, achievement, or merit, but on faith alone.[10]

That faith is not merely assent to the creed, although it is that as well.

7. From "Sermon Number Six," preached at St. Paul's Upon Christmas Day, 1621, in *John Donne's Sermons on the Psalms and Gospels*, ed. Evelyn M. Simpson (University of California Press, 1963), 149.

8. On Augustine see Gerhard Strauss, *Schriftgebrauch, Schriftauslegung und Schriftbeweiss bei Augustin*. (Tübingen: J. C. B. Mohr, 1959): 42-43; W. J. Sparrow Simpson, *St. Augustine on the Spirit and the Letter* (London: SPCK, 1925); P. Philipp Platz, *Letter to the Romans in St. Augustine's Teaching on Grace* (Würzburg, n.p., 1937), 140-45.

9. For the impact of Augustine's book on the medieval church, see "Letter and Spirit," anon., *Dictionary of Biblical Tradition* (Grand Rapids, Mich.: Eerdmans, 1999), 445-47.

10. For a thorough study of this topic, see Rollin Stely Armour, *Anabaptist Baptism* (Scottdale, Pa.: Herald Press, 1966).

More importantly, it is the readiness to participate in the very life of Christ, his mind and action. It is more than simply a literal following, the *imitatio Christi*. Specifically, the believer becomes, by baptism, part of the body of which Jesus is the head, an incorporated part of the body of Christ, so that the believer is directed by Jesus, the head. None of this was unique to Marpeck. It can all be found again and again at various points and times in the teaching of the church. But it was absent in most Protestant churches in the sixteenth century.

Departure from Teachings

Marpeck's departure from the Protestant and Catholic teaching of the time comes especially in the conclusions he drew from what constituted the central characteristic of divine revelation in Jesus. He called that characteristic the deep humility of God. The whole of Jesus' life, he wrote, revealed this divine trait: born in obscurity to parents of no social account, associating not with the mighty but with lowly suffering humanity, his disciples fishermen and tax collectors, claiming no rights for himself when arrested and put on trial, and dying a shameful death without resisting but praying for his tormentors. Jesus died willingly and was buried. The depth of Christ's humiliation was his descent to the dead, the antithesis of divine life and presence. His return in the resurrection revealed him as the one who mediated the grace and forgiveness of God. Now he was exalted as Lord of all to God's right hand, to which he brought his holy humanity, now glorified by his resurrection.

The path of the disciple in the world, continued Marpeck, also goes through humiliation and self-denial on to glorification and resurrection. There is no glory except that one passes first through the humiliation of the surrender of all self-will and all claims to power over others. It is this vision of discipleship that Marpeck tirelessly described in his writings. It is the vision he also had for the church. Along with other Anabaptists, Marpeck not only believed in a disciplined church, as did Catholics and Protestants, but also that internal discipline was one of the marks of the church. Yet he totally rejected the practice of Catholics and Protestants to compel internal conformity by force if it could not be done by persuasion.

What Anabaptists called persecution, Catholics and Protestants called church discipline. In Marpeck's time, the means of discipline were too often imprisonment, exile, and—especially in Catholic jurisdictions—death by fire and sword.[11] In order to establish church discipline without coercion, Marpeck gave extensive attention to finding a middle way

11. Marpeck's nemesis, Ferdinand, remained steadfast in his bloody enforcement of church discipline throughout his life. In a 1562 letter to a son-in-law six years after

between legalism and licence, which he called the liberty of Christ. That liberty was given by the Holy Spirit, who, in the practice of church discipline, led the Christian community in the active process of discerning the difference between forced and free obedience, and between liberty and licence. This was a process fraught with pitfalls for the unity of the church but which, if it could be achieved, would avert the danger of relapsing into coercion when resolving conflicts.

⌐

In the twenty-first century it is not possible, like it was in the sixteenth, to impose conformity in the church by coercion. The result too often has been the neglect to call Christians to live as disciples of Jesus and to adhere to the classic creeds. Today's church desperately needs to develop a process by which conflicts over moral and doctrinal issues can be resolved while preserving the liberty of Christ for all. Unless the church can be seen to be a model of patience and charity both in its process as well as its outcome, it will have failed at a vital point in its ministry to the world.

One of the weightiest items on the church's agenda, closely related to the foregoing, is the relationship between the Christian community and secular society and government. Marpeck radically separated the church with Christ as its head, and the civic community, which he saw as ruled by law and protected by the sanction of the sword. Only the sword of the Spirit may be used in the church, wrote Marpeck. The sword of steel that coerces has no place in the church. He totally rejected the ancient view that government, appointed by God, carries out disciplinary measures for the church. The sword of justice wielded by government, he wrote, is limited by God to keeping order in unregenerate society. It may never be used to coerce religious conformity, nor may it be used to promote the gospel through war in the name of Christ. He offered this vision especially to Protestant leaders in the empire. He called on them as Christians to abandon their view that it was necessary to defend the church of Christ with weapons of war.

The twentieth-century Russian religious philosopher Nikolai Berdyaev echoed this interpretation when he wrote: "Truth nailed upon the cross

---

Marpeck's death, Ferdinand observed that the sects considered themselves the true church, but in fact they were "pigsties." He cited the story in 2 Samuel of Uzzah, who tried to steady the ark of the covenant when it wobbled and was immediately struck dead, as the appropriate fate for all who thought they could step in and touch that which had been deemed holy. See Ernst Laubach, "Ein Religiöses Mahnschreiben Kaiser Ferdinands I," *Archiv für Reformationsgeschichte* 87 (1996), 90-118.

compels nobody. . . . Every time in history that man has tried to turn crucified Truth into coercive truth he has betrayed the fundamental principle
of Christ." [12]

This is a live issue today, not only for Christians and people of other
faiths under autocratic governments, but for those living in democracies as
well. We in the West are quick to point to Islamic nations where religion is
enforced by the power of the state and the gun. But many western nations
also have their own state-sanctioned expressions of religious zeal. Even
today, soldiers in some democratic nations are sent into battle in the name
of Christ to maim and kill. And even today, Christians defend as just warfare in which 95 percent of the casualties are defenceless civilians, including mothers and children. How long will modern Christians be sceptical of
Christ's authority in this matter?

Scripture says that the faithful witnesses of the past, being dead, yet
speak. Pilgram Marpeck is one of those witnesses.

---

12. Quoted from N. Berdyaev, *Dostoevsky*, by V. Gollancz, in *Man and God*
(Boston: Houghton Mifflin, 1951), 51.

Epilogue

Marpeck's Legacy

Human beings have a strong inclination to conform to the society in which we live. But we also have an indomitable urge to dissent from the norms of the majority and especially to challenge the authority of those who rule, even when rulers are chosen voluntarily and after due deliberation. The urge to dissent is especially strong when claims of infallibility are made of documents or people. Monotheism came into existence in Egypt as a result of such dissent, and Socrates led humanity to new concepts of ethics and philosophy as he dissented from the ruling establishment in his society in Athens.

Historians generally agree the Hebrews were the first "community of dissent"—an entire people who carved out a distinctive existence by splitting off from their society and affirming that one must observe certain days and restrict certain foods and practices because they as an entire people had been called by God. The ancient Hebrews are also recognized by many scholars as introducing the concepts of history and conscience to humankind. Across the millennia, many Jews and courageous people of other traditions have paid with their lives for "being different" and for following their conscience in the service of their God.

It is with this historical community of dissent that Pilgram Marpeck belonged. Born fifteen centuries after Jesus, he drew from the same well. Abraham and Sarah, Isaiah, Judith, and Mary Magdalene were familiar to Marpeck as a result of his upbringing in the Catholic parish of Rattenberg in the heart of the Austrian Tirol. Because Marpeck loved the church, he left its Roman form and practice when it no longer nourished his soul and was mired in its sense of self-importance, unable to adapt to the spiritual needs of the people. He parted company mainly because it had joined with political power, and together they were burning dissenters at the stake.

Marpeck's Enduring Values

Marpeck had the courage to stand against forces that stifle rather than allow the Spirit of God to move freely among the people of God. He also joined the act of dissent to the consistent rejection of violence. His writings and practices drew substance and inspiration from what he learned in his twenties from his parish priest in Rattenberg. Stefan Castenbaur repeatedly called attention to a text of the prophet Isaiah in which God states that the ultimate weapon of the Almighty is the spoken word. Marpeck's commitment to a better way than violence was rooted in the Hebrew Bible and New Testament. He remembered these teachings throughout his life and never settled for anything else. Marpeck wrote energetically for much of his adult life, spurred on by the conviction that, whether successful or not, his ministry of the word was patterned upon the way in which Jesus sent forth his message.

One important part of Marpeck's immediate legacy was to build God's community among the working people. He began in the mines, one of the most dangerous places in the world to work. He would have often experienced the loss of mining colleagues, and he sought parents for orphaned children, several of whom he and his wife adopted. But the mines also taught him that seemingly insurmountable obstacles could be overcome by people patiently working together. He built public works projects in various cities, resulting in the direct improvement in people's living and working conditions. But it was the spiritual realm that consumed his greatest energies.

In the sixteenth century, hopes were raised and then dashed in the spiritual quest of many people. Early in the century, Martin Luther listed as his first concern the relation of the inner to the outer in the quest for freedom from the burden of guilt and the bondage of sin. In 1515-18, he challenged and then defied a solidly entrenched system of church and state, and in doing so, opened a path for Marpeck and thousands of others to begin their own spiritual quest. Joining with the Anabaptist movement, Marpeck and others made bold to seek forgiveness without the mediation of priest or bishop. Rather, they saw forgiveness as being channelled through the people of God.

When dissent became an issue within the Anabaptist community, Marpeck became impatient with those who sought to build Christian community around regulations and restrictions. "I will not allow you to place a yoke on my conscience," he told the Swiss.[1] To dissent was not to be rebuked, he argued, because the dissenter also has the Spirit of Christ and

---

1. Fast and Rothkegel, *Kunstbuch*, 241.

in that very act may be speaking the mind of Christ. When he was accused by Martin Bucer and Caspar Schwenckfeld of breaking the unity of the church and thereby lacking love, he said: "I will never separate myself from them any more than I would separate myself from my Christ. I am prepared to show human love to everyone according to the word of Paul [Gal. 5:13], to serve everyone from the heart and not to hurt anyone's feelings."[2]

One area in which Marpeck took an enormous step forward is in his view of the role of women in the church. Jesus had commissioned women to declare the resurrection, he noted. Why should they not be spokespeople for the resurrected Christ today? Helena von Freyberg was one of the leading members of his Anabaptist community in Augsburg. We can find no examples of gender being an issue in his relations with other Anabaptists or in his messages to them.

The most important part of Marpeck's legacy was his refusal to split religious realities into inner and outer, spiritual and material. For him the whole of human existence was redeemed by a living Christ, and it was the task of the church to affirm joy and make peace and justice available not just to members of the kingdom of God but to all humanity.

A Challenged Legacy

After Pilgram Marpeck's death, some of his most important letters were placed in the *Kunstbuch* in a larger context of dissenting movements of the time, as well as the very early Reformation movement. These, along with clear reminders of patristic and medieval Christianity, were a legacy that had to be preserved.

But the legacy would not be retained and nurtured in Augsburg. Martin Rothkegel, a historian now based in Germany and final editor of the modern edition of the *Kunstbuch*, contends that Marpeck had a vision of a bourgeois, urban Anabaptism, which Rothkegel suggests was no longer viable at the time of his death. Centred in Protestant cities like Strasbourg or Augsburg, Anabaptism could not survive the relentless pressure of city governments for religious conformity.

"The future of Anabaptism lay elsewhere," Rothkegel writes, "in the marginal, ineradicable sectarianism of the Swiss Anabaptists; in the tenacious struggle of Netherlands Anabaptists for a place at the centre of society; until 1620 in tolerant Moravia, and then, a century later, in America."[3] It should

2. Klassen and Klaassen, *WPM*, 156-57. It is interesting to note that a description of the rebel by Albert Camus fits Marpeck: The rebel is compelled toward "transformation" and "rebellion must be accompanied with a strange form of love and be free of all resentment." See Camus, *The Rebel: An Essay on Man in Revolt* (New York: Knopf, 1971), 10-16; cf. 304.

3. "Randglossen," 62.

be pointed out, however, that the only urban group in the Marpeck circle was in Augsburg. All the others were in small towns or rural centres.

We don't know if Jörg Maler, the compiler of the *Kunstbuch*, turned away from Marpeck's Anabaptism-in-the-cities Anabaptism, but he emphatically did not abandon Marpeck's theological accomplishment as out-of-date and unworkable. The *Kunstbuch* was the last, herculean effort of an aging follower to give the Marpeck legacy new life in a radically different setting.

The fact is, though, that the churches associated with Marpeck's name disappeared as separate entities. Why did this happen? Martin Rothkegel suggested that they were no longer viable. But that judgment merely begs the question, and some effort must be made to respond to the question. Attempting to account for the disappearance of those fellowships and, with them, the name of Pilgram Marpeck, can only be conjectural at this time. Two considerations may move us closer to the truth of what happened, but there are likely others that wait to be discovered.

Of these two, the first had to do with church discipline in the Marpeck churches. Letters of his community reveal the tension between legalism[4] and its opposite,[5] both of which contain Marpeck's warnings of taking extreme positions. Either there was a proclivity to regulate church life by laws (as among the Swiss Brethren of Appenzell), or there was a temptation by some of his followers at Austerlitz to imagine that there were no moral constraints at all. Given the lures of "the blessed rage for order" and the yearning to be free of moral restraints, any attempt at a middle way easily recognizable by all was doomed to continual struggle or perhaps even failure.

Anabaptists almost always opted for order through law, a system of church discipline that penalized infractions but rarely took account of motives or circumstances. Both the Hutterites and the Mennonites of the Netherlands chose that way. It is at least arguable that the rigid internal discipline in those communions had something to do with surviving the fires of persecution. Absolute certainty about moral and theological truth armoured by strict internal discipline increases chances of survival.

Modern political movements give evidence of similar dynamics. Guerrilla movements regularly execute their own for nonconformity, thus maintaining discipline. Another example is modern Cuba, which has survived as an independent state due in considerable degree to inflexible internal political and economic discipline. It may be, therefore, that the absence of a legalistic discipline in the Marpeck fellowships hastened their decline. There would always be the temptation to minimize the differences between

4. Klassen and Klaassen, *WPM*, 309-69.
5. Ibid., 402-6.

Anabaptists and their Reformed neighbours. Leupold Scharnschlager's letters to his church at Ilanz warn of this temptation and provide some evidence of it.[6]

The other consideration centres on Marpeck's view of the church. While there are passages in his writings about this topic,[7] there is no single writing devoted to the concept of the church as one finds in Dirk Philips[8] or Peter Rideman.[9] The church is seen by Marpeck to be an extension of the incarnation and is therefore always discussed in the context of christology.[10] Perhaps the lack of a description in Marpeck's writings of the church with institutional forms and an Anabaptist version of a code of canon law contributed to blurring the lines of demarcation between Anabaptists and their Protestant neighbours. This blurring is best documented in the Scharnschlager letter "Admonition and Reminder,"[11] which suggests that their problems were rooted in inadequate congregational process and the irregularity of their clandestine gatherings, as well as in their advanced social integration into the surrounding society. Recent discoveries shed further light on the fortunes of the Marpeck circle.

New Insights

In 1993 historian Arnold Snyder made an astonishing discovery in the state archives in Zürich. He found a handwritten book carrying the following title and inscription: "*A Simple Confession*. To the mayor and council of the city of Zürich, concerning the reason for the great division and disagreement among all who boast of Christ and the Holy Gospel." It was dated 1588.

This led to the further important discovery that most of *A Simple Confession* was a verbatim copy of another manuscript in Bern titled *A short, simple understanding concerning the thirteen articles as they were disputed in this past year 1572 (sic) at Frankenthal in the Palatinate.* This manuscript of nearly five hundred pages was a response to the official printed version of the proceedings of a well-known disputation between evangelical clergy and Anabaptists held in Frankenthal in 1571.[12]

6. Fast and Rothkegel, *Kunstbuch*, 522-23, 446-50.

7. Klassen and Klaassen, *WPM*, 199-202, 390-401, 521-27; Rempel, *Later Writings by Pilgram Marpeck*, 96-99.

8. *The Writings of Dirk Philips*, ed. C. J. Dyck (Scottdale, Pa.: Herald Press, 1992), 350-82.

9. Peter Rideman, *Confession of Faith* (Hodder and Stoughton, 1950), 139-225.

10. For this, see Neal Blough, *Christ in Our Midst*.

11. Fast and Rothkegel, *Kunstbuch*, 446-50.

12. For detailed description of these manuscripts, their complex interrelationships, and analysis of their content see C. A. Snyder, "The (Not-so) 'Simple Confession' of the

Snyder's discoveries throw a bright floodlight on what happened to the Marpeck legacy in central Europe. There is much more here than a protective move by Anabaptists from urban Augsburg to rural Bern. Snyder suggests that "members of the Marpeck circle emerge as the most probable authors/editors of many of the [Swiss Brethren] writings that were copied and circulated" in the last decades of the sixteenth century.[13] We learn that members of the Marpeck circle wrote major portions of the *Simple Confession*.

Of particular importance are Marpeckian formulations on the role of secular government and the statement that a ruler may be a Christian, as well as the familiar plea of the Marpeck circle for freedom of conscience in matters of faith. Arguments for these formulations come from Marpeck's *Exposé of the Babylonian Whore* and Scharnschlager's *Plea for Tolerance to the Strasbourg Council* of 1534. Of equal importance was the discussion of the relationship between the Old and New Testaments, couched in words unmistakably Marpeckian:

> The Old [Testament] has an outer, fleshly mediator, namely Moses; it had an outer priesthood, outer unction, an outer kingdom, sword, law and judgement. The New has an inner, spiritual mediator, namely the person Jesus Christ. It has an inner kingdom and priesthood, the kingdom of our Lord Jesus Christ which he establishes in the newly reborn person, in justice, peace and joy in the Holy Spirit, Romans 14.[14]

This view represented what Snyder calls "a new and more sophisticated exegetical tool" for biblical interpretation which the Swiss Brethren had lacked even at Frankenthal. From the textual evidence Snyder draws the conclusion that "the mystery of the 'disappearance' of the Marpeck community may be explained by the absorption and integration of followers of Marpeck into the later Swiss Brethren, where they appear to have exerted a significant literary influence."[15]

Marpeck's theology came to have a growing role among the Swiss Brethren from 1573 onward. As Snyder suggests, this theology provided a more "culture-friendly alternative" to the rigid exclusivist understanding of church and world that they had inherited from the Schleitheim

---

Later Swiss Brethren, Pt. 1: Manuscripts and Marpeckites in an Age of Print," *MQR* 73 (1999), 677-722; Pt. 2: "The Evolution of Separatist Anabaptism," *MQR* 74 (2000), 87-122.
    13. *Simple Confession* 1, 721.
    14. *Simple Confession* 2, 99.
    15. *Simple Confession* 1, 708.

Confession. It encouraged a careful accommodation to the political realities in late sixteenth-century Switzerland.

No claim is made here for the collection of Anabaptist writings known as the *Kunstbuch* as the direct transmitter for all this. It was an integral part of a movement of people and convictions, participating in the inner spiritual reality of the survival of the Marpeck legacy. Even as the churches associated with Marpeck's name declined and vanished, his legacy remained alive among the Swiss Anabaptists. Amazingly, only the original autographed version of the text by Maler himself survived the persecution, book-burnings, and wear and tear of time. No copies of this original manuscript have surfaced thus far.

'Not What, but That'

We are left in the end with the passion, insight, and deep spirituality of Pilgram Marpeck that infuses the *Kunstbuch* and has helped to foster an Anabaptist vision that endures however imperfectly to this day. Although the author of a poem in the *Kunstbuch* is not known, much of the poem breathes the Marpeck spirit, especially his emphasis on careful judgment. It could well have been written by him. Marpeck's motto, "It is not what, but that" (*Es ist nit was sonnder das*—see chapter 7), forms a title for the poem.[16]

> The gifts of God are manifold
> and often seem against each other.
> If you desire the help of God
> don't judge before the proper time.
> God is the judge in today's strife. . . .
> Keep what is good, let the rest go.
> Have careful watch over your tongue.
> And don't blaspheme what you don't know. . . .
> Above all let us take to heart
> that God accepts our faith in him;
> that we cling to his truth alone;
> receive His Spirit to discern
> and understand this perilous time.

May he rest in peace and may the theology that he so passionately espoused continue to guide in a world still troubled by violence and political-religious animosity.

---

16. Klassen and Klaassen, *WPM*, 70 and n5. The motto "Not what, but that" was a key phrase used in one of Marpeck's first books, *A Clear and Useful Instruction*.

Appendix A

The *Response*

All the main subjects of Pilgram Marpeck's theology, such as baptism, the Lord's Supper, covenant, original sin, the Christian and government, the church, the faith of the patriarchs, and Christ as man and God, have been touched on in this biography. This appendix offers a summary of Marpeck's mature thought on these issues.[1] It is based on a translation by John Rempel of selections from the *Response* from which we can follow the main lines of Marpeck's argument against Schwenckfeld.[2]

The sequence of subjects in the *Response* was determined by their order and format in Schwenckfeld's *Judgement*.[3] This summary will follow another order to avoid repetition, taking care not to distort Marpeck's theological understanding of these issues.

God and Christ

Marpeck was very concerned about being theologically orthodox; that is, being part of a tradition shaped by the great creeds and therefore casting his views in traditional terms, firmly based on Scripture. Even when, as on the question of the Christian and the exercise of violence, he departed from the church's just war tradition, he was convinced that he was simply drawing out the implications of the traditional doctrine of the incarnation.[4] Marpeck's ethical views were derived strictly from his theology.

Marpeck began with the incarnation and from there went on to for-

1. This appendix refers to Marpeck as the author of the *Response*, but it is important to recognize (see chapter 13) that others in his community, especially Leupold Scharnschlager, may also have contributed to the text.
2. Rempel, *Later Writings by Pilgram Marpeck*, 75-144.
3. See Loserth, *Quellen und Forschungen*, 585-86. Similarly, Marpeck follows the outline of Schwenckfeld's *Judicium* of 1530 in his *Clear and Useful Instruction* of 1531.
4. See, for example, Klassen and Klaassen, *WPM*, 432-33.

mulate his views on God, the Holy Trinity. In Jesus "God took on flesh and lived in it." In his earthly life Jesus was not the Trinity, although by Spirit and Word he was God. "He was born out of God and the Holy Spirit and out of a remarkable act of God the Father, from his nature and essence, and from the Virgin Mary, full of grace and blessing under the sway of the Holy Spirit." Because of his supernatural conception and birth, he was not bound by sin. "There was no deceit, lust, evil inclination, or inherited remnants from Adam's fall in him." But for all that, he was a human being with flesh and blood, words and actions, and died a natural human death. He was tempted but was without sin. As a human being Christ was the grace of God himself, not merely a sign of grace. But "Christ's flesh is also God, as it is also the Holy Spirit, in the oneness of the Trinity, a life-giving power yet without annulling his true humanity and flesh."

In his resurrection, Christ's body was transfigured and glorified. "In its divinity, his human body now has eyes and face and comeliness in fullness, without blemish." He took his transfigured flesh with him to the right hand of God, and because he was still a human with flesh, he could be at only one place at a time. Thus he could never be bodily in the bread and wine. "It is," wrote Marpeck, "no small comfort and hope to the human race that human flesh and blood as part of Christ's humanity now sits at the right hand of God in heavenly glory."

The glorified Christ now acts "through the Holy Spirit as God the Father worked from the beginning of creation through the Holy Spirit. The Spirit has become the Son's arm and finger." Jesus works his will from heaven through the Spirit. But "even today he works through his unglorified body (which is the church). It is the very temple of God." This "untransfigured body (in other words, his church) . . . is his outward work: teaching, baptism, Lord's Supper, admonition, ban, discipline, evidence of love and service for the common good, a handclasp, improving and retaining Christ's commands and teachings." The church was, in Marpeck's understanding, the extension of the incarnation in the world. As Christ in his flesh worked as a human being outwardly, so did the church.

How Does God Work?

Salvation, wrote Marpeck, was through Christ alone.

> For that reason the Son assumed human nature, to do human bodily works: speaking words and doing deeds. Thus, physical eyes could see him, physical ears hear him, the physical body grasp and perceive him. All this the Father has placed in the Son's hands, so that the outward works of God the Son, like the inward work of the Father, is one work and essence.

That seeing and touching became possible through "the outward apostolic office and ministry of the Spirit." Part of that apostolic ministry was Scripture.

> The invisible, spiritual content and meaning of Holy Scripture and the outwardly preached word is the very word [to] which Scripture . . . gives glory and power as God's natural, almighty word. It is spirit and life, yes God himself. It is not a visible, perishing book of paper and ink; it is the eternal, living, essential word of God. The Scriptures and outward preaching don't only witness to it . . . but they themselves are that word.

Marpeck had no time for the separation of Scripture from the Word of God, which was a mark of the spiritualizers from Hans Denck onward.

In this book we have discussed in a number of places Marpeck's insistence on the proper view of the relationship of the external to the internal. "The truth lies in never separating or dividing the inward from the outward." Whatever the Holy Spirit attests internally is attested through the outward person.

> Inwardly, Christians are made holy and moved by the Holy Spirit; their life is hidden with Christ in God (Col. 3[:3]). No creature in heaven or on earth may judge that life. Through the Holy Spirit that life comes to outward expression, revealed in the flesh and through the body for obedience to the word, to which we testify before the world. . . . Through faith in Christ we become holy in heart and spirit; in flesh—with our mouth—we make confession and are saved (Rom. 10[:9]). This happens externally, in the flesh as the external word of teaching or preaching, as well as baptism, the Lord's Supper, admonition, discipline, punishment, the ban, and more. It brings about the salvation of the confessor and others, just as Jesus and the apostles first brought salvation to humanity.

The outward actions, insisted Marpeck, were of fundamental importance because they were co-witnesses to the internal work of the Spirit, and directly participated in the work of salvation. For this reason, the believer's "use of outer things is joy, peace, and comfort—delight in sorrow, suffering, and remorse for sin. They receive forgiveness unto salvation and assurance through the Holy Spirit." All this is reminiscent of the words of Martin Luther that he flung at the devil when assailed by doubt: "I am baptized!"

Faith of the Patriarchs[5]
Marpeck defended himself against Schwenckfeld's charge that he

5. John Rempel did not include this topic in his translation, but it seemed wise to include it here directly from Loserth, *Quellen und Forschungen*, 317-24, 333-408.

denied the patriarchs the privilege of being "Christians, children of God, and friends" and that they had neither forgiveness, a peaceable conscience, nor the Holy Spirit. Marpeck responded that

> Now, after the resurrection and ascension of Jesus Christ, we confess the salvation of the patriarchs and all those of ancient humanity who had persevered to the end in the hope of the incarnation and advent of Christ, and went down to Sheol after physical death. . . . When the Lord preached the gospel to them in the Depths, they received grace, comfort, salvation, peace and redemption because their sins were now expiated through him. The Lord led their captivity captive Eph. 4[:8-10] and they ascended with him out of the Depth to the Height.[6]

Marpeck's teaching about the patriarchs in the time of the Old Testament was that they had not received the benefits of Christ's passion as did those who believed following his death, resurrection, and ascension. They lived in hope of God's redemption through Christ and saw it from afar. They did not have the fullness of the Spirit because he was given only after Christ's exaltation. The whole argument, as Schwenckfeld correctly pointed out, was developed to reject the evangelical equivalence between circumcision and infant baptism and to assert the discontinuity of the old dispensation and the new. All this was copiously documented in the *Explanation of the Testaments* (*Testamenterleutterung*), a massive topical concordance that was being prepared by Marpeck and his associates during the early 1540s.[7] Its purpose was to show the difference between the Old and New Testaments, and especially to demonstrate that the Old Testament was a long preparation for the coming of Christ.

The Sacraments

The sacraments of baptism and the Lord's Supper best illustrate the relationship of outer and inner in Marpeck's theology.

Baptism. In his discussion of baptism Marpeck agreed with Schwenckfeld that water baptism was not necessary to salvation and also that nothing was accomplished by baptism if faith was absent. In order to meet the arguments of the infant baptizers, Marpeck had to address the question of original sin. Schwenckfeld had charged Marpeck with what was called "the Pelagian heresy," the belief that one could become godly by personal effort. Marpeck responded that he and his fellow believers taught no such thing.

---

6. Loserth, *Quellen und Forschungen*, 317.
7. Ibid., especially 129-37, 181-82, 320-21, 322-25.

He began by dismissing existing theories about the origin of original sin because he did not accept the concept at all. There was no need to baptize an infant to remove original sin because the child was sinless, as were Adam and Eve before the fall. "There is no more condemnation for [infants] through Adam and Eve's fall. Nor do they have an inheritance which leads to condemnation; the wrath of God is not upon such children *until they reach understanding, that is, the common knowledge of good and evil.*"[8] Only when that knowledge set in could repentance and faith be born and water baptism become necessary.

Water baptism was therefore reserved for those who were able to testify to personal faith. The water was the external co-witness to the inward faith. "Under the Holy Spirit inward and outward obedience flow together." But the faith of the one baptized did not somehow stand alone and fill the baptismal horizon. The confession of faith in baptism was the outward response indivisible from the *prior* inner work of God the Holy Spirit. Significantly, this "baptism is not into remorse, regret, or sadness but into comfort, forgiveness, peace, and joy in conscience in the Holy Spirit in the name of the Holy Trinity." With these words, Marpeck refuted the claim of the spiritualizers that John's baptism to repentance was the only model for the present. Marpeck's view was that baptism in the name of Jesus promised forgiveness of sins and resurrection to a new life.

The Lord's Supper. In the eucharistic controversies of the time, the ongoing question concerned the meaning of the bread and wine. Was the substance of the bread and wine changed into the actual body and blood of Jesus, as taught by Catholics, or were bread and wine memorial symbols pointing to the suffering and death of Jesus, as the Zwinglians taught? Marpeck rejected both views.

> As we have said, life-giving and sin-forgiving faith focuses on the time and history of Christ's death for the forgiveness of sins and the offering up of his untransfigured body, flesh and blood. Only his death . . . feeds, strengthens, and consoles the mourning soul and conscience through faith. The flesh and blood of Christ, which was offered up in death, is the right food in the Lord's Supper. . . . It's clear that the flesh and blood which the Lord Jesus Christ bade us eat and drink was his untransfigured mortal body and blood unto reconciliation and favour with God. . . . It is not the transfigured, spiritual, exalted flesh and blood!

This language could strike the reader as proving nothing, until it is remembered that Marpeck was defending an objective view of the Lord's

8. Emphasis is that of the authors.

Supper against Schwenckfeld's subjective view—in other words, that material bread and wine were an essential part of the rite, against Schwenckfeld's view that the Lord's Supper was an entirely inward experience. Moreover, Marpeck was as comprehensible as anyone else in that long controversy. Listen to Martin Luther's formulations on the Lord's Supper, which clearly influenced Marpeck. For Martin Luther, Jesus "did not say *this represents*, is *a symbol* of, or *stands for* my body. Rather, this is body, metaphysically and inexplicably—not essential as Rome declared, but somehow truly, fully, my body, my flesh and blood."[9]

The only true communion, continued Marpeck, was one that was celebrated by those truly filled with love. "He offered up his soul, his very life for us in death, that we might offer up our bodies in love like his as an act of true thanksgiving with everything we possess." One is reminded of Thomas Cranmer's formulation in the *Book of Common Prayer*: "And here we offer and present unto thee, O Lord, ourselves, our souls and bodies."[10] Again, Marpeck draws attention to the outer and inner in the use of the bread and wine.

> These and other forms of creatures[11] . . . succeed, through the spiritual use made of them and through the understanding of faith, in making the breaking of the bread and the drinking of the cup into a true communion or participation in the body and blood of Christ. He brings it about in truth and is an outer and inner, a single communion. . . . Yet bread and wine remain what they are, namely, mere creatures; by themselves they are not the Lord's Supper.

That was to protect the Lord's Supper from the error on the Catholic side. On the other hand, "his flesh and blood is not a memorial but that which one remembers. It is not a thanksgiving but he whom one thanks; not a proclamation but he whose death one proclaims. It is not a figurative food and drink . . . but the essential food and drink itself." That was to distinguish his understanding from the Zwinglian memorialist view.[12]

Marpeck considered both baptism and the Supper to be integral to the church and its ongoing life.

> What is given to the spouse of Christ is applied through apostles, prophets, teachers, bishops, admonishers, and the like. This is the

9. Oyer, '*They Harry the Good People out of the Land*,' 10.

10. *Book of Common Prayer* (Toronto: Anglican Book Centre, 1959), 85.

11. Again one is reminded of Cranmer's words in the communion service: "these thy creatures of bread and wine."

12. A careful statement of Zwingli's teaching about the Lord's Supper is found in Cyril C. Richardson, *Zwingli and Cranmer on the Eucharist* (Evanston: Seabury-Western Theological Seminary, 1949), 11-13.

service of the whole congregation, carried out in and through the
Holy Spirit, as members grow as branches on the Vine, who gives
them guidance; without him they can do nothing, externally or
internally (John 15[:5]; Eph. 4; Col. 2)—neither baptism, communion, laying on of hands, footwashing, brotherly love, discipline, the
ban, and the like. All these issue from one spirit to the praise of the
one essence, that is, the God who is in all things, who wins us to
and sustains us in eternal life unto salvation—one essence and one
glory.

Marpeck deliberately attempted to find a middle way between the
Catholic and Zwinglian views that incorporated parts of the positions he
rejected. He accepted from Catholicism an objective view of the sacraments and from Protestantism the view that without the faith of the recipient there was no sacrament. He saw his attempt as another part in the
unified church he was trying to encourage among Anabaptists. In the end
this attempt came to nothing through ethnic and theological differences
among Anabaptists, and it was forgotten. Only in the twentieth century
would some of his spiritual descendants rediscover his vision.

Church and Government

Schwenckfeld had charged Marpeck with wrongfully saying that a
Christian could not be a secular ruler. This was a serious matter, Schwenckfeld said, because it was finding fault with God's order. Marpeck responded
by pointing back to the *Admonition*. There he had written:

> For the kingdom of Christ is not of this world. Thus no true
> Christian is allowed to occupy or defend either city, land, or peo-
> ple, as earthly lords do, nor to carry on with violence, for such
> belongs to the earthly and temporal rulers and not at all to the true
> Christians, who show forth the faith in Christ. Many false people
> in our time have attempted, as the papists and evangelicals (as they
> call themselves) still try to show today, that city rulers, princes, and
> lords (in the appearance of defending the faith) use all earthly
> power. It is to be feared that they shall suffer the same fate as did
> those who engaged in the Peasants' War.[13]

It would be hard, wrote Marpeck further, "for a Christian to be a worldly
ruler. . . . How long will he remain a ruler of this world? . . . How long
would his conscience let him be a ruler?" For rulers, he believed, are compelled to use violence. That is part of the order of God, and God gives rulers

13. Translation slightly amended: Rempel, *Later Writings by Pilgram Marpeck*,
96-97; Loserth, *Quellen und Forschungen*, 303.

special wisdom to exercise their rule. But "true Christians have no order or commandment in the Gospel to rule over the kingdom of this world with violence in the name or in the light of Christ."

When Marpeck referred again and again to "the true Christian," in this context he meant Christians who were able to distinguish between the kingdom of Christ and the kingdoms of this world. The kingdom of Christ had become visible in the church.

> Through the divine Spirit the human spirit bridles his body for servanthood and cross bearing (Rom. 6[:13], 8[:10-11], 12[:1-2]; 1 Cor. 9; Gal. 5[:16-18]; James 4[:7-8]). The external obedience of a wholly believing person makes him—spirit, soul, and body—a partaker of the obedience of the whole body of Christ, that is, his holy congregation. He becomes a member of the body of which Christ is the head, the lord, the ruler. Each one serves the other to the betterment of the body of Christ.

Violence and coercion could not be part of servanthood and cross bearing, and could not serve the betterment of the body of Christ. The ruler who by God is given the mandate to use violence for the punishment of evil could, as ruler, have no role in the life of the church.

When Marpeck denied government (today we would also say state) any religious role, he desacralized it. He was among the few in the sixteenth century who drew this radical conclusion from reading the New Testament. This concept was not accepted by Catholics and Protestants until they were compelled to do so by secular government in the eighteenth and nineteenth centuries.

Marpeck had more empathy for rulers than most Anabaptists. After all, he had been a magistrate himself in several offices. But he objected to justifying the use of violence and coercion as expressing the mind of Christ. On that basis, many years before, he had resigned his influential office of mining superintendent.

Finally, it is worth another reminder that Anabaptists, along with Catholics and Protestants, were concerned about the reform of the church. In the conclusion of the *Response*, Marpeck expressed the daring conviction that this reform had happened.

> Through the might of his Holy Spirit in true believers—his apostles, his true church—[God] has reformed and built up Christendom and restored it as the sacrament of the New Testament. Even today, he upholds this reformation and restoration through his believers, who are his members, his congregation, until he comes in judgement.[14]

14. Translation slightly amended: Rempel, *Later Writings by Pilgram Marpeck*, 138; Loserth, *Quellen und Forschungen*, 569.

Appendix B

The *Kunstbuch*

The sixteen letters of Pilgram Marpeck and the eleven letters by other members of the Marpeck-affiliated churches have already been discussed elsewhere in this book. There is no need to give further attention to them here. The other twenty items included by Maler in the *Kunstbuch* and placed throughout the collection are of equal interest, if not of equal importance. There are three groupings (not in chronological order):

- five items from the early South German Anabaptist movement
- six non-Anabaptist writings and
- ten "fillers" (Zwischenstück), two of which are by the compiler Jörg Maler, three might be by Maler, and the remaining five by others.

The first group involves witnesses from the early Anabaptist movement. These are: one tract by Hans Hut, three by Lienhart Schiemer, and one by Hans Schlaffer. Schiemer and Schlaffer were the early missionaries responsible for Marpeck's conversion to Anabaptism.

The inclusion of these witnesses was the acknowledgment by Maler of their importance for the beginnings of the Marpeck circle. Schiemer and Schlaffer had been present at the confrontation between Hubmaier and Hut in Nikolsburg in May 1527. Both had sided with Hut and accepted his mystical spiritualism.

Hans Hut

Hans Hut's "The Beginning of a Genuine Christian Life,"[1] was part of a longer work known as "The Mystery of Baptism," and concentrated mostly on the process of how a person came to believe. Almost six pages were devoted to a detailed description of what Hut called the "gospel of

---

1. Fast and Rothkegel, *Kunstbuch*, 164-99.

the creatures." He found these words in Mark 16:15 in Martin Luther's translation: "das Euangelion aller Creaturn."[2] He took that to mean not that the gospel should be preached to every creature or to the whole creation, as it is now normally read, but rather as the gospel of the presence and working of God in all created things. It was a version of a natural theology because this gospel was accessible to every human being.[3] But then he taught that even as the creatures, trees, or animals have to be killed and prepared for human use, so the action of God in the soul was to kill all self-will and to lead the soul to dependence on God only. This work of God was the suffering of the cross that Christ had first endured, which everyone who desired to be his disciple also had to endure. And this, taught Hut, was the true baptism, of which water baptism was the sign. This teaching was found also in Schiemer's writings and was adopted to a degree by Marpeck.[4] It contributed to Marpeck's theological principle that the inner, spiritual truth is given by God only through external, material means.

Maler also took the trouble to edit Hut's work so that it was compatible with the teaching of the Marpeck community. In particular, references to baptism as a sign were eliminated. For example, Hut's "the sign and essence of baptism" was amended by Maler to "the external and internal work and essence." He also omitted a passage in which Hut, describing water baptism, completed the passage with the words: "the true baptism then follows," that is, the baptism of spiritual tribulation. He deleted Hut's statement that Adam already had experienced the baptism of tribulation.[5] Where Hut had written: "Where are such Christians? It is a little flock," Maler exclaimed thirty years later, "O God, it is a little flock!" Such Christians by 1560 had shrunk to a small remnant in Augsburg.

Hans Schlaffer

Maler included the penitential prayer Hans Schlaffer composed on the eve of his execution in Schwaz on February 3, 1528.[6] The reasons for the inclusion of this burning, fervent, eloquent prayer are obvious, for it touched on numerous themes so common in South German Anabaptism of the Marpeck decades. It began with a prayer for all the sisters and brothers in persecution.

2. The Froschauer Bible of 1526 has "aller Creatur."
3. For more on this subject see Walter Klaassen, "'Gelassenheit' and Creation," *The Conrad Grebel Review*, Winter 1991, 23-35. Anabaptist writers derived this particular use of the term "creatures" from the late medieval mystics.
4. Klassen and Klaassen, *WPM*, 352-59.
5. Lydia Müller, *Glausbenszeugnisse* 1, 21.
6. Fast and Rothkegel, *Kunstbuch*, 344-70.

O merciful God, we pray for our brothers and sisters wherever they are in the whole world, persecuted, exiled, scattered, imprisoned, and daily put to death. Look upon them and us from your holy place and heavenly dwelling with the eyes of fatherly mercy and goodness, that we be not swallowed up, body and soul, and exterminated by the lions, wolves, and the seven-headed Beast and Dragon.

Schlaffer prayed for all people of goodwill that they may know God's truth, and he prayed for all governments and rulers that they will protect the poor and righteous, and punish evildoers. Finally he prayed that in the hour of death he may be patient and at rest.

Then followed a confession of sin made in the consciousness that he will soon be in the presence of the holy God. The confession is most reminiscent of *The Confessions of St. Augustine*. Again and again Schlaffer confessed that despite all his waywardness from his youth to the days of being a priest, God never left him but kept drawing him to Christ crucified. Repeatedly he reverted to his imminent death in "the desert of this cruel world." He comforted himself with the reflection that Christ sweated blood in Gethsemane in his great anxiety and that made his own suffering easier to bear. To eat the body and drink the blood is a severe meal indeed! People everywhere want Christ as a gift, but they won't take on his cross of suffering. Then followed what sounds like a description of how the Lord's Supper was celebrated in those first years of the Anabaptist movement, using the eucharistic words from the Gospel of Matthew and 1 Corinthians 11. "Thus we have observed it," he wrote.

Could we assume that this prayer was also the prayer of Jörg Maler in the sufferings and struggles of his own life? Certainly it spoke for the Anabaptist martyrs in the great tribulation that was not yet over when Maler included this prayer for Christian posterity.

Lienhart Schiemer

Lienhart Schiemer's writings and their influence on Marpeck and his group have already been discussed in chapter 4. The tracts "Concerning the Grace of God," "The Bottle," "The Twelve Articles of the Christian Faith," "Concerning True Baptism," and "A Summary of the Gospel to be Preached to the World"[7] represent the full range of Schiemer's teaching. The last piece is not found anywhere except in the *Kunstbuch*.[8]

Copies of Schiemer's works probably came into Marpeck's hands

7. "Von der Gnade Gottes," "Vom Fläschlein," "Die Zwölf Artikel des christlichen Glaubens," "Von der wahren taufe Christi," "Ein wahrhaftig, kurz Evangelium, heut der Welt zu Predigen."

8. Fast and Rothkegel, *Kunstbuch*, 242-343.

directly as claimed earlier in chapter 4. They were copied both in Moravia and by Maler with minor differences between the various copies. Schiemer's closing greeting became the signature regularly used by Marpeck in his letters: "Your servant and comrade in the tribulation which is in Christ."

Valentin Ickelsamer

Full attention needs to be given here to the broad spectrum of the writings by non-Anabaptists. Following Maler's poem preface "I am the book of sacred art," he placed what must be seen as the introduction to the whole *Kunstbuch* collection, the double-rhymed poem in tetrameter "Die Gelehrten die Verkehrten" (The more education, the more fabrication)[9] by Valentin Ickelsamer. At an early point in the Reform movement, Ickelsamer parted company with Martin Luther and became an independent dissenter in the company of Sebastian Franck and Caspar Schwenckfeld. He was a schoolmaster in Augsburg where Maler most likely met him. The poem is a long interpretation of the adage found in Sebastian Franck's collection of proverbs, *Sibent halbhundert Sprichwörter* (Seven Hundred Fifty Adages), published in 1532.

The views expressed by Ickelsamer in his poem are found extensively in Anabaptist writings of the sixteenth century. It is therefore not surprising to find the poem here. Close to its beginning, readers are admonished to test the teachings of scholars to determine whether they are true or not. This also served as Maler's invitation to test the contents of the *Kunstbuch*.

According to Ickelsamer, the betrayal of the scholars began soon after the time of the apostles and continued unabated until the present. Who, he asked, caused the division of the church between West and East? Who created the enmity between Christianity and Islam? The scholars in Rome! And now the evangelical scholars call everyone who disagrees with them enthusiasts, rebels, and heretics! Even worse, he continued, they seek to control people's faith by government coercion to create uniformity of faith, and they defend it all with the letter of Scripture. Of course, not all scholars are like that. God uses some to exercise the true *Kunst* (artistry) for the kingdom of God. For *Kunst* to be genuine it must be united with love; otherwise it is poison.

The last 110 lines (480-590) are an interpolation, likely by Maler himself, alluding to events of 1547, a year after Ickelsamer's death. The interpolation expressed Marpeck's views concerning evangelical military resistance to the emperor in the Schmalcald War. Those who take the sword will perish by it; they will be judged like the rebellion of Korah (see Num. 16:31ff.). True Christians should pray for their enemies, not kill them.

9. Ibid., 451-63.

At first sight the most surprising item of this group of non-Anabaptist writers comes with the title "Military Orders of the Heavenly Emperor for His Captains (*Kriegsordnung des himmlischen Kaisers für seine Hauptleute*).[10] The Maler text had as its core an early Reformation pamphlet with a similar title by the Lutheran knight and layman Hartmut von Cronberg. Written in 1522, it was an allegorical text of the spiritual warfare of the early years of the Reformation. Maler may have come into possession of the printed pamphlet through his association with the von Pappenheims, noble members of the Augsburg Anabaptist group who were known to have received von Cronberg's pamphlets.[11] As happened often in the sixteenth century before the advent of copyright, Maler took the pamphlet and made it his own by providing it with an introduction and a conclusion without divulging the name of the original author.[12] Maler's additions reflect the difference in context. The euphoria of the early years of the Reformation is absent. It was now no longer a call to overthrow the papal and scholastic enemies of the truth but an admonition to preserve faithfulness in response to the assaults of the powers of evil. These powers are no longer actual armies waging war on actual countries. This spiritual warfare calls for the weapons and armour described in Ephesians 6.

> Let everyone beware that [the orders] of the heavenly emperor are received with thanksgiving as becomes a true soldier and knight of Christ. Also, one raises the shield of faith against the satanic enemy, the two Beasts. . . . It extinguishes all the fiery arrows [of the wicked one]. If one believe in Christ, living water will flow from the body of faith, which will extinguish all of Satan's cunning warfare, temptation, and fire.

The link between this work of Maler and Marpeck may be Marpeck's letter to Magdalena von Pappenheim of 1547, where he uses the allegory of the true knighthood in the service of the true liege lord, Jesus Christ.[13] In Marpeck's writings, the rich military imagery of 2 Corinthians 10 appears more than twenty times. Other biblical texts that attracted Marpeck and Scharnschlager were Isaiah 61, Wisdom of Solomon 6 and, to a lesser extent, Ephesians 6.[14]

10. Ibid., 451-63.

11. Victor Thiessen, "Flugschriften eines Ritters im Kunstbuch des Marpeck-Kreises," *MGBl* 60 (2003), 65-79.

12. The name was likely muted because Cronberg had apparently returned to fighting "real" wars.

13. Klassen and Klaassen, *WPM*, 464-83.

14. The *Admonition* began with a clarion call to arms (*WPM*, 184-90), a fact that did not escape Schwenckfeld, who called the Anabaptists incompetent soldiers of

Hans Has

More "familiar" is the letter of encouragement by the evangelical preacher Hans Has to his followers in the midst of persecution. Written just before his execution by hanging, "Comfort for Christians in Persecution" (*Vom Trost der Christen in der Verfolgung*) is an early non-Anabaptist witness dated late 1527.[15] Hans Has had begun preaching in 1525 and attempted a Zwinglian reform in Windischgraz. This strong, confident letter is known to us only from the *Kunstbuch*. Its never-flagging encouragement to be faithful in persecution, written in a captivating, articulate style by a man under sentence of death, must have made it especially attractive to Anabaptists. Has's follower Kaspar Maler, who became an Anabaptist in 1528, may have been the letter's preserver.

Has sought especially to help his followers face the fierce deadliness of Ferdinand's persecution, which began in his domains in 1527. First of all he assured them, as did Ickelsamer, that all things happen through, from, and in God. The persecution was not arbitrary or accidental. "Wherever there are Christians, there is and must be, the cross [of persecution]. Where that cross is absent, there are no true Christians." This assertion, so familiar in Anabaptist writings, places the tyrants in the context of God's providence. The blind, miserable tyrants are the instruments of God whose power, because it is from God, need be feared no more than the falling of a leaf from a tree. All their tyranny, he wrote, only drives true Christians to search the Scriptures more diligently and to tell others about it. The tyrants serve our salvation without intending it, because they are in God's hands just as we are. In the end it is the faithful witnesses who, even in death, are conquerors and rulers with Christ over all creatures.

No doubt Maler included this letter also because it had supported his own struggle with tyranny.

Christian Entfelder

Marpeck's controversy with Christian Entfelder lay three decades in the past. Marpeck's concern in the confrontation (see chapter 6) had been to defend the external ministrations of the church, which Entfelder had regarded as dispensable. But Marpeck himself would not likely have objected to including in the *Kunstbuch* Entfelder's mystical discourse "Concerning True Blessedness" (*Von wahrer Gottseligkeit*), written in

---

Christ. The fact that many modern Christians have expunged military imagery from their hymns should not deter scholars from trying to understand why it had such an attraction to Marpeck and his associates. This could be a tantalizing area of research.

15. Fast and Rothkegel, *Kunstbuch*, 464-75.

1530.[16] The ancient quarrel was over, and the writings of the two could now be read side by side.[17]

Entfelder's concern in this tract was describing the process by which a person arrived at true blessedness, a totally interior event unrelated to external circumstances. It expresses mystical themes found in Schlaffer and Schiemer, perhaps derived from them in his early Anabaptist days, and found also in Marpeck. Among these themes is Entfelder's version of the gospel of the creatures, that even as the creatures are subject to suffer the human will, so those who desire the rest that God gives must first suffer the painful process of transferring dependence from the creatures to God alone. When that is complete, one has entered the condition of *Gelassenheit*, the absence of strife, and rest in God. In this early work by Entfelder, there is still an echo of his earlier Anabaptist involvement when he wrote that in this process of moving toward blessedness, "the external often accompanies and promotes the internal."

As Heinold Fast has suggested, now that Maler had come to his rest after long, exhausting conflict, he found comfort by accommodating himself to the political and ecclesiastical realities of his city.

Epistle of Comfort

"An Epistle of Comfort" (*Eine Trostepistel*), from 1533, was also likely by Valentin Ickelsamer.[18] The tract is a collection of Scripture passages under three headings: first, nothing happens to believers except what God has determined; second, God has set an end goal for believers; and third, suffering is the only way to blessedness. This piece was included because it expressed so well the sentiments of Anabaptists including the Marpeck circle. The expression "mouth Christians, not cross Christians" (*maulchristen nicht creuz christen*) would especially commend itself to Maler as echoed by Marpeck.

Several sentences in the concluding section on the gospel of the creatures ruled out the claim that Schwenckfeld could have been its author.[19] This part could also have been an interpolation by Maler, a possibility strengthened when, on the next page, the text changes to the first person

16. Ibid., 643-60.
17. In 1560, Schwenckfeld spoke of "our beloved brother Christianus who has still not been able to see things" as Schwenckfeld did (see *CS* 8, 423-25, and *CS* 17, 214-33). Note *CS* 17, 221, where Entfelder is mentioned alongside of Hans Denck, whom Schwenckfeld refers to as "martyred" in 1527!
18. Ibid., 610-36.
19. See *CS* 5, 804. The argument for the authorship of Ickelsamer is made in Fast and Rothkegel, *Kunstbuch*, 610-11.

plural, making that section autobiographical. He announces that he will follow Christ and help him bear his shame.

The last sentences read: "On this path I will remain, which he has himself sprinkled and marked with his rose-coloured blood and walked before me. It is my true path, my true path! Let no one any longer seek to turn me from it! On this path I cannot go astray!"

If this is Maler's passionate signature, it was probably added to the text before his final resolve in 1559 to fight no longer. Then follows a description of the joys of the just in paradise and of the dismay of the persecutors in hell. Like smoke they will vanish while the just rule eternally with Christ. He ends with the famous words from Wisdom of Solomon 3:1-7, "The souls of the righteous are in the hands of God" (v. 1). This section is reminiscent of similar sentiments in the writings of Jacob Hutter and Menno Simons.[20] The resentment against their persecutors was so common in Anabaptism that this passage too has all the marks of an Anabaptist interpolation and, given Maler's suffering, perhaps by him. The last words read: "The Lord knows my name."

Creed of Athanasius

Why would Maler have included the Creed of Athanasius,[21] the third of the official Christian creeds, and not the Nicene Creed? He reproduced it with literal exactness, adding only a few comments in parentheses, an example of which appears right near the end: "This is the Christian faith, which, as said above, except everyone faithfully and steadfastly believes (here Maler adds in parentheses, 'keeps, does, and confesses') one cannot be saved." The answer to the question seems to lie in the words about the incarnation with the creed's emphasis on "one Christ, one not by conversion of the Godhead into flesh, but by taking the manhood into God" (*einer, aber nit verwandlet die gotheit inn das fleisch, sonder inn annemung der menscheit in Got*).

These words from Christian antiquity may well have been the source for Marpeck's argument against Schwenckfeld that not only did the glory of Christ not brush aside his humanity but that the humanity itself was taken up into God. Following the creedal words "Who suffered for our salvation," Maler adds for emphasis, "and died a natural death because of our sins," to underscore again the Marpeckian theme of the true humanity of Christ.

---

20. *Brotherly Faithfulness. Epistles from a Time of Persecution*, [Jacob Hutter] (Rifton, N.Y.: Plough Publishing House, 1978), 60-61, 96-99; *The Complete Writings of Menno Simons*, ed. J. C. Wenger (Scottdale, Pa.: Herald Press, 1956), 613, 1058-59, 1067.

21. Fast and Rothkegel, *Kunstbuch*, 506-7.

Collection of Poems

Maler was a lover of poetry. He placed a collection of short poems and adages at the end of the introductory pieces following his warning to the reader that the world will not last forever, and the devil is smarter than you think.[22] Maler seems to have made his selection from available late medieval anthologies. Verses by church fathers Gregory the Great, Jerome, Ambrose, and Augustine appear, along with those of medieval theologian Bonaventure and the Roman Seneca. One of the better poems in terms of poetic merit addresses avarice, one of the seven deadly sins. The overarching theme of the poems is to do what God commands or face the consequences. Several deal specifically with death and its gravity as the gateway to heaven or hell. All of these were common themes of a late medieval piety that appears to have been nurtured among Augsburg poets. The strong ethical cast of these poems commended them to Anabaptists.[23]

It is significant that Maler included one of his own poems reflecting his own long experience of suffering at the hands of rulers.

> Force masquerades as justice.
> This is my lament,
> Miserable bondsman that I am.
> Preferential privilege has won the day
> And many a person is forced into exile.

Lienhart Schienherr, a cousin of Jörg Maler, wrote the final poem, "The Two Golden Calves and the Two Beasts," (*Von den zwei goldenen Kälber und von den zwei Tieren*), based respectively on 1 Kings 12 and Revelation 13.[24] Schienherr is nowhere identified as an Anabaptist, but his views locate him in the separatist Anabaptist-Spiritualist milieu in Augsburg. Internal evidence suggests that the poem was written between 1528 and 1546. It has the same rhyming metre as the opening poem of the *Kunstbuch*.

The conviction that the end of all things was near was universal in Anabaptism, and the poem's inclusion here likely expresses Maler's own conviction. It is a theme we hear in the *Kunstbuch* collection at numerous points. The two golden calves of the first part of the poem were erected by King Jeroboam I of Israel at Bethel and Dan, the two extremities of the kingdom. These two calves, the occasion of idolatry in Israel, were then matched by the poet with the two beasts of Revelation 13. He identified the calf at Bethel and the first beast of the Apocalypse with the pope, the calf at Dan

---

22. Ibid., 129. Three more poems are inserted at p. 661.
23. Martin Rothkegel, "Randglossen zum Kunstbuch," in *MGBl* 61 (2004), 59-61.
24. Fast and Rothkegel, *Kunstbuch*, 662-75.

and the second beast with Martin Luther. Those who would not worship the first beast were put to death. Those who disagreed with the second, Luther, were all condemned by him. Anyone who does not agree with these two is rendered a notorious heretic and rebel.

A gloss by Maler reflected that the whole world wants "golden" worship accepted by all, but without the cross. The pope and Luther have set guards at Christ's tomb to prevent him whom they have crucified with their false teaching from rising again to judge them. But no matter; Christ will arise and save his flock from the power of the beasts.

Brief Reflections

The copying of the texts and their arrangement by Maler[25] repeatedly left space on a page. Into these spaces Maler inserted short reflections, among them a paragraph from some Anabaptist work on baptism, a short collage of biblical passages, and a collection of four medieval aphorisms. A curious inclusion is a prophecy by an unknown prognosticator named Albrecht Gleicheisen from the year 1372. A usurper will become emperor, goes the prophecy, with the help of the imperial cities in 1528. But there is nothing that obviously links this prediction with either Maler or Marpeck. It was truly a filler. Maler's two confessions of faith and his short account of clergy visiting him in prison have already been discussed in the text.

There are three more reflections, also used as fillers, but more substantial. The first is by Maler explaining why he changed his view on the oath.[26] It seems to have happened after he became part of the Marpeck group in Augsburg. Once he held to a literal rejection of all swearing, but now he had learned that a Christian is subject to no law where the honour of God and love of the neighbour is concerned.

The second is a little reflection on true patience.[27] It is stylistically very accomplished and seems to come from some mystical writing. But it is also something one might expect Marpeck to write.

The last piece is clearly more than a filler. It has the title "The Time is Near" (*Die Zeit ist nah*) and begins with the gospel words about the coming judgment.[28] Then follow what appear to be Maler's own words, as the writer used the first person singular. The signs of the approaching end are visible, although the writer does not identify them. Every person will have to tend the oil in his or her own lamp.

25. See Rothkegel, "Randglossen," 56-58.
26. Fast and Rothkegel, *Kunstbuch*, 407.
27. Ibid., 428.
28. Ibid., 438-39.

We have enough reason not to look to individuals nor churches for help since all are unreliable and no one can judge with certainty, according to the words of the prophet [Dan. 12:4]. Many churches want to be churches of Christ and claim the right to include and exclude, but are at strife with each other.

Every Christian should pray for light so that he or she does not stumble in the darkness and that the light within be not extinguished. It appears that the Lord will soon close the door and whoever hesitates will be left standing outside. The Lord "alone knows who and where [his own] are."

There is no doubt that Maler was disillusioned with the many competing Christian voices with their claims and counterclaims. This fact, and the exhaustion of his struggle with the Augsburg council, had reduced him to tending his own lamp. Even though he was alone, he wrote, the Lord knows him and his place.

Bibliography

I. Encyclopedias, Dictionaries, and Reference Works

Anabaptist Bibliography 1520-1630. Edited by Hans Hillerbrand. St. Louis: Center for Reformation Research, 1991.

Augsburger Stadtlexikon. Augsburg: Perlachverlag, 1998.

Catholic Encyclopedia, The. New York: Robert Appleton Company, 1911.

Dictionary of Biblical Interpretation 1-2. Edited by John H. Hayes. Nashville: Abingdon Press, 1999.

Dictionary of Biblical Tradition in English Literature. Edited by David Lyle Jeffrey. Grand Rapids: Eerdmans, 1992.

Dictionary of the Middle Ages 3. Edited by J. R. Strayer. New York: Charles Scribner's Sons, 1985.

Encyclopedia of Protestantism 1-4. Edited by Hans J. Hillerbrand. New York: Routledge, 2004.

Encyclopedia of the History of Technology. Edited by Ian McNeil. London: Routledge, 1990.

Global Anabaptist Mennonite Encyclopedia Online. http://www.gameo.org/encyclopedia/contents/D39ME.html. 1989.

History of Technology 2-3. Edited by C. Singer, et al. New York: Oxford University Press, 1957.

Holy Bible. New Revised Standard Version. New York: Oxford University Press, 1989.

Lexikon des Mittelalters 7. Edited by Norbert Angermann. Munich: LexMA Verlag, 1995.

Mennonite Encyclopedia 1-5. Edited by Harold Bender, et al. Scottdale: Herald Press, 1955-1990.

Müller, Gerhard, ed. *Theologische Realenzyclopädie* 36. New York: de Gruyter, 1976-2004.

Oxford Encyclopedia of the Reformation 1-4. Edited by H. J. Hillerbrand. New York: Oxford University Press, 1996.

Siebmacher, Johannes. *General-Index zu den Siebmacherischen Wappenbucher, 1605-1964.* Graz, Austria: Akademischer Drucker, 1964: 363 (Tirol), Bgl 28.

————. *Grosses Wappenbuch* 28, *Die Wappen des Adels in Salzburg, Steiermark und Tirol*. Neustadt an der Aisch: Bauer and Raspe, 1979.

von Stetten, Paul. *Augsburger Stadtlexikon*. Edited by Günther Grünsteudel. Augsburg: Perlachverlag, 1998.

Widmoser, Eduard, ed. *Tirol A bis Z*. Innsbruck: Südtirol-Verlag, 1970.

II. Primary Sources

Adler, Clemens. "Das Urteil von dem Schwert mit unterschidlichem gewalt dreier fürstenthum der Welt, Juden, und Christen, mit anderen Anligender sachen. Beschrieben durch Clemens Adler im Jahr MDXXIX" ["The Judgment Concerning the Sword"]. "Kopie eines Handschriftenbandes von Liedern und Glaubensartikel der Täufer," a typewritten transcription by Samuel Geiser, Mennonite Historical Library, Goshen College, Goshen, Ind. Made available by Joe Springer, curator of the Mennonite Historical Library.

Agricola, Georgius, *De re metallica*. Translated by H. C. and L. H. Hoover. New York: Dover, 1950.

Bauer, Wilhelm, ed. *Kommission für neuere Geschichte Österreichs* 2. Vienna: Adolf Holzhausen, 1912.

————. *Die Anfänge Ferdinands I*. Vienna: Adolf Holzhausen, 1907.

————, and R. Lacroix, eds. *Die Korrespondenz Ferdinands I* 2. Vienna: Adolf Holzhausen, 1912.

Bauman, Clarence, ed. *The Spiritual Legacy of Hans Denck: Interpretation and Translation of Key Texts*. Leiden: E. J. Brill, 1991.

Beck, Joseph, ed. *Die Geschichtsbücher der Wiedertäufer in Österreich-Ungarn, 1526-1785*. 1883. Reprint, Nieuwkoop, The Netherlands: B. De Graaf, 1967.

Beck, Sammlung. "Wiedertäuferischen Gesindleins in Mähren und Schlesien seltsame Beschaffenheit." 1535. G 10149, no. 68, 22v. State Archive, Brno, Slovakia.

Bergsten, Torsten, and Gunnar Westin, eds. *Hubmaier, Balthasar: Schriften*. *Quellen zur Geschichte der Täufer* 9. Gütersloh, Germany: Mohn, 1962.

Bossert, Sr., Gustav, and Gustav Bossert Jr., eds. *Quellen zur Geschichte der Wiedertäufer, I. Band. Herzogtum Württemberg*. Leipzig, Germany: M. Heinius Nachfolger, 1930.

Braght, Thieleman J. van. *The Martyrs Mirror*. Translated by Joseph Sohn. Scottdale: Herald Press, 1951.

Braitmichel, Caspar. *Von der Zerspaltung der Gemein. Sampt den Artikeln und Beschuldigungen, die wir wider den Philip und Gabriel haben*. 1571. Codex Hab. 5, 371 MICA 274. Reel 87 of the Eastern

European Anabaptist Collection. Arts Library, University of Waterloo.

Bullinger, Heinrich. *Von dem einigen vnnd ewigen Testament oder Pundt Gottes. Hierinn findt du welches der vralt recht wolbegründt vnd vnbefleckt Christen gloub: welches der eltist pundt vnnd der waar wolgefellig Gottes dienst sye: woruf ouch all Biblische gschrift reiche vnd sähe.Iesvs. Das ist min lieber Sun in dem ich versönet bin jm sind gehörig. Matth. XVII.* Zürich: Christoph Froschauer, 1534.

Bünderlin, Hans. *Erklärung durch vergleichung der Biblischen geschrifft, das der wassertauff sampt andern eusserlichen gebreuchen, in der Apostolischen kirchen geübet. On Gottes befelch und zeügniss der geschrifft, von etlichen diser zeit, wider eefert [eingeführt] wirt. Sintemalen der Antichrist dieselben all, zehend nach der Apostel abgang verwüst hat. Welche Verwüstung dann biss an das ende bleibt* [Explanation through Comparison of the Biblical Scripture]. 1530: n.p.

Castenbaur, Stefan. *Ain köstlicher guter Sermon vom Sterben.* Augsburg: Steiner, 1523.

———. *Artickel Wider S. Castenbaur auch was er darauf geantwortet hat.* Augsburg: Steiner, 1523.

———. *Schlussreden and Artickel wider Doctor Steffan Castenpaur,* 1523.

———. *Ein Bedencken des Agricola Boius wie der wahrhaftig Gottesdienst von Gott selbst gebotten möcht wiederumb auffgericht.* Leipzig, Germany: Stoeckl, 1520.

Chronicle of the Hutterian Brethren 1525-1665 1. Farmington, Pa.: Plough Publishing House, 1987.

Chroniken der deutschen Städte vom 14. Bis ins 16. Jahrhundert, Bd. 32 *Augsburg* 7. Bd. Göttingen, Germany: Vandenhoeck u. Ruprecht, 1917/1966: 27-31. 8. Bd., 1928/1966: 70, 326-27, 330-31.

Corpus Schwenkfeldianorum 1-19. Edited by Chester David Hartranft, Elmer Ellsworth Schultz Johnson, and Selina Gerhard Schultz. Leipzig, Germany: Breitkopf & Härtel, and Pennsburg, Pa.: Board of Publication of the Schwenkfelder Church, 1907-1961.

Die Zürcher Bibel von 1531. Facsimile print by Theologischer Verlag Zürich, 1983, of *Die gantze Bibel der ursprüngliche Ebraischen und Griechischen warrheyt nach, auffs aller treüwlichest verdeutschet.* Zürich: Chr. Froschauer, 1531.

Dyck, C. J., ed. *Spiritual Life in Anabaptism.* Scottdale: Herald Press, 1995.

———. *The Writings of Dirk Philips.* Scottdale: Herald Press, 1992.

Eleutherobius, Stoffel [Christoph Freisleben]. *Vom warhafftigen Tauf Joannis Christi und der Aposteln.* Worms: Peter Schöffer, 1528.

Elsass 1: Strasbourg, 1522-1532. Edited by Manfred Krebs and Jean-George Rott. In *Quellen zur Geschichte der Täufer* 7. Gütersloh, Germany: Mohn, 1959.

Elsass 2: Stadt Strasbourg, 1533-1535. Edited by Manfred Krebs and Jean-George Rott. In *Quellen zur Geschichte der Täufer* 8. Gütersloh, Germany: Mohn, 1960.

Elsass 3: Stadt Strasbourg, 1536-1542. Edited by Marc Lienhard, Stephen Nelson, and Hans-Georg Rott. In *Quellen zur Geschichte der Täufer* 15. Gütersloh, Germany: Mohn, 1986.

Elsass 4: Stadt Strasbourg, 1543-1552. Edited by Marc Lienhard, Stephen Nelson, and Hans-Georg Rott. In *Quellen zur Geschichte der Täufer* 16. Gütersloh, Germany: Mohn, 1988.

"Endscheid zwischen denn Perckh-und Lanndgericht zu Ratemberg." In *Rattenberger Bergbuch*, HS 6248.

Entfelder, Christian. *Von den manigfaltigen im glauben zerspaltungen/dise far erstanden. Inn sonderhait von der Tauff spaltung und iren urtail/Ain bedacht* [Of the Manifold Divisions in the Faith]. 71/I:E7. Strasbourg: Microfiche BME, n.d.

———. *Von Gottes und Christi Jesus unsers Herr enerkandtnuss, ain bedacht/Allen schulern des hailigen gaists weiter zebendencken auffgezaichnet/mit freyem urthail.* Strasbourg, 1533.

Faber, Johann (Dominican, Heilbronn). *Von dem Ayd Schwören. Auch von der Widertäuffer Marter/ vnd woher entspring/ das sie also frölich vnnd getröst die peyn des tods leyden. Vnd von der gemainschafft der Widertäuffer.* Augsburg, 1550.

Fabri, Johan. *Ettliche Sermon von Doctor Johan Fabri geprediget, wider die gotlossen Widertauffer zu Znaym auf dem Lanndtag der Marggratschafft Merhern, im Monat April.* Vienna: Hans Singrietter, 1528. Victor Thiessen graciously provided a copy from the University Library, Munich.

———. Letter 286. 23 May 1526, Strasbourg. The Strasbourg Preachers to Johannes Fabri, *Epistola v. Fabritii Capitonis ad Hulderichum Zuinglium.* Strasbourg: W. Köpfel, 1526.

———. *Malleus in haeresim Lutheranam.* Available in the original Latin (Cologne, 1524) in the series Corpus Catholicorum 25-26. Muenster: Aschendorff, 1952.

———. *Several Sermons on the Eight Beatitudes Preached at the Stift Church during the Diet of Speyer* [*Etlich Sermon von den Acht seligkeiten: gepredigt in der hohen Stift, zu Speyer auff dem Reichstag*]. Vienna: Hans Singrietter, 1528.

———. *Ursache warum der Wiederteuffer Patron und erster Anfänger,*

Doktor Balthasar Hubmaier zu Wien auf den 10. Tag März, anno 1528 verbrannt wurde. Leipzig, Germany, 1528.

Fast, Heinold. *Der Linke Flügel der Reformation: Glaubenszeugnisse der Täufer, Spiritualisten, Schwärmer und Antitrinitarier.* Bremen: Carl Schünemann Verlag, 1962.

————, and Martin Rothkegel, eds. *Briefe und Schriften oberdeutscher Täufer 1527-1555, Das Kunstbuch des Jörg Probst Rotenfelder gen. Maler.* Quellen zur Geschichte der Täufer Band 17. Heidelberg: Gütersloher Verlagshaus Gerd Mohn, 2007.

Fellmann, Walter, ed. *TA: Denck 2, Hans Denck: Religiöse Schriften.* Gütersloh, Germany: Bertelsmann, 1956.

Franck, Sebastian. *Zeytbuch und geschichtbibel von anbegyn bisz inn disz gegenwertig M. D. Xxxj. Jar.* Darmstadt: Wissenschaftlicher Verlag, 1969.

————. *Paradoxa*, 1534.

Franz, Günther, ed. *Urkundliche Quellen zur hessischen Reformations-geschichte 4. Wiedertäuferakten 1527-1626.* Marburg, Germany: Elwertsche Verlagsbuchhandlung, 1951.

————. *Thomas Müntzer: Schriften und Briefe.* Edited by Günther Franz. Gütersloh, Germany: Mohn, 1968.

Friedmann, Robert. "The Oldest Church Discipline of the Anabaptists." *Mennonite Quarterly Review* 29 (1955): 162-66.

Furcha, Edward J. *Selected Writings of Hans Denck 1500-1527.* 1975. Reprint, Queenston, Ont.: Edwin Mellen, 1989.

Glaidt, Oswald. *Enntschuldigung Osvaldi Glaidt von Chamb. Etwan zu Leybm in Oesterreich. Yetz predicannt zu Nicolspurg . . . etlicher Artickel Verklärung* [Apology Oswaldt Glaidt]. 1527. Nicolsburg: Simprecht Sorg. Original at the State Archive, Brno, Slovakia. Made available by Dr. M. Coupek.

————. *Handlung yetz den XIV tag Marcij dis XXVI jars, so zu Osterlitz in Merhern durch erforderte versammlung viles pfarrer und priester-schaften . . . in syben artickeln beschlossen.* 1526. Nicolsburg: Simprecht Sorg. Radical Reformation Microfiche Project, Section 1, Mennonite and Related Sources up to 1600, ID CAG, Zug, Switzerland. Conrad Grebel College Library.

Haffner, Hans. *Von einem Wahrhaften Ritter Christi, und womit er gewappnet muss sein, damit er überwinden möge die / welt das / fleisch und den Teufel* [Concerning a True Knight of Christ]. Undated. A type-written copy with introduction by Robert Friedmann. Mennonite Archive in Goshen, Ind. Made available by Dr. Leonard Gross.

Harder, Leland, ed. *The Sources of Swiss Anabaptism.* Scottdale: Herald Press, 1985.

Hätzer, Ludwig. *Ein urteil gottes . . . wie man sich mit allen götzen und bildnussen halten sol, uss der heiligen gschrifft gezogen durch Ludwig Hätzer.* Zürich: Froschauer, 1523.

Hein, Gerhard. "Two Letters by Leupold Scharnschlager." *Mennonite Quarterly Review* 17 (1943): 165-68.

Hillerbrand, Hans. An early Anabaptist treatise on the Christian and the state. *Mennonite Quarterly Review* 32 (1958): 28-47.

Hutter, Jacob. *Brotherly Faithfulness. Epistles from a Time of Persecution.* Rifton, NY: Plough Publishing House, 1978.

Kempis, Thomas à. *The Imitation of Christ.* Translated and edited by Leo Sherley-Price. New York: Penguin Classics Books, 1956.

Kessler, Johannes. *Sabbata. St. Galler Reformationschronik 1523-1539.* Bearb. Von Traugott Schiess, Leipzig, Germany, 1911.

Kinthis, Jobst. *Gesprächbüchlein.* Worms, 1553.

Klaassen, Walter. *Anabaptism in Outline: Selected Primary Sources.* Scottdale: Herald Press, 1981.

———. "The Exposé of the Babylonian Whore." *Later Writings by Pilgram Marpeck and His Circle* 1. Translated by Walter Klaassen. Kitchener: Pandora Press, 1999: 24-44, 42-43.

Klassen, William, and Walter Klaassen, trans. and eds. *The Writings of Pilgram Marpeck.* Kitchener: Herald Press, 1978.

Klassen, William, trans. "Two Letters by Pilgram Marpeck." Edited by Torsten Bergsten. *Mennonite Quarterly Review* 32 (1958): 192-210.

Krebs, Manfred, ed. *Baden und Pfalz* 4. *Quellen zur Geschichte der Täufer* 4. Gütersloh, Germany: Bertelsmann Verlag, 1951.

Laubach, Ernst. "Ein Religiöses Mahnschreiben Kaiser Ferdinands I." *Archiv für Reformationsgeschichte* 87 (1996): 90-118.

Laube, Adolf, ed. "Von den mannigfaltigen Zerspaltungen im Glauben, die in diesen Jahren enstanden sind." In *Flugschriften vom Bauernkrieg zum Täuferreich (1526-1535).* Berlin: Akademie Verlag, 2002: 708-27.

Loserth, Johann, ed. "Pilgram Marbecks Antwort auf Kaspar Schwenckfelds Beurteilung des Buches der Bundesbezeugung von 1542." In *Quellen und Forschungen zur Geschichte der oberdeutschen Taufgesinnten im 16. Jahrhundert.* Vienna: Carl Fromme, 1929, 55-578.

Louthan, Howard. *The Quest for Compromise: Peacemakers in Counter-reformation Vienna.* New York: Cambridge University Press, 1997.

Luther, Martin. "An Appeal to the Ruling Class of the German Nation," 1520. From *Martin Luther. Selections from His Writings*, John Dillenberger, ed. New York: Doubleday, 1961, 403-85.

———. *Biblia/das ist/die gantze Heilige Schrifft Deudsch.* Wittemberg,

Germany: Hans Lufft, 1534. Facsimile print by Verlag Philipp Reklam. Leipzig, Germany, 1983.

———. "Secular Authority: To What Extent it Should be Obeyed," in *Martin Luther: Selections from His Writings*, John Dillenberger, ed. New York: Doubleday, 1961, 363-402.

Mantz, Felix. "Petition of Defense." In *The Sources of Swiss Anabaptism*. Scottdale: Herald Press, 1985: 311ff.

Marpeck, Pilgram. *Ain klarer / vast nützlicher unterricht / wider ettlicher Trück / und schleichendt Geyster* [A Clear and Useful Instruction]. 1531. English translation by William Klassen and Walter Klaassen in *The Writings of Pilgram Marpeck*. Scottdale: Herald Press, 1978, 69-106.

———. *Aufdeckung der babylonischen Hurn.* Strasbourg: Cammerlander, n.d.

———. *Clare verantwurtung ettlicher Artickel / so jetzt durch jrrige geyster schrifflich unnd mündtlich ausschweben* [A Clear Refutation]. 1531. English translation in *The Writings of Pilgram Marpeck* (1978): 43-68.

———. *Wie die Gschrifft verstendiglich soll underschieden / un erklärt werden / die von Tauff saget* [How the Scriptures Are to Be Distinguished]. English edition: John H. Yoder, trans., *Legacy of Michael Sattler*. Scottdale: Herald Press, 1978: 150-77.

Martin Luther Studienausgabe. Hrsg. Von Karl Gerhard Steck. Frankfurt: Fischer-Bücherei, 1970.

Matheson, Peter, trans. and ed. *Argula von Grumbach, A Woman's Voice in the Reformation*. Edinburgh: T & T Clark, 1995.

Melanchton, Philipp. *Whether Christian Princes are obligated to apply physical punishment and the Sword against the Unchristian Sect of the Anabaptists*. 1536. Translated by Leonard Gross. *Mennonite Quarterly Review* 76 (2002): 315-36.

Meyer, Christian. "Zur Geschichte der Wiedertäufer in Oberschwaben." Part 1. "Die Anfänge des Wiedertäufertums in Augsburg." In *Zeitschift des historischen Vereins für Schwaben und Neuburg* 1 (1874): 207-56.

Montana Codex [Braitmichel]. 1566. MICA 274. Reel 22 of the East European Anabaptist Collection. Arts Library, University of Waterloo.

Mosham, Ruprecht. *Ain Christliche warhafftige, gründtliche Entschuldigung Herrn Rueprechten von Moshaim*. Aschaffenburg, Germany, 1539.

Müller, Lydia, ed. *Glaubenszeugnisse oberdeutscher Taufgesinnter 1. Quellen zur Geschichte der Täufer 3*. Leipzig, Germany: M. Heinius Nachfolger; and New York: Johnson Reprint Corporation, 1971.

Nationalbibliothek Wien, Sammelband medizinischer Schriften, Codex Nr. 11.

Österreich 1. Edited by Grete Mecenseffy. *Quellen zur Geschichte der Täufer* 11. Gütersloh, Germany: Mohn, 1964.

Österreich 2. Edited by Grete Mecenseffy. *Quellen zur Geschichte der Täufer* 13. Gütersloh, Germany: Mohn, 1972.

Österreich 3. Edited by Grete Mecenseffy. *Quellen zur Geschichte der Täufer* 14. Gütersloh, Germany: Mohn, 1983.

Ostschweiz. Edited by Heinold Fast. *Quellen zur Geschichte der Täufer* 2. Zürich: Theologischer Verlag, 1973.

Otter, Jacob. *Das erst buch Mosi, gepredigt durch Jacob Otthern zu Steynach*. Hagenau, 1528.

Pipkin, H. Wayne, and John H. Yoder, trans. and eds. *Balthasar Hubmaier: Theologian of Anabaptism*. Scottdale: Herald Press, 1989.

Prophetische gesicht vnd Offenbarung, der götlichen würckung zu diser letsten zeit, die vom xxiiij. jar biss in dz. Einer gottes liebhaberin durch den heiligen geist geoffenbart seind, welcher hie in disem büchlin lxxvij verzeichnet seind. 1530. Published with an introduction by Melchior Hoffman.

Rattenberger Bergbuch, Handschrift 63, Tiroler Landesarchiv.

Rempel, John D., ed. *Later Writings by Pilgram Marpeck and His Circle* 1. Kitchener: Pandora Press, 1999.

Rideman, Peter. *Confession of Faith*. London: Hodder & Stoughton, 1950.

Roth, Friedrich. *Augsburgs Reformationsgeschichte, 1547-1555* 4. Munich: Theodor Ackermann, 1911.

———. Zur Geschichte der Wiedertäufer in Oberschwaben. Part 3. Der Höhepunkt der Bewegung in Augsburg und der Niedergang im Jahre. 1528. In *Zeitschift des historischen Vereins für Schwaben und Neuburg* 28 (1901): 1-154.

Rothmann, Bernhard. "Restitution rechter gesunder christlicher Lehre." *Die schriften Bernhard Rothmanns*. Edited by Robert Stupperich. Münster: Aschendorff Verlagsbuchhandlung, 1970.

Sailer, Wolfgang. Letter dated June 4, 1540, mailed to Caspar Schwenckfeld. Translated by Victor Thiessen. Wolfenbüttel Library, Germany.

Scharnschlager, Leupold. "A Church Order for Members of Christ's Body." Translated by William Klassen. *Mennonite Quarterly Review* 38 (1964): 354-56, 386.

———. "Scharnschlager's Farewell to the Strasbourg Council." Translated by William Klassen. *Mennonite Quarterly Review* 42 (1968): 211-18.

———, and Pilgram Marpeck. *Testamenterläuterung. Erleuttterung durch ausszug/aus Heiliger Biblischer schrifft*. Augsburg, 1549.

Schiemer, Lienhart. "Die dritt epistel Lienhart Schiemer, darinnen wirt begriffen von dreyerley Tauf im Neuen Testament ganz clärlich entdeckt." *Glaubenszeugnisse* 1 (n.d.): 77ff.

———. "Erstlich ein Epistl an die gemain zu Rottenburg [Rattenberg], darinnen hübsche erklärungen der 12 hauptstück unsers Christlichen Glaubens begriffen sein." *Glaubenszeugnisse* 1 (n.d.): 44ff.

———. "Letter to the Church of God at Rattenberg." Available in English in *Sources of South German\Austrian Anabaptism*. Edited by W. Klaassen. Kitchener: Pandora Press, 2001: 64-80, 85-88.

Schiess, Traugott. "Aus dem Leben eines Ilanzer Schulmeisters." *Bündnerisches Monatsblatt* 3 (1916): 73-89.

Schornbaum, Karl, ed. "Bayern." *Quellen zur Geschichte der Täufer* 2. Gütersloh, Germany: Bertelsmann, 1951.

———. "Bayern." *Quellen zur Geschichte der Täufer* 1. Leipzig, Germany: M. Heinius Nachfolger, 1934.

Schweiz 1: Zürich. Edited by Leonhard von Muralt and Walter Schmid. *Quellen zur Geschichte der Täufer*. Zürich: Hirzel, 1952.

Schweiz 4: Drei Täufergespräche. Edited by Martin Haas. *Quellen zur Geschichte der Täufer*. Zürich: Hirzel, 1974.

Schwenckfeld, Caspar. "Der andre Sendbrieff an alle Christgleubige geschrieben." *Corpus Schwenckfeldianorum* 4 (1531): 71-83.

———. "Judicium de Anabaptistis." *Corpus Schwenckfeldianorum* 3 (1530): 830-34.

———. "Vom Christlichen Sabbath und Unterschaidt des alten und newen Testaments." *Corpus Schwenckfeldianorum* 4 (1532): 452-518.

Sider, Ronald J., ed. *Karlstadt's Battle with Luther*. Philadelphia: Fortress Press, 1978.

Snyder, C. Arnold, ed. *Sources of South-German/Austrian Anabaptism*. Kitchener: Pandora Press, 2001.

Spittelmaier, Johann. *Entschuldigung Joannis Spitelmayer Prediger zu Nicolspurg von wegen etlichen artickeln, jne von de Clöster d'stat Veldsper sunnderlich feind, des creuz Christi on alle ursach zue gemessen. Gro Shirken rukopisu 49, raa*. State Archive, Brno, Slovakia. Made available by Dr. M. Coupek.

Springer, Nelson, and Joe Springer. "The Testimony of a Bernese Anabaptist." *Mennonite Quarterly Review* 60 (1986): 289-303.

Stadler, Ulrich. "Von ordnungen der heiligen in irer gmainschaft und leben mit den güetern ires vaters alhie in dem Herren." *Glaubenszeugnisse* 1 (n.d.): 222-27.

Staupitz, Johann. "Gutachten von Staupitz aus dem Jahre 1523." *In Historisches Jahrbuch der Görresgesellschaft* 12. Written in November 1523. N. Paulus, 1891: 273, 773-77.

Strauss, J. *Christenlich vnd wolgegrundet antwurt . . . D. Johannis Coclei*, n.d.

———. *Das wucher zu nemen vnd geben vnserm Christlichen glauben vnd brüderlicher lieb . . . entgegen yst . . .* 1524.

———. *Ein kurtz Christenlich unterricht des grossen jrrthumbs . . .* 1523.

———. *Ein neuw wunderbarlcih Beychtbuechlin*, 1523: A2v, B2r.

———. *Eyn Sermon vber das Euangelium Luce . . .* 1523.

———. *Eyn verstendig trostlich leer vber das wort Sanct Paulus. Der mensch sol sich selbs probieren . . .* Remberg, Sachsen, 1522: A2r.

———. *Haubtstuck vn artickel Christenlicher leer wider den . . . wucher . . .* 1523.

———. *Von dem ynnerlichen vnnd ausserlichen Tauff . . .* 1523.

———. *Vnderricht D. Jacob Straussen wartzu die Bruderschaften . . .* 1522.

———. *Widder den Simonieschen Tauff . . .* 1523.

Stupperich, Robert. *Martin Bucer's Deutsche Schriften, #7, Schriften der Jahre 1538-39.* Gütersloh, Germany: Gerd Mohn, 1967. Especially his "Ratschlag ob Christlicher Oberkait gebüren müge, dass sye die Juden unter den Christen zuwonen gedulden und was sie zu gedulden. Welcher gestalt und Mass."

Swiss Order: "A Congregational Order." *The Legacy of Michael Sattler.* Translated and edited by John H. Yoder. Scottdale: Herald Press, 1973.

Tschackert, Paul. *Urkundenbuch zur Reformationsgeschichte des Herzogthums Preussen* 1. 1890. Reprint, Osnabrück: Otto Zeller, 1965.

Wappler, Paul, ed. *Die Täuferbewegung in Thüringen von 1529-1584.* Jena: G. Fischer, 1913.

Wenger, John C., ed. "Letter from Wilhelm Reublin to Pilgram Marpeck." *Mennonite Quarterly Review* 23 (1949): 67-75.

———. "Menno Simons' Meditation on the Twenty-Fifth Psalm." *The Complete Writings of Menno Simons.* Scottdale: Herald Press, 1956: 63-86.

Williams, George H., and Angel Mergal. *Spiritual and Anabaptist Writers.* Library of Christian Classics 25. Philadelphia: Westminster Press, 1957.

Wolfram, Henrig, and Christiane Thomas, eds. *Die Korrespondenz Ferdinand I: Familienkorrespondenz 1531 und 1532* 3. Vienna: Adolf Holzhausen, 1977.

Württemberg. Manuscripts collected by Gustav Bossert and Gustav Bossert Jr., intended as a future *Quellen zur Geschichte der Täufer* 2. Karlsruhe Staatsarchiv, sig. GLA, Abt S, Verein für Reformationsgeschichte.

Yetelhauser, Michael [Jedelshauser]. "Ain Christliche Bekhantnus und widerueff Michael Yetelhauser." In *Ain Christliche warhafftige, gründtliche Entschuldigung Herrn Rueprechten von Moshaim.* Aschaffenburg, Germany 1539.

Yoder, John H., trans. and ed. *The Legacy of Michael Sattler.* Scottdale: Herald Press, 1973.

Zaunring, Jörg. "Ain kurtze anzaignung des abentmals Christy." *Glaubenszeugnisse* 1 (n.d.): 143ff.

———. "Eine schöne Epistel." Codex Hab. 5, 334ff. Reel 87 of the Eastern European Anabaptist Collection. Arts Library, University of Waterloo.

Zieglschmid, A. J. F., ed. *Die älteste Chronik der Hutterischen Brüder. (Ein Sprachdenkmal aus frühneuhochdeutscher Zeit).* Ithaca: Cayugan Press, 1943.

III. Secondary Sources, Including Studies on Marpeck, Members of His Community, Anabaptism, and the Reformation

Abray, Lorna Jane. *The People's Reformation: Magistrates, Clergy, and Commons in Strasbourg 1500-1598.* Ithaca: Cornell University Press, 1985.

Als Frieden Möglich War: 450 Jahre Augsburger Religionsfrieden. Augsburg: Maximilianmuseum, 2005.

Aries, Philippe. *The Hour of Our Death.* New York: Knopf, 1981.

Armour, Rollin Stely. *Anabaptist Baptism.* Scottdale: Herald Press, 1966.

Armstrong, B. G. *Who's Who in Christian History.* Wheaton, Ill.: Tyndale House, n.d.

Augustine. "Letter and Spirit." *Dictionary of Biblical Tradition.* Grand Rapids: Eerdmans, 1999: 445-47.

Bainton, Roland H. *Here I Stand.* New York: Mentor, 1950.

———. *Women of the Reformation.* Minneapolis: Augsburg Publishing House, 1971.

Barge, Hermann. *Jakob Strauss: Ein Kämpfer für das Evangelium in Tirol, Thüringen und Süddeutschland.* Leipzig, Germany: M. Heinsius Nachfolger, 1937.

Barth, Ludwig. *Die Geschichte der Flösserei im Flussgebiet der oberen Kinzig.* Karlsruhe, Germany 1895.

Barrett, Lois. "Ursula Jost and Barbara Rebstock of Strasbourg." *Profiles of Anabaptist Women* 3, C. Edited by Arnold Snyder and Linda A. Huebert Hecht. Waterloo: Wilfrid Laurier University Press, 1996: 277, 283.

Baum, J. W. *Capito und Butzer, Strassburger Reformatoren, in Leben und Ausgewählte Schriften der Väter und Begründer der reformierten Kirche.* Teil III. Elberfeld, 1860.

Bauman, Clarence. *Gewaltlosigkeit im Täufertum: Eine Untersuchung zur theologischen Ethik des Oberdeutschen Täufertums der Reformationszeit.* Leiden: Brill, 1968.

Beck, James. "The Anabaptists and the Jews: The Case of Hätzer, Denck and the Worms Prophets." *Mennonite Quarterly Review* 75 (2001): 407-27.

Bell, Dean Phillip, and Stephen Burnett, eds. *Jews, Judaism and the Reformation in the Sixteenth Century.* Leiden: Brill, 2006.

Bellot, Josef. "Humanismus—Bildungswesen—Buchdruck und Verlagsgeschichte." *Geschichte der Stadt Augsburg.* 2nd edition. Edited by G. Gottlieb, et al. Stuttgart: Konrad Theiss Verlag, 1985.

Bender, Harold. "The Anabaptist Vision." *Church History* 13 (1944): 147-50.

Berdyaev, V. Gollancz. *Man and God.* Boston: Houghton Mifflin, 1951.

Bergen, Jeremy M., Paul G. Doerksen, and Karl Koop, eds. *Creed and Conscience. Essays in Honour of A. James Reimer.* Kitchener: Pandora Press, 2007.

Bergier, Jean-Jacques. "Wachstum, Energie, Verkehr vor der industriellen Revolution im Raume der heutigen Schweiz und der Zentralalpen." In *Wirtschaftliches Wachstum, Energie und Verkehr vom Mittelalter bis ins 19. Jahrhundert.* Bericht über die 6. Arbeitstagung der Gesellschaft für Sozial- und Wirtschaftsgeschichte. Edited by Hermann Kellenbenz. Stuttgart: Gustav Fischer Verlag, 1978: 21-22.

Bergsten, T. *Pilgram Marpeck und seine Auseinandersetzung mit Caspar Schwenckfeld.* Uppsala, Sweden: Almquist & Wiksells Boktrykeri, 1958.

Berman, Morris. *The Reenchantment of the World.* Ithaca: Cornell University Press, 1981.

Bietenholz, Pieter C. *The Correspondence of Erasmus.* Toronto: University of Toronto Press, 1988.

Blanke, Fritz. *Brothers in Christ: The History of the Oldest Anabaptist Congregation, Zollikon, Near Zürich, Switzerland.* Scottdale: Herald Press, 1961.

Blough, Neal. *Christ in Our Midst.* Kitchener: Pandora Press, 2007.

———. *Christologie Anabaptiste.* Pilgram Marpeck et l'humanité du Christ. Geneva: Editions Labor et Fides, 1984.

———. "Pilgram Marpeck and Caspar Schwenckfeld: The Strasbourg Years." In *Bibliotheka Dissidentum: 16th Century Anabaptism and Radical Reformation.* Baden-Baden, Germany: Koerner, 1987: 371-80.

———. "'The Uncovering of the Babylonian Whore': Confessionalization and Politics Seen from the Underside." *Mennonite Quarterly Review* 75 (2001): 37-55.

Book of Common Prayer. Toronto: Anglican Book Centre, 1959.

Bornkamm, Heinrich. *Martin Bucer's Bedeutung für die europäische Reformationsgeschichte*. Gütersloh, Germany: Bertelsmann Verlag, 1952.

Boyd, Stephen B. *Pilgram Marpeck, His Life and Social Theology*. Durham: Duke University Press, 1992.

———. "Anabaptism and Social Radicalism in Strasbourg, 1528-1532. Pilgram Marpeck on the Civil Oath." *Mennonite Quarterly Review* 64 (1989): 58-76.

Brady, Jr., Thomas A. "Architect of Persecution: Jacob Sturm and the Fall of the Sects at Strasbourg." *Archiv für Reformationsgeschichte* 79 (1988): 262-81.

———. "Jacob Sturm of Strasbourg and the Lutherans at the Diet of Augsburg, 1530." *Church History* 42 (1973): 183-202.

———. *The Politics of the Reformation in Germany. Jacob Sturm (1489-1553) of Strasbourg*. New Jersey: Humanities Press, 1997.

———. *Ruling Class, Regime and Reformation at Strasbourg 1520-1555*. Leiden: Brill, 1978.

———. "Social History." In *Reformation Europe: A Guide to Research*. Edited by Steven Ozment. St. Louis: Center for Reformation Research, 1982: 161-82.

———. *Turning Swiss: Cities and Empire, 1450-1550*. New York: Cambridge University Press, 1985.

Brandi, Karl. *Deutsche Geschichte im Zeitalter der Reformation und Gegenreformation*. Munich: Bruckmann, 1969.

———. *The Emperor Charles V*. Norwich: Fletcher and Son, 1967.

Braudel, Fernand. *The Structures of Everyday Life: Civilization and Capitalism 15th–18th Century* 1. New York: Harper & Row, 1981.

Brensinger, Terry L., and E. Morris Sider, eds. "Erasmus, the Anabaptists and the Idea of Peace." *Within the Perfection of Christ*. Nappanee: Evangel Press, 1989: 106-18.

Buchholtz, Franz-Bernhard, ed. *Geschichte der Regierung Ferdinands des Ersten* 9. Vienna, 1831-1838.

Bücking, Jürgen. *Frühabsolutismus und Kirchenreform in Tirol (1565-1665): Ein Beitrag zum Ringen zwischen "Staat" und "Kirche" in der frühen Neuzeit*. Wiesbaden, Germany: F. Steiner, 1972.

Burke, James. *Connections*. Boston: Little, Brown, 1978.

Burkert, Günther R. *Landesfürst und Stände: Karl V., Ferdinand I. Und die österreichischen Erbländer im Ringen um Gesamtstaat und Landesinteressen*. Graz, Austria, 1987.

Burnett, Amy Nelson. "Martin Bucer and the Anabaptist Context of

Evangelical Confirmation." *Mennonite Quarterly Review* 68 (1994): 95-122.

Camus, Albert. *The Rebel. An Essay on Man in Revolt*. New York: Knopf, 1971.

Chrisman, Miriam Usher. *Lay Culture, Learned Culture: Books and Social Change in Strasbourg, 1480-1599*. New Haven: Yale University Press, 1982.

———. *Strasbourg and the Reform*. New Haven: Yale University Press, 1967.

Christianson, Paul. *Reformers and Babylon: English Apocalyptic Visions from the Reformation to the Eve of the Civil War*. Toronto: University of Toronto Press, 1978.

Collins, John J. *The Apocalyptic Imagination: An Introduction to Jewish Apocalyptic Literature*. Grand Rapids: Eerdmans, 1998: 215.

Cipolla, C. M. *Before the Industrial Revolution. European Society and Economy 1000-1700*, 3rd edition. New York: Morton, 1994.

———, ed. *The Fontana Economic History of Europe: The Sixteenth and Seventeenth Centuries*. Glasgow: Collins/Fontana, 1974.

Clasen, Claus-Peter. *Anabaptism, A Social History, 1525-1618*. Ithaca: Cornell University Press, 1972.

———. "The Anabaptists in South and Central Germany, Switzerland, and Austria: A Statistical Study." *Mennonite Quarterly Review* 52 (1978): 5-38.

———. *Die Wiedertäufer im Herzogtum Württemberg*. Stuttgart: W. Kohlhammer Verlag, 1965.

Cleaver, Robert. "A Godly Form of Household Government (London, 1598)." Joyce L. Irwin, *Womanhood in Radical Protestantism 1525-1675*. New York: Edwin Mellen Press, 1979: 70-86.

Cramer, U. "Die Verfassung und Verwaltung Strassburgs von der Reformationszeit bis zum Fall der Reichsstadt (1521-1681)." In *Schriften des Wissenschaftlichen Instituts der Elsass-Lothringer im Reich*, n.s. 3. Frankfurt, 1931.

Daumas, Maurice, ed. *A History of Technology and Invention*. New York: Crown Publishers, 1969.

de Gamez, Diaz. "The Chivalric Ideal." *The Portable Medieval Reader*. New York: Viking Press, 1949, 91-92.

de Wind, H. "A Sixteenth-Century Description of Religious Sects in Austerlitz, Moravia." *Mennonite Quarterly Review* 29 (1955): 44-54.

Denck, Hans. *Schriften*. Edited by Walter Fellmann. Gütersloh, Germany: C. Bertelsmann Verlag, 1956.

Deppermann, Klaus. *Melchior Hoffman, Soziale Unruhen und apokalyptische Visionen im Zeitalter der Reformation.* Göttingen, Germany: Vandenhoeck und Ruprecht, 1979.

————. "Schwenckfeld and Leo Jud on the Advantages and Disadvantages of the State Church." *Schwenckfeld and Early Schwenkfeldianism.* Edited by Peter C. Erb. Pennsburg, Pa.: Schwenkfelder Library, 1986: 211-36.

Diederichs, Eugen. *Deutsches Leben der Vergangenheit in Bildern* 1. Jena, Germany, 1908.

Dittrich, Christoph. "Katholische Kontroverstheologen im Kampf gegen Reformation und Täufertum." *Mennonitische Geschichtsblätter* 47/48 (1990-91): 71-88.

Dipple, Geoffrey. "Pilgram Marpeck, the Spiritualizers, and the Anabaptist View of Church History." *Commoners and Community, Essays in Honour of Werner O. Packull.* Edited by C. Arnold Snyder. Kitchener: Pandora Press and Scottdale: Herald Press, 2002.

————. "Sebastian Franck in Strasbourg." *Mennonite Quarterly Review* 73 (1999): 783-802.

Driedger, Michael. "The Intensification of Religious Commitment: Jews, Anabaptists and Radical Reform, and Confessionalization." Edited by Bell and Burnett. *Jews, Judaism Reform in the Sixteenth Century.* Leiden: Brill, 2006: 269-99.

Dülmen, Richard van. *Reformation als Revolution. Soziale Bewegung und religiöser Radikalismus in der deutschen Reformation.* Munich: Deutscher Taschenbuch, 1977.

Edwards, Jr., Mark U. *Printing, Propaganda and Martin Luther.* Berkeley: University of California Press, 1994.

Eire, Carlos M. *War Against the Idols: The Reformation of Worship from Erasmus to Calvin.* New York: Cambridge University Press, 1990.

Enzenberger, Josef Franz. "Das österreichische Täufertum im Spiegel der modernen Historiographie." Essay, University of Vienna, 1979.

Erb, Peter C. "Schwenckfeld, the Anabaptists and the Sixteenth-Century Crisis of Knowing." In *Bibliotheka Dissidentum: Anabaptists and the Radical Reformation.* Edited by J. G. Rott and S. L. Verheus. Baden-Baden, Germany: Koerner, 1987: 131-47.

————, ed. *Schwenckfeld in His Reformation Setting.* Pennsburg, Pa.: Schwenkfelder Library, 1978.

Farmer, Craig S. "Reformation-Era Polemics against Anabaptist Oath Refusal." *Mennonite Quarterly Review* 81 (2007): 207-26.

Fast, Heinold. "Hans Krüsis Büchlein über Glauben und Taufe: Ein Täuferdruck von 1525." *The Heritage of Menno Simons: A Legacy of*

Faith. Edited by C. J. Dyck. Newton: Mennonite Publication Office, 1962: 213-31.

———. *Heinrich Bullinger und die Täufer*. Weierhof: Mennonitischer Geschichtsverein, 1959.

———. "Nicht was sondern Das: Marpeckhs Motto wider den Spiritualismus." *Evangelischer Glaube und Geschichte: Grete Mecenseffy zum 85 Geburtstag*. Vienna: Evangelischer Oberkirchenrat, 1984: 66-74.

———. "Pilgram Marbeck und das oberdeutsche Täufertum. Ein neuer Handschriftenfund." *Archiv für Reformationsgeschichte* 47 (1956): 212-41.

———. "Reformation durch Provokation: Predigtstörung in den ersten Jahren der Reformation in der Schweiz." *Umstrittenes Täufertum 1525-1975: Neue Forschungen*. Hans-Jürgen Goertz, ed. Göttingen, Germany: Vandenhoeck and Ruprecht, 1975: 79-110.

———. "Vom Amt des 'Lesers' zum Kompilator des sogenannten Kunstbuches. Auf den Spuren Jörg Malers." *Aussenseiter zwischen Mittelalter und Neuzeit*. Edited by N. Fischer and M. Kobelt-Groch. Leiden: Brill, 1997: 187-217.

Fichtner, Paula Sutter. *Ferdinand I of Austria: The Politics of Dynasticism in the Age of the Reformation*. Boulder, Colo.: Westview University Press, 1982.

Finger, Tom. *A Contemporary Anabaptist Theology*. Downers Grove, Ill.: InterVarsity Press, 2004.

Fischer, David H. *Historians' Fallacies*. New York: Harper & Row, 1970.

Fischer-Gallati, Stephen A. *Ottoman Imperialism and German Protestantism, 1521-1555*. Cambridge: Harvard University Press, 1959.

Fox, R. L. *Alexander the Great*. London: Dial Press, 1974.

Friedmann, Robert. "Anabaptism in Moravia." *Hutterite Studies: Essays by Robert Friedmann*. Edited by H. S. Bender. Goshen: Mennonite Historical Society, 1961: 58ff.

———. "The Christian Communism of the Hutterian Brethren." *Archiv für Reformationsgeschichte* 52 (1995): 196-208.

———. "Concerning the True Soldier of Christ: A Hitherto Unknown Tract of the Philipite Brethren in Moravia." *Mennonite Quarterly Review* 5 (1931): 87-99.

———. "Jacob Hutter's Epistle Concerning Schism in Moravia in 1533." *Mennonite Quarterly Review* 38 (1964): 329-43.

———. "Leonhard Schiemer and Hans Schlaffer: Two Tyrolean Anabaptist Martyr-Apostles of 1528." *Mennonite Quarterly Review* 33 (1959): 31-41.

————. *Mennonite Piety through the Centuries*. Goshen, Ind.: Mennonite Historical Society, 1949.

————, trans. "The Oldest Church Discipline of the Anabaptists." *Mennonite Quarterly Review* 29 (1955): 162-66.

————. "The Philipite Brethren: A Chapter in Anabaptist History." *Mennonite Quarterly Review* 32 (1958): 272-97.

Friesen, Abraham. "Acts 10: The Baptism of Cornelius as Interpreted by Thomas Müntzer and Felix Manz." *Mennonite Quarterly Review* 64 (1990): 5-22.

————. *Erasmus, the Anabaptists, and the Great Commission*. Grand Rapids: Eerdmans, 1998.

————. "The Radical Reformation Revisited." *Journal for Mennonite Studies* 2 (1984): 124-76.

Fritzius, John M. "Biography Martin Bucer (1491-1551), Early Protestant Reformer." *Journal Theology Thru Technology*. 2005. www.tlogical.net/biobucer.htm.

Gäbler, Ulrich. *Huldrich Zwingli. Eine Einführung in sein Leben und sein Werk*. Munich: Beck, 1983.

Gaventa, Beverley. "Cornelius." In *Anchor Dictionary of the Bible* 1. New York: Doubleday, 1992: 1154-56.

Geisberg, Max. *Die Münsterischen Wiedertäufer und Aldegrever. Eine Ikonographische und Numismatische Studie*. Baden-Baden, Germany: Verlag Valentin Koerner, 1977.

Geiser, Samuel. "An Ancient Anabaptist Witness for Nonresistance." *Mennonite Quarterly Review* 25 (1951): 66-69, 72.

Goertz, H. J. "The Confessional Heritage in Its New Mold: What Is Mennonite Self-understanding Today." *Mennonite Identity, Historical and Contemporary Perspectives*. Edited by Calvin W. Redekop and Samuel J. Steiner. Lanham, Md.: University Press of America, 1988: 109ff.

————. *Die Täufer, Geschichte und Deutung*. Munich: Beck, 1980.

————. "Ketzer, Aufrührer und Märtyrer. Der Zweite Speyerer Reichstag und die Täufer." *Mennonitische Geschichtsblätter* 36 N.F. 31, 1979: 7-26.

————, ed. *Profiles of Radical Reformers: Biographical Sketches from Thomas Müntzer to Paracelsus*. Scottdale: Herald Press, 1982.

Gothein, E. "Zur Geschichte des Bergbaues im Schwarzwald." *Zeitschrift für die Geschichte des Ober-Rheins*. N.F. 2, 1887: 385-448.

Gottlieb, Gunther, et al., eds. *Geschichte der Stadt Augsburg. 2000 Jahre von der Römerzeit bis zur Gegenwart*, 2nd ed. Stuttgart: Konrad Theiss Verlag, 1985.

Götzinger, Ernst. *Joachim Vadian der Reformator und Geschichtsschreiber von St. Gallen*. Halle, 1895.

Gregory, Brad S. *Salvation at Stake. Christian Martyrdom in Early Modern Europe*. Cambridge: Harvard University Press, 1999.

Greschat, Martin. *Martin Bucer. Ein Reformator und seine Zeit*. Munich: Beck, 1990.

Grimm, H. J. *The Reformation Era*. New York: Macmillan, 1954.

Guderian, Hans. *Die Täufer in Augsburg: Ihre Geschichte und Ihr Erbe: ein Beitrag zur 2000-Jahr-Feier der Stadt Augsburg*. Pfaffenhofen: W. Ludwig Verlag, 1984.

Haas, Martin. "The Path of Anabaptists into Separation: The Interdependence of Theology and Social Behavior." *The Anabaptists and Thomas Müntzer*. Edited by James M. Stayer and Werner O. Packull. Dubuque, Iowa: Kendall/Hunt, 1980: 72ff.

Halbach, Silke. *Argula von Grumbach als Verfasserin reformatorischer Flugschriften*. *European Highschool Writings*. Series 23, Theology 468. Frankfurt: Peter Lang Publishers, 1992.

Hall, Douglas J. *Thinking the Faith. Christian Theology in a North American Context*. Minneapolis: Fortress Press, 1991.

Hantsch, Hugo. *Die Geschichte Österreichs. Bd. 1 bis 1648*. 2nd edition. Graz-Vienna: Styria Steirische Verlagsanstalt, 1947.

Hartman, Franz. *Paracelsus. His Life and Prophecies*. New York: Rudolf Steiner Publications, 1973.

Hartung, Fritz. *Deutsche Verfassungsgeschichte vom 15. Jahrhundert bis zur Gegenwart*. Stuttgart: K. F. Koehler Verlag, 1959.

Hege, Christian. "Pilgram Marbeck und die oberdeutschen Taufgesinnten." *Archiv für Reformationsgeschichte* 38 (1940): 249-57.

Hege, Lydie. "Täufertour in Strassburg." *Mennonitisches Jahrbuch* 1999: 97-102.

Herlihy, David. *Medieval Households*. Cambridge: Harvard University Press, 1985.

Hilger, Wolfgang. *Ikonographie Kaiser Ferdinands I (1503-1564)*. Vienna: Böhlau, 1969.

Hillerbrand, Hans. "The Radical Reformation: Reflections on the Occasion of an Anniversary." *Mennonite Quarterly Review* 58 (1993): 408-20.

———, ed. "Radicalism in the Early Reformation." In *Radical Tendencies in the Reformation: Divergent Perspectives*. Kirksville, Mo.: Sixteenth-Century Journal Publishers, 1988: 7-42.

Holl, Karl. "Luther und die Schwärmer." In *Gesammelte Aufsätze zur Kirchengeschichte* 1. *Luther*. Tübingen: Mohr Verlag, 1923.

Homan, Gerlof D. "Orie Benjamin Gerig: Mennonite Rebel, Peace Activist,

International Civil Servant and American Diplomat, 1894-1976." *Mennonite Quarterly Review* 73 (1999): 751-82.

Hruby, Frantisek. *Die Wiedertäufer in Mähren*. Leipzig, Germany: Separatdruck, n.d. Originally published in *Archiv für Reformationsgeschichte* 30 (1933): 1-36, 170-211; and 32 (1935): 1-40.

Hulshof, Abraham. *Geschiedenis van de Doopsgezinden te Straatsburg van 1525 tot 1557*. Amsterdam: J. Clausen, 1905.

Husser, Daniel. "Caspar Schwenckfeld et ses Adeptes entre l'Église et les sectes à Strasbourg." *Strasbourg au coeur réligieux du XVI siècle*. Edited by G. Livet and F. Rapp. Strasbourg: Librarie Istra, 1977: 511-35.

Illich, Ivan. *Tools of Conviviality*. New York: Harper & Row, 1973.

Immenkötter, H. "Kirche zwischen Reformation und Parität." *Geschichte der Stadt Augsburg*. Edited by Gunther Gottlieb, et al. Stuttgart: Konrad Theiss Verlag Stuttgart, 1985: 391-412.

Iongh, Jane de. *Mary of Hungary, Second Regent of the Netherlands*. London: Faber & Faber, 1959.

Isaak, Helmut. *Menno Simons and the New Jerusalem*. Kitchener: Pandora Press, 2006.

Janz, Denis. "Johannes Fabri." In *Contemporaries of Erasmus 2*. Edited by P. Bietenholz and T. Deutscher. Toronto: University of Toronto Press: 5-8.

Johnson, Galen. "The Development of John Calvin's Doctrine of Infant Baptism in Reaction to the Anabaptists." *Mennonite Quarterly Review* 73 (1999): 803-23.

Jones, Michael, ed. *The New Cambridge Medieval History* 6. Cambridge: Cambridge University Press, 2000.

Jones, Rufus M. *Spiritual Reformers in the 16th and 17th Centuries*. Boston: Beacon Press, 1914.

Kantorowicz, Ernst. *Kaiser Friedrich der Zweite*. 3rd edition. Stuttgart: Klett-Cotta, 1992.

Kawerau, G. "Zur Reformationsgeschichte Augsburgs." *Beiträge zur bayerischen Kirchengeschichte* 2 (1896): 131-32.

Kellenbenz, Hermann, ed. "Technology in the Age of the Scientific Revolution 1500-1700." *Fontana Economic History of Europe. The Sixteenth and Seventeenth Centuries*. Edited by Carlo M. Cipolla. Glasgow: Collins/Fontana, 1974.

———. "Wirtschaftsleben der Blütezeit." *Geschichte der Stadt Augsburg*. Edited by G. Gottlieb, et al. Stuttgart: Konrad Theiss Verlag Stuttgart, 258-301.

———. *Wirtschaftliches Wachstum, Energie und Vekehr vom Mittelalter bis ins 19. Jahrhundert*. Bericht über die 6. Arbeitstagung der Gesellschaft für Sozial- und Wirtschaftsgeschichte. Stuttgart: Gustav Fischer Verlag, 1978.

Kiwiet, Jan. *Pilgram Marpeck*. Kassel: Oncken Verlag, 1957.

Klaassen, Walter. "Anabaptist Hermeneutics: Presuppositions, Principles, and Practice." *Essays in Biblical Interpretation*. Edited by Willard Swartley. Elkhart, Ind.: Institute of Mennonite Studies, 1989: 1-13.

———. "Anna Scharnschlager." *Profiles of Anabaptist Women*. Waterloo: Wilfrid Laurier University Press, 1996: 58-63.

———. *Armageddon and the Peaceable Kingdom*. Kitchener: Herald Press, 1999.

———. "Church Discipline and the Spirit in Pilgram Marpeck." *De Geest in het geding*. Alphen aan den Rijn, The Netherlands: Tjeenk Willink, 1978: 169-80.

———. "Die Taufe im Schweizer Täufe." *Mennonitische Geschichtsblätter* 46 (1989b): 75-89.

———. "Hans Hut and Thomas Müntzer." *Baptist Quarterly Review* 19 (1962): 207-27.

———. "Investigation into the Authorship and the Historical Background of the Anabaptist Tract. 'Aufdeckung der Babylonischen Hurn.'" *Mennonite Quarterly Review* 61 (1987): 251-61.

———. *Living at the End of the Ages: Apocalyptic Expectation in the Radical Reformation*. Lanham, Md.: University Press of America, 1992.

———. *Michael Gaismair: Revolutionary and Reformer*. Leiden: Brill, 1978.

———. "The Modern Relevance of Anabaptism." *Umstrittenes Täufertum 1525-1975*. Edited by Hans-Jürgen Goertz. Göttingen, Germany: Vandenhoeck and Ruprecht, 1975: 290-304.

———. "Of Divine and Human Justice: The Early Swiss Brethren and Government." *Conrad Grebel Review*, 10 (1992a): 169-86.

———. "Schwenckfeld and the Anabaptists." *Schwenckfeld and Early Schwenkfeldianism*. Edited by Peter C. Erb. Pennsburg, Pa.: Schwenkfelder Library, 1986: 389ff.

Klassen, John. *The Mobility and the Making of the Hussite Revolution*. New York: Columbia University Press, 1978.

Klassen, William. *Covenant and Community. The Life, Writings and Hermeneutics of Pilgram Marpeck*. Grand Rapids: Eerdmans, 1968.

———. *The Forgiving Community*. Philadelphia: Westminster Press, 1966.

———. "The Legacy of the Marpeck Community in Anabaptist Scholarship." *Mennonite Quarterly Review* 78 (2004): 7-28.

————. "The Limits of Political Authority in Pilgram Marpeck." *Mennonite Quarterly Review* 56 (1982): 342-64.

————. "Pilgram Marpeck: Liberty without Coercion." *Profiles of Radical Reformers*. Edited by Hans-Jürgen Goertz. Scottdale: Herald Press, 1978: 168-77.

————. "Pilgram Marpeck's Two Books of 1531." *Mennonite Quarterly Review* 33 (1959): 18-30.

————. "The Role of the Child in Anabaptism." *Mennonite Images*. Edited by Harry Loewen. Winnipeg: Hyperion Press, 1980: 17-32.

Klötzer, Ralf. "The Melchiorites and Münster." *A Companion to Anabaptism and Spiritualism, 1521-1700*. Edited by John D. Roth and James M. Stayer. Leiden: Brill, 2007: 217-56.

Kobelt-Groch, Marion. *Judith macht Geschichte*. München: Wilhelm Fink Verlag, 2005.

————. "Unter Zechern, Spielern und Häschern. Täufer im Wirtshaus." *Aussenseiter Zwischen Mittelalter und Neuzeit. Festschrift für Hans-Jürgen Goertz Zum 60. Geburtstag*. Edited by Norbert Fischer and Marion Kobelt-Groch. Leiden: Brill, 1997: 111-26.

Koenigsberger, H. G. "The Empire of Charles V in Europe." *The New Cambridge Modern History* 2, *The Reformation*. Edited by G. R. Elton. Cambridge: Cambridge University Press, 1958: 312-13.

Köfler, Werner. *Rattenberg*. Rattenberg: Verlag Buchhandlung Robert Armitter, 1973.

Köfler, Gretl. "Täufertum in Tirol." *Michael Gaismair und Seine Zeit*. Edited by Christoph von Hartungen and Günther Pallaver. Verona: Cierre Editrice Nuova Grafica, 1983: 112-22.

Kohler, Alfred. *Die Korrespondenzen Ferdinands* 2. Family correspondence until 1526. Vienna: Kern reprint, 1970.

————. *Ferdinand I. 1503-1564. Fürst, König und Kaiser*. Munich: C. H. Beck, 2003.

————. *Ferdinand I Herrscher zwischen Blutgericht und Türkenkriegen*. Wiener Neustadt, Austria: Statutarstadt, 2003.

Kopialbuch, *Missiven und Befelch 1520*, Tiroler Landesarchiv Innsbruck, fol. 3r.

————. Tiroler Landarchiv. *Bekennen 1525*, Tiroler Landesarchiv, fol. 81v-82r.

Koppensteiner, Norbert. "Das Neustädter 'Blutgericht' und die Folgen für die Niederösterreichischen Stände." *Ferdinand I*, a chapter in Museum Wiener Neustadt (Austria) catalogue: 26-33, 2003.

————, ed. *Ferdinand I Herrscher zwischen Blutgericht und Türkenkriegen*. Wiener Neustadt, Austria: Statutarstadt, 2003.

Krüger, Friedhelm. "Bucer and Erasmus." *Mennonite Quarterly Review* 8 (1994): 11-23.

Laferl, Christopher F., and Christina Lutter, eds. *Die Korrespondenz Ferdinands I. Bd. 4: Familienkorrespondenz 1533 und 1534 4.* Vienna: Böblau, 2000.

Lassmann, Wolfgang. "Die Frühphase der Süddeutsch-Öesterreichischen Täuferbewegung: Unter BesondererBerücksichtigung von Salzburg, Niederösterreich und Oberösterreich." Unpublished paper, University of Vienna, 1980.

———. "Möglichkeiten einer Modellbildung zur Verlaufsstruktur des Tirolischen Anabaptismus." *Anabaptistes et Dissidents.* Edited by Jean-George Rott and Simon L. Verheus. Baden-Baden, Germany: Koerner, 1987: 297-310.

Laubach, Ernst. *Ferdinand I. als Kaiser. Politik und Herrscherauffassung des Nachfolgers Karls V.* Münster: Aschendorff, 2001.

Laube, Adolf. "Radicalism as a Research Problem in the History of Early Reformation." *Radical Tendencies in the Reformation: Divergent Perspectives.* Edited by Hans Hillerbrand. Kirksville, Mo.: Sixteenth-Century Journal Publishers, 1988: 7-42.

Lhotsky, Alphons. *Des Zeitalter des Hauses Österreich: die ersten Jahre der Regierung Ferdinand I in Österreich 1520-1527.* Vienna In Kommission bei H. Böhlaus Nachf, 1971.

Liebmann, Maximilian. *Urbanus Rhegius und die Anfänge der Reformation.* Münster: Aschendorffer Verlagbuchhandlung, 1980.

Liechty, Daniel. *Andreas Fischer and the Sabbatarian Anabaptists: An Early Reformation Episode in East Central Europe.* Scottdale: Herald Press, 1988.

———. "The Origins of Sabbatarianism among East Central European Anabaptists in the Sixteenth Century." *Anabaptistes et Dissidentes.* Edited by Jean-George Rott and Simon L. Verheus. Baden-Baden, Germany: Koerner, 1987: 361-69.

———. "Oswald Glaidt, Simone Simoni, and Juan de Valdes." *Bibliotheca Dissidentium* 9. Edited by André Séquenny. Baden-Baden, Germany: Koerner, 1988.

———. "Schwenckfelders and Sabbatarian Anabaptists: A Tragedy of the Early Reformation." *Schwenckfeld and Early Schwenkfeldianism.* Edited by Peter Erb. Pennsburg, Pa.: Schwenkfelder Library, 1986: 135ff.

Lieder der Hutterischen Brüder. 5th edition. Cayley, Alta.: Macmillan Colony, 1983.

Lienhard, Marc, ed. *The Origins and Characteristics of Anabaptism.* The Hague: MartinusNijhoff, 1977.

Locher, Gottfried W. *Die Theologie Huldrych Zwinglis im Lichte seiner Christologie.* Zürich: Zwingli-Verlag, 1952.

Lortz, Joseph. *Die Reformation in Deutschland 2.* 5th edition. Freiburg, Germany: Herder, 1962.

Loserth, Johann. "Der Anabaptismus in Tirol vom Jahre 1536 bis zu seinem Erlöschen." *Archiv für österreichische Geschichte* 79 (1893): 127-276.

———. "Der Anabaptismus in Tirol von seinen Anfängen bis zum Tode Jacob Huters." *Archiv für österreichische Geschichte* 78 (1892b): 430-604.

———. "Ferdinand I." In *Mennonitisches Lexicon* 1, ed. C. Hege and C. Neff, Frankfurt a. M. and Weierhof: privately published, 1913, 638-41.

———. "Georg Blaurock und die Anfänge des Anabaptismus in Graubünden und Tirol." *Vorträge und Aufsätze aus der Comenius-Gesellschaft* 7 (1899): 1-30.

———. "Oswald Glaydt." *Zeitschrift des Vereins für die Geschichte Mährens und Schlesien* 1 (1897): 70-73.

———. "Reichsgesetze gegen die 'Wiedertäufer.'" *Mennonitische Geschichtsblätter* 1 (1936): 27-28.

Ludwig, Karl-Heinz und Fritz Gruber. *Gold und Silberbau im Übergang vom Mittelalter zurNeuzeit. Das Salzburger Revier von Gastein und Rauris.* Köln, Germany: Bohlau, 1987.

Lutterbach, Hubertus. *Der Weg in das Täuferreich von Münster. Ein Ringen um die heilige Stadt.* Münster: Dialogverlag, 2006: 147-48.

Lutz, Heinrich. "Augsburg und seine politische Umwelt 1490-1555." In *Geschichte der Stadt Augsburg. 2000 Jahre von der Römerzeit bis zur Gegenwart.* 2nd edition. Edited by G. Gottlieb. Stuttgart: Konrad Theiss Verlag, 1985.

MacCulloch, Diarmaid. *The Reformation: A History.* New York: Viking Penguin, 2003.

Macek, Josef. *Der Tiroler Bauernkrieg und Michael Gaismair.* Berlin: VEB Deutscher Verlag der Wissenschaften, 1965.

Machiavelli, Niccolo. *The Prince.* Translated by George Bull. Harmondsworth: Penguin Classics (U.K.), 1961.

Martin, Dennis. "Catholic Spirituality and Anabaptists and Mennonite Discipleship." *Mennonite Quarterly Review* 62 (1988): 5-25.

Mattern, Marlies. *Leben im Abseits: Frauen und Männer im Täufertum (1525-1550). Eine Studie zur Alltagsgeschichte.* Frankfurt a. M.: Peter Lang: Europäischer Verlag der Wissenschaften, 1998.

Maurer, W. "M. Butzer und die Judenfrage in Hessen." *Zeitschrift Vereins für Hess. Geschichte u. Landeskunde* 64 (1953).

McGinn, Bernard. *The Calabrian Abbot. Joachim of Fiore in Western Thought*. New York: Macmillan, 1985.

McKee, Elsie Anne. *Katharina Schütz Zell 2*. Leiden: Brill, 1999.

McLaughlin, Emmet. *Caspar Schwenckfeld, Reluctant Radical: His Life to 1540*. New Haven: Yale University Press, 1986.

———. "Schwenckfeld and the South German Eucharist Controversy, 1526-1529." *Schwenckfeld and Early Schwenkfeldianism*. Edited by Peter Erb. Pennsburg, Pa.: Schwenkfelder Library, 1986: 181-210.

———. "Schwenckfeld and the Strasbourg Radicals." *Mennonite Quarterly Review* 59 (1985): 133, 268-78.

Mecenseffy, Grete. "Die Täufer in Rattenberg." *Das Buch von Kramsach, Schlernschriften* 262 (1972): 197-214.

———. "The Origin of Upper Austrian Anabaptism." *The Anabaptists and Thomas Müntzer*. Edited by James M. Stayer and Werner O. Packull. Dubuque, Iowa: Kendall/Hunt, 1980: 152-54.

———. "Ursprünge und Strömungen des Täufertums in Österreich." *Mitteilungen des oberösterreichischen Landesarchivs* 14 (1984): 77-94.

———. "Wiedertäufer in Kitzbühl." *Stadtbuch Kitzbühl* 4 (1971): 155ff. Edited by Eduard Widmoser.

Moeller, Bernd. "Bucer und die Geschwister Blarer." *Martin Bucer and Sixteenth Century Europe* 1. Leiden: Brill, 1993: 441-50.

Moger, Travis J. "Pamphlets, Preaching and Politics: The Image Controversy in Reformation Wittenberg, Zürich and Strassburg." *Mennonite Quarterly Review* 75 (2001): 325-52.

Mols, Roger. "Population in Europe 1500-1700." *Fontana Economic History of Europe. The Sixteenth and Seventeenth Centuries*. Edited by Carlo M. Cipolla. Glasgow: Collins/Fontana, 1974: 15-82.

Müller, Johannes. *Martin Bucer's Hermeneutik*. Quellen und Forschungen zur Reformationsgeschichte 32. Gütersloh, Germany: Verlaghaus Gerd Mohn, 1965.

Müsing, Hans-Werner. "The Anabaptist Movement in Strasbourg from Early 1526 to July 1527." *Mennonite Quarterly Review* 51 (1977): 91-126.

Mutschlechner, Georg. "Die Verwendung der Schneeberger und Gossensasser Erze." *Der Schlern* 67, Heft 5 (Mai 1993): 333-39.

———. *Erzbergbau und Bergwesen im Berggericht Rattenberg*. Im Selbstverlag der Gemeinden Alpbach, Brixlegg, Rattenberg, Reith im Alpbachtal 32, 1984.

Nelson, Stephen, and Jean Rott. "Strasbourg: The Anabaptist City in the Sixteenth Century." *Mennonite Quarterly Review* 58 (1984): 230-41.

Nicoladoni, Alexander. *Johannes Bünderlin von Linz und die*

Oberösterreichischen Täufergemeinden in den Jahren 1525-1531. Berlin: R. Gärtners Verlag, 1893.

Nipperdey, Thomas. *Reformation, Revolution, Utopie.* Göttingen, Germany: Vandenhoeck & Ruprecht, 1975.

Noflatscher, Heinz. "Heresy and Revolt: The Early Anabaptists in the Tyrol and in Zürich." *Mennonite Quarterly Review* 68 (1994): 291-317.

Oberleitner, K. "Österreichs Finanzen und Kriegswesen unter Ferdinand I von Jahren 1522 bis 1564." *Archiv für Kunde Österreichischer Geschichtsquellen* 22. Vienna: Akademie der Wissenschaften, 1860.

Oberman, Heiko. *The Harvest of Medieval Theology.* Grand Rapids: Eerdmans, 1967.

———. *The Roots of Antisemitism in the Age of Renaissance and Reformation.* Translated by James Porter. Philadelphia: Fortress Press, 1984.

Oyer, John S. "Bucer Opposes the Anabaptists." *Mennonite Quarterly Review* 68 (1994): 24-50.

———. "Bucer and the Anabaptists." In *Martin Bucer and Sixteenth Century Europe* 2. Edited by Christian Krieger and Marc Lienhard. New York: Brill, 1993: 603-13.

———. *Lutheran Reformers against Anabaptists: Luther, Melanchthon, and Menius and the Anabaptists of Central Germany.* The Hague: Martinus Nijhoff, 1964.

———. *"They Harry the Good People Out of the Land."* Essays on the Persecution, Survival and Flourishing of Anabaptists and Mennonites. Edited by John D. Roth. Goshen, Ind.: Mennonite Historical Society, 2000.

Ozment, Steven. *The Bürgermeister's Daughter, Scandal in a Sixteenth-Century German Town.* New York: Harper, 1996.

———. *Flesh and Spirit, Private Life in Early Modern Germany.* New York: Penguin, 1999.

———. *Three Behaim Boys: Growing Up in Early Modern Germany.* New Haven: Yale University Press.

Packull, Werner O. "The Beginning of Anabaptism in Southern Tyrol." *Sixteenth-Century Journal* 21, (1991b): 717-26.

———. "Clemens Adler's Judgment Concerning the Sword: A Swiss Connection to Silesian Anabaptism?" *Conrad Grebel Review* 9 (1991a): 243-50.

———. "Denck, Hans (ca. 1490-1527)." *Theologische Realenzyklopädie* 8 (1981): 488-90.

———. "Die Anfänge des Täufertums im Tirol." *Wegscheiden der Reformation: Vom 16. bis zum 18 Jahrhundert.* Edited by Günter Vogler. Weimar, Germany: Bohlaus, 1994: 179-209.

————. *Hutterite Beginnings: Communitarian Experiments during the Reformation*. Baltimore: Johns Hopkins University Press, 1995.

————. *Mysticism and the Early South German-Austrian Anabaptist Movement, 1525-1531*. Scottdale: Herald Press: 1977.

————. "Preliminary Report on Pilgram Marpeck's Sponsorship of Anabaptist *Flugschriften*." *Mennonite Quarterly Review* 75 (2001): 75-88.

————. "A Reinterpretation of Melchior Hoffman's *Exposition* against the Background of Spiritualist-Franciscan Eschatology with Special Reference to Peter John Olivi." *The Dutch Dissenters: Contributions to a Reassessment of Their History and Ideas*. Edited by Irvin Horst. Leiden: Brill, 1986: 32-61.

————. Research Note: "Pilgram Marpeck's *Uncovering the Babylonian Whore* and Other Anonymous Tracts." *Mennonite Quarterly Review* 67 (1993): 351-55.

————. "In Search of the 'Common Man' in Early German Anabaptist Ideology." *Sixteenth-Century Journal* 18 (1986a): 51-68.

————. "Some Reflections on the State of Anabaptist History: The Demise of a Normative Vision." *Studies in Religion* 8 (1979): 313-23.

————. Swiss Anabaptism in the Context of the Reformation of the Common Man." *Journal for Mennonite Studies* 3 (1985): 36-59.

————. "Thomas Müntzer and das Hutsche Täufertum." *Mennonitische Geschichtsblätter* 46 (1989): 30-42.

————. "'We Are Born to Work Like the Birds to Fly': The Anabaptist-Hutterite Ideal Woman." *Mennonite Quarterly Review* 73 (1999): 75-86.

Palme, Rudolph. "Zur Täuferbewegung in Tirol." *Mennonitische Geschichtsblätter* 43/44 (1986-87): 47-61.

————. "Zur Täuferbewegung in Tirol." *Die Täuferbewegung. Tagung zum 450. Todestag Jakob Huters (1536-1986)*. Edited by Christoph von Hartungen and Günther Pallaver. Bolzano: Collana di Documentazione, 1986: 66-81.

Panek, Jaroslav. "Die Täufer in den böhmischen Ländern, insbesondere in Mähren im 16. und 17. Jahrhundert." *Schlern* 63 (1989): 648-61.

Parker, T. H. *Commentaries on the Epistle to the Romans 1532-1542*. Edinburgh: T & T Clark, 1986.

Parry, J. H. "Transport and Trade Routes." *The Cambridge Economic History of Europe* 4. Edited by E. E. Rich and C. H. Wilson. Cambridge: Cambridge University Press, 1967: 155-222.

Pauck, W. "Martin Bucer's Conception of a Christian State." *Princeton Theological Review* 1928: 80ff.

Pelikan, J. *The Growth of Medieval Theology*. Chicago: University of Chicago Press, 1978.

Pfaffenbichler, Matthias. "Ferdinand I der Aufstieg eines Kaisers." In *Ferdinand I*. Museum Wiener Neustadt (Austria) catalogue: 19-24.

———. "'Fiat iustitia aut pereat mundus,' Ferdinand und das 'Wiener Neustadt Blutgericht'." In *Kaiser Ferdinand I, 1503–1564, Das Werden der Habsburgermonarchie*. Vienna: Kunsthistorisches Museum Vienna, 2003: 85-88.

Platz, P. Philipp. *Der Römerbrief in St. Augustin's Gnadenbegriff*. Würzburg, Germany, 1937.

Pries, Edmund. "Anabaptist Oath Refusal: Basel, Bern and Strasbourg, 1525-1538." PhD dissertation, University of Waterloo, 1995.

Quiring, Horst. "Die Anthropologie Pilgram Marbecks." *Mennonitische Geschichtsblätter* 2 (1937): 10-17.

Reimer, A. James. "Law, Conscience and Civil Responsibility: Marpeck, Mennonites and Contemporary Social Ethics." *Commoners and Community, Essays in Honour of Werner O. Packull*. Edited by C. Arnold Snyder. Kitchener: Pandora Press, 2002.

Rempel, John D. *The Lord's Supper in Anabaptism. A Study in the Christology of Balthasar Hubmaier, Pilgram Marpeck, and Dirk Philips*. Waterloo: Herald Press, 1993.

Richardson, Cyril C. Richardson. *Zwingli and Cranmer on the Eucharist*. Evanston, Ill.: Seabury-Western Theological Seminar, 1949.

Rischar, Klaus. "Das Leben und Sterben der Wiedertäufer in Salzburg und Süddeutschland. Nach einem Brief des Prof. Johannes Eck an Herzog Georg von Sachsen aus dem Jahre 1527." *Mitteilungen der Gesellschaft für Salzburger Landeskunde* 108 (1968): 197-207.

Rogge, Joachim. *Der Beitrag des Predigers Jacob Strauss zur Frühen Reformationsgeschichte*. Berlin: Evangelische Verlagsanstalt, 1957.

Roper, Lyndal. *The Holy Household, Women and Morals in Reformation Augsburg*. Oxford: Clarendon Press, 1989.

Roth, Friedrich. *Augsburgs Reformationsgeschichte* 4. Munich: Theodor Ackermann, 1904.

Rothkegel, Martin. "Anabaptism in Moravia and Silesia." In *A Companion to Anabaptism and Spiritualism, 1521-1700*. Edited by John D. Roth and James M. Stayer. Leiden: Brill, 2007: 165-89.

———. "Beneš Optàt on Baptism and the Lord's Supper." *Mennonite Quarterly Review* 79 (2005): 359-81.

———. "The Hutterian Brethren and the Printed Book: A Contribution to Anabaptist Bibliography." *Mennonite Quarterly Review* 74 (2000): 51-85.

———. "Randglossen zum Kunstbuch." *Mennonitische Geschichtsblätter* 61 (2004): 49-64.

Rott, Hans-Georg and Stephen F. Nelson. "Strassburg—die Täuferstadt im 16. Jahrhundert." *Mennonitisches Jahrbuch* 1984: 31-40.

Ruckdeschel, Wilhelm. "Das untere Brunnenwerk zu Augsburg durch vier Jahrhunderte." *Zeitschrift des historischen Vereins für Schwaben* 75 (1981): 87-113.

———. "Die Brunnenwerke am Roten Tor zu Augsburg zur Zeit des Brunnenmeisters Caspar Walter." *Zeitschrift des historischen Vereins für Schwaben* 69 (1975): 61-90.

Rummel, Erika, ed. *Erasmus' Annotations on the New Testament: From Philologist to Theologian.* Toronto: University of Toronto Press, 1986.

———. *Erasmus on Women.* Toronto: University of Toronto Press, 1996.

Rupp, E. G. *Patterns of Reformation.* London: Epworth, 1969.

———. "The Reformation in Zürich, Strassburg and Geneva." *The New Cambridge Modern History II. The Reformation 1520-1559.* Edited by G. R. Elton. Cambridge: Cambridge University Press, 1975.

St. Galler Geschichts- und Wirtschaftschronik, n.d: n.p.

Sallaberger, Johann. *Kardinal Matthäus Lang von Wellenburg (1468-1540), Staatsmann und Kirchenfürst im Zeitalter von Renaissance, Reformation und Bauernkriegen.* Salzburg: Verlag Anton Pustet, 1997.

Schimmelpfennig, Bernhard. "Religiöses Leben im späten Mittelalter." *Geschichte der Stadt Augsburg.* 2nd edition. Edited by G. Gottlieb. Stuttgart: Konrad Theiss Verlag, 1985: 220-24.

Schmelzer, Matthias. "Jakob Huters Wirken im Lichte von Bekenntnissen gefangener Täufer." *Der Schlern* 63 (1989): 596-618.

Schottenloher, Karl. *Philip Ulhart: Ein Augsburger Winkeldrucker und Helfershelfer der "Schwärmer" und "Wiedertäufer" (1523-1529).* 1921. Reprint, Nieuwkoop, The Netherlands: de Graaf, 1967.

Schraepler, Horst W. *Die Rechtliche Behandlung der Täufer in der deutschen Schweiz, Südwestdeutschland und Hessen 1525-1618.* Tübingen, Germany: Mennonitischer Geschichtsverein, 1957.

Schultz, R. *Martin Bucer's Anschauung von der Christlichen Obrigkeit.* 1932.

Schulze, Winfried. "Augsburg 1555-1648: Eine Stadt im Heiligen Römischen Reich." *Geschichte der Stadt Augsburg.* 2nd edition. Edited by G. Gottlieb. Stuttgart: Konrad Theiss Verlag Stuttgart, 1985: 433-47.

Schwartz, Hillel. "Early Anabaptist Ideas about the Nature of Children." *Mennonite Quarterly Review* 47 (1973): 102-14.

Seebaß, Gottfried. "Bauernkrieg und Täufertum in Franken." *Zeitschrift für Kirchengeschichte* 85 (1974): 284-300.

————. "Caspar Schwenckfeld's Understanding of the Old Testament." In *Schwenckfeld and Early Schwenkfeldianism*. Edited by Peter C. Erb. Pennsburg, Pa.: Schwenkfelder Library, 1986: 97-102.

————. "Das Zeichen der Erwählten. Zum Verständnis der Taufe bei Hans Hut." *Umstrittenes Täufertum, 1525-1975. Neue Forschungen.* Hans-Jürgen Goertz, ed. Göttingen, Germany: Vandenhoeck and Ruprecht, 1975: 138-64.

————. "Hans Hut: The Suffering Avenger." *Profiles of Radical Reformers*. Edited by H. J. Goertz. Scottdale: Herald Press, 1982: 54-61.

————. *Müntzers Erbe: Werk, Leben und Theologie des Hans Hut.* Göttingen, Germany: Gütersloher Verlagshaus, 2002.

Seiling, Jonathan, ed. and trans. "Christoph Freisleben's 'On the Genuine Baptism of John, Christ and the Apostles,'" *Mennonite Quarterly Review* 81 (2007): 623-54.

Short Title Catalogue of Books Printed in the German-speaking Countries and German Books Printed in Other Countries in the British Museum, 1455-1600. London: British Museum, 1962. This volume refers to the *Vermanung* dated 1542 as under Christian Confederation Union: 209, 593. There is no reference to Marpeck's *Klarer Vast Nützlicher Unterricht* (1531). The Short Title book is in University of Toronto Library.

Simpson, Evelyn M., ed. "Sermon Number Six." *John Donne's Sermons on the Psalms and Gospels*. Berkeley: University of California Press, 1963.

Simpson, W. J. Sparrow. *St. Augustine on the Spirit and the Letter*. London: SPCK, 1925.

Simyani, Tibor. *Er schuf das Reich: Ferdinand von Habsburg*. Vienna: Amalthen, 1987.

Snyder, C. Arnold. *Anabaptist History and Theology*. Kitchener: Pandora Press, 1995.

————, ed. *Biblical Concordance of the Swiss Brethren, 1540*. Translated by Gilbert Fast and Galen F. Peters. Kitchener: Pandora Press, 2001.

————. "Biblical Text and Social Context: Anabaptist Anticlericalism in Reformation Zürich." *Mennonite Quarterly Review* 65 (1991): 169-91.

————. "The Birth and Evolution of Swiss Brethren Anabaptism (1520-1530)." *Mennonite Quarterly Review* 80 (2006): 501-645.

————. "Communication and the People: The Case of Reformation St. Gall." *Mennonite Quarterly Review* 67 (1993): 152-73.

————. "The Influence of the Schleitheim Articles on the Anabaptist Movement: A Historical Evaluation." *Mennonite Quarterly Review* 58 (1989): 323-34.

————. *The Life and Thought of Michael Sattler*. Scottdale: Herald Press, 1984.

————. "The (Not-so) 'Simple Confession' of the Later Swiss Brethren, Manuscripts and Marpeckites in an Age of Print." Part 1. *Mennonite Quarterly Review* 73 (1999): 677-722.

————. Part 2. "The Evolution of Separatist Anabaptism." *Mennonite Quarterly Review* 74 (2000): 87-122.

————. "Word and Power in Reformation Zürich." *Archiv für Reformationsgeschichte* 81 (1990): 263-85.

Snyder, C. Arnold, and Linda H. Hecht, eds. *Profiles of Anabaptist Women. Sixteenth-Century Reforming Pioneers* 3. Waterloo: Wilfrid Laurier Press, 1996.

Sölch, Georg. "Die Holzbringung im oberen Kinzigtal." *Der Forstmann in Baden-Württemberg* 7 (1957): 158-63.

Speck, Dieter. *Die vorderösterreichischen Landstände* 2. Freiburg, Germany: Plaetz, 1994.

Stayer, James M. "The Anabaptists." *Reformation Europe: A Guide to Research*. Edited by Steven Ozment. St. Louis: Center for Reformation Research, 1982: 135-59.

————. "Anabaptists and Future Anabaptists in the Peasants' War." *Mennonite Quarterly Review* 62 (1988): 98-139.

————. *Anabaptists and the Sword*. Lawrence, Kan.: Coronado, 1971.

————. Book review of Adolf Laube, et al. *Flugschriften vom Bauernkrieg zum Täuferreich (1526- 1535)* 2. *Mennonite Quarterly Review* 68 (1994): 123-26.

————. "Die Anfänge des Schweizerischen Täufertums im Kongregationalismus." *Umstrittenes Täufertum, 1525-1975*. Neue Forschungen. Edited by Hans-Jürgen Goertz. Göttingen, Germany: Vandenhoeck and Ruprecht, 1975: 19-49.

————. "The Easy Demise of a Normative Vision of Anabaptism. *Mennonite Identity: Historical and Contemporary Perspectives*. Edited by Calvin W. Redekop and Samuel J. Steiner. Lanham, Md.: University Press of America, 1992: 109ff.

————. "Reublin and Brötli: The Revolutionary Beginnings of Swiss Anabaptism." *The Origins and Characteristics of Anabaptism*. Edited by M. Lienhard. The Hague: Martinus Nijhoff, 1977: 83-102.

————. *Schriften von katholischer Seite gegen die Täufer; die Schriften der Münsterischen Täufer und ihrer Gegner*. Edited by Robert Stupperich. Book review in *Mennonite Quarterly Review* 56 (1982c): 388-90.

————. "Wilhelm Reublin: A Picaresque Journey through Early

Anabaptism." *Profiles of Radical Reformers: Biographical Sketches from Thomas Müntzer to Paracelus.* Edited by Hans-Jürgen Goertz. Translated by Walter Klaassen. Scottdale: Herald Press, 1982: 107-17.

Stayer, James M., and Werner O. Packull, eds. *The Anabaptists and Thomas Müntzer.* Dubuque, Iowa: Kendall/Hunt, 1980.

Stayer, James M., Klaus Deppermann, and Werner O. Packull. "From Monogenesis to Polygenesis: The Historical Discussion of Anabaptist Origins." *Mennonite Quarterly Review* 49 (1975): 83-121.

Stein, Paul. *Die Industrie des Kantons St. Gallen. Chronik des Kantons St. Gallen.* Zürich: Verlag Franz Brun, 1945.

Steinmetz, David Curtis. *Reformers in the Wings: From Geiler von Kaysersberg to Theodore Beza.* Philadelphia: Fortress Press, 1971.

Steinmetz, Max. "Die dritte Etappe der frühbürgerlichen Revolution. Der Deutsche Bauernkrieg 1524 bis 1526." In *Der Bauernkrieg 1524-1526.* Edited by Rainer Wohlfeil. München: Nymphenburger Verlagshandlung, 1975.

Stolz, Otto. "Zur Geschichte des Bergbaues im Elsass im 15 and 16. Jahrhundert." *Elsass-Lothringisches Jahrbuch* 18 (1939): 116-71.

Stops, Friedrich. *Rattenberg: Chronik der alten Stadt am Inn.* Österreichischer Kulturverlag, 1981.

Strauss, Gerhard, *Schriftgebrauch, Schriftbeweis und Schriftauslegung bei Augustin.* Tübingen: J. C. B. Mohr, 1959.

Stuart, Murray. *Biblical Interpretation in the Anabaptist Tradition.* Kitchener: Pandora Press, 2000. Reviewed by D. Jonathan Grieser in *Mennonite Quarterly Review* 75 (1971): 123-25.

Stupperich, Robert. *Geschichte der Reformation.* Munich: Deutscher Taschenbuch, 1967.

Ten Doornkaat Koolman, J. "Leupold Scharnschlager und die verborgene Täufergemeinde in Graubünden." *Zwingliana* 4 (1926): 329-37.

Text of a guided tour of the Museum Area Schneeberg Ridnaun. Printed, n.d.

Thavis, John. "Limbo teaching a 'restrictive view of salvation.'" *The Catholic Register*, Toronto, week of May 6, 2007.

Theuer, Franz. *Blutiges Erbe: Die Habsburger im Kampf mit Franzosen, Päpsten, Ungarn und Türken um die Vorherrschaft in Italien und Ungarn, die Reformation, der Untergang Ungarns im Türkensturm und seine Eingliederung in das Osmanische Reich.* Eisenstadt: Edition Röetzer, 1996.

Thiessen, Bernhard. *Kirchengeschichtliches Hauptseminar bei Prof Doktor C. Augustijn,* SS 1982. Universität Tübingen, 1982. Cited in Fast and Rothkegel, Kunstbuch, 57, n62.

Vogelsang, Erich. "Weltbild und Kreuzestheologie in den Höllenfahrtsstreit-igkeiten der Reformationszeit." *Archiv für Reformationsgeschichte* 38 (1941): 90-132.

von Muralt, Leonhard. *Glaube und Lehre der Schweizerischen Wiedertäufer in der Reformationszeit*. Zurich: Kommissionsverlag Beer & Co., 1938.

Wagner, Murray L. *Petr Chelcický: A Radical Separatist in Hussite Bohemia*. Scottdale: Herald Press, 1983.

Waite, Gary K. *David Joris and Dutch Anabaptism, 1524-1543*. Waterloo: Wilfrid Laurier University Press, 1990.

Walde, Kurt. *Ein heimatliches Sammelwerk*, 4. Heft, *Rattenberg*, 1956.

Waldner, F. "Dr. Jakob Strauss in Hall und seine Predigt vom Grünen Donnerstag . . ." *Zeitschrift des Ferdinandeums für Tirol und Vorarlberg*. Series 3, 26. Innsbruck, 1882: 3-39.

Walton, Robert C. "Was There a Turning Point of the Zwinglian Refor-mation?" *The Anabaptists and Thomas Müntzer*. Edited by James M. Stayer and Werner O. Packull. Dubuque, Iowa: Kendall/Hunt, 1980: 66-71.

Watt, Tessa. *Cheap Print and Popular Piety, 1550-1660*. New York: Cambridge University Press, 1991.

Weber, Franz Michael. *Kaspar Schwenckfeld und seine Anhänger in den freybergishcen Herrschaften Justingen und Oepfingen*. Stuttgart: W. Kohlhammer Verlag, 1962.

Wenger, John C. "The Life and Work of Pilgram Marpeck." *Mennonite Quarterly Review* 12 (1938): 137-66, 186.

Werner, Anton. *Die Wasserkräfte der Stadt Augsburg im Dienste von Industrie und Gewerbe*. Augsburg: Verlag der Math. Rieger'schen Buchhandlung, 1905.

Widmoser, Eduard. "Das Tiroler Täufertum." *Tiroler Heimat. Jahrbuch für Geschichte und Volkskunde* 15 (1951): pt. 1, 45-89; pt. 2, 103-28.

Wiebe, Rudy. *The Blue Mountains of China*. Toronto: McClelland and Stewart, 1970.

Wiesner, Merry E. *Working Women in Renaissance Germany*. New Bruns-wick: Rutgers State University Press, 1986.

Williams, George H. *The Radical Reformation*. 3rd edition. Kirksville, Mo.: Sixteenth-Century Journal Publishers, 1992: 205-8.

Wolf, H. H. *Die Einheit des Bundes. Das Verhältnis des alten und neuen Bundes bei Calvin*. Neukirchen Kreis Moers: Verlag der Buchhandlung des Erziehungsvereins, 1958.

Wray, Frank J. "The 'Vermanung' of 1542 and Rothmanns 'Bekenntnisse.'" *Archiv für Reformationsgeschichte* 47 (1956): 243-51.

Yoder, John H. "Hermeneutics of the Anabaptists." *Mennonite Quarterly Review* 43 (1967): 291-308.

———. *The Legacy of Michael Sattler*. Scottdale: Herald Press, 1973.

———. *Täufertum und Reformation in der Schweiz. Die Gespräche zwischen Täufern und Reformatoren 1523-1538*. Karlsruhe, Germany: Schneider, 1962.

———. "The turning point in the Zwinglian Reformation." *The Anabaptists and Thomas Müntzer*. Edited by James M. Stayer and Werner O. Packull. Dubuque, Iowa: Kendall/Hunt, 1980: 61-65.

———. "The turning point in the Zwinglian Reformation." *Mennonite Quarterly Review* 32 (1958): 128-40.

Zeman, Jarold. *The Anabaptists and the Czech Brethren in Moravia, 1526-1628: A Study of Origin and Contacts*. The Hague: Mouton, 1969.

———. "Historical topography of Moravian Anabaptism." *Mennonite Quarterly Review* 40 (1966): 266-78; 41 (1967): 40-78.

Zürcher, Isaac. *Die Täufer um Bern in den ersten Jahrhunderten nach der Reformation und die Toleranz*. Sonderdruck Informationsblätter des Schweizerischen Vereins für Täufergeschichte 9, 1986.

Scripture Index

Subject Index

415

The Authors

Walter Klaassen is an adjunct professor at the College of Emmanuel and St. Chad and an adjunct professor of history at the University of Saskatchewan. He holds graduate degrees from McMaster University, McMaster Divinity College, and Oxford University. He has taught Bible and church history at Bethel College, Conrad Grebel University College and Okanagan University College. He is editor of the widely used source book *Anabaptism in Outline*.

William Klassen is adjunct professor and Principal Emeritus at St. Paul's College, University of Waterloo, Ontario. He has been professor of New Testament and Peace Studies at Associated Mennonite Biblical Seminary, the University of Manitoba, Simon Fraser University, the University of Toronto, and the École Biblique, Jerusalem. He is the author of *The Forgiving Community*, *Covenant and Community*, and *Judas: Betrayer or Friend of Jesus*.

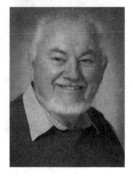